To Bob Gross,
a dear...

♡ ...nd COUNTING),

Best wishes,

Rob Thomas

Also by Robert David Thomas

The Man Who Would Be Perfect:
John Humphrey Noyes and the Utopian Impulse (1977)

"With Bleeding Footsteps"

Portrait of Mary Baker Eddy by Edwin T. Billings, 1889.
(National Portrait Gallery, Washington, D.C. / Art Resource, N.Y.)

"WITH BLEEDING FOOTSTEPS"

Mary Baker Eddy's
Path to Religious Leadership

Robert David Thomas

Alfred A. Knopf
New York
1994

This Is a Borzoi Book
Published by Alfred A. Knopf, Inc.

Grateful acknowledgment is made to the following for permission
to reprint previously published material:
De Vorss & Co.: Excerpts from *Phineas Parkhurst Quimby: The Complete Writings,*
edited by Ervin Seale (DeVorss & Co., 1988). Reprinted by permission.
International Universities Press, Inc.: Excerpts from *The Annual of Psychoanalysis,*
Volumes XII/XIII, by The Chicago Institute for Psychoanalysis, copyright © 1985 by
The Institute for Psychoanalysis of Chicago; excerpt from "The Concept of Projective
Identification," from *Projection, Identification, Projective Identification* by Joseph
Sandler, copyright © 1987 by Joseph Sandler. Reprinted by permission of
International Universities Press, Inc.
Longyear Museum and Historical Society: Excerpts from unpublished letters and
essays. Reprinted by permission of Longyear Museum and Historical Society,
Brookline, Mass.

Library of Congress Cataloging-in-Publication Data
Thomas, Robert David.
"With bleeding footsteps": Mary Baker Eddy's path to religious leadership
/ by Robert David Thomas.—1st ed.
p.   cm.
Includes bibliographical references and index
ISBN 0-679-41495-9
1. Eddy, Mary Baker, 1821–1910.
2. Christian Scientists—United States—Biography.
3. Christian Science—United States—History.
I. Title.
BX6995.T46   1994
289.5'092—dc20
[B]
92-39053
CIP

Manufactured in the United States of America
First Edition

This book is dedicated to Fred Weinstein
in respect and admiration

*Prayer means that we desire to walk and will walk in the light
so far as we receive it, even though with bleeding footsteps,
and that waiting patiently on the Lord, we will leave our
real desires to be rewarded by him.*

Mary Baker Eddy,
Science and Health with Key to the Scriptures

In those places where *"hard old New England divines . . .
tread with sublime assurance, woman often follows
with bleeding footsteps."*

Harriet Beecher Stowe,
The Minister's Wooing

CONTENTS

ACKNOWLEDGMENTS

IN PUTTING A BOOK TOGETHER—the years of research, the writing, rewriting, and more rewriting—there are times when one feels like some kind of monk in a cell, quill in hand, bent over the parchment, squinting in the flickering candlelight. A computer, of course, is not a quill, and today the isolation is not so intense; it only feels that way. When an author is finished with his work, he can then sit up, look around, and recognize the fact that all along he has had a great deal of help. I want to thank a number of people and organizations for supporting me, in one way or another, in this project. At University School, Pat Aliazzi, my department chairman, kept me on track with his encouragement. Pat is a superb scholar, and he knows how much focused, concentrated time is needed to produce a book. He got precious time off for me when I ran into last-minute snags. Scott Smith, with his complete understanding of computers, not only kept the machine running but also kept me from going off the edge because of damaged disks and irretrievable material. My old friend Roger Erickson is a gifted English teacher at Friends Academy in Locust Valley, New York. Roger agreed to read several drafts of the manuscript; his eye for tight phrasing considerably strengthened it. Unfortunately, he did not get to see my final revisions; so I accept full blame for any clumsiness in the wording.

For nearly ten summers I was in Boston doing research at the Archives of the Mother Church. Many people made it easier for me financially by finding me cheap quarters or, better yet, allowing me to stay with them. My appreciation goes to two former students, Steve Szarasz and

Kerrick Johnson, and two former colleagues at Friends Academy, Bob and Jackie Cressey.

While at the Archives I met Christian Scientists who were courteous and helpful. I looked forward to my trips to Boston in large part because of the generosity of these people. Before he left for Japan, Steve Howard, in the early years, worked closely with me in the Archives. With unwearying patience Steve shared his vast knowledge of Mrs. Eddy and Christian Science, and I felt a real sense of loss after his departure. Each year I eagerly anticipated my discussions with Lee Johnson, former director of the Archives, and with Robert Peel, now deceased. Both Lee and Bob read an early version of the manuscript. When they believed I had gone astray, they did not hesitate to show me where and how. One has not lived until one has received a sample of Bob's ten-page, single-spaced critiques; I never knew anyone who could find so much to say about two or three chapters. Bob could be blunt, but his frankness was always in the spirit of trying to improve the manuscript. Bob and Lee also saved me from making embarrassing mistakes regarding such simple things as proper names and chronology. If any of these mistakes remain, they do so because of my carelessness. One of my disappointments is that Bob Peel will never read this book. I had looked forward to the day when I could present him with a copy, even knowing that he would not have agreed with everything in its pages.

On my sojourns to the Archives, I also profited from my talks with Stephen Gottschalk. He has written a fine book on Christian Science, and he gave freely of his time and shared his considerable knowledge on the subject. Steve also provided a strong critical reading of an early version of the manuscript. I came to know Tom Johnsen better during the last few years. He read a late draft and made me rethink a number of points. Like Lee, Bob, and Steve, Tom is a Christian Scientist, meaning that he, too, had strong reservations regarding parts of my assessment of Mrs. Eddy.

In my first year of research on Mrs. Eddy, I spent time at the Longyear Museum and Historical Society in Brookline, Massachusetts. I appreciate the efforts of Robert A. Conrads, the director, and his staff. I would also like to acknowledge Jane Zimring, librarian at the Cleveland Psychoanalytic Institute, for gathering materials for me, often on short notice.

Ron Numbers read an early and a late version of the manuscript. There was a time when Ron saw greater possibilities in this project than I did. Whether he knew it or not, he encouraged me to keep writing long after I had grown weary of the process, and his criticisms greatly strengthened the work. Jane Garrett, my editor, has been a tremendous help from the moment she put down the first draft I had sent her. She has read each subsequent one and has provided much-needed counsel and encouragement. Also at Knopf, Paul Schnee, Melvin Rosenthal, and Barbara Perris have taught me the difference between a completed manuscript and a book. I deeply appreciate their work in transforming my manuscript into this book.

My wife, Becky, had to put up with my disappearances into the research and the writing. There is no adequate acknowledgment for tolerating this kind of withdrawal. From beginning to end, I am deeply indebted to Fred Weinstein. Sometime in their academic careers, all students should be lucky enough to have a teacher like Fred. Encouraging, supportive, and yet demanding, Fred would not accept anything less than a student's best effort. Fred's insights and suggestions always kept me on my intellectual toes; I could not have gotten as far as I did without his help.

To all of these people: thank you. What strengths this book has in large part belong to you; its flaws are mine.

R.D.T.

Preface

ONE OF MARY BAKER EDDY'S contemporaries, Mark Twain, the celebrated author of *Huckleberry Finn* and *Tom Sawyer*, was so disconcerted by her and Christian Science that he devoted a book to the subject Occasionally in a sentence or a paragraph one can find grudging praise for Mrs. Eddy and her accomplishments, but one does not have to search long and hard to encounter his sardonic and far more frequent attacks. He could dismiss Mrs. Eddy's lifework with a wicked dash of the pen, as he does in the following passage:

> Mrs. Eddy's known and undisputed writings are very limited in bulk; they exhibit no depth, no analytical quality, no thought above school-composition size, and but juvenile ability in handling thoughts of even the modest magnitude. She has a fine commercial ability, and could govern a vast railway system in great style; she could draft a set of rules that Satan himself would say could not be improved on—for devilish effectiveness—by his staff; but we know, by our excursions among the Mother Church's By-laws, that their English would discredit the deputy baggage-smasher. I am quite sure that Mrs. Eddy cannot write well upon any subject, even a commercial one.[1]

Nearly forty years later Mrs. Eddy became the target of Noël Coward's rapier-like wit. "The poor woman," he said, being more cruel than funny, "was obviously mentally adrift from the age of five, querulous, hysterical, unscrupulous, snobbish, and almost unbelievably stupid. . . . To be a moral thief, an unblushing liar, a supreme dictator, and a cruel self-satisfied monster, and attain, in the minds of millions, the status of a deity, is not only remarkable but a dismal reflection on the human race. She had much in common with Hitler, only no mustache." Recently, in his quirky book on the current state of religion in America, Harold Bloom branded Mrs. Eddy "a monumental hysteric of classical dimensions."[2]

From Twain to Bloom—from the past to the present—from her first fame in the 1870s to the day she died, December 3, 1910, and after, Mary Baker Eddy and her religion have had the capacity to stir deep and conflicting feelings. Over the years a number of biographies of her have been written. Some embrace her in loving praise; others hold her skeptically at arm's length or launch an outright attack. Robert Peel, a Christian Scientist, has written the most thoroughgoing and comprehensive biography, and it is indispensable for those who wish to follow the twists and turns of her career from New Hampshire farm girl to religious leader.[3]

And yet, however substantial the merits of Peel's work, he cannot be said to have written the last word on Mrs. Eddy. No one has, and my guess is that no one will. In his book Mark Twain admitted that "it is hard to locate her, she shifts about so much. She is a shining drop of quicksilver which you put your finger on and it isn't there." As we shall see, Twain was in no way flattering Mrs. Eddy with this observation, but in a roundabout way he was right: something about Mrs. Eddy makes her elusive for the historian.[4]

That something does not lie in the complexity of Mrs. Eddy's character; indeed, a biographer expects to find unresolvable contradictions in his or her subject, and Mrs. Eddy is no exception. For instance, she loved children, but could not be an effective mother to her own son and to her adopted son. She could be delicately feminine, even childlike, yet almost instantaneously become assertively masculine. In public she could appear to be a powerful, charismatic figure, but behind closed doors she sometimes seemed to sag under the weight of her duties, to be weak and vulnerable. Her life could be used as an example of the American myth of success, yet she was uncomfortable with direct ties to the material world.

Besides these various contradictions, there is something else about Mrs. Eddy that makes her difficult to grasp. Some of the most important information about her comes from the reminiscences of those who knew her best, but many of these recollections were recorded decades after the fact, when the people were quite old, and even the sharpest memory is not necessarily a reliable guide to the past. This is especially true of Mrs. Eddy's own memories, which are sometimes crucial. As she grew older and more prominent as a religious leader, one could argue that she was actively reinventing herself by reconstructing her past. She played with her memories in a creative way, altering them into spiritual folk tales, into religious myths. At this point, the historian begins to appreciate Twain's quicksilver analogy. It is as though a fog bank has rolled in and wrapped itself around Mrs. Eddy. Where once there stood a complete, flesh-and-blood person there now remains the dim outline of a receding figure.

In this book, I do not pretend to be able to reach into the fog bank, take Mrs. Eddy by the hand, and reintroduce her to readers as the "real" Mrs. Eddy. Over the fifteen years it has taken me to research and write this book, I have been one of the few non–Christian Scientists granted wide access to documents in the Archives of the Mother Church. During the same period, I embarked upon and completed a training program at the Cleveland Psychoanalytic Institute. By preference and training, therefore, I have asked psychoanalytic questions about the Eddy material. Partly because my focus has been on ideas in a social and psychological context, and partly to limit the scope of the narrative, I have not included much in the way of institutional history.

Quite early in my research, I realized that there would be no way to categorize Mrs. Eddy. In a way, psychoanalytic training prepares one to tolerate ambiguity, uncertainty, and confusion. While I have necessarily brought a sense of shape and order to Mrs. Eddy's life, I have tried to preserve the complexities and inconsistencies that were a part of her and her life so that the reader can appreciate why Mary Baker Eddy became for some people the object of veneration, admiration, and love, and why for others she became the object of ridicule, vilification, and hate.

Fifteen years is a long time to live with anyone. My years with Mrs. Eddy have been rewarding, frustrating, and exhausting. At times I found myself alternating between the poles described above, and in those instances I would step back and try to understand what was pulling me in one direction or the other. I know that I was not always successful in reaching a neutral middle ground. Indeed, when it comes to some of her statements and actions, I remain torn in my ambivalence. I hope that it becomes clear in the pages ahead, however, that I have taken Mrs. Eddy seriously and treated her respectfully but critically.

"With Bleeding Footsteps"

The Baker Family: Ornaments and Chains

My son, hear the instruction of thy father, and forsake not the law of thy mother:

For they shall be an ornament of grace unto thy head, and chains about thy neck.

Proverbs 1:8–9

In the early 1890s, a visitor to Pleasant View, Mary Baker Eddy's spacious home in Concord, New Hampshire, made a passing comment that the home and its ample grounds matched "the ideal" of Mrs. Eddy's nature. Whether they did or not is not the issue for the moment; instead let us try to imagine the number of instances when Mrs. Eddy stepped out on her balcony—perhaps troubled in thought—and gazed over the gently rolling hills. As her eye sought the horizon she could make out the contours of the hills that embraced her childhood home in Bow, New Hampshire. With the trees, rocks, and hills in the distance growing fainter, her memory's eye, colored by nostalgia, grew sharper. In her autobiography, *Retrospection and Introspection*, Mrs. Eddy painted such a childhood home, suffused in soft, autumnal hues, perched on the summit of a hill, and commanding a sweeping view of the Merrimac River Valley. Surrounding the house were ample fields of grain and orchards bearing their cornucopia of apples, pears, and cherries. A veritable Eden, indeed![1]

Her recollections of her family, especially the highly selective ones of her father and mother, were similarly affecting. Late in life she described her father, Mark Baker, as "uniformly dignified—a well-informed, intellectual man, cultivated in mind and manner." Thoughts about her mother, Abigail Ambrose Baker, left her with such an aching sense of loss that words failed to capture her mother's loving, nurturing qualities.[2]

These retrospective views of home and family served a present need rather than accurately reflecting historical truth. However, over the years a number of historians and biographers have in the main accepted these descriptions of her parents. Her father is often depicted as the stern Calvinist, embodying the harsher qualities of our Puritan past, while her mother represents the loving, accepting qualities of Jesus that nineteenth-century Protestantism was to embrace. In reconciling these traits within herself, so the story goes, Mrs. Eddy forged them anew in her Christian Science.

No doubt there is some kernel of truth in all this, but one suspects that these images of her parents fit the cultural stereotypes too snugly. They were neither the ideal that Mrs. Eddy created in her later years nor the "ideal typical" characters that some historians have made them out to be. On the contrary, the letters of the Baker family suggest that the seeds of Mrs. Eddy's contents and discontents resist such simple answers. If we wish to understand some of the important early influences on Mrs. Eddy's character, we need look more closely at the New England family and culture from which she emerged. Let us, therefore, direct our attention to her family: to her parents, Mark and Abigail; to her brothers, Samuel (born 1808), Albert (born 1810), and George (born 1812); and to her two sisters, Abigail Barnard (born 1816) and Martha (born 1819). Once we possess more sharply etched images of them, we can then focus on the youngest member of the family, Mary Morse Baker (born 1821).[3]

Physically Mark Baker bore a strong resemblance to Andrew Jackson: the shock of unkempt hair, the high forehead, the deep-set, piercing eyes, the tightly drawn, razor-thin lips, the lanky, sinewy frame. And if Jackson was "Old Hickory," then surely Mark might have been nicknamed "Old Granite."

As his youngest daughter, Mary, once recollected, Mark Baker was a man used to voicing his opinions, and he was as flinty as the New England soil. When he was not tilling his fields, he carried these attributes into his participation in community affairs, ranging over the years from clerk of the Congregational Church of Bow, to coroner for the County of Rockingham, to justice of the peace for the County of Belknap. The firmness of his mettle, however, was never more evident than when he engaged his neighbors, nearby friends, and local ministers in doctrinal disputes. Mark relished these squabbles, and he could be cantankerous in defending his Calvinistic beliefs in the absolute sovereignty of God, the fallen, sinful nature of man, and man's inability to ameliorate his condition.[4]

The Bible almost wholly absorbed Mark's reading time; he could cite chapter and verse with the best of them. There is little doubt that he took seriously that part of the Congregational Church's confession of faith which commanded that fathers train their children to accept God by "all good precepts and examples and by praying with and for them night and morning." Mark breathed life into these dry words, for as Mrs. Eddy recalled late in her life, "Father kept the family in the tightest hands I have ever known."[5]

During the week Mark would solemnly open the family Bible to the appropriate text and lead the family in morning and evening prayers. As he warmed to the task, Mark's prayers, carried in his rich, full voice, would occasionally blossom into full-fledged sermons. All the while his wife and six children, heads bowed, knelt on the hard wooden floor, no doubt straining to maintain rapt attention while their backs stiffened and their knees ached. Decades later, long after she had become the established leader of Christian Science, Mrs. Eddy was once asked whether her mother ever spoke during these prayer sessions. Not once, she answered emphatically. In those days women were expected to defer to their husbands, their masters.[6]

For Mark and his family, Sunday was a special day. It was God's day—seemingly all twenty-four hours of it—and Mark often had his family attending both morning and afternoon services at the Meeting House on White Rock Hill, where the minister would reinforce Mark's daily lessons. Unquestionably, at home Mark was a dominant force; what he wanted from his children was obedience and submission. No doubt that as an adult and a parent Mark was expressing the Calvinism he had learned at his own father's knee. And no doubt that the strictness of Mark's voice contributed to his image as the stern, distant father. Mark would learn, however, that a parent may preach his "relentless theology," but his children are not supple clay to be molded as he pleases.[7]

It is telling that none of the children, save Mary, ever made the confession of faith and joined the Congregational Church. There is also some evidence that as the family trundled off to those interminable Sunday meetings, some of the sons were not along for the ride. So, while Mark had them on their knees in family prayer, the children in time found their feet and were determined not to march like little chicks obediently accepting their father's brand of Calvinism.[8]

Mark always counseled an inner simplicity and paid little heed to the fashions of the world. His daughters Martha and Abigail might have heard his words on this score, but they were lured to the social world and wished to keep up with the Joneses. When the family moved to Sanbornton Bridge in 1836, Abigail wrote to one of her brothers how impressed she was with the friendly people, and she assured him that they hobnobbed with the better sort. Gradually moving into the social whirl of the town, the attractive Baker girls had gentlemen "of the first rank" calling upon them. Any of these young men who essayed to take out one of the girls, however, was likely to confront a daunting paternal admonition. As they were ready to depart for the evening, Mark would strongly caution his daughter and her escort that all the evening's activities should be pleasing in the eyes of God.[9]

If Abigail was a bit chagrined that their home and furnishings did not compare to the town's finest, she was absolutely mortified that the family went to church in a lowly wagon rather than in a chaise. Abigail would rather have died than be seen in the wagon, and she threatened to stay home. On this issue the usually quiet Martha sided with her sister. Martha thought she knew how to persuade Mark; she would tease him by threatening not to go to church until he bought a chaise. Maybe the girls knew something about Mark that others failed to see; in time he put his money down for a chaise and eventually he expended a somewhat larger sum for a carriage.[10]

While Mark did not seem to mind his daughters' attending local parties and welcoming gentlemen callers to his home, he was opposed to dancing. Martha yearned to go to a dancing school not far from their home, but Mark forbade it. That was hardly the end of it. In the late summer of 1836, Abigail wrote to her brother George that Martha had gone to a ball on the Fourth of July: "I suppose she would not have gone if she had asked consent; but she went without leave or license." And, Abigail sniffed, she would have gone, too, if she had not been ill and afraid that she might not be able to finish teaching school. That fall, Martha received an invitation to another dance. She went again. Later, she wrote George, "Do you stare, and wonder how it happened?" Well, she explained, luckily Mark was in Concord at the time, and she did not ask for his permission to go until it was too late for him to say no.[11]

If his daughters were able to tease and tweak him, Mark did not find it much easier asserting his will over his sons. Mark himself had been the youngest male in his family; he had worked long and hard at his father's side, and eventually inherited part of the farm. For years Mark's mother, Mary Ann, continued to live with them in the small Baker home, until she died in January 1835. Mark was thus freed from a tie to the past, and by the first of 1836 he had loosened other ties by selling the family farm and moving to the larger farm one mile north of Sanbornton Bridge where he had hopes of improving his fortunes.

In one sense, then, Mark was comfortable with the forces of commercialization that were changing the face of rural society; indeed, part of him sought success in the outside world. Yet the moral and religious side remained more firmly anchored in his Calvinist past, and Mark never saw the irony that his quest for material improvement would help undermine his cherished values. Nor is there any evidence that Mark was plagued by doubts or suffered any strain from these conflicting wishes. On some level they were emotionally compatible to him. Mark could thus wish for self-improvement and autonomy while asking his sons to replicate the filial dependency he had once experienced.[12]

Mark had reason to hope that at least one of his three sons would gladly join him in the fields. But Samuel, the oldest brother, had already taken the road to Boston, where he was engaged in the contracting business. Albert's path had led to college, and he was well on his way to becoming a lawyer. That left George. Or did it? In the summer of 1835, George fled to Connecticut without telling anyone. This sudden departure, as it was dealt with in a series of letters, opens the family door sufficiently to enable us to glimpse the interaction of a nineteenth-century father and his sons.

When George hied off to the Nutmeg State, the family was thrown into turmoil. Mark thundered about; Albert was called home for his advice; and the women, acting as a mollifying chorus, urged Mark to calm down and to consider George's health. In the letters among the brothers and sisters, everyone seemed to have something to say about the affair, and their words to George tend to belie the image of Mark as a forbidding, austerely paternalistic figure.

Abigail, in her no-nonsense manner, urged George to stay put; "if you can do better than work on a farm I advise you to stay." Surely Mark would have winced had he read this. Had he seen Albert's advice to George, Mark would have reddened in anger. Albert surmised that Mark was deluded in thinking that he could appreciably improve his circumstances by moving from one farm to another. While Albert acknowledged that Mark could manage a farm competently enough and could avoid debt, he was the "least qualified to *make money*, of any man that ever I saw of his natural abilities." Mark might know his soil, but he was woefully naïve in the ways of the world. Albert even boasted to George that had he, Albert, been running the farm, he could have cleared $200 that year, which was $200 more than Mark did. As the letter drew to a close, Albert encouraged George to make up his own mind, but if he chose to return, he should make sure to manage the farm and "*manage it right*." He also held out a warning of sorts. If George did return to Bow, and if he did take over the farm, he could not remain in the role of the obedient son. As Albert phrased it, "You never can live with him to advantage as you have lived."[13]

Fortunately, Mark, submerged in his own thoughts and feelings about

George's leaving, never saw these letters. At first he tried to sell George on the idea of the new farm; profits were to be made, because property values were on the rise around Sanbornton Bridge. He wished his son would return, but Mark also recognized that George's newly acquired freedom might be one reason for not returning to his father's roof. Nevertheless, this did not stop Mark from offering his paternal advice about George's "youthful vanities."[14]

While Mark eventually accepted George's decision to stay in Connecticut, and while he seemed to accept that it might also be better for George's health, almost a year later he was still upset and hurt. George had earlier written about his quest for personal happiness, and this inspired Mark to write a letter that seemed to say, "Your happiness? What about mine?" If, Mark's letter began, George wished to know the true meaning of happiness, then he should turn to Job, Chapter 28, where it is clearly spelled out that happiness can never be found in secular pursuits. Rather, true wisdom and happiness can be found only in God, and as the final verse warns: "Behold, the fear of the Lord, that is wisdom; and to depart from evil is understanding."

Mark may well have known that George was struggling with inner conflicts, that he was trying to make sense of his own life. In this light, Mark's reference to Job, to finding one's self in God rather than in material things, was appropriate advice and consistent with his Calvinism. Yet one does not have to read too deeply between the lines to see that on another level Mark was referring to their own situation: the errant son had gone out into the world to seek his own fortune, when true wealth, as measured by wisdom and happiness, was to be found not in the city by himself but at home by his father's side.

Mark went on to note that he had hired a young man to help work the fields, but he was proving so inept that Mark could not find the words to express his disappointment and anger. But, indirectly, he did express himself. He said that he desperately needed someone to work with him, to take on some of the burden and to "console my drooping spirits." Then, with a Calvinistic sigh of resignation, and with words evidently calculated to stir up whatever guilt George might have felt, Mark declared he had no right to complain, for his suffering and recent hardships were condign punishment for his sins.[15]

The Mark Baker who emerges from the family letters forces us to modify one writer's characterization of him as "a rigid, narrow, inflexible, grudging, controlling, litigious, and angry man, obsessed with his granitic religious beliefs, austere and scrupulously moral in his observance on his family." As we have seen, there was clearly both much more and much less to Mark. He was indeed a hard-working, moral man, but was far less successful in imposing his strict morality on his children than he might have wished. By the 1820s and 1830s, Calvinism had begun to lose its force on a wider social level, as well as within his own home. In public Mark presented one image: an Old Testament patriarch thunderously upholding the old faith. At home his children saw a more complex man: in traditional rituals, such as the daily Bible readings, he exercised dominance, but in other areas where the world seemed to be passing him by, he appeared hesitant and uncertain. In the end Mark, like most parents, discovered that the parent-child relationship was a give-and-take affair, for at the very moment he was trying to shape them, they were manipulating him. Ultimately, he could not fully impose his worldview on them, for too many things were enticing them away from it.[16]

While Mark comes to us as a strongly drawn figure, Abigail Ambrose, his wife, is lost in the softer shadows of Mrs. Eddy's later idealizations of her as well as through the wider cultural tendency to idealize women and motherhood. At the turn of this century, Georgine Milmine, muckraker's pen firmly in hand, trekked through the hills of New Hampshire jotting down the recollections of surviving witnesses to these earlier times. Some of the memories pertaining to the Baker family were quite nasty, except when it came to Mother Abigail. Even Milmine had to conclude in her *McClure's* articles that Mrs. Eddy's mother was a "gentle, capable, conscientious New England housewife. . . . In the community and in her home she was always a peaceful and inspiring influence." Abigail's obituary echoed these sentiments. The *New Hampshire Patriot and State Gazette* eulogized her as "kind and conciliatory in manner, wise and prudent in counsel, at all times cheerful and hopeful." Indeed, she was "the presiding genius of a lovely circle and a happy home."[17]

Physically, Mark and Abigail presented a striking contrast. He was tall and lean, with steel-gray eyes; she was short and plump, with blue eyes set off by her soft blond hair. In so many respects it seems as if they were opposites, or, in Robert Peel's mellifluous phrase, "Abigail was the summer to Mark's winter, the New Testament to his Old." But was the demarcation really this sharp?[18]

In an older history of Sanbornton Bridge, a writer spelled out the routine chores of a typical farm wife. With the help of her daughters, she was in charge of the kitchen, and in her spare time she did what "spinning and weaving, sewing and knitting, washing and mending" needed to be done. In the Baker letters we catch glimpses of Abigail in many of these activities, and a family friend, Mahala Sanborn, once wrote that she and Abigail had been kept busy that spring with the usual chores of "cleaning house, quilting, scraping back the chips. . . ." When we readily concede that Abigail had a nurturing, loving side, it might seem that she is not that far removed from the ideal figure in the obituary. As we probe the family letters, however, a more complex, more human figure begins to emerge.[19]

If Mark had problems letting go of George, Abigail also, for her own reasons, had difficulty with separations, with accepting the fact that her children had grown, married, and begun lives of their own. In one letter to George, long after he had left home, Abigail questioned whether time or distance could ever intervene between a mother's love and her children. Never. Her "desires will follow them and her *voice* at the throne of mercy pleading for their safety." In one particularly poignant letter, she wrote to George after one of his brief visits that she missed him so much that as she gazed wistfully upon his picture, "I almost converse with it."[20]

The loss of her daughters weighed just as heavily upon Abigail. Mahala Sanborn, the friend who had been helping Abigail with the house chores, stated that she was being asked to become a combination of daughter and maid to Abigail, but that she could not fulfill this role because Abigail constantly talked about her absent daughters. After a lengthy separation from Martha, Abigail wondered whether Martha had lost sight of the fact that she even had a mother. Martha's absence and Abigail's failure to write had left such a void that, Abigail offered, "you must almost think one silent in the grave."[21]

In many ways Abigail viewed the outside, secular world with apprehension, for it was pulling her children away from her, and it threatened to seduce them away from God. When George had reason to leave New York City, where he was living in the late 1840s, Abigail rejoiced that he was fleeing this modern Babylon, an "unhealthy dissipated sink of wickedness," for a healthier, less tempting spot in Baltimore. Much like Mark, she was conflicted about her son's struggle to become independent; she urged him to restrain himself, to curb his quest for status, prestige, and riches. Sounding more like a variation of Ben Franklin than a farmer's wife, she cautioned George with the maxim: "He that is content with his situation will smile upon his stool while Alexander weeps upon the Throne of the World."[22]

Abigail's reservations about secular progress were matched by her resignation to the exigencies of life. In one despairing moment she told George that while each member of the Baker family had his or her respective strengths, "we all perverted our talents," and she for one felt that she should humble herself daily before God, asking for His forgiveness. She once advised Martha never to forget that no matter how much Martha might suffer from her tribulations, Christ had also endured suffering, and He was rewarded with the Resurrection. In some respects, then, while Abigail's voice may have been softer than Mark's, she, too, counseled a resignation to the pain and afflictions of this world, while holding out the promise of a better life at the Father's side in the next.[23]

From our vantage point in the late twentieth century, we can see that Mark and Abigail Baker found themselves in a changing world, one not always to their liking. These changes produced anxieties and inconsistencies in the ways they dealt with their children, but overall one could argue that they did something right, for their children genuinely cared for one another. In some ways they functioned as a support group as they moved into the world of work and marriage. The extant letters and reminiscences, however, are not spread equally among the Baker children. We virtually lose sight of Samuel, but get a sharper look at Albert and George and, to a lesser extent, Abigail and Martha.

The path Albert's life took seems to embody the American success story. As a farm boy he attended a school near his home; then came Pembroke Academy, and finally graduation Phi Beta Kappa from Dartmouth. To help defray his educational expenses he taught school, and for a while he was principal of Hillsborough Academy. After Dartmouth he practiced law with Franklin Pierce's office in Hillsborough, New Hampshire. A rising star in law and politics, Albert was elected to the New Hampshire legislature in 1839, and two years later was seriously considered as a possible Democratic candidate for a U.S. congressional seat. From 1836 on, however, Albert had battled a number of severe illnesses, and in October 1841 he died. Nevertheless, these are impressive credentials for such a brief career, and on the surface Albert comes across as a self-possessed, confident young man on the move. Albert never tried to hide the fact that he had little respect for the life of a farmer. Perhaps trying to distance himself from his farm days in Bow, Albert, in a college essay on character, once described a lawyer as shrewd, discriminating, and highly perceptive, while he denigrated the occupation of his father, a farmer, as uninspiring, dull, and plodding. If indeed Mark's view of the world was enclosed by his rural past and if he understood it predominantly through his biblical metaphors, Albert, the lawyer, was apparently more at ease with secular idioms. Where Mark and Abigail would have urged their children to put their fate in the hands of God, Albert apparently placed his trust in man's rational mind. He could not have made his point clearer than when he noted, "Religion is the handmaid of philosophy, not [its] mistress; her duty is to aid and assist in the affairs of life, not lead."[24]

Bright and energetic, blessed with a superb analytical mind, Albert seemed ready to ride the wave of rapid change and progress in Jacksonian America with nary a look over his shoulder to his rural past. College offered the chance not only to leave his father's world but to surpass it.

Taking a break from his busy law practice, Albert wrote to a friend, absolutely distressed by his recent achievements. In a self-castigating tone, Albert lamented that he had drunk too deeply from a mug of flattery and self-pride, and this heady brew had knocked him off the straight and narrow path. He confessed that his "overweening confidence" had gotten the upper hand, and having lost his emotional equilibrium, he had acted like an inebriate: he teetered and then fell into agonizing self-doubt. Yet, Albert mused, a person must have confidence in himself and be reasonably assured that he can accomplish what he sets out to do. A man had to be watchful, however, for confidence should never mushroom into arrogance, and excessive enthusiasm could unwittingly subvert reason.[25]

Part of this developed emphasis on self-restraint stemmed from his belief that the internal reality of man and the external reality of objects affected each other. The inner wishes and passions of man could, without the steadying hand of reason, distort and warp his judgment and lead him into the most damaging mistakes. In this respect, obedience to the immutable laws of nature assured man of his physical and moral health, of an inner and outer harmony that might lead to perfectibility. Such obedience, according to Albert's firm convictions, was rewarded with pleasure, disobedience with pain.[26]

If Albert's meteoric success in his law practice led to some momentary emotional disequilibrium, then the hurly-burly of Jacksonian politics promised to be even more disconcerting. Seemingly, this was a period of potentially unlimited growth. Science and philosophy were unfolding their truths to man's reason, while antiquated political systems and theories were being discarded, Albert surmised. Yet the perfection of society was still out of reach because of selfish, crass individuals and because of the new corporations which threatened to destroy true individualism. Like the promising Jacksonian that he was, Albert railed against the Second Bank of the United States, and in that wonderfully inflated and inflammatory Jacksonian rhetoric, he compared the bank to a slaveholder depriving a man of his liberties. He excoriated monopolies as "that excrescence, that fungus upon the body politic, that deepest, blackest, direst curse of the age," which unless curbed would "swallow up all that is worth the name of liberty."[27]

Albert's inflated prose must be understood in two contexts. On the one hand, his bodily and health metaphors and his oral imagery were employed by many other young men of the period. Language reflected the need for a stable sense of self, and it was being employed for the same purpose. Historian Martha Verbrugge has put it as clearly as anyone: "For some, the language and philosophy of health enabled them to make sense of external events, and the practice of good habits restored order to their lives. One way Americans comprehend and cope with the world around themselves is through the world within."[28]

No doubt Verbrugge is correct, but Albert Baker's case is an eerie one. When he used those words in a political speech, he was a year away from death. As his brother George wrote after Albert had died, when they performed an autopsy on Albert, they found an infected kidney. That horrible excrescence that Albert espied on the body politic was actually in him; Albert may not have been speaking as metaphorically or abstractly as it appeared. Nevertheless, he placed his faith in Jackson and his party; the Democrats would be the party of the future, restoring morality and health to America.[29]

Albert was never shy about counseling self-control in others, and his moral didacticism comes across in an exchange of letters with his brother George, who was often considered the most engaging and high-spirited of the Baker children. Shortly after George had made his quick retreat from Bow, Albert wrote him a letter of advice; in it we discover that George's dash to Connecticut was prompted in part by a wish to escape a delicate situation with a certain young woman. Albert was emphatic on this point: every scrape that George had fallen into was his own fault, and, in one way or another, it was linked to "some damn fool of a girl."[30]

Several years later George received more unsolicited advice from Albert. "Will you allow me to mention to you what I think a radical defect in your character?" Naturally, Albert did not wait for a reply. One of George's serious flaws was that he lacked restraint and "prudence" in his relationships with people. Too often George wore his emotions on his sleeve; either he trusted people naïvely or he hated them too vehemently. One way or the other, the intensity of George's feelings made him vulnerable. This was all wrong, said Albert. George must learn to select a few friends quite carefully the way Albert had done, and then make sure never to allow himself to be placed in a situation in which what they said or did could devastate him. What George needed was a degree of self-restraint. Try not to be so open, so exposed, Albert counseled. George was to keep cool and to keep a rein on his feelings, especially with the women. If he followed this advice and did his job honestly, then, Albert assured him, everything would be all right.[31]

Albert's moral advice was restrained in this letter, but in later ones he grew more insistent. At times George got angry with his brother for lecturing him like a parent. On one occasion he "took cold" reading Albert's letter. Albert countered by saying that he was being harsh only out of his love and concern. Besides, "No man can have his weaknesses, and foibles, too often passed in review before him." He raised a question as to whether his younger brother had been guilty of any "disgraceful act," or had perhaps failed to do his duty in some way. Albert suspected that George's passions had once again gained the upper hand, and he urged him to master his impetuous outbursts. If he was successful in these endeavors, Albert assured George, he would be the master of himself and others.[32]

Even if Albert's tone sometimes rubbed George the wrong way, he knew that Albert's advice was well-intentioned, and, more important, was dead right on the issue of self-restraint. When George had settled in Connecticut, he got a job teaching textile weaving to inmates in the Connecticut State Prison. Away from home, George revealed that there was more to him than a devil-may-care philanderer; not surprisingly, and in his own way, George wrestled with many of the same inner demons that Albert did.

George had "left the familiar scenes of home and fled to society," hoping that his new surroundings would erase the painful memories of Bow. Yet his past would not go away; it intruded into his thoughts, and made it hard to concentrate on his current situation and his dreams for the future. To control those thoughts that conjured uncertainty and despair—that was George's pressing need. In searching for answers, he convinced himself that he had to sidestep the entrapments of his culture. And the place to begin was with his reading. Modern novels and stories had the capacity to overstimulate the imagination, to dredge up those concealed, painful memories that lay in the past, and to leave a person swamped in "gloomy, revolting reflections." If read and pondered too much, such novels could unleash the passions that would submerge reason. Avoiding this loss of control was critical to George, so he vowed to replace his seductive reading with Shakespeare and other morally elevating classics.[33]

Albert was pleased to hear about George's efforts at self-improvement, and Albert's encouraging words reinforced the moral seriousness in studying the past and its great figures. As he put it, we use the past for didactic purposes; to help us "regulate our lives, to influence our minds, our manners, and our conduct." Good advice, though it took George some time to learn this lesson. Several years later in a letter to a friend, George sounded like an echo of Albert. He, too, had very little regard for "prating upon religious tenets and pious dogmas." Nevertheless, he would encourage those very truths by urging youths to seek pleasure in those subjects best calculated to thwart personal corruption. Sobriety, carried into all walks of life, he solemnly declared to his friend Jeremiah C. Tilton, would guarantee success in all endeavors.[34]

As George moved into the workaday world and was swept into the helter-skelter pace of the city, he found it hard to adjust to the changes. The very strength of his inner conflicts seemed to plunge him "into a stream of mist and confusion," which threatened to overwhelm him. He had to endure passively being "borne down its current reckless of the shoals upon which it may cast me." Despite these dark moments, George, as had Albert, regained an active sense of hope that with a proper marshaling of his inner strengths, things would get better.[35]

In the family letters Abigail never comes across as suffering the angst that gripped George and Albert. She has often been pictured as the tough-minded sister, the one eager for status and wealth. She was that, certainly. In an early letter to one of her brothers, she was more than ready to outgrow Bow. When Mark decided to buy the farm in Sanbornton Bridge, she was overjoyed as long as he did not get a smaller house. But, she remarked sardonically, there was little chance of that. She then shared her excitement about attending school in Hillsborough; here was a chance to make something of herself; she was not about to return home until she graduated or had received a diploma "or some mark of distinction." Not only that, Abigail had set her sights on capturing the most eligible bachelor in Sanbornton Bridge, Alexander Hamilton Tilton, a successful businessman. She landed him and in time became a prominent member of the town's elite.[36]

Marriage may have been a step upward for Abigail, but it was also a step away from home, and this separation cracked her tough veneer. In the fall of 1837, shortly after her marriage, she wrote George that the time was fraught with so many mixed feelings, and when you added the trip to Boston, well, she was "fairly faded out" and had been intermittently sick. Recently, though, she had begun to regain her strength and to deal with her new role as a married woman. She took some pride in her adjustment. In a light, pleased tone she said to George, "O! do come and see me, Sullivan, and witness how well I manage my household affairs. I imagine you will be surprised to see how domesticated I am." She concluded her letter by reassuring her brother that her marriage did not mean that she was leaving him or the family, or that she loved them any less. Finally, Abigail's social ambitions had their limits. For instance, she was not lured by the glitter and hubbub of Boston. When she returned from her honeymoon, she seemed to share her mother's opinion about city life. Boston, she declared, was filled with "such noise and confusion" that she had no desire ever to live there. In fact, in later years Abigail seemed content to wear Boston's fashions a year late in her New Hampshire hometown.[37]

If even Abigail, with her tough edges, felt the pangs of separation, the gentle Martha could be expected to feel them more deeply, as she apparently did. She comes across in the letters as a sensitive, affectionate young lady who cherished her close family ties. We see some of the lighter, more relaxed, even teasing moments among the Baker children through her eyes. When George left home, her letter to him carried the usual family news, and then she spoke directly about her sadness. While certainly life would eventually go on as usual, for the moment there was no denying that the once-full family circle had "shrunk" into a "nothingness."[38]

The trek from Bow to Sanbornton Bridge was not any easier on Martha, in the early days. Whereas Abigail had looked forward to better things, Martha felt the loss of old roots and bemoaned the fact that they now lived "in a strange land and among strangers." As time went by, she willingly stepped out the front door into the town's social life. Dancing and courting might eventually lead to marriage, a momentous step for any young woman, and Martha could not hide her apprehensions about Abigail's nuptials. On the day of Abigail's marriage, Martha sent a letter to George telling him that the wedding ceremony was to be that morning, and then the bride and groom would leave for Boston. Martha was thrilled to be a member of the wedding party, but her excitement was tempered by her musings on what marriage meant. It signaled, among other things, that a girl had become a woman and was leaving the home of her childhood, leaving the secure and the familiar for the uncertain and the unknown. Some of these unsettling thoughts may have been going through Martha's mind as she and the rest of the wedding party accompanied Abigail and her new husband to Concord. At that point they waved goodbye, leaving them "to their own destruction, or all the happiness of a new married pair."[39]

With the exception of Samuel, the oldest, and Mary, the youngest, we have been introduced to the Baker family. Perhaps we should pause here and place the Bakers' thoughts and feelings in a wider social context. While Bow and Sanbornton Bridge may sound like sleepy New England villages, untouched by the social changes transforming Boston to the south, this was not so. We have already seen how the Baker family, parents and children alike, reacted to these currents of change as they flowed into their communities and their home. Their move to Sanbornton Bridge, the actions and the departure of their children, told Mark and Abigail that the times were changing, and so, too, was their relationship to their children. Nevertheless, they clung to the modified Calvinism of their youth, with its emphasis on God's omnipotence and man's relative weakness and passivity. Mark's and Abigail's optimism was thus often sheathed in a "gentle melancholy" and resignation to whatever befell them in life. If things went wrong, if mistakes were made, if one became ill, then one surely had no right to blame God the Father. He did not err; man did. Mark and Abigail probably encouraged this attitude of submission in their offspring. They taught, that is, a critical self-examination of one's words and deeds, a turning inward to wrestle with a guilty or shameful self. We are perhaps asking too much of Abigail, then, if we wish to see her as a representative of the nineteenth century's sentimental Christianity. She simply could not wrench herself from her past to be that. Rather, if Mark and Abigail are any indication, Lewis Saum is correct when he argues that on the level of popular culture a "vestigial Puritanism" kept a firm hold on America well into the nineteenth century.[40]

If Albert had lived and fulfilled the promise of his early career, he probably would have been a worthy figure for a biography. Far more worldly-wise than either of his parents, wearing a secular optimism the way he would a new cut of clothes, Albert seemed closer to the attitudes of Boston than Bow, for he clearly felt comfortable with a number of the cultural shifts taking place. In an essay on why poetry would not find a fertile soil in America, Albert declared that religion had significantly molded the American character. The religion of our Puritan forefathers taught man not to enjoy life in the world but to prepare for a hereafter. Hence, whatever was thought, said, or done "must be in reference to the tremendous issues of eternity." This older concept of religion was "at war with the light, buoyant temper" of the day.[41]

Despite his prescience, Albert was never able to lift his oars and let himself be carried by the current of secular optimism. If we recall his inner struggles, his efforts to moderate his feelings and sentiments, then we can see that his boat was borne back, and that his conflicts resonated with Mark's struggles with his God. After one of the times when Albert had wrestled with inner conflicts and doubts, he exclaimed to a friend that the lessons of his past had taken on a new meaning. The rules and regulations, the dos and don'ts, that parents and teachers had drummed into his ears as a boy, along with the "grave maxims" from his philosophy texts in college, had been just so many dry words or intellectual exercises to him. But when "the hard hand of misfortune is laid upon us, and we feel [its] truth," then those old warnings take on new meaning, which we believe and obey. In other words, when his current painful experiences enlivened the religious strictures from his past, Albert was probably closer to his father than he realized.[42]

George, too, was closer. Although he protested that he had no use for pious religious truths, he was not above employing them when the occasion called for it. When Abigail had informed him that she was mortified to ride in the family wagon, George replied with words that would have brought an approving nod from Mark. He urged his sister to read the twenty-eighth chapter of Job and for good measure the eleventh of Samuel.[43]

Seen from another perspective, the Baker brothers' balancing of optimism and pessimism puts them squarely in the ranks of those nineteenth-century Americans whom Marvin Meyers called "venturous conservatives," or, as John William Ward said about Americans of this period: they were Janus-faced, looking back to the past and forward to the future simultaneously. In the same vein, Albert's and George's preoccupation with issues of self-control and health can also be placed in a wider cultural context. Self-control and temperance in all aspects of life were vital issues for many in this period as they sought to keep a personal and social balance in a world that to them was spinning at a dizzy pace. The words of the two Baker brothers were repeated countless times in the proscriptive literature of the day. Good health for Albert, and for many others, signaled a redeemed self and ultimately a redeemed nation. Perfection was, in fact, just around the corner. As we move into the chapters on Mary Baker Eddy, we will have ample reason to return to these issues surrounding health.[44]

One of the central themes of this chapter has been the issue of separation and loss in the lives of the Bakers, and how they individually responded to it. Each in his or her own way coped, some with more difficulty than others. We must be cautious with the feelings expressed by the Bakers, however. Much of the excess one encounters in the letters stems from the florid, idiomatic expression of nineteenth-century writers. Part of what strikes the modern ear as exaggerated sentiment comes from the fact that when families separated, distance and space were real obstacles. There was no phone to pick up, no plane to catch. Written expression thus took on special meaning: so much had to be said in so few lines to close the distance. These qualifications are not meant to diminish the feelings people experienced when a loved one left home, whether in a rite of passage from the farm to the city or a young woman's marriage, or an escape such as George's. The emotions were there, but in some instances the people may not have been as profoundly distraught as the letters sound.

Martha and her mother, Abigail, were the most open in their feelings about missing a brother or sister, a son or daughter. Even Albert, who wished to place reason above enthusiasm, could be effusive when writing his sisters. "If there is a brother in the world who is happy in the love of his sisters, it is I," he wrote longingly. To him they were "the *oasis* in the desert of life," the only spot in a demanding, hectic world where, in his imagination, he could "rest with *entire* safety." He knew that he could find "*honesty* and *sincerity* in a sister's love."[45]

If we can cut through Albert's sentiment in this letter, we can see that life in his "modern" world was not all that it was cracked up to be, that he wished for self-acceptance, and that perhaps in an idealized way he yearned for the secure embrace of his sisters. Even beyond his sisters, however, Albert yearned—again, in his imagination—for Home, for a temporary, edenic retreat from the harshness of everyday reality. He was hardly alone in this longing; many across America were expressing the same sentiment.[46]

Long after she had become the established leader of Christian Science, Mrs. Eddy reminisced with one of her most reliable and devoted followers. She told him that when she was still a child, her older brothers frequently got into arguments that spilled over into fistfights. Her role was to be the peacemaker, carrying messages back and forth until tranquillity was restored in the home. It is hard to know what to do with this isolated memory. If we dip back into the family letters, we do not find corroboration of it, so it would be easy to dismiss. Yet her memory leads one to wonder: where are the flare-ups, the jealousies and wounded feelings that we might expect to find among brothers and sisters living in relatively cramped quarters? As effusive as the Bakers were on some topics, one must suspect that they were guarded on others. The Baker children's letters to one another, then, not only expressed an ideal of attachment, a concern and fondness often more polite than real, a way to be reassuring and courteous, but they also functioned as a way to maintain a tie to the past while the children lived in the present and hoped for the future.[47]

With this, it is time to turn the spotlight on the youngest of the family, Mary Morse Baker. She, too, would experience the hopes and desires of growing up, as well as the conflicts that this growth and change bring. She, too, would marry and leave the family; she, too, would have to cope with a society that was proving disruptive to familiar expectations and patterns of behavior. And she would know more than she ever wanted to know about illness and death.

MARY BAKER'S YOUTH:
A TIME TO WEEP,
LAUGH, MOURN, DANCE

To every thing there is a season, and a time to every purpose under the heaven:

A time to weep, and a time to laugh; a time to mourn, and a time to dance.

Ecclesiastes 3:1&4

NOT LONG AFTER THE PUBLICATION of *Science and Health* in the late 1870s, Mrs. Eddy's cousin D. Russell Ambrose reminisced fondly about their ties some forty years earlier. She was, he mused, young and frail; her white, clear skin highlighted her "brilliant blue eyes." In the early 1900s, Georgine Milmine unearthed some old-timers who remembered Mary Baker as a young girl. They concurred with Ambrose's assessment: Mary was "a most interesting and beautiful child," they said. She was also, they thought, "dainty, fragile and precocious in development." The most striking aspect of young Mary's features was her "big gray eyes." Deep-set and protected by dark lashes, they had a remarkable "gift of immediate expression." When Mary got angry, an old neighbor recalled, her eyes became "fairly black."[1]

A number of letters exchanged among the Baker children indicate that they had their lighter moments, enjoyed one another's company, and relished a good laugh together. It is also evident from the family correspondence that Mary deeply admired her two older brothers. Though George was never as successful in the outside world as Albert was, he was affectionate with Mary and shared her interest in writing poetry. She trusted and depended upon George's caring, brotherly advice; writing to him from Sanbornton Bridge, Mary closed a lengthy letter with a plea that he give her all the advice he could, for his was "the genuine growth of experience." Albert, of course, was never shy about passing on his advice, and in his letters he comes across as a bit more polished, and a bit stuffier, than George. He had his gayer moments, though, and in one instance he sent a letter with a friend of his who was going to be attending school in Sanbornton Bridge. Albert also tweaked Mary's nose by telling her that his friend was a good student, and like Mary he had a tendency for "discursive talking," although he did not have "so much poetry at his command" as she did.[2]

While Mary could be mirthful and occasionally spontaneous, there were, of course, other facets of her character. In her later teens one senses a young woman who wished to make something of herself, a woman not wholly content to remain in the Bows and Sanbornton Bridges of her home state. Her family subscribed to the *New Hampshire Patriot and State Gazette*, and its pages were open to her. Even though George could never pass as a scholar, he was a reader and sometimes would encourage the girls back home in their intellectual endeavors by mailing them a book. Albert, though, had the most profound effect upon Mary's desire to learn and excel as a student.[3]

In a later reminiscence, Mrs. Eddy recalled that her father often put up roadblocks in the path of her learning. On his visits home from Dartmouth College, Albert would occasionally bring with him some of his college books, and sometimes father Mark bristled when his son introduced secular texts into the home. The family Bible was sufficient literature for Mark; if he thought Albert's books too secular in spirit, he would strongly object to Mary's reading them. But, though Mark may have intercepted some books, others did filter through to Mary. Indeed, there was no way Mark could effectively block the steady stream of cultural knowledge that flowed into his home and threatened to liberate his children from their traditional ties to his authority, the family, and the community.[4]

Albert stimulated Mary's desire to learn in other ways as well; in fact, he was the first to encourage Mary in her writing. While Mary loved to curl up with a book, and while she was a budding poet in her teen years, letter writing was often a struggle for her. No matter how hard she tried, she had insurmountable difficulty mastering the syntax, grammar, and punctuation that would allow her to express herself with clarity and precision. Mary would have found little consolation in knowing that many literate people in the nineteenth century had the same problem; to her this inability was a source of frustration and embarrassment. She often apologized to her brothers for her poor writing; in one letter she expressed her envy of Martha's skill with the pen. Despite this drawback, Mary was an eager learner. In a letter to George, she disclosed that she had been studying every free moment she had during the chilly days of that winter, and if her health permitted, she would be attending school in the summer.[5]

Learning may have been important to Mary, but so were social activities and friendships. In the late 1830s, during her middle and late teen years, Mary was hardly content to stay at home. In letters to George, we catch glimpses of her in a round of activities. She attended a party with some of the town's other young ladies, but this was not as exciting as the news about a young man who recently had come from Boston to Sanbornton Bridge to study medicine with a local doctor. She had met this certain young man at a party the previous winter and in her estimation he was as fine a gentleman as one could find. He had invited Mary to go with him to visit a Shaker community in nearby Canterbury, but her "superiors" scotched this idea because they considered it a violation of the Sabbath. While this put a minor crimp in her social schedule, not too long thereafter she attended a wedding with another man, John Bartlett.[6]

Mary also established some relationships with girls her own age, and she had a close friend in Augusta Holmes, a schoolmate who was two years older. Mary's fondness for and deep attachment to Augusta come through clearly in the letters, and in one of them she bemoaned the fact that she had not seen Augusta for two whole days. Mary could share with Augusta her interest in reading, her love of poetry, and perhaps some secrets of the heart.[7]

Mary's ill health sometimes cut into this round of activities. In the summer of her fifteenth year, we learn, Mary was able to attend school. As Abigail said to George, this was more than anyone could have expected, given Mary's usual state of poor health. The letters from the Baker children indicate that no one in the family, parents included, escaped the fevers, colds, and ravages of more serious maladies. In the depths of the winter of 1836, Abigail informed George, who had already made his escape to Connecticut, that severe colds had passed through the family, with mother Abigail and sisters Martha and Mary succumbing.[8]

We have already learned of Albert's losing medical battles, and from Connecticut George sprinkled his journal with worries about his failing health. A hacking cough seemed to prey upon his lungs, wearing away "the pitiful remnant of a once generous condition now rent by disease." Abigail and Martha both missed school repeatedly with colds and fevers. Martha once disclosed in a letter that for almost three weeks she had stopped doing everything and had gone to bed with a severe cough. Just when it seemed as if Martha would slip into a more desperate condition, she bounced back with the cheery words that it was not such a distressing illness after all. It was, in fact, a cough that had left her "comfortably ill."[9]

Outside the Baker family, poor health was visiting just about everyone in the nineteenth century, or so it seemed. Sarah Gates, a friend of Augusta Holmes, wrote to her that her health was so bad that her father thought she must stay home and not attend school. Augusta herself was laid low by a severe cough and cold, while another friend was "quite sick with the mumps today."[10]

In the context of her friends' and family's bouts with poor health, one is hard put to find anything distinctive about Mary. Similarly, if we place her social and intellectual development in a wider context, there does not seem to be much to distinguish her from other nineteenth-century adolescents. Yet the ever-critical Georgine Milmine was convinced that she had unearthed something singular about the character of the youthful Mary Baker. From the bits and pieces of recollections about Mary's childhood, Milmine drew a composite picture of a disturbed, rather unpleasant little girl: young Mary Baker was a spoiled, willful child, who would do anything to get her way, even use illness to manipulate others. Her anger flared at any insult to her self-esteem, but in the blink of an eye her ire would subside, and one might be faced with a coy, charming, even seductive young girl. For Milmine all of these characteristics added up to one thing: Mary's "girl-hood had been a fruitless, hysterical revolt against order and discipline."[11]

The family letters do not reach far back into Mary's childhood; they pick up the story when Mary enters her early teen years. So there is no way to confirm Milmine's findings about Mary's childhood days. We do not really know whether Milmine's informants were talking about a general, everyday pattern of behavior or about isolated but vivid moments. Furthermore, labeling Mary a "hysteric" does not reveal what might have been special about her, except in judgmental, negative terms.[12]

Even if we are skeptical about Milmine's purposes (she was writing an exposé), and even if we do not wholeheartedly accept what the old-timers had to say, it is instructive to note that after so many years, more than a few people would have such vivid stories to tell. Clearly, there was something highly memorable about Mrs. Eddy's personality, even as a child.[13]

The Baker family letters may provide us with some clues as to what it was, though they are an incomplete guide to the past. Illness was accepted as a part of life, but during her adolescent years, Mary's brothers and sisters sensed that her illnesses were not of the usual run. In July

1837, Martha apologized to brother George for not writing sooner, but she had been very anxious about Mary's declining health. That fall, Abigail told George that Mary's health had improved a little, but "the poor girl can never enjoy life, as most of us can should she live any time, and this is altogether uncertain." Then, in words ringing with Christian resignation, she said that while all of them had a fragile hold on life, it seemed that Mary's grip was much weaker. As it was, Mary was able to maintain the semblance of health only by dieting and other "simple expedients."[14]

In 1840, Albert, who had not many more days to live himself, received a distressing letter from Abigail that suggested Mary was in desperate straits again. Alarmed, Albert immediately wrote Mary with the hope that Abigail had exaggerated out of her deep concern, and that Mary's suffering was not as severe as he was led to believe. It is to the ever-sensitive Martha that we must turn for a chilling description of one of Mary's earlier sieges, one that had more than matched Albert's fears. In the summer of 1837, Mary's declining health again alarmed her family. On top of her usual ailments, Martha wrote, "her stomach became most shockingly cankered, and an ulcer collected on her lungs, causing the most severe distress you can conceive of; the physician with the family thought her cure was impossible, but she was a good deal recovered for two weeks past, and this morning was carried out to ride." Three months later Martha could sigh with relief that Mary was beginning to recover slowly on a diet of bread and water.[15]

Martha's optimism was guarded, for Mary was often susceptible to illness, and in the months and years ahead she would suffer a variety of maladies. The above incident, however, should not be shuffled in with all the other illnesses and thereby dismissed as a typical health problem of the nineteenth century. Because the doctor and the Baker family were well acquainted with disease and death, there is little doubt that they knew a life-threatening illness when they saw it. What this severe bodily illness meant to Mary as she moved from girlhood to womanhood is, of course, the critical issue.[16]

Robert Peel has located a deep, existential anguish in Mary during these years. While one would expect philosophical ruminations to be a part of adolescence, Peel recognizes that Mary felt something more than adolescent angst. One strongly suspects that the continuous assaults on her body by illness—especially the times when she and others thought she was dying—took their emotional toll. When as a teenager she lay in bed near death, these overwhelming experiences left her in an emotionally precarious position. The repeated assaults hammered away at her; they sapped her emotional resistance; they reawakened and then revitalized her earlier childhood experiences dealing with loss and death.[17]*

Precisely what the earlier experiences were, we will never know; there is a gap here that we simply cannot close. We can, however, approach the issue indirectly by looking at what psychoanalysis has to say about overwhelmed children. Once we have this general background, we can briefly examine Mrs. Eddy's later writings that comment upon this issue.

We know that severe illness brings any child face to face with his or her helplessness, with the recognition that his or her world is not secure, and with the horrifying realization that annihilation or death could occur at any moment. D. W. Winnicott called this kind of trauma "the un-thinkable anxiety." One might add that most adults flinch when con-templating the fact that their own lives could be snuffed out at any moment. If this is unthinkable for most adults, then try to imagine what it must be like for a child. Words fail to capture the profound sadness, the deep anxiety, and the intense rage; Winnicott would have been justified in calling it the "unspeakable anxiety."[18]

Children thus threatened will be affected on all levels of their per-sonality. Each stage of development contains its own set of conflicts revolving around issues of separation and growth. Sadness, anxiety, and anger, which we associate with separation, are at times in conflict with the state of "feeling good," which we associate with the potential ac-complishments that lie ahead. For most people the feelings associated with separation are experienced and managed, and the pleasure of doing well wins out. The threatened child, however, is especially vulnerable to the feelings of separation, for instead of tamable passions, they become lions and tigers threatening an inner fragmentation and possible anni-hilation. Separation thus touches upon fears of profound loss, even death, making normal separation conflicts all the more difficult to resolve.[19]

The sick child is engaged in a continuing struggle to make sense of suffering, to integrate the significance of suffering, to close the wound, to make the self whole. Above all else, the child must protect his or her fragile self from those internal and external forces that threaten to over-whelm it. The child must constantly check and silently monitor his or

* David E. Stannard comments on the differences between the ways the Puritan child and the child of the nineteenth century were instructed in the meaning of death. The Puritan child was encouraged to imagine the terrors of separation, the finality of death, and the torments of hell. The nineteenth-century child was urged to see death as a transformation and a reunion with loved ones. Mary Baker, because of life's experi-ences, could not shake the former to embrace fully the latter. See Stannard's *The Puritan Way of Death: A Study in Religion, Culture, and Social Change* (New York: Oxford University Press, 1977), pp. 171, 174.

her feelings and the feelings of others, making sure that none aggravate the wound. To aid him or her in these efforts the child resurrects in the imagination a sense of the omnipotence of the self and important figures in his or her life. Children so affected may then appear haughty, arrogant, controlling, self-centered, and quick to anger at the slightest insult to their self-esteem.[20]

Just as important, some of these children will harbor a secret knowledge within themselves. While one plus one equals two and two plus two equals four, a threatened child has reason to believe that this is not true. Such children will know, in fact, that the permanence assigned to external reality (no matter what social and economic shifts there might be, the world is there) is in some ways an illusion. Psychic reality, which tells such children that nothing is permanent, nothing is safe from loss and death, is just as real to them—if not more so—than conventional reality. We recall that those old folks interviewed by Georgine Milmine commented upon young Mary's precocity. They probably did not mean it the way we are using the word here, but Mary's too early—precocious—awareness of the unpredictability and fragility of life left its indelible mark upon her.

Just as the deep psychic wound contains the germs of potential pathology, it may also be the source of certain strengths. By keeping open early phases of childhood where the boundaries between the self and the outside world are fluid, where there is a strong mixing of primary and secondary process thinking that results in a perception of the world colored by feeling, intuition, metaphor, and symbol, and where the capacity exists to enter into and reemerge from fusion states, one may not be looking only at the earmarks of pathology in the adult; one may also be seeing the signs of strength and creativity.[21]

This precocious awareness of suffering and death contributed to Mary's bottomless empathy for children, which was virtually lifelong. While a number of cultural and personal sources fed into this strong identification, we will focus here on the personal factors dealing with a precocious awareness of suffering and death. Her sensitivity to childhood suffering might have been one of the reasons that she chose to include the life of Kaspar Hauser in her *Science and Health with Key to the Scriptures*. From 1830 on, this true account of a deprived, abused, primitive boy and his attempts to fit into society was a captivating, well-known story in Europe and America. Mrs. Eddy used it to illustrate the "frailty and inadequacy of mortal mind"; yet her words betray an awareness that goes well beyond the Christian Science lesson she was teaching. When she talked about Hauser's isolated imprisonment as a child, she betrayed her deep understanding of what an abandoned infant felt. She made a special point of capturing this lonely, terrifying feeling by quoting Tennyson:

> *An infant crying in the night:*
> *An infant crying for the light:*
> *And with no language but a cry.*[22]

This was the epitome of abandonment. No wonder that when Hauser entered society, he ultimately found it a threatening place and wished to withdraw from it, and Mrs. Eddy fully grasped why reality could be so threatening:

> Outside of dismal darkness and cold silence he found no peace. Every sound convulsed him with anguish. All that he ate, except his black crust, produced violent retchings. All that gives pleasure to our educated sense, gave him pain through those very senses, trained in an opposite direction.[23]*

There are other places in *Science and Health* where Mrs. Eddy draws upon the parent-child relationship to illustrate the Christian Science point she is making. In the process of showing how the attitude of a parent toward his child's beliefs can affect the way the child perceives reality, Mrs. Eddy again reveals that she knew all too well that sometimes even the well-intentioned parent could not protect the child from illness, anxiety, or despair:

> Children, like adults, *ought* to fear a reality which can harm them and which they do not understand, for at any moment they may become its helpless victims; but instead of increasing children's fears by declaring ghosts to be real, merciless, and powerful, thus watering the very roots of childish timidity, children should be assured that their fears are groundless, that ghosts are not realities, but traditional beliefs, erroneous and man-made.[24]

---

* The suffering that Mary experienced in her illnesses would have made it very difficult for her to bear the painful affects of sadness, loneliness, and depression. Her incapacity to tolerate these feelings and to master normal developmental conflicts left gaping wounds. While one can see them as sources for later pathology, it is also important to note that these unresolved conflicts pushed her to seek different ways of healing herself. The depressive affect and how it is differentiated from other feelings like sadness, and what its role is in normal and pathological development, are ably discussed in Erna Furman, "What Is Depression in Childhood? A Discussion of Definition, Assessment and Some Developmental Factors," *Child Analysis* 3 (June 1992), pp. 101–23.

Mary's struggles to manage the issues surrounding loss and death played an important role in what Milmine and others have labeled her hysterical manifestations. And this inner struggle might also help to explain the apparent paradox of how little Mary could be willful and obstreperous and yet obsessed with order. It was once reported that in her childhood, Mary was so preoccupied with appearing neat that she would break into tears over "a wrinkle in her dress." This demand for excessive neatness and order was to be a lifelong trait, and during her childhood and adolescence, it served many purposes. The horror at the wrinkle in the dress, for instance, probably reflected the wish not to appear flawed in any respect, for any flaw, no matter how minor, threatened to expose that fragile inner self. And we should recall that Mary was equally sensitive about other kinds of "wrinkles," such as mistakes in her writing. To maintain external order would also be a way of keeping internal order, of making sure that one was not overwhelmed by inner impulses. In this light perhaps we can better understand Mary's use of the Graham diet as a way of curbing her illnesses and improving her health.[25]*

We do not know precisely when Mary began the regimen of the Graham diet, although two historians have recently suggested that it was in 1837, when she turned sixteen. Her obedience to Graham's dietary laws was, of course, as much a wider cultural expression as it was a personal experience. It is logical to assume, for instance, that her parents' Calvinism encouraged self-control and simple tastes in all aspects of life, including what one ate. By the early 1830s Graham had established himself as a leader of the Christian physiology movement.[26]

According to historian Robert Fuller, Graham came to view the stomach as the "physiological agent responsible for delivering "vital power" to the organism in its quest to overcome the various causes of disease and death." Consequently, proper diet became Graham's sine qua non for health and salvation. To ensure a healthy body and spirit, he argued, one must shun all stimulating food and drink. Coffee, tea, alcohol, condiments, salt, butter, and meat were forbidden. In their place Graham offered his brand of natural food: a bread made from unsifted wheat flour, vegetables, and water. His meals were an orgy of self-restraint and control; to ensure that the digestive system was not overtaxed, Graham urged that six hours should lapse between one meal and the next, and that one should never eat a meal shortly before going to bed.[27]

Along with other Christian physiologists like William Alcott, Graham

---

* Mrs. Eddy's neatness will be discussed more fully in later chapters. What this material suggests is that Mrs. Eddy, like virtually everyone else, embodied a mixture of hysterical and obsessional traits. Rather than pinning labels on her, we are better off focusing on how she coped with injuries, slights, and overwhelmings.

was quick to make symbolic connections between ills affecting the social body and maladies afflicting the human body. He established links among man's mental, physiological, and spiritual natures, asserting that any overstimulation from one of these sources could contaminate the others and lead to a mental breakdown or physical illness. Illness thus became an external symbol of internal disorder and conflict, of disintegration rather than integration. Conversely, in the antebellum period good health became a moral imperative. Through self-discipline and self-control, people were told, they could achieve a perfect relationship to their own bodies, to their outer world, and to their spiritual world.[28]

Given her own inner struggles and conflicts, one can see why Mary found the Graham diet appealing. However, she did not require a remote cultural figure like Graham to lecture her about the benefits of self-restraint and self-discipline. In one of her childhood schoolbooks, Lindley Murray's *Grammar*, all students were reminded that a "temperate spirit and moderate expectations, are excellent safeguards of the mind, in this uncertain and changing state." Albert preached the same message in a letter from 1840: "Be careful that you do not sacrifice too often at the shrine of the muses," he cautioned Mary. "Your health is of paramount importance, yet, though you may think yourself pretty well." From Graham to Albert, then, Mary's culture reinforced the metaphoric use of the body for the representation and expression of emotional conflicts.[29]

Mary listened raptly to what these cultural authorities had to say on the issues of health and wholeness. One of her earliest poems, "Resolutions for the Morning," written when she was twelve years old, reflects her concern over these very issues. It is a long poem, stretching eight stanzas. The opening lines have Mary, the narrator, awakening in the morning, drinking in the freshness of the day and the sublime beauty of nature. Her imagery is sharp and gives us the feeling that we are standing before one of Thomas Cole's or Asher B. Durand's landscapes.

As Mary's eye imbibes the becalming beauty of God's nature, her gaze moves upward, away from the flora and fauna to the spiritual realm of God, where she hopes that "His beam" will inspire her writing. By the time we reach the third stanza, the worries of twelve-year-old Mary break through and become the central concern of the poem. She firmly resolves, as long as she has God's help, to maintain an inner self-control so that she may enjoy physical, mental, and emotional health. The next three stanzas, however, reflect lingering doubts about her capacity for self-mastery and her ability to fulfill her resolutions. In these stanzas she redoubles her prayers to God, asking Him to deliver her from egotism and self-indulgence, from earthly ambition and "all that is wrong."

In the penultimate stanza, Mary's need for self-control has led to the wish to annihilate a material self, a conflicted self. These feelings in turn stimulate thoughts about loss and death, and she vows to remember and to pray for her "*dear absent* friends" even though they are separated by time and distance. In the final stanza, Mary acknowledges that if she has successfully kept her resolutions, that if her spiritual side has been able to overcome her material cravings, then even though her days may be numbered, she will not be anxious because she will be carried away to God's side.[30]

Between the time when Mary inhaled the morning air in the first verse to the time when she exhaled her prayer in the penultimate verse, she breathed life into her personal conflicts and desires. Her quest to bring all conflicting wishes and impulses under control quickly moved from the resolution to master the physical laws of health to an obedience to the spiritual laws of God. And here we can see the culture's and Mary's intimate link between the physical body and the spiritual body, between physical health and wholeness, between spiritual health and holiness.[31]

This is what Mary was attempting to do in her poem. The final two verses impart a mood of sadness that encompasses loss and death. The absence of her dear friends and her feelings of sorrow no doubt reflected a departure in the outside world, perhaps a chum who moved or her brothers and sisters who were leaving the family home. These separations also reflected inner strains related to psychic loss. To overcome the sense of isolation, to help her manage her conflicting wishes and impulses, Mary turned to God. In the final verse, Mary's merger into the loving, protecting arms of God seems to quell her inner division and strife. With God, she attains her wished-for completeness and wholeness.*

Mary's experiences with real as well as psychic loss and death, however, left her very vulnerable as she moved into her adolescent years. In the throes of her many severe illnesses, she may have wished for a special somebody to hold and contain her feelings; someone who could assure her that the world was safe and that she would not die. Despite the genuine concern of her family, all of them, to one degree or another,

---

* This poem illustrates many of the central issues in adolescent separation and individuation. An important article in this context is Anny Katan's "The Role of 'Displacement' in Agoraphobia," *International Journal of Psychoanalysis* 32 (1951), pp. 32–41. Note particularly her discussion of the concept of object removal. Also see Robert Furman's "Object Removal Revisited," *International Journal of Psychoanalysis* 15 (1988), pp. 165–75, especially his discussion of the adolescent's inner sense of loneliness while in the process of object removal. Finally, see the discussion of boundaries and boundary experiences in adolescence in H. Shmuel Erlich, "Boundaries, Limitations, and the Wish for Fusion in the Treatment of Adolescents," *Psychoanalytic Study of the Child* 45 (1990), pp. 195–212.

reminded her of the precariousness of her existence. Albert spoke elo-
quently for the family on this score. During one of her prolonged illnesses, he wrote Mary in 1840 assuring her that she was getting the best
bedside care that she could. He encouraged his plucky sister to keep up
her "usual fortitude," and then reminded her that as difficult as it might
be for her to accept her suffering, it was for her own good. Though the
hand of God meted out the chastisement, He punished in mercy. Albert
closed his letter hoping that Mary would recover, but no matter which
course her illness took, she should accept the consequences "with calmness and resignation."[32]

As Mary lay ill in bed, her brow must have furrowed and her eyes
narrowed on reading Albert's well-intentioned words. Wracked as she
was by bodily illness and emotional stress, Albert's advice was like a
cup of sand offered to a woman dying of thirst. How could a merciful
God permit suffering and the terror of death? How could a just God
permit the inner sense of annihilation that she felt? Perhaps God's angry
hand was something more than mere appearance. To trust a God like
this could leave her at the mercy of the confusion, anger, and anxiety
she felt. Calmness and resignation? As she was to express it years later:
predestination was "the doctrine of annihilation."[33]

This, of course, was not the first or only time she had to struggle with
her family's and the culture's Calvinism. In a later reminiscence, colored
by time, Mrs. Eddy recalled an exchange she had with her mother at
the age of twelve. Previously her mother had taught her to say, after
being punished for naughtiness, that she was sorry and would never
commit the transgression again. One day, trying to come to terms with
her feelings and doubts, Mary asked her mother whether she really
believed in eternal punishment. Mary's mother replied that it was probably true, whereupon Mary wondered: What if we told God that we
are sorry and that we would never do it again? Would God still punish?
If so, then God was not as kind and decent as her mother, and He had
better watch His step. Whether this incident really took place as described, no one now can say for certain. But whether literally true or
not, the story contains important psychological truth, manifesting two
key aspects of the young Mary's emotional and spiritual life: her struggle
with an unyielding God who will not accept atonement for one's guilty
thoughts and actions; and, in conjunction with her rising anger, her
idealization of her mother.[34]

Some of these same emotional issues surfaced in another memory that
an elderly Mrs. Eddy shared with one of her favorite students, Julia
Bartlett. When she was a young girl, Mrs. Eddy told Bartlett, she was
in the habit of praying seven times a day, and on occasion her friends

would tease her, doing "the most aggravating things" to disrupt her rituals, trying to get her to do or say something that she would feel guilty about. In this same reminiscence, Mrs. Eddy intimated that at a very early age she had the capacity to heal her playmates' suffering, and she would beg her mother's permission to do so. Letting her thoughts skip freely, Mrs. Eddy also recalled that she loved to read, but her father thought her fragile health might be impaired, so he hid the books. But Mary apparently had no trouble finding the books, even when her father placed them between mattresses. As Julia Bartlett jotted it down in her reminiscences, Mrs. Eddy, as a young girl, "could find anything" when she put her mind to it.

Mrs. Eddy's thoughts then drifted to another memory of her father. He was a deacon in the Congregational Church, and when young Mary began to spout her unorthodox religious views, he would scold her, telling her that it was the devil's work and she had to pray to God for His forgiveness. Her comforting mother, however, saw something more than a rebellious child; her daughter was special. In the threads of these memories, it is evident that Mrs. Eddy, the leader of Christian Science, was stitching together a seamless past, a religious and healing precocity that probably was not evident as early as she remembered it. Nevertheless, some important themes recurred in these reminiscences: a guilty conscience, an angry father entrenched in his Calvinistic orthodoxy, and an understanding, encouraging mother who recognized her daughter's uniqueness.[35]

A variation of this scenario dominated a number of Mrs. Eddy's reminiscences about her childhood and adolescence. The events she recalled seemed to mimic the gut-wrenching scenes of a nineteenth-century melodrama. As the curtain rises on the final act, we see Mark, a stern Calvinistic father, looming over his frail young daughter. They are engaged in a heated debate over the meaning of predestination and the fate of the soul. To one side of the besieged and emotionally battered young child sits her mother, wringing her hands, silently suffering through the epic struggle. As the heated words swirl about the room, they create an emotional whirlpool in Mary, and, as if on cue, she faints. Barely has her prostrate body touched the floor when the parents spring into action. Mark races out to fetch the doctor, and Abigail rushes to her fallen daughter's side. As she bathes Mary's fevered brow, Abigail urges Mary to "lean on God's love." Nurtured in her mother's arms and in God's love, Mary recovers. The curtain falls.[36]

One battle was over, but this would be a long war. When she turned from the world of her parents to her schoolbooks, Mary could not avoid the message of resignation. Her temper must have flared when she read these words in Murray's *Grammar*: "The best preparation for all the uncertainties of futurity, consists in a well-ordered mind, a good conscience, and a cheerful submission to the will of heaven."[37]

As Mary well knew, it was nigh impossible to have a well-ordered mind without a good conscience. And it is quite difficult for a young adolescent to have a good conscience at all times. The inner struggles to master the thoughts and wishes that come with life's conflicts, the feelings of love and anger, and the guilt may make a young person feel temporarily that there is not much order within. As we have seen, Mary's previous experiences with loss and death would have made an integration of these conflicts even more difficult; but she did arrive at a solution.

We have previously seen that Abigail Baker preached her own brand of Calvinism. Although her softer tones may have blunted the impact of Mark's sternness, the message was still unmistakably there. In a brief anecdote that Mrs. Eddy recalled late in her life, she said that once when she was coming home from school, she found a pitch-pine knot in the woods of a neighbor. She picked it up and took it home, looking forward to watching it burn in the fireplace. Mary's fantasy of the hearth's warmth was chilled by her mother's inquiry: Where had she gotten the pine knot? And had she asked the neighbor's permission to take it? Mary gulped. No, she had not asked permission. Abigail told Mary to take it back because she had stolen it, and God did not permit theft. Mary balked, saying that she was too tired to return it at that moment, whereupon her mother retorted, would Mary really like having God and Mother think until the following day that she had broken His commandment?

Twenty-four hours of guilt would have been about twenty-three hours and fifty-nine minutes too much, so we must assume that a contrite Mary restored the pine knot to the neighbor's woods posthaste. A clearer and fuller picture of Mary's interaction with her mother now begins to come into focus. Besides holding to a doctrine of Christian resignation, Mother Abigail could also imbue a child with a strong imperative, "I should." The punishing eye of Abigail's Calvinistic God apparently observed all acts, no matter how insignificant, and passed judgment accordingly. What a burden for any child! And on the face of things, at least, there seems little here to differentiate the punishing aspect of Abigail's God from Mark's.[38]*

---

* As I have tried to suggest in this chapter, Mary's guilt in a number of these reminiscences has complex origins. While the cultural factors are important—the struggle against her parents' Calvinism—we should always keep in mind that the sources of an individual's guilt do not all stem from the external world. According to Erna Furman, to some degree a child's conscience "also depends on him or herself, on how he perceives

Nonetheless, Mary reacted quite differently to her mother in the capacity of moral preceptor than she did to her father in that role. The struggles with her father were noisier and were, in a sense, carried on in an open arena over a wider cultural issue. Her mother was the less dramatic figure, ever-present but unobtrusive, standing patiently to the side as her husband and daughter engaged in their emotional tugs-of-war. One cannot really blame Abigail for such acquiescence, for it was substantially determined by her culture's expectations concerning proper wifely behavior. Calvinism, and orthodox Christianity generally, granted women respect as long as they remained in the position assigned to them: subordinate to men. By necessity, then, Abigail had to wait for Mary to faint before she herself could become active and rush in. But the damage would by then have already been done, and no matter how caring Abigail was, Mary must have wondered: How can my mother stand aside and permit this? Even though social convention dictates that she stand by my father's side, why doesn't she defend me? Why doesn't she speak up about the loving and protecting side of Jesus? Does she *want* me to be overwhelmed? defeated? humiliated?[39]

Such agonizing questions would have provoked a deep anger in Mary, as they would in any child, but Mary could not safely direct hostile or critical thoughts and feelings toward her mother. For children in those awkward preadolescent and early adolescent years, one of the central tasks is to begin unraveling the psychic ties to the mother. This was proving too difficult for Mary, because the prospect of such inner separation called up too painfully her profound fears of loss and death. To keep herself together, Mary had to exaggerate the differences between her parents and, in her own mind, see them as diametrical opposites. She created a negative ideal which then became safe to attack; her father thus became the stern one, the sole representative of an inscrutable, harsh Calvinistic God. Mary simultaneously created a positive ideal in her mother; Abigail became the nurturing one, the representative of a loving God. With her expressions of anger muffled in this idealization, Mary could see her mother as "perfect," feel consciously nothing but love and admiration for her, and do her best to be like her.

Mary's way of thinking about her parents, one good and forgiving, the other mean and harsh, safeguarded her sense of self, and, as in her dieting, her solution revealed her capacity to use what the culture offered

---

the parents and feels about them, on his life experiences with and apart from them, and on his individual makeup." Erna Furman, *Helping Young Children Grow: "I Never Knew Parents Did So Much"* (Madison, Conn.: International Universities Press, 1987), p. 241. Her chapter "Conscience," pp. 229–46, succeeds in showing what an extremely complicated process the attainment of a conscience is.

in a creative way. That is, the nineteenth century tended to ascribe the same characteristics to the genders that she attached to Mark's masculine, Calvinistic God and Abigail's feminine, loving God. Interestingly enough, the well-known nineteenth-century writer Fanny Fern resolved her conflicts in much the same manner. In Fanny's struggles with Calvinism and her subsequent rebellion against it, she "mentally pitted her mother . . . as a 'Christian' against her father as a 'Calvinist,' " as the historian Ann Wood has noted. This split aided Fanny in quelling her inner turmoil, for in her relationship with her mother "Hell was forgotten, harshness was softened, fear was cast out."[40]

Mary's struggles with the dictates of Calvinism were not confined to the family circle, and they did not cease at the age of twelve. Sanbornton Bridge, like many other New England villages on the fringe of the "burned-over district," felt the warmth of the religious revivals that blazed through parts of New England in the 1830s. In 1837 one of these religious brushfires was ignited in Sanbornton Bridge, and its spiritual heat seared Mary at a time when she was in the throes of emotional and spiritual turmoil. In mid-April of that revival year, Mary wrote George a letter that indicated issues of separation and loss were once again troubling her. She was distressed about the social changes that were rocking her formerly stable family. Over the past year, she recounted, marriage and business ventures had greatly circumscribed the once-wide family circle. Within a year's time, she lamented, "the full family circle" had been so reduced that they were barely able "to form a semicircle."[41]

As we saw in Chapter 1, this loss of family unity was a real one; there was more to it than sons and daughters literally leaving the home. The Jacksonian world had intruded into homes like the Bakers', leading sons and daughters to think twice about accepting the wisdom of the past and the unquestioned authority of parents, especially of the father as head of the family. He stood for the old ways; they for the new. As we also saw, however, these changes did not come without a psychological price. The revival, then, could be very alluring to a young adult trying to make sense of his or her social and psychological worlds.

When sister Abigail wrote Albert to inform him that the evangelical fervor was exercising its seductive appeal upon Mary, Albert took it upon himself to write her a cautionary letter. There was nothing wrong with religion per se, he counseled her; in fact, he believed that a woman simply could not be complete without it. But Albert expressed his disdain for religious excess. Mary, he cautioned, must watch her spiritual step, for in the enthusiasm of a revival, she could easily stumble into "bigotry or fanaticism."[42]

Mary, of course, was not the only adolescent grappling with the meaning of salvation in this period. Ellen G. White, who rose to the leadership of the Seventh-Day Adventists, was plagued by ill health in childhood, and she, too, wrestled with the terrors of death and the uncertainty of salvation. Lucy Colman, the abolitionist, was a young girl in the late 1820s when she began to question her mother about God's goodness. How could He let any of His children be slaves? How could He permit eternal damnation? In her teens, Colman could not find the answers to these questions in the orthodoxy of her Universalist Church, and she left it. Elizabeth Cady Stanton was swayed by the revival message of Charles Grandison Finney, and his preaching helped her first to question her Calvinist heritage and then to reject it.[43]

Recently the historian Barbara Epstein has focused on the gender differences in nineteenth-century conversion experiences. Women, she has discovered, had great difficulty managing their ambivalence regarding active-passive issues. The wish for change, for an assertion of the self, contained an aggressive wish for authority, especially the paternal authority of the Calvinistic God. But this wish conflicted with an equally strong desire to be secure, to be cared for, and to submit to authority. According to Epstein, for a number of nineteenth-century women, "conversion meant the conquest of angry, rebellious feelings and their replacement with joyful submission." One might argue that this active-passive dilemma was not gender-specific, that both women and men faced the dilemma but resolved it differently. Nevertheless, Epstein's findings are relevant to Mary Baker's revival experience.[44]

Caught up in the excitement of the revival, Mary might have had thoughts of sweeping Albert's conservative advice aside, for she was attracted to the Methodist Church with its more lenient doctrines on sin and depravity. But this very option produced even more turmoil within Mary. To embrace Methodism meant to sever the ties to her Calvinistic past—but we need to be cautious here. It would be a mistake to reduce her inner conflict to the pat formula in which the Congregational Church symbolizes her father's strict Calvinism and submission to paternal authority while the Methodist Church represents her feminist strivings and her mother's kinder, gentler God; in reality, the strands of her mother's and father's Calvinism hung around her neck like a tightly woven lanyard. This made it doubly difficult for her to remove it, to cope with the anxiety and guilt engendered by her aggressive wish and transgression.

Mary has left us with one clue that suggests the kind of inner turmoil she suffered as she contemplated surrendering herself to the revival. "Shade and Sunshine," a poem whose very title speaks of a divided self and world, was written by Mary in 1837, and in it she spoke to these issues of separation and loss. Some of the tensions she had filtered into her poem five years earlier had changed, but they had not abated. We find in this more recent poem many of the inner struggles and conflicts that we would expect to find in a girl her age. Her ruminations have become darker than they were in the earlier poem; the sense that resolutions and a firm determination can provide happiness is not so evident. As she looks back nostalgically on her younger years, sadness rather than joy floods her. The reader senses in this poem a young adolescent girl who has learned to put on the appearance of cheerfulness, who wears a social smile easily, but underneath carries a profound sadness that few if any ever see. It is indeed as if her life's experiences had formed her "to suffer in the crowd more gay."[45]

In these opening verses Mary ruminated about the meaning of life, the sense of loss relating to the past and childhood. Her spontaneous transformation into a budding young woman heightened her awareness that she was no longer who she once was, but who was she to be? Her hopes for a brighter future were dampened; in fact, they were "delusive." Indeed, if we did not know that Mary deeply suffered from her illnesses and from her early encounters with the meaning of death, then we might dismiss her line "Though formed to suffer in the crowd more gay" as nothing more than adolescent anguish.*

This last line, however, also suggests that the depth of her suffering had set her apart from others, from "the crowd more gay." Mary pursued this theme in the poem's next verses. She wished to still her inner turmoil, to gain a sense of self-mastery that the social world demanded. Alone she sought—but could not really find—sustenance for her "lonely mind," something that might quell her anxieties. The sense of inner peace and wholeness that Mary yearned for could not be found in solitude, and she turned to a merger fantasy as a way of healing herself. She wanted to become a part of the gentle lap of the ocean's wave, to be embraced by moon and stars whose bright light beckoned to her in the night. She yearned, in fact, to merge and become a part of the universe, "To feel a fellowship of mystic tie."

In these fervent hopes, Mary was influenced by one of her favorite

---

* One of the bodily-psychological changes for Mary may have been the onset of her menses. In 1833 "the normative age of menarche in the United States may have been as high as seventeen," according to Joan Jacobs Brumberg. This important change would have intensified the feelings Mary had begun to express in the poem she wrote in her preteens. See Brumberg, "Chlorotic Girls, 1870–1920: A Historical Perspective on Female Adolescence," in Judith Walzer Leavitt, ed., *Women and Health in America: Historical Readings* (Madison: University of Wisconsin Press, 1984), p. 186.

poets of the sublime, Edward Young. As Marjorie Nicholson has written
about this eighteenth-century poet, "No poet was ever more 'space in-
toxicated' " than he was, nor did any other eighteenth-century poet
"equal him in his obsession with the 'psychology of infinity'—the effect
of vastness and the vast upon the soul of man." Like Young, Mary also
invested the universe, the sky, with "a noble pathos," and her "mystic
tie" was a way of overcoming the unpredictability and uncertainty of
her life.[46]

If one of the central tasks of a sixteen-year-old is to redefine herself
in relationship to her parents, and in this process to define her spiritual
and worldly standards, then Mary addressed herself to these issues in
the last lines of the poem when she described a stream whose gentle
waters, like a mother's love, bathed her cares and concerns. The source
of this stream, again much like her mother's love, was in her childhood,
and as it tranquilly wended its way through her life, it linked her past
and present as it flowed into and merged with the eternal "ocean depths"
of the future. The awareness of eternity as a source of personal fulfillment
in these last lines reflects Edward Young's influence on Mary. In his
popular "Night Thoughts," which Mary read thoroughly and absorbed,
the poem's movement suggested the breaking out of restraints, the expansion into infinite space, the reaching toward perfection.[47]

Mary may have wished for this kind of inner freedom for herself, but
the end of her own poem indicates that she settled for far less. There is
a certain quietness in these lines; one does not feel energy bursting
constraints. The gently flowing stream mingling in the ocean depths
conveys not quite a stasis, but a restful merging. There is not a thrust
into infinite space to overcome limitations; rather, there is a calm bathing
of all woes. There is also no sad farewell to the past or reshaping of it
in order to move on. In Mary's poem, childhood is not lost; it is not
given up, and neither are the ties to the important figures, mother and
father. Where Young sought the expansion of the self in space and
eternity, Mary changed the meaning of these terms. The woe and fears
that she experienced in the first part of the poem are now soothed in a
mother's love.

It was this all-embracing love that allowed Mary to step from the
coolness of the shade (death) to the warmth of the sunshine, thus in-
dicating that no matter how dark her life got, she kept a beacon of hope
alive. Her mother's love (or more correctly, what life experiences, feelings, wishes, and fantasies Mary brought to the love that her mother
gave her) was the bedrock of this hope, the part of Mary that always
shook her small fist against the forces that threatened to overwhelm her.

Abigail's Calvinism was more muted than her husband's, but in her later years Mrs. Eddy tended to exaggerate how liberal her mother was on this issue. This exaggeration probably reflected the emotional needs of the young daughter rather than any advanced theological position of the mother. Even as she stumbled and collapsed in the darkness of her suffering, Mary would keep moving forward, looking for that elusive sense of well-being. And thus the apparent paradox: On the one hand, her tie to her idealized mother kept Mary enmeshed in the past, and she was afraid to let go. On the other hand, this very same idealization, once she projected it into the future, offered the hope for change and a better world. This was a perplexing problem, for Mary could not move in both directions simultaneously. If the two previously cited historians are correct about the year when Mary took her first bite of Graham's bread, then surely we cannot pass it off as a coincidence that she began the diet in the same year that she was trying to find a solution to this emotional conundrum. And it was the same year that she suffered from illness and the religious revival hit Sanbornton Bridge.

The religious revival thus offered Mary a chance to find consolation for her troubled soul and to heal her self. On both a social and a psychological level this was potentially a move toward independence for Mary. This momentous step did not escape her parents' notice, and when Mark had had enough, he brought his Congregational foot down on the whole matter. What Mary felt about all of this has been lost to history. She caved in to his demands, but we cannot place all of the blame for this on Mark's assertion of his paternal authority. Mary had her own reasons for giving in to Mark's demands, and they had much to do with her fears of what might happen if she did "let go" in the revival. Would she be able to control her aggression? Would she be able to channel it into a constructive experience? Or would her aggression threaten to destroy the ties she had to both parents and leave her feeling unable to cope on any level? The risks were great—too great. In the end, she chose not to take the plunge.[48]

There is a coda to this discordant religious episode. In the fall of 1837, the Reverend Enoch Corser became the pastor of the Congregational Church, and he was a minister to reckon with. A "strong, blunt, eloquent, and thoroughly devoted man," Corser was noted for his rousing sermons. As his strong voice reverberated throughout the church, inveighing against evil, he would punctuate his preaching by dramatically slamming his fist down on his lectern or Bible. Mark and Abigail understood Corser's muscular orthodoxy, and they joined the Congregational Church at Sanbornton Bridge in June 1838. A little more than a month later, Mary also joined.[49]

Mary may have paid a price for this gesture to family unity. Late in life, Mrs. Eddy repeated the story that Reverend Corser would not take her into the church unless she accepted the doctrine of predestination. So the struggle with Mark and Abigail was rejoined, and the struggle between Mary and her minister over the meaning of predestination must have been just as severe, because she fell ill. Eventually, Mary was admitted to the church, but her acquiescence to outward forms was deceiving. To be reunited with her parents on the social level, much as she had reunited with her mother's love in her poem, did not necessarily imply that her rebellion had been squelched or that she had been truly integrated within.[50]*

As she moved into her late teens and early twenties, Mary channeled her deepest thoughts into her poetry. In 1841 one of her former teachers married the editor of a local weekly, the *Belknap Gazette*, and not long thereafter Mary's poems began to appear in its pages. During this period some of Mary's poetry was also accepted for publication in the *New Hampshire Patriot and State Gazette*. As her words reached out to a wider world from her home in small Sanbornton Bridge, Mary surely felt a sense of satisfaction and pleasure at being accepted as a writer.

---

* Mary Baker Eddy's recollections about her youth and adolescence reveal that her most intense conflicts centered on issues revolving around paternal authority. Whatever anger she felt toward her mother was deeply buried in the idealization of her. This was not a gender-specific issue. Walt Whitman had the same response to his parents. His anger toward his father was on the surface; it became the stuff of his writing. But there were no real mothers in Whitman's writing, "only a voluminous mother-legend." Paul Zweig, *Walt Whitman: The Making of a Poet* (New York: Basic Books, 1984), p. 39.

Fred Weinstein and Gerald M. Platt, in *The Wish to Be Free: Society, Psyche, and Value Change* (Berkeley: University of California Press, 1969), pp. 144–53, discuss the wider social circumstances that explain why the father in the nineteenth century came under conscious critical examination, whereas dissatisfaction with the mother remained deeply repressed for both men and women. In two books, *The Language of Puritan Feeling* (New Brunswick, N.J.: Rutgers University Press, 1980) and *Manhood and the American Renaissance* (Ithaca, N.Y.: Cornell University Press, 1989), David Leverenz finds similar forces at work in the changing world of the Puritans and among nineteenth-century writers. In the case of the Puritans, Leverenz sees a weakening of paternal authority, a growing ambivalence about the father's role in the family, which led to the construction of a compensating fantasy about God's omnipotent, paternal authority.

One can see some striking parallels in Mary Baker's life. Her father's position in the family was weakened; gender roles were undergoing changes; men in the outside world were anxious about failure. No doubt these wider social issues contributed to the intensity of Mary's struggle with her father's Calvinism. Social and personal factors thus worked in Mary to keep the idealization of her mother intact. The developing person's struggle for individuation and independence may contribute significantly to both genders' need to keep the psychic mother repressed. A thoughtful essay on this topic is Roy Schafer, *Retelling a Life: Narration and Dialogue in Psychoanalysis* (New York: Basic Books, 1992), pp. 82–99.

These refreshing moments, however, were overweighed by her bouts with poor health and the departure of both her sister Martha and her friend Augusta into married life. And, as distressing as these losses were to her, they were minor compared to the shattering news of Albert's death on October 17, 1841. A month later, in the throes of her grief, Mary scratched a poem in her notebook. Albert had died of kidney disease, and Mary's thoughts turned to her own disease and the perpetual imminence of death. In her close identification with Albert, it is as if she took her reading of Isaac Watts's *The Improvement of the Mind* to heart, especially when he urged his readers to view life as unstable and uncertain. The only certainty was death. "From a coffin and a funeral," he counseled, "learn to meditate upon your own departure."[51]

Early in the poem we find Mary lamenting the loss of her health and wondering about the purpose of her "silent suffering," even fearing that she may be destined to an early grave. And, she questions, when it comes time for her to die, will anyone be there to mourn her? One way Mary might have answered this question would have been to create a reunion with Albert in heaven, so that if she felt abandoned here on earth, heaven would hold its own consolations. But surprisingly, Mary's poem takes a much more somber turn. Death held no consolations; it was nothingness; it was annihilation. Is her life to end meaninglessly "as some fated blank"? Is she to be wrenched from life, coldly buried, and then forgotten?[52]

These thoughts are terrifying, and her words, if we are not careful, could be lost in the reams of graveyard poetry that glutted the newspapers and women's magazines of the day. If we place her words in a more personal context—the death of an admired brother, and the traumatic meaning of death to her—then we can more fully appreciate the depth of the anxiety that lay behind these words. Fortunately for Mary, as she mourned the loss of one brother, she had the comforting arms of another. George had returned to Sanbornton Bridge in 1838 to go into partnership with Alexander Tilton, Abigail's husband. As it turned out, George was not the only man in Mary's life during the early 1840s. Hildreth Smith, a cousin, shared her intellectual interests and her love of poetry, and in time he felt deeper stirrings. As Robert Peel delicately put it, Smith's "consanguinity seemed to him an insuperable obstacle to his proposing marriage"; so he left her and journeyed to the South.[53]

Mary, too, probably felt that the relationship was uncomfortably close, that it pressed against forbidden boundaries. In 1840 she published a poem anonymously in Hill's *New Hampshire Patriot and Gazette* which intimated that a cousin had pursued his amorous feelings too far:

"When I Was a Wee Little Slip of a Girl"

When I was a wee little slip of a girl,
  Too artless and young for a prude;
The men as I passed would exclaim, "pretty dear,"
  Which, I must say, I thought rather rude;
  Rather rude, so I did;
Which, I must say, I thought rather rude.

However, said I, when I'm once in my teens,
  They'll sure, cease to worry me then:
But as I grew the older, so they grew the bolder
  Such impudent things are the men;
  Are the men, are the men,
Such impudent things are the men.

But of all the bold things I could ever suppose,
  (Yet how could I take it amiss?)
Was that of my impudent cousin last night,
  When he actually gave me a kiss;
  Ay, a kiss, so he did;
When he actually gave me a kiss!

I quickly reproved him, but ah, in such tones,
  That ere we were half through the glen,
My anger to smother, he gave me another—
  Such strange, coaxing things, are the men;
  Are the men, are the men,
Such strange, coaxing things, are the men.[54]

This is an intriguing poem, for it is unlike any other she wrote. In her other poetic efforts she could take whatever troublesome feelings she had—sadness, depression, anger, excitement—and mask them in the literary conventions of the day. Much of her inner woe was sublimated into the rubescent skies of nature's sublime, and she was proud to put her name below the title of the poem. In this ditty, however, she chose to remain anonymous. Compared to her other work, the poem is explicit; it barely hides the authoress's excitement and anxiety about sexual advances from men. Being attractive or beautiful might be every girl's wish, but such attractiveness invited unwanted advances—rude advances—from others.

As much as she wished to forget the rudeness of men in her early childhood days, she could not do so when she became a teenager, for the effrontery of men grew bolder as she blossomed into womanhood.

The final two stanzas might have contained the event that triggered her associations to the rude men in her past. Her "impudent cousin" kissed her, an act so unsettling that she was not certain whether she read it correctly or not. Her cousin's impudence did not stop with one kiss; despite her anger, he coaxed and took another. This time, and in this poem, nature—the enclosure of the glen—was no protection for her, unlike the way it and her mother combined to shelter her in "Shade and Sunshine."

Even though "When I Was a Wee Little Slip of a Girl" seems so open and direct, it also camouflaged whatever disturbed Mary so deeply. One can sense a young girl—and then an adolescent—being confronted with a situation that aroused excitement and anxiety. In the poem she responds with anger, but anger and resistance are not enough to ward off another advance from her cousin. She is alone and unprotected in this stroll through the glen, and while we may be led to believe that things never progressed beyond the stolen kisses, one senses a young girl about to be overwhelmed. Mary's concern over her relationship with her cousin Hildreth triggered the central worry that fed into the writing of this poem, but one must be suspicious that there were other overwhelmings, hidden and unstated, that found indirect expression in the poem.

In July 1843, Mary and George took a trip to the White Mountains. As their coach tilted and rocked over the mountain roads, this seemed to be nothing more than an ordinary trip that a brother and sister might take. Yet as their bodies were being jostled in the coach, so were the thoughts, feelings, and wishes in Mary's mind. This week's journey would become something much more than she could have anticipated. To appreciate more fully Mary's responses to this trip, let us go back seven years to a trip that her sister Abigail took to the same area.

Abigail and her husband, along with three other couples, had taken a week's expedition to the White Mountains. On one day's journey through the hills, the party ascended Mount Washington and stood atop the majestic peak, breathing in the brisk, clean air, gazing over a sea of luxuriant trees that stretched their limbs to the horizon. Ah, the romantic sublime! Maybe in Emerson's or Thoreau's imagination, but not in the highly practical Abigail's. To her, a tree was a tree. Besides, the ride itself hardly prepared the mind to appreciate nature's beauty. These weekend travelers had to traverse seven bumpy miles on horseback and then trudge the final three miles to the summit. Abigail's reward for becoming one with nature was a pair of badly blistered feet. Once they reached the pinnacle, she grumbled that the view was obscured by a cloud of pollution. To top it off, there was not a house in sight.[55]

If one has read Emerson and Thoreau, Bryant and Cooper, then there is something refreshing about Abigail's sour description of nature, if only the reminder that not everyone in the nineteenth century got swept along by the swift currents of romanticism. Mary's encounter with nature would be an entirely different one, as one might expect knowing the differences between the sisters. In the early stages of her trip with George, Mary cried out that the sad whisperings of the night wind matched the sadness and loneliness in her heart. Even the breathtaking beauty of the White Mountains failed to lift her spirits. If she only felt better, then she might be able to experience the world differently. She had carried a nosegay with her, but it had become withered, much like her own inner spirit. The last thing Mary needed was a reminder from nature about decay and death.

Several days into the journey, Mary's spirits began to lift, and as they did she saw nature differently. It was now suffused with beauty, and Mary wished she could be a bird soaring to the highest peak to drink in God's presence manifested in every aspect. The better Mary felt about herself inside, the more she invested nature with "symbols of invisible power." The pure mountain air served as an elixir, and as her spirits lifted, her lungs felt to her as if they were "an inflated balloon." Mary was soaring. At Littleton she and George separated, but Mary was still feeling so "high" that she suspended her Graham diet and wolfed down some food. She then took the coach to Haverhill to visit Augusta Holmes and her husband. When she arrived, she was met with enthusiasm and affection. For a couple of days Mary enjoyed herself by indulging her sweet tooth and having long, intimate conversations with Augusta. Sadly, there were gnawing worms in this delicious fruit. As we shall see, some of the villagers upset her, thereby undermining her health and prompting her to cut her visit short.

On the trip home alone, Mary could not sustain her good feelings, and blackness began to fill her. When the coach arrived at a small village, she stepped out exhausted, but her tortured mind would not let her sleep. At one in the morning she lay in her room feeling fragile and abandoned, desperately wanting to see her brother. She vowed that she would never again ride alone in a coach at night. Once she got back safely to Sanbornton Bridge, Mary copied a poem of Barry Cornwall's; its final stanza, filled with existential doubts about the meaning of life, seemed to mirror her dark mood at journey's end. And in the margin of her notebook, close to the lines of the poem, she wrote plaintively: to live, to endure pain, to love, to die—was this all there was to life?[56]

The week's trip up, down, and around the White Mountains jarred Mary's emotional equilibrium and led to changes in the way she felt about herself and others. If we retrace Mary's path, perhaps we can grasp why she fell so rapidly from the peak to the valley.

For a while George's guidance and support protected her and, feeling whole and alive, Mary began to view nature similarly. When her inner "nature" and the world's nature mirrored one another, Mary felt ecstatic. In the midst of jotting down these happy feelings in her journal, Mary casually mentioned that she had met some people at an inn who had known her brother Albert. The very mention of his name released her pangs of sadness, and they soon swamped whatever happiness she had been feeling.[57]

By the time Mary got to Augusta's, she was having great difficulty controlling her roller coaster rides from elation to depression. On her first night with Augusta, the sheer joy of being with her friend seemed to blot out all dark thoughts. She had been separated so long from Augusta, and they had so much to talk about, that they stayed up all night—"slept together, or rather *talked*"—until Augusta's husband came home. Mary, however, was starting to have trouble maintaining her emotional balance. Near the end of her visit, she described two women whom she had met who seemed to reflect the very forces warring within her. In their respective ways, both women were daring and assertive, but one Mary liked, the other she disliked. A certain Miss Ann Bryant did not fare well under Mary's critical eye. She thought that she was a very "flippant lady," lacking "feminine softness and dignity." On the other hand, there was a certain Mrs. R. who voiced her politics in a forceful way, but she also conveyed a feeling of genuine warmth. These two women, then, reflected the conflicting sides within Mary. When she could no longer keep them in balance, she was overwhelmed by the darker impulses and thoughts.[58]

This is not quite the whole picture, however. Mary did not disclose everything in her journal; some thoughts she kept even from herself. At the very moment she was riding with George in the coach, she was engaged to another George, a young man named George Washington Glover. Just who was this beau? Mrs. Eddy once told Gilbert C. Carpenter, at one time a secretary to her, that she had met George when she was ten and he was twenty-one. The occasion was her brother Samuel's wedding to Eliza Ann Glover, George's sister. George was apparently attracted to Mary, the pretty little girl, and he sat her on his knee and asked her how old she was. When she told him, he jokingly said that he would return in five years. George returned often, the last time when Mary was twenty-two. As she told Carpenter, she was walking along the streets of Tilton when she thought she saw her brother George strolling ahead of her. Catching up to him, she slapped him on the back and gushed about how well dressed he was. When he turned around, Mary was mortified; it was George Glover. With the passing years, this became an amusing vignette to Mrs. Eddy, but to a nubile Mary Baker, the close resemblance between the two Georges and her approaching nuptials were more than a little thrilling and a little distressing. She was having more than her share of difficulty managing these feelings.[59]

Brother George especially sensed that a cloud of melancholy hung over Mary as her wedding day approached. At Thanksgiving, a few weeks away from the momentous day, George wrote her a poem expressing his worry about her apparent sadness. His concern must have been consoling, but George could not have been expected to understand what a woman would feel about an impending marriage.[60]

We have previously seen that marriage for her sister Abigail—as well as for other women in the nineteenth century—was fraught with anticipation and anxiety. As the historian Ellen K. Rothman has observed, in the nineteenth century women often shared with one another their deepest fears of losing their childhood home once they were married. Childhood probably "stood for the close connection with parents, for safety and familiarity, all of which were at risk in marriage." Mary's deep sadness no doubt stemmed partly from this impending separation, which increasingly began to feel to her like a profound loss. And we should not be surprised that Mary would paste a poem in her notebook whose lines carried the lament of a young woman who slipped a wedding band onto her finger, left her father's home for her new husband's, but anxiously wondered, "What sorrows wait her there?"[61]

As the wedding day drew near, Mary became preoccupied with thoughts of loss and death. She paid a last visit to Albert's grave and wrote a poem which acknowledged that while Albert's strife was over, hers was about to begin: "Thou too may soon follow the spirit that fled/ When far from thy kindred and place of the dead." Mary's earlier experiences with separation and loss may have darkly colored her feelings about her forthcoming marriage, but her fantasies and ruminations about death were not all that unusual. Lydia Maria Child, who had no children of her own, fully understood the pain and loss a mother experienced when her daughter was about to marry. True, congratulations were in order, but Child also recognized that marriage sundered the tie between a mother and her child; indeed, it was "the severest trial a woman can meet, except the death of her loved ones."[62]

On December 10, 1843, George and Mary were wed in her home in Sanbornton Bridge, and on Christmas Day they sailed for Charleston, South Carolina, where George had established a successful contracting business. While the journey south with her new husband seemed to signify Mary's break with the family of her childhood, one senses that she was not able to cut those bonds effectively. George Glover's ties to the Baker family and his resemblance to brother George assured her that at least some ties would never be severed. More important, because we have seen how difficult separations were for her mother, Abigail made certain that time and distance would not cut her off from her youngest child. Some months before the wedding, Abigail asked Mary to write down a poem. Once they were actually apart, Abigail wanted Mary to look at the poem every night and to think of her as she read it. We do not know whether Mary obeyed her mother's wish, but it is interesting to note that in one stanza the drumbeat of Calvinism was insistent. The speaker wanted to know what she had done for Christ, who had died to save her "guilty soul." Obviously very little, for she then asked for God's forgiveness, asked for His help that she might live closer to Him, and that she "offend *no more*."[63]

Abigail had one more piece of maternal advice. As Mary lay seasick in their cabin on the voyage south, George, in obedience to Mrs. Baker's instructions, read to her a poem by Lydia Sigourney. "The Mother's Injunction" brought tears to Mary's eyes, especially the verse that went:

> *A mother yields her gem to thee,*
> *On the true breast to sparkle rare*
> *She places 'neath thy household tree*
> *The idol of her fondest care;*
> *And by trust to be forgiven,*
> *When judgment wakes in terror wild,*
> *By all thy treasured hopes of heaven,*
> *Deal gently with my darling child.*[64]

Mary's tears may well have been for the sentimentality in Sigourney's lines, but they were also for herself. Through her marriage to George, her tie to her mother had not been broken; in fact, it had been reknit. There is more than a little irony in the fact that the mother's voice came through George while Mary lay sick. And rougher times lay ahead for Mary Baker Glover. "It may also be that what was most frightening about the transition to marriage," Ellen Rothman has noted, "was the motherhood it would almost certainly—and almost immediately— bring."[65]

3

BLIND GUIDES FULL OF EXCESS

Ye blind guides, which strain at a gnat, and swallow a camel.

Woe unto you, scribes and Pharisees, hypocrites! for ye make clean the outside of the cup and of the platter, but within they are full of extortion and excess.

Matthew 23:24–25

AFTER A FEW WEEKS in Charleston, business interests lured George Glover and his bride to Wilmington, North Carolina. Once they had settled in, Mary continued to write poetry, and she submitted occasional pieces to the local paper. Back in Sanbornton Bridge, the Bakers had not forgotten their youngest daughter. In their letters, Abigail and Mark expressed to Mary their worries about her continuing poor health. They encouraged her in her efforts to adapt to the ways of the South, and they reminded her how much she was missed. When Mary informed them about a recent misfortune, Mark could not resist dispensing a small dose of Calvinism. He wanted his daughter and son-in-law to trust in God just as Job had done. He gave them his best wishes "both for life and death," and urged them to turn to the punishing yet merciful God they had known in childhood.[1]

The strongest tugs on the cord that tied Mary to her childhood days came, not surprisingly, from her mother. Not long after arriving in the South, Mary sent Abigail a touching poem, "To my Mother, after a long separation." Alone and so many miles from the Sanbornton Bridge hearth, Mary missed her mother's gentle voice and longed for her counsel. As feelings for home and mother grew stronger in the poem, Mary worried that the separation might portend an irretrievable loss, that she might be replaced in her mother's affections by one of her sisters, or even worse, that if she was out of Abigail's sight, she might be out of Abigail's mind. In the next verse she used her memory to salve the wounds of time by recalling the family's singing of an evening hymn and the "family bible" near her father. Her deepest longings, however, drifted back poignantly to her mother and a wish to be close to her once more.[2]

Mary closed her poem with the hope that she and her mother would see each other again, and they would, for Mary had no other place to turn but home. In mid-June the honeymoon was over. George's business went under; he contracted yellow fever; on June 27, 1844, he died. Alone, penniless, and six months pregnant, Mary was truly a stranger in a strange land. With no one to comfort her, she turned to home, as did so many other young women who found themselves in dire straits.[3]

Before setting out on the arduous trip North, Mary put her grief into a poem, "Thoughts at a Grave." And shortly before departing North Carolina in July, Mary talked about severing her ties to the South. The loss here—the leaving of her husband's grave—was assuaged by the thoughts that she would be returning to her childhood home, where her mother's "fondest welcome" would surely dry her tears. Abigail, the comforting mother, would make everything all right.[4]

In early September, just as the leaves were beginning to give a hint of the crisp splendor of New Hampshire's woods, Mary, as she had done in the early stages of her trip to the White Mountains, found it impossible to appreciate the beauty in nature when she felt so ill and in so much turmoil. Abigail might have succeeded in dabbing Mary's tears, but the revival of old dependency conflicts between mother and child was inevitable once the coach deposited Mary in Sanbornton Bridge. There was a major difference this time, though: the child-daughter Mary was about to become a mother herself. This was the stuff of fiction, and the situation fueled Mary's literary imagination.

In a romantic short story that Mary wrote for *The Covenant* in 1846, her heroine, Emma Clinton, experiences some of the intense feelings occasioned by a marriage, death, and birth. Emma disobeys her father's wishes and marries Colonel Beaumont. At the wedding, her father takes in the ceremony with tightly pressed lips, and his eyes alight upon his new son-in-law with "deflected pride and resentment." As her father steps to one side and offers Emma's hand to the bridegroom, she is filled with "bliss and pain," the pain of sadness and separation. Once the ceremony is over, she has to leave her weeping mother, "the guardian angel of her youth, the constant companion of her riper years."

Time passes, and then Emma is jolted by the untimely deaths of her husband and mother. These losses conspire to bring her back home, where she is at last reconciled with her father. The "painful, yet joyful" reunion with him helps to alleviate her profound grief—but, more important, Emma is pregnant. A mother-to-be. With that "holy name [of mother] there was music to her ear, wild aeolian melancholy music, such as lingers when the pulse of life moves slower, but to rekindle its dying embers, to replenish hope with one more blossom." It is this, apparently, this impending motherhood, the promise of a child, that heals Emma's wounded heart, that lifts her spirits and repairs the losses she has so recently suffered.[5]

That was fiction; Mary's reality two years earlier had been strikingly different. On September 12, 1844, she gave birth to a son named George Washington Glover. We do not know Mary's thoughts and feelings regarding her pregnancy, her delivery, and her first months with and without her baby. The historian Judith Leavitt has noted that during the nineteenth century women feared not only the intense suffering of childbirth but also the real possibility of dying. Certainly many women shared Hallie Nelson's feelings as she awaited the birth of her first child: "I began to look forward to the event with dread—if not actual horror." Such emotions were actually fostered and encouraged in the wider culture. Nineteenth-century fiction constantly told women readers to prepare themselves for suffering during childbirth; more important, the Calvinistic strains in their Protestantism taught that childbirth was to be regarded as God's punishment to women. "Countless women, either explicitly or implicitly, related their fears and their pregnancy-related trials to God's will and accepted it as such," observes Leavitt.[6]

We have good reason to doubt whether Mary passively accepted this Calvinistic resignation, for she had already been struggling with it for many years. Emotionally, the conflicts over it that were revived in her pregnancy and childbirth must have contributed to her agony. After giving birth, Mary remained virtually incapacitated for several months. During this period, her son was nursed by a Mrs. Morrison, who had borne infant twins, one of whom had died. While her baby was being nursed by another woman, Mary in turn was being taken care of by family friend and helper Mahala Sanborn. As soon as Mary was well enough, her son was returned to her, but still not all was well, for baby George was thrust into a home with three competing mothers: Mary; her own mother, Abigail; and Mahala.[7]

Mary's anguish, if not depression, must have been considerable. Ideally, the nine months of pregnancy, of carrying the child and feeling it as a part of oneself, help a woman prepare psychologically for motherhood. The unborn child also comes to represent a part of the mother's own body that she will eventually lose, and this impending loss triggers fantasies regarding her own earlier experiences with separation and loss. Thus, even though the earliest mother-child relationships are revived unconsciously in the mother-to-be, she is not locked hopelessly in a regressive struggle; rather, these returns into the past are more than balanced by her new role as a wife and future mother, which, it is hoped, prepares her for motherliness.[8]

Mary's continuing poor health in North Carolina, the death of her husband, and her intermittent illness at home in Sanbornton Bridge all combined to exacerbate the usual ups and downs that women experience during pregnancy. Especially vulnerable to the issues of separation and loss, Mary was not in good enough physical and psychological shape to make the transition from a child/daughter to a mother. While she may have announced in her poetry that she was relieved to be returning to the open arms of her family, this was only partly true. Another part of Mary had wished to establish a sense of independence in her marriage, and by having a child of her own, she could perhaps rework some of those deep ties to her mother. Instead of reworking them and moving forward, Mary was once again overwhelmed by her inner conflicts. As much as Mary wished to take this self-liberating step, she was even more afraid to do it, and thus she remained emotionally attached to the mother of her childhood.[9]

Mary must have felt even worse when she compared herself to her sisters. Martha, who had married Luther Pilsbury, had given birth to a daughter, Ellen, a number of months earlier. Abigail Tilton delivered a son, Albert, several months after Mary's son was born. And here was poor Mary, ill and depressed, unable to care for and to nurse her own child. Not only did she have a hard time measuring up to her sisters, but she fell far short of the cultural ideal for young mothers. Nursing an infant, according to Mary Ryan, was regarded as "one of the most hallowed and inviolate episodes in a woman's life." Moreover, the milk that passed through the mother's breast to the child contained more than mere nourishment. Indeed, the milk and "warmth with which she offered it also conveyed the child's first moral lessons."[10]

And what moral lessons was little George receiving? He was handed to a surrogate mother, returned to Mary when she felt better, and then turned over to Mahala when Mary suffered one of her frequent relapses. One can also assume that in the Baker household, Mother Abigail did not sit idly by while all of this was transpiring, and that she probably helped care for Mary's baby. Given that he seemed to have no single, consistent maternal figure over a prolonged period, it is little wonder that Mary's infant was a difficult child. Decades later, when she was the established leader of Christian Science, Mrs. Eddy told one of her closest helpers, Clara Shannon, that her baby boy had seemed "unhappy, crying, and sometimes screaming piteously." Apparently, no one was able to comfort him. According to Robert Peel, when Mary's baby was born, he cried much longer than one might reasonably expect, for he was "born into a house of gloom, to a mother who remained deathly ill."[11]

It is evident that much interfered with the knitting of a strong tie between Mary Glover and her son. Withdrawn into her illness and depressed, Mary could not fully invest in him and therefore could not satisfy his needs. His crying, his frustration, and his tantrums further served to drive mother and child apart, for his angry cries struck at her own fragility. In those moments when her responses to him failed to console him, as his cries grew louder and angrier, she could not help feeling frustrated, ineffective, and depressed.[12]

Interestingly, when George was two, Mary opened an "infant school" in an attempt to earn some money. Sarah Clement Kimball remembered being in Mary's class. A lonely girl without playmates, Sarah clung to Mary, spending as much time with her as she could. Sarah could recall only one time when she felt afraid of Mrs. Glover. Once in a while Sarah acted up in class, and one day Mrs. Glover decided enough was enough; Sarah would have to be whipped, and Mary sent her to fetch a stick. Her fear mounting, Sarah found the smallest twig she could and brought it to Mrs. Glover, whose eyes darted from the twig to Sarah. Then slowly a smile broke across her face, and she told Sarah to take her seat. That ended the incident. In this episode we can see that Sarah, for her own reasons, needed Mary and loved her. Her dependence and love in turn reinforced in Mary that she was a good teacher (mother), and when she felt good about herself in this way, Mary could handle a disobedient child in a caring manner. In fact, this is one of the first instances we have of one of the great ironies in Mary Baker Eddy's life. With her own son, George, and later with her adopted son, Foster, the parent-child relationship was badly strained. With children other than her own, however, she exuded a glowing warmth and love, a sense of humor, and a gentle firmness.[13]

If only things could have run as smoothly at home with little George. Over the next five years there were times when she was unable to give herself fully to him. As we have seen, when he was two years old, Mary was separated from him for part of the day when she became a teacher. In 1847, when he was three years old, we learn from a family letter that Mary was again down with an illness, and although often too weak to make her own bed, she was able to sit up and do some work.[14]

The next year, Luther Pilsbury, her brother-in-law, encouraged Mary to keep her spirits up and not submit to her "gloomy forebodings." She conveyed some of her depressed feelings to her brother George's fiancée, Martha Rand, but Martha had her own worries. George, who had left home in 1848, was now ill himself. Mary wished she could be there to comfort him, but she was hardly in condition to do that. Her own somber thoughts and feelings had weakened her so that she was in no shape to reach out to others. Moreover, she confided that her heart harbored its own dark secrets, and when she was by herself, they were "unfriendly to [her] eyes." Fate, she sadly mused, had surely conspired against her. Would she ever be able to be what she wanted to be?[15]

In a letter to her sister Martha several months earlier, Mary readily admitted that she closely identified with anyone overcome by misfortune. She surely knew what it meant to be "sick and alone" while living away from home, but she also knew what it felt like to be "completely unhappy" while living at home. There was always the hope that she might get better with the help of her friends; yet she had lost a husband and her son a father, and as her tears fell, she confessed to Martha that she was depressed. She was tired of living; life held no joy for her. Other people might be happy, but she felt so bereft that she might as well die.[16]

By the summer of 1849, when George was approaching his fifth birthday, his grandmother Abigail told her son George Baker that Mary had been gone for the past seven weeks with a Dr. Whidden to Warner and the surrounding area in an attempt to cure her illnesses. According to Abigail, the doctor said that Mary would not live long the way she was. While his mother was away, and in those times when she was depressed and withdrawn, young George tried to attach himself to a male figure. Evidently Mark Baker could not be the caring, protective father figure George needed. The letters tell of no brief moments when Mark might have taken his grandson's hand to go on a walk, to fix a toy, or to mend a field tool. All the evidence indicates that Mark, set in his Calvinistic notions of what constituted proper behavior in a child, could not tolerate his young grandson's outbursts.[17]

To fill the gap left by the lost father, little George created a hero in his Uncle George, at least in his fantasies. In a letter to Martha Rand, Mary said that her rambunctious son often asked about his favorite uncle, and whenever they were in the parlor, he begged her to raise him up so that he could kiss the picture of Uncle George. Mother Abigail related virtually the same story in several letters to George. She relished telling him that she had seen her young grandson standing on a chair kissing George's picture, and in another instance had watched him in the parlor gazing at George's picture and asking for him.

One can well imagine a small child's frustration and anger in knowing that his mother was in the house, but that, for reasons he could not fully understand, he was not permitted to be with her. She was there, but she was not. Despite being surrounded by his grandfather and grandmother, his mother and Mahala, George Washington Glover was almost an abandoned child craving love.[18]

During these pre–Civil War years Mary Glover was, of course, doing more than idly counting her days at home, submerged in conflicts with her parents and struggling to be a parent herself. In the very same letter in which she talked about her son and his love of little Nell, her sister Martha's daughter, she informed Martha that there had been a sleigh-ride party, and in a joyful spirit they were driven to Concord. After dinner they came home, but the rush of the cold New England air must have warmed Mary's spirits because, as she told Martha, they had "a real spree," even though there were no young gentlemen. Maybe there were no young men along for the ride this time, but after an appropriate period of mourning, the young men came courting. Despite some potential suitors—at one point it looked as if another marriage might be in the offing—it all came to nought.[19*]

If for one reason or another the men failed to hold Mary's interest, the same cannot be said for the attention she gave to a number of fads and movements that surfaced in the antebellum landscape. Many of these movements—diet and health, hydropathy, and mesmerism—had their subtle differences, but they also shared a number of points. Each, in its own way, was quasi-religious; each promised an integrated physical and emotional self; each incorporated the period's growing fascination with science—at least the current definition of it—in the quest for harmony and perfection. If these movements harped upon a familiar refrain, no wonder a number of people hopscotched their way from one movement to the next when their expectations were not fulfilled.

In 1848 Mary attended a lecture on phrenology. It is not surprising to find her in the audience for at least one lecture on this short-lived fad. Sarah Josepha Hale, then the editor of Boston's *Ladies' Magazine*, flatly declared that "excepting Christianity, phrenology will do more to elevate women than any other system has ever done. It gives her a participation in the labors of the mind." Hale's optimism was based on the phrenologists' assertion that the brain could be divided into compartments or faculties; each of these faculties they assumed to be the center of a distinct personality trait. By measuring the particular areas on a person's skull, a phrenologist could with assurance predict his or

---

* A letter dated September 2, 1848, indicates that Mary was apparently close to marrying John Bartlett, but he moved to California and died there (Longyear). According to Lyman Powell, at one point Mary's name was linked to that of John Burt, and a certain James Smith seemed interested in her. See Powell, *Mary Baker Eddy: A Life Size Portrait* (New York: Macmillan, 1930), p. 88.

her character traits. Phrenologists argued that such an external, "scientific" reading of the skull provided a way to penetrate beneath the surface to discern the inner psychological, moral, and spiritual qualities.[20]

Phrenology succeeded in drawing a sharp connection between body and mind, and attempted to integrate the two at a time when conventional religion was under attack. As one historian of the movement pointed out many years ago, American phrenologists, unlike their English counterparts, were not antireligious; to the contrary, in America phrenology became a substitute for a failed religious orthodoxy. With its semireligious base, phrenology aligned itself with the proponents of temperance, fresh air and exercise buffs, water curists, and believers in mesmerism.[21]*

No one had to remind Mary that there was a close link between the pain she felt in her body and the pain she felt in her heart. While Sarah Hale may have harbored the wish to elevate women, Mary would have settled for a less conflicted self. The orthodox Christian faith to which she adhered—the Congregational Church—had not brought her the healing she sought. And while phrenology attracted the great educational reformer Horace Mann, the celebrated writer Mark Twain, and the most influential minister of his day, Henry Ward Beecher, Mary Glover's interest apparently ended that night in the lecture hall. But two things about that evening lecture registered strongly: the phrenologist's reading of her traits and the response of the man who escorted her.[22]

The lecturer had asked for a female volunteer, and several of Mary's friends urged her to go up onstage. She did, and the phrenologist, after carefully examining and measuring her skull, said that she was very attached to her friends and that she would stick with them through thick and thin, even die for one if need be. He then announced that Mary had several major aspects to her character: "*Philosophy*—truth combined with conscience—and affection." Finally, he asked whether anyone in the audience could verify his reading. Dr. Nathaniel Ladd, who had been the Baker family's physician ever since Mary was a young girl, testified that the phrenologist could not have been more accurate.

Mary herself knew otherwise. Standing there onstage, she may well have been momentarily pleased when the phrenologist described her

---

* Despite the tendency of some Americans to turn phrenology into a religion, it could never have fulfilled Mary in that way. If the phrenologists in their materialistic assumptions wished to create a church in the body, Mary's wracked body and soul told her that this was a flimsy foundation to build on. While the Congregational Church might not have been meeting all her needs, it continued to preach that there was a higher spiritual reality above corporeality.

character in such flattering terms. After all, this was an age that was increasingly nervous about the meaning of "character"; how one got it, showed it, and recognized it in others. In a world of shifting realities, as Karen Halttunen has shown, "confidence men and painted women" in the 1840s stood as reminders that beneath pleasing and glittering surfaces might lurk deception and danger. But whatever initial glow Mary may have felt quickly faded. She certainly did not need to probe very deeply within herself to know that there was much more to her than this. Did not the contours of her skull reflect anything of her inner turmoil?[23]

The glibness of the phrenologist was not the only thing bothering Mary that night; there was also the evident disingenuousness of Dr. Ladd's response that the phrenologist had been right on the mark. As she wrote to her brother George indignantly—her earlier encounters with the family doctor clearly in mind—could he, George, ever imagine Dr. Ladd saying that about her and meaning it? What hypocrisy, what dishonesty! And so, what had started out as a light, inconsequential evening for Mary ended by calling up memories freighted with personal and cultural meaning.[24]

For a brief moment, let us return to Mary's childhood, when, we recall, she and her father would get into emotional, drawn-out arguments over matters of faith. Sometimes, as we know, in the heat of battle Mary would faint. The horrified Mark would then frantically hitch up the horses and race off to fetch a doctor. In earlier recountings of this family melodrama, the doctor was a weakly defined character, a shadowy figure who made a hurried entrance after all the action had taken place, after the child had been overcome. That doctor, however, was none other than Dr. Ladd, and as it turns out, he had something much more than a walk-on role.

When he was summoned by Mark, Dr. Ladd was being asked to restore not only Mary's health but order and Mark's authority within the family. Historians have noted that by the late nineteenth century doctors were beginning to assume the advisory role heretofore reserved for ministers, "to act," as John Harley Warner points out, "as a moral agent in a religious sense"; but well before that time Dr. Ladd had been functioning in just this role for the Bakers. By bringing Mary to her senses, Dr. Ladd would be reaffirming Mark's Calvinism and the kind of cultural authority it represented. His diagnosis of Mary, then, was never medically impartial; it was loaded with moral/spiritual and gender implications.[25]

After a brief examination, Dr. Ladd would usually dismiss Mary's spells as manifestations of hysteria, but on other occasions he seemed genuinely alarmed about her health. At some point Dr. Ladd came to sense that young Mary was a highly impressionable girl, and, since he had become interested in mesmerism around that time (with its quasi-religious overtones), he decided to try it out on Mary. Through mental suggestion he discovered that he could indeed influence her to some extent, although to friends he bragged that he could stop Mary in the streets merely by thinking.[26]

Today Dr. Ladd would be branded a quack, but in the early decades of the last century he was a respected physician. People would have shaken their heads knowingly in sympathy with the difficulties he was experiencing in helping the intractable Mary Baker. No matter how hard he tried, Dr. Ladd could not bring her "disease" under control. Indirectly, she was challenging his expertise and upsetting the traditional doctor-patient relationship he was accustomed to. Baffled and perturbed as he was by his failure to diagnose her properly and to alleviate her suffering, it is understandable why, in his most frustrated moments, Dr. Ladd might pin the label of hysteria on Mary. It said that he was competent and she was willfully disobedient.[27]

There were times when Mary's relationship to Dr. Ladd was laden unconsciously with other wishes and fantasies. In 1848 Mary wrote her sister Martha a letter that mingled the sigh of despair with the fresh breath of hope. She was weary of drifting through life, a passive vessel being either gently nudged by a friendly breeze or tossed to and fro by a rough gale. She was tired of being sick and dependent upon others. If she could only start something new, something that would allow her a measure of independence. She shared a fantasy along these lines with Martha, confiding that she wanted to learn to play the piano so that she could return to the South and teach. It might not sound like much, especially compared to the success of Abigail, but it would be hers, and if her health allowed, she would be standing on her own two feet.

Dr. Ladd's daughter, Helen, had recently graduated from a school in Vermont, where she had specialized in music. Her father bought her a piano, and this act of paternal pride and love, which would also give his daughter her independence as a music teacher, unsettled Mary. In words tinged with sadness and anger, she wished that her own father had been "*ever* willing to let me know something." It is safe to argue that Mary brought some of these conflicted feelings regarding parental love and autonomy into her relationship with Dr. Ladd. He, in turn, easily read her vulnerability. His casting his mesmerizing spell over Mary and his boasting that he could do anything mentally to her that he wanted clearly indicated that more was at stake in this relationship than a simple diagnosis. No wonder, then, that Mary wrote to her brother about Dr.

Ladd's deceptive flattery at the phrenology lecture. What she could not see, of course, was how deeply involved she was in the relationship.[28]

By the 1840s, Dr. Ladd's diagnoses of Mary's illnesses had become more tempered. Her dyspepsia, which constituted her main complaint, was caused by "a disease of the spinal nerves," since he assumed that there was an intimate connection between the stomach and the spine; nevertheless, he still could not bring her suffering under control. Neither could some of the other doctors who attended her. Her health was not restored on the trip with Dr. Whidden, nor did he provide much relief when he treated her during the summer of 1849. In another instance, in late January 1848, Mary told Martha Rand that even though Dr. Renton had told her that she would be better in a few days, she suspected that her "old pains" were now centered in her right kidney. She was also convinced that if she did not improve, she, like Albert seven years before, would die from a kidney ailment. Later in the year Mary had to stand by helplessly and watch her mother suffer an attack of dysentery. When Dr. Woodbury was called in, he provided immediate relief, but his dose of calomel was too strong, and it blistered Abigail's mouth so badly that she could barely eat or talk.[29]

Mary, like so many other Americans during this period, had little reason to trust in the efficacy of doctors. Historians have offered a number of compelling reasons why many Americans lost faith in the capacity of doctors and medicine to heal in the first half of the nineteenth century, but even if Mary had been privy to this knowledge, it would not have offered her much comfort. No matter what they tried, her doctors, with their pills and drugs, and their advice, failed to heal her body and her emotional wounds. Given this failure, we should not be surprised to learn that in the late 1840s Mary's curiosity was pricked by spiritualism. Indeed, from the time the Fox sisters heard those mysterious rappings in Rochester in 1848, to roughly ten years after the Civil War, spiritualism found a ready audience in America.[30]

For centuries the rational-empirical approach to knowledge moved slowly and unevenly across Western Europe and America. The increasing tempo of secularization, abetted by science and technology in the nineteenth century, strengthened man's grip on the forces of nature as it weakened religion's hold on man. "On an unarticulated level," the historian James Turner has written, "religion came to be felt as disjoined from the tangible realities of everyday life." Where conventional religion was once able to bridge the gap between the rational and the nonrational, between the secular and the spiritual, many Americans anxiously sensed that the gap was yawning wider and conventional religion was losing its explanatory power.[31]

Increasing numbers of people—the poet William Cullen Bryant, the writer Harriet Beecher Stowe, the abolitionist William Lloyd Garrison, and women's rights advocate Elizabeth Cady Stanton, among others—gravitated therefore to the doctrine of spiritualism, which held that the living could communicate with the spirits of the dead through scientific laws, not miracles. If Americans could invest a religious, transcendental meaning in the machine and the electrical mystery of the telegraph, the reasoning went, then other invisible lines that obliterated conventional time, distance, and space—the line between the living and the dead—could be "rationally" explored, explained, and crossed.[32]

As odd as spiritualism may sound to us today, it had a compelling inner logic to many Americans in the nineteenth century. For those who found regular church rituals increasingly dry and empty, there was not much solace to be found in medical science, either. Its track record against disease and death was at best discouraging, at worst terrifying. The people who were enticed into spiritualism were advocates of science, but, according to R. Laurence Moore, they "feared a science without direction and a world without meaning. They called spiritualism science, but it was also a surrogate religion." The voices of the spirits were all they had to keep them from falling into the pit of despair.[33]

Despair and surrender were no strangers to Mary Glover. With each incapacitating illness came the silent reminder that death was always close by. These factors alone, of course, would not necessarily make her accept spiritualism with open arms. In fact, two of her sympathetic biographers argue that she never embraced it; she got close enough to see what it was and then pushed it away. According to Robert Peel, back in Sanbornton Bridge Mrs. Glover "shared in the general interest in the new phenomenon. Apparently her natural curiosity was soon satisfied," for shortly thereafter she was indifferent to it, then actually argued against it. Sibyl Wilbur, an earlier biographer, also acknowledged that Mary lived "fully and deeply" in that New England atmosphere where the pros and cons of spiritualism were debated. Wilbur even argued that a person like Mary who was willing to challenge her father's political opinions "most certainly had ideas concerning Spiritualism." But "to connect her life seriously at any period with Spiritualism is to make use of unwarrantable conjecture," Wilbur cautioned in no uncertain terms.[34]

We do not want to engage in "unwarrantable conjecture," but Mary Baker Eddy's record on spiritualism was not as black-and-white as Wilbur thought. Ann Braude, for one, has recently shown that Mrs. Eddy's and Christian Science's relationship to spiritualism was complex and ambiguous. But that is getting ahead of our story. For the time being,

we need to understand what first drew her "natural curiosity" to spiritualism, whether it was a fleeting interest or not.[35]

As with other people drawn to spiritualism to one degree or another,
Mary had struggled with the tenets of Calvinism, and though she had
joined her parents' church, a silent canker of mistrust, anger, and rebellion gnawed within her. The church's modified Calvinism provided
little comfort for her tortured body and mind, and it failed to silence
the inner voice of despair. She masked her inner turmoil in a brief passage
in *Science and Health*. In her early years she had been a member of the
Congregational Church, but later life's experiences had taught her that:

> her own devout prayers failed to heal her as did the pray-
> ers of her devout parents and the church; but when the
> spiritual sense of the creed was discerned in the Science
> of Christianity, this spiritual sense was a *present help*. It
> was the living palpitating presence of Christ, Truth, which
> healed the sick.[36]

While this terse account leaves much unsaid, Mrs. Eddy does convey
her growing sense of psychological detachment from the church of her
childhood and the church of her parents. Outside the family, this was
the key institution in her life, because it kept her rooted to the past and
to authority. No matter how much suffering she had undergone, it was
not severe enough yet for her to snap the chain of this anchor and set
herself adrift. (Officially, she would not withdraw her membership from
the Tilton Congregational Church until 1875.) Her "Science of Christianity" and the "palpitating presence of Christ" were not yet within
her grasp; she would have to reach out for other possible solutions to
her crisis.

In 1847 she wrote for *The Covenant* a short essay, "Immortality of
the Soul," which was couched in terms of the orthodox Christian doctrine of eternal life after death, a theme which we have already seen in
some of her early poems and letters. Death and decay were stamped on
all earthly things, she declared. What man or woman did not contemplate
the meaning of death and the horrible prospect of an empty eternity?
But, Mary assured her readers, while annihilation and nothingness might
claim the body, man's "inner faculties" continued to grow stronger even
as the body died; the mind would continue its march toward perfection.
The further man progressed, she said, the closer he would come to a
higher way of knowing that simply could not be fully grasped "by
material reasoning and reality."

This higher spiritual truth—the "boundless ocean of truth" that
would fill the deathlike stillness and emptiness of eternity—would ul-

timately be fathomed and investigated by men whose intellectual heritage stretched back to the Enlightenment and the world of Newton. Science was not at war with religion; man's body was not at war with his mind. Scientific experiments could in fact reaffirm the spiritual meaning of life. At some future point, she told her readers, the limitations of language would be overcome; words as we knew them would no longer be needed for communication. Man's intelligence—the words he used in his rational thinking—once "refined, etherealized," would communicate directly "with material objects." Through this "scientific" way of knowing, "all will be accessible, permanent, eternal." When he reached this level, man's passions, his terror of death and eternity, would be eased because of this new level of harmony and integration; things would be rational and understandable.[37]

By the end of this essay, it is clear that Mary has begun to move in another direction. She has incorporated something new in the traditional Christian message about the afterlife. She has given a scientific twist to the conventional Christian belief, and is beginning to question matter's reality. She was, in fact, being driven by the very forces that drove the celebrated Beecher family to take spiritualism seriously if not wholeheartedly. "Painful bereavement, on the one hand, and the desperate hunger for empirical verification of immortality, on the other," Marie Caskey has written, "animated their inquiries and undoubtedly colored their conclusions" about spiritualism.[38]

Spiritualism's belief in a supermundane reality and man's ability to communicate directly with it through that special combination of reason and feeling resonated deeply with Mary Glover. By the late 1840s, Mary's experiences with illness, suffering, and death had begun to reawaken some of those early patterns of thinking and knowing that had never been completely buried in her. In 1848, when she was informed that her brother George was sick, she sent a letter immediately. The coincidence of George's illness and her own dreams bordered on the uncanny. George had no idea "what a strange spirit" she had in such matters. Just about the time she received his letter with the news of his illness, she had a dream about him for three successive nights, and each night she awoke anxious and upset. Somehow she *knew* that something was wrong with George.

This was not the only time Mary had an experience of empathic precognition. The preceding fall, she continued in the letter, she had visited their oldest brother, Samuel, in Boston, and she had had a feeling—a premonition—that somebody in the family was sick. She wished she could be with George, for something in her told her she might be able to help him, but her own poor health precluded that. Fate, often disguised as an incapacitating illness, had always prevented her from fulfilling her destiny. Only once in her life had she known the sweet feeling of having her deep sorrows relieved by her efforts. But at this moment even this thought was too much for her, because she associated her feelings with the death of a person she had trusted and loved. This memory evoked too many powerful emotions, and her thoughts trailed off.[39]

It is evident that Mary's sense that she could feel and know others on an intuitive, preverbal level was being reawakened at a time when spiritualism made bold promises that it could string a line of communication between the living and the dead. This affinity in the ways of knowing and communicating would have drawn Mary's interest to spiritualism. She revealed this unintentionally later in her life. In responding to a number of attacks on her beliefs by conservative ministers in the early 1880s, she disavowed any tie to or interest in spiritualism. She understood the impossibility of communication between the living and the dead. Nevertheless, her life had been punctuated with "phenomena of an uncommon order" which spiritualists had attributed to the power of a medium. She clearly understood, however, that "no human agencies" played a part in her case.[40]

No matter how well she might have been able to "read" people and her environment, Mary was not prepared for the events that befell her in 1849. In the autumn of that year her father decided to sell the family farm; he was planning to move to a new house in Sanbornton Bridge, where things might be easier for his wife, whose health was failing. Brother George married Martha Rand in November, and they left for Baltimore, where he had a job waiting. On November 21, just before her mother and father were to move into their new home, Abigail Baker died. Mary's brief letter to her brother the next day conveyed her overwhelming loss and grief. Words were inadequate; they simply could not begin to impart her anguish.[41]

On December 20—within a month of Abigail's death—Mary had a poem, "To My Mother in Heaven," published in the *Patriot*. Considering that the poem was written shortly after her mother's death, it was remarkable in that it distilled the complex interweaving of thoughts and feelings that accompany the death of a parent into the sentimental and religious conventions of the day. In the last stanza she yearned for "the soft vision" of her mother to come to her, bearing "some balm for human woes" until that day when she would be reunified with her in heaven.[42]

Again, these lines can be read in light of traditional Christian sentiments about loss, death, and reunification. And we can hear much the same two months earlier in a letter Mary wrote to her friend Priscilla

Wheeler on hearing of the death of Priscilla's mother. Mary urged Priscilla to rejoice; in death her mother's joy was "unspeakable" and filled with "glory." Mary fully understood Priscilla's temptation to surrender to her sorrow. But a well-disciplined mind such as hers should not "dwell with aching memory on the past," for the past was gone; yet that which was lost could be recovered. "The virtues of the parent stem dwell in the fruit and blossom, and the Mother still *lives* in her daughter—and with what pleasure (I had almost [said] pride) you may perpetuate the living remembrance." Thus, in the presence of overpowering grief, Mary counseled her friend to deny the sadness and transform it into happiness and rejoicing. The loss, furthermore, could be denied through a strong connection with the mother. Broken harp strings would be restrung; the mother would continue to live through the daughter and the daughter through the mother.[43]

Overtly there is nothing to indicate that Mary turned to spiritualism in her advice to Priscilla. More important, she did not embrace it when attempting to deal with the crushing death of her own mother. In the privacy of her notebook, however, Mary confronted feelings within herself that sometimes were too strong to be easily disguised in prose and poetry. In a poem titled "My Soul Is Dark," Mary ruminated about her own dead mother, and she admitted that she had "a strange strange yearning to mingle with the dead." It is difficult to know how to interpret this deep anguish. The title of the poem and Mary's repetition of "strange" suggest that her thoughts, and perhaps the depth of her feeling, were shocking and unnerving even to her. Was she reaching a level of despair that might make spiritualism attractive? At this point in her life, the evidence does not indicate so. Even if she could no longer count on the institutional church as a safe harbor from her inner storms, her Bible continued to provide such protection.[44]

Potential spiritualism aside, death continued to hover over the Baker household. Luther Pilsbury, Martha Baker's husband, died suddenly of cholera. Widowed and left with two children, Martha moved into Mark's house, where she was greeted by Mary and her son, George. Less than a month later, at Thanksgiving, the family gathering was a somber one. In a letter to George, Mary noted that the holiday had come and gone, and where, she questioned pointedly, were "the absent and the *dead*"? The empty chairs around the Baker table were mute testimony to absence and death. Although Abigail Tilton had joined her sisters, Mary had the dark feeling that before another Thanksgiving passed further separations and deaths would take their toll on the family.

The family was not as united in grief as it first appeared. As Mary continued in her letter to her brother George, she had had a misunder-

standing with her sister Abigail; it had resulted in some angry words
and hurt feelings. Furthermore, she did not know why George had
spoken so "cruelly" about her to Abigail, and she was incensed that she
and her young son were treated so unfairly. Mary's feelings were bruised,
but she found it in her heart to forgive her brother. Then, almost as if
it were an afterthought, Mary told him that next Thursday their father
was going to marry Elizabeth Patterson Duncan of Candia, New Hampshire. She had already begun to move in some of her furnishings.

Mary might have been upset with her brother and sister in the early
paragraphs of the letter, but here, mingled in with her other complaints,
was where she harbored her deepest resentment and anger. Barely a year
before, she had been the one who had helped her father clean the house
and arrange the furniture. Then she had lived with him and a servant
girl all winter long. Apparently being cooped up with his grandson for
the winter months had been too much for Mark, because at one point
in the spring he told Mary that if her son was not sent away he would
put him in the poorhouse. How, Mary wondered, after he had threatened
to throw her son out of the house, could he ask her to help him get the
home ready for his new bride? She would rather see her father and
Elizabeth "in the bottomless pit" before lifting a hand to get the house
ready. It is clear that Mary resented her father's happiness. To her, the
marriage meant not only that her mother would be replaced but that
she, too, would have to go.[45]

Feeling enraged at her father and his new bride, tasting the fears of
being displaced and abandoned once more, what was Mary to do? Since
her father refused to allow her six-year-old son to stay in the house, the
tensions in the home would only get worse with the new Mrs. Baker
taking her place at Mark's side. Abigail Tilton opened her doors to
Mary, but the invitation was not extended to young George. Unable to
stay at home, unable to manage her son, and unable to make her own
way in the world, Mary chose to live with Abigail and her family. This
was a hard decision, for she would have to surrender her son to others.
It was decided, probably by Mark, that George should live with Mahala
Sanborn, who had taken care of him when he was an infant. Mahala
had recently married one Russell Cheney, and the two of them were
moving to the village of North Groton, some forty miles away in the
foothills of the White Mountains.

Some of Mary's conflicted feelings found their way into her notebook,
in a poem written on May 9, 1851, the day she and her son were
separated. As he set out on his new voyage of life without her, Mary
urged him to keep God as his guide and the Bible as his anchor. She
acknowledged that his early years had been stormy; he had never known

a father's love, and he had often been frail and sick. She prayed that he would not be burdened by "the early blight of [his] unprotected years."[46]

Mary revealed the fuller extent of her pain in a letter almost two weeks later. While her son was staying with his aunt and uncle in Concord, Mary wrote them saying that Mrs. Cheney had stopped by and would be returning the following week. She was very fond of children and was anxious to have George with her when she returned to North Groton, so Mary asked the Glovers to please have George back by the latter part of the week. Mahala had told Mary that the schoolhouse was only about a quarter of a mile from their home, and Mary wanted him to attend.

This was the nuts-and-bolts part of the letter, but the separation from her son touched upon past associations with loss and death. The memories and feelings were almost too much for Mary, and her anguish spilled out on the page. She desperately missed George. Every day at twilight the feelings would become more intense. Often she stood by her window and gazed at "the sacred spot" where her mother was buried. Silently to herself she sought her mother's "blessing and counsel," while all the while envying "her repose." The connections and associations dredged up in Mary's mind by the loss of her son must have run a troubling gamut: young George's relationship to his mother, Mary, and young Mary's relationship to her mother, Abigail. She could not, she admitted, write on this subject anymore; words were "impotent things" to convey the depth of her feelings.[47]

These ineffable feelings eventually found expression, albeit indirectly, in bodily illness. In early January 1852, Martha Pilsbury passed on the dreary news to George's wife that they had found Mary very ill, suffering a particularly severe attack of "dispepsia, liver-complaint and nervous disease." Martha found it impossible to chronicle the ebb and flow of Mary's illness over the past few months, or even to describe the fluctuating hopes and doubts that they all felt regarding the course of her suffering. Mary had been so ill that she was bedridden, except for an occasional carriage ride. As for the state of her health at that very moment, the prognosis was not good at all. Mary's strength seemed to be declining every day, and whatever energy she had was being consumed by the disease. Even the strongest person, Martha wrote, would be affected by Mary's suffering; her pain and agony were indescribable.[48]*

---

* As painful as her psychosomatic episodes were, they need to be seen in another context. Irving Schiffer, *The Trauma of Time* (New York: International Universities Press, 1978), p. 83, makes this point about using the body to express deep emotional pain: "I would emphasize a more positive aspect of somatization, where the body ego, in acute distress, acts as a bastion against more serious disturbances, sacrificing a part in order to protect

She had so many personal wounds to bear: the loss of both husband and mother, her father's remarriage, the separation from her son as an unwelcome reminder that she was not a maternal ideal, and her illnesses. Some members of her family did their best to comfort her; sometimes one can get the impression from the family letters that Mary's life was one disaster after another. While her physical and mental anguish did tend to dominate, this is far from the whole story. Her scrapbooks indicate that she was an avid, promiscuous reader. Scattered among the graveyard poems and other dirgeful ditties were recipes, an article on the history of California, a phrenological study of Lydia Sigourney, a poem by John Greenleaf Whittier, and pithy quotations from Shakespeare, Byron, and Pope. Both varied and virtually endless, her reading list stretched from the classical to the romantic.

While living with Abigail's family in Sanbornton Bridge, Mary borrowed books from a neighbor's library, and, like most everyone else in the North, she read Harriet Beecher Stowe's *Uncle Tom's Cabin*, though she was not overly impressed with this best-seller. The *Patriot* kept her informed on current issues. She kept a keen eye on the divisive Mexican War, the boisterous elections in the 1840s and 1850s, the noisy protests of the antislavery movement, the growing strength of the women's movement, as well as a host of other reform movements.[49]

As we have seen, Mary had her private quarrel with established institutions, so it should not surprise us that she was attracted to a number of reform activities, especially after they had become infected with the spirit of romanticism. Imbued with a moral and religious fervor, many women in the antebellum period eagerly joined a wide variety of benevolent associations, temperance groups, and reform movements of every stripe. As Sarah Evans has recently noted, in creating these voluntary associations, women began "carving out a public space located between the private sphere of the home and public life of formal institutions of government." In these cultural spaces, comforted and emboldened by the support of other women, they were able to create and try out new roles for themselves, to test new boundaries of self-expression and (limited) autonomy. Elizabeth Cady Stanton, Dorothea Dix, Mary Gove Nichols, the Grimké sisters: they were the highly recognizable tip of a very large iceberg.[50]

Mary never marched in this parade of women. One may argue that her illnesses prevented her from joining their ranks, but one can point

---

the whole." From what is known of Mary's traumas and the narrow avenues of expression afforded by her culture, one can argue that in the midst of all her suffering, she found a way to protect herself from her overwhelming fears of death.

to Mary Gove Nichols of water cure fame, and to a certain extent Catharine Beecher, as women who overcame frail constitutions to leave their strong imprints on reform. Yet indirectly Mary's poor health was a critical factor. The sense of social upheaval, the bitter conflict and intense excitement that were unleashed in the 1840s and 1850s, might have opened the door for change and growth for some people, but that highly disruptive social world could be emotionally threatening and undermining for others. As for Mary, she was always a deeply sensitive "reader" of the outside world, but she was not always able to regulate her feelings and responses to people and events. She was, therefore, at risk of being made helpless by the social turmoil and by her agitated feelings.[51]*

Mary lost the chance to participate in the activism of social reform, to have roots in new friendships and institutions even as old attachments were falling away, to know that she could be competent and effective in the outside world, because she never attached herself to these networks of women. To be sure, she was also spared the frustrations and defeats that come from any reform activity as one's hard work is met by indifference or entrenched foes. Everyone's life, of course, consists of roads not taken, but Mary's isolation from close contact with women's reform organizations had important consequences that were not immediately apparent. Lori Ginsberg's recent work on women's moral reform movements before, during, and after the Civil War helps us to understand what those consequences were.

According to Ginsberg, as America edged closer to the Civil War increasing numbers of female reformers recognized the limitations of moral suasion, which had been couched in the language of female values. Men controlled political and economic power, and they were not persuaded to change their ways. Sometime during the 1840s and 1850s a number of younger women came to the conclusion that for benevolent reform to work, women, like men, would have to get their hands dirty: "Benevolent women began to speak less of moral regeneration and increasingly of shortcuts to reform. Like men, they focused more and more

---

* On the role of one's perception of reality and the notion of safety as a feeling state (and why Mary would have had trouble managing the social tensions and disorder of the period), see Joseph Sandler, "The Background of Safety," in his *From Safety to Superego: Selected Papers of Joseph Sandler* (New York: Guilford Press, 1987), pp. 1–8. Mary P. Ryan, *Cradle of the Middle Class: The Family in Oneida County, 1790–1865* (New York: Cambridge University Press, 1981), points out that the reform associations seemed to vie with the middle-class family as an agent of socialization, and during the 1830s and 1840s these organizations helped individuals adjust to the changing world around them. Without this kind of support, Mary was thrown largely upon her own resources.

on electoral and institutional strategies with which to accomplish the work of benevolence."[52]

This kind of practical dirt never got under Mary's nails, and her hands never bore the calluses from the hard work of reform. In turn, this meant that her impressionistic way of knowing reality would remain protected from the hard knocks of the real world. Mary, however, did not seal herself off in her home, prostrate with illness. If, as Sarah Evans has told us, other women were able to create real and psychological spaces for themselves in the world as a way of enhancing their development, then in narrower quarters Mary creatively played her version of this game. That is, she used her poetry as a way of simultaneously interacting with the world and remaining a safe distance from it. The range of topics in her poetry was wide: graveyard elegies, the romantic's mountain gloom and mountain glory, nationalistic fervor, war heroes, woman's rights, the candidacy of Franklin Pierce, the coming of the Civil War, and so on. To one degree or another, each of her poems allowed her imagination to roam over feelings and thoughts, and in integrating them into the structure of the poem (along with her idealism, which was not directly challenged by outside reality), she was able to feel that she was being active, that in the act of creating the poem she had accomplished something.[53]

In one sense, Mary's poetry functioned like a mirror in that the poem—the shaping and reshaping of the words, the rhythms of the lines, the harmony and symmetry of the form—became an image that reflected to her a momentarily whole self. Mary's poems, furthermore, would be read and reflected in others' eyes, and her creations (she hoped) would be praised and admired. One can well imagine the deep sense of satisfaction Mary had when her poem "Woman's Rights" was accepted in *Gleason's Pictorial Drawing-Room Companion* in February 1853, and even more impressive was her publication of "Lake Winnipiseogee" in the more prestigious *Godey's Lady's Book*. *Gems for You*, an anthology of prose and poetry by New Hampshire authors, included two of her earlier poems. It was hard to believe, but there she was, Mary Glover sharing the pages with Sarah Josepha Hale, *Godey's* editor.[54]*

---

* Years after I had first written this paragraph, I discovered Thomas Simmons's *The Unseen Shore: Memories of a Christian Science Childhood* (Boston: Beacon Press, 1991). On page 108 he talks about his own writing of poetry in strikingly similar terms. This is a lovely passage and worth a full reading:

> For me the beauty of poetry was inseparable from the beauty of bodies, yet it had one essential advantage: it did not require contact with beautiful bodies. It required contact instead with words, sounds, methods, ideas, music. It was sensuous without being sensual. Thus it bought me time as I wrestled with passions that drew me

In another, related sense, Mary's poetry acted as a bridge to the outside world, a transitional object that allowed her to link life's real events (with her conscious and unconscious thoughts, wishes, and feelings about them) to the world of her creative imagination. Psychically speaking, the two crossed paths in a specially created space: a transitional sphere. This metaphorical space lies between the illusionary space of imagination and dreams and the space of hard reality. (Or perhaps more accurately, in the transitional space a person can creatively stitch together the usually incompatible worlds of illusion and reality.) In the safety of this transitional space, Mary could work on the unstable equilibrium between her wishes to merge and be dependent and her countervailing wishes to be separate and independent.

These concepts—transitional object, transitional space—are D. W. Winnicott's, and this British pediatrician/psychoanalyst had the gift of making the complex beguilingly simple. "This intermediate area of experience," Winnicott said, "unchallenged in respect of its belonging to inner or external (shared) reality, constitutes the greater part of the infant's experience, and throughout life is retained in the intense experiencing that belongs to the arts and to religion and to imaginative living and to creative scientific work." Mary Glover's poems served many of these same creative functions, and she was beginning to frame an allegiance to a self she could not yet name.[55]

A number of Mary's poems, for example, continued to dwell on the themes of loss and death, and on the wish for a reunification with a lost loved one, especially her mother. Yet in some of her Civil War poems, Mary boldly championed the cause of the Union, which, of course, many Northerners were doing. In Mary's case a more personal element was involved: though her father thought that slavery was a sin, he was an adamant defender of states' rights. Mary's celebration of the Union's cause put her at odds with her father's political position and thus may have represented a modest assertion of her wish for independence.

The assaults on the body politic, the increasing social fragmentation, and the growing rift in the house divided resonated metaphorically with Mary's own bodily infirmity, her own inner conflicts, and the tensions within her own family. The harmony she wished for herself was extended to the nation. For instance, the poem "The Flag of Our Union," written

more and more ardently to bodies themselves—to their fragrances, their caresses, their private and fundamental responses to love. I did not see myself as walking a tightrope between Christian Science and sexuality, but of course I was. Poetry was my balancing pole. In words I could give a sublimated shape and context to my passions; I could engage the spirituality of my religion without abandoning the intensity of my life in the world.

for the *Patriot* in 1852, ignores the social and political fragmentation in the country as it moves inexorably toward war. The poem instead focuses on the flag as a symbol of unity, tying together the past, present, and future generations. In "The Grave of Ringgold," "Lines on the Death of Colonel Ransom," "American Heroes' Festival," "Our Country," and "To General Cass," all published in the 1840s and 1850s, the death and destruction of war are transformed into a healing process for the nation. In her graveyard poems and more somber pieces, the sense of loss and death is contained within the embrace of a loving figure, whether it be a mother, nature, God, or a condensed image of the three.

In one poem, "Voices in Spring," which was also carried in the *Patriot*, Mary treats spring as a metaphor for the heart or psyche. On the surface, she is thrilled to hear the chirping of the birds, to feel the gentle breeze, to smell the delicate flowers; indeed, life is invigorating. But Mary's winter memories have not completely receded; soon colder, darker thoughts begin to surface. "Strange yearnings from the soul's deep cell gush for loved voices gone," she laments. And these lonely, sad feelings, these terrifying feelings associated with death, begin to merge with the happier feelings associated with spring. By the end of the poem, Mary, confused by the conflicted stirrings in her soul, asks, "Oh! Spring, what wakest thou in the heart?"[56]

In a poem inspired by the appearance of a wild rose in her garden, Mary created some of her lushest romantic imagery. When she turned to nature, it whispered to her in a special way. Mary's words were tinged with transcendental feeling, especially when she wrote, "Where all nature in converse with Deity speaks/In soft symbols of beauty. . . ." When she listened to the comforting message of God in nature, she found a solace that life failed to provide.[57]

Mary clearly infused nature with religious meaning, and while it may never have become an outdoor church for her the way it did for Emerson, Thoreau, and other transcendentalists, Mary's imagination invented a deeper devotional experience in her poetry than she had experienced as a seventeen-year-old joining the Congregational Church. In her poetry, her words were like a mirror held up to nature; they might reflect God, but since He surpassed His world and the human language seeking to mirror it, she knew the imperfections and limitations of her writing. But there was something she did share generally with other romantic writers: her sentimental effusions contained both the longing to merge with a parental figure and a rebellious wish to break from the past. For the time being, there was no resolution for this paradox; thus she stayed rooted in her home and church.[58]

In 1853 Mary's thoughts about her writing were temporarily interrupted, for she had become attracted to her dentist, Dr. Daniel Patterson, a relative of Mark Baker's second wife, who resided in Franklin, a small village several miles north of Sanbornton Bridge. Raised as a hard-working farm boy in Maine, he was trying now to eke out an existence as a peripatetic dentist. One young town resident remembered her mother telling her how Patterson courted Mary: he was "very much a ladies' man" and was persistent in his wooing of her. With much pomp and splendor, he used to drive up to the Tiltons' home with "white horse and carry all." Patterson would then, like a dashing knight, carry the weakened Mrs. Glover out of the house and place her in the carriage. Mary would always wear white gloves, and with her hands folded properly in her lap, she rode erect and proud as Patterson slowly walked the horse through the town.[59]

When one considers the tensions in the Tilton home, Patterson's calls must have been a soothing tonic to Mary. Six years earlier she had written a short piece for *The Covenant*, a romantic tale that may have foreshadowed her growing interest in Patterson. Her heroine, Martha Graham, did not quite fit the feminine stereotype. She was beautiful but not capricious; her femininity was cast "in a superior mold." Many young men sought her hand, and she devised a scheme to determine the best suitor. She wrote each one a letter saying that she was destitute and then sat back to see how each would respond. Sifting through the responses, she felt that only one person, Frank Cleaveland, genuinely cared about her welfare. Some of Martha's suitors had more money, a better education, and a better pedigree than Frank, but he was the only one to open his heart totally to her.

When Frank finally summoned enough courage to propose to her, Martha did not blush, become giddy, or swoon. Instead, "a glow of pride and gratification" touched her cheek and then "frankly extending her soft white hand, as it clasped in his," she softly whispered, "the friend of the widow and fatherless cannot fail to make a sincere lover and worthy husband." Frank's response also confounded typical expectations for manly behavior. He, rather than the maiden, blushed. He had courted his ideal, and he had won her. Martha, the fair but strong damsel, had also found something worthy in Frank, her persistent knight.[60]

Many years later Mrs. Eddy discussed her marriage to Daniel Patterson in much more practical terms: she wanted a father for her son, George. While this may have been her paramount consideration, the exchange of letters between Mary and Patterson in 1853 suggests that there were other factors as well. One of Mrs. Eddy's biographers is at least partly right when he says that they each got married "to images

out of their own ideal conceptions." Another possible motive is hinted
at in the inversion of gender characteristics in the short story described
above. Part of Mary was marrying out of a quiet rebellion against the
conventional patterns of authority she had known. Daniel Patterson was
a Baptist; Mary Glover was a Congregationalist. After they became
engaged in March, Mary began to have second thoughts. Despite her
own struggles within Congregationalism, she was not ready to throw it
aside and accept Patterson's faith. She wrote him a letter to this effect,
and also told him that she had discussed the forthcoming marriage with
her father, implying that Mark was less than sanguine about his youngest
daughter's marrying a Baptist.[61]

Over the next month their relationship traveled a rocky road, but
near the end of April their engagement was on again. The tensions and
excitement attendant upon the forthcoming marriage may have been
too much for Mary, because she lapsed into illness. On April 29, she
wrote to her fiancé that she could not see him because her health had
declined. Some of the old plaints had returned; "neuralgia in the spine
and stomach" had flared up again, causing a condition of "nervous
inflammation." She was becoming increasingly anxious that she might
be bedridden for several months, and her only relief, she disclosed to
Patterson, came from the morphine her doctor had prescribed. Though
the drug did its work, she disapproved of it. A few days later she wrote
Patterson with the news that she had switched doctors. Her cousin Dr.
Alpheus Morrill, a homeopath, had prescribed cold water, and some of
his remedies apparently began to have some effect, although she remained bedridden.[62]

On June 11, 1853, Mary and Patterson were married in the Tiltons'
home. Mary was far too ill to walk down the stairs for the ceremony.
Patterson carried her, and as soon as their vows were exchanged, he
carried her back to bed. If Mary had hoped that her second marriage
might help to get her back on her feet, this was not an auspicious beginning.[63]

Mary did not snap back from her illness. After several months she
was finally able to join him in Franklin, where they lived at first in "a
dingy tenement" underneath a tailor's shop. A little later they bought a
small house, and Patterson had a horse for his dental rounds. If Mary
had expected Patterson to play Frank Cleaveland's role and become a
"friend of the fatherless," she was quickly disabused of this notion, for
Patterson wanted nothing to do with young George Glover. Even when
they moved from Franklin to North Groton in 1855 so that Mary could
be closer to her son, who was still living with Mahala and Russell
Cheney, Patterson refused to allow George to live with them. Just why

he rejected George is unclear, although the boy would have been a handful for anyone, and Patterson realized that George's antics had a way of driving his mother into emotional and physical relapses.[64]

George was now eleven years old and showed none of the signs of a well-adjusted boy. Living with the Cheneys apparently was no bargain. Mahala loved him, but her husband, Russell, was known as a hard taskmaster and a strict disciplinarian. According to Jewel Spangler Smaus, Russell "treated the boy more like a hired hand than a foster son." Myra Wilson, a blind girl who served the Pattersons in these years, clearly remembered young George and the trouble he caused. Her brother had worked for the Cheneys, and he had to bunk with George. They did not get along because George was "rough and would not mind anyone." George, Wilson said, was equally disliked by the children at school, and the Cheneys finally stopped making him go. George evidently had the ability to provoke more people than his mother.[65]

A niece of the Cheneys, Mrs. Sarah C. Turner, recalled a telling incident involving Mary and her son that may have been acted out more than once. One time when George paid a visit to his mother, Mary was in her room with the door locked, lying in bed ill, unable to move. Finding himself locked out and separated from her, George moved to the side of the house and tried to enter through the window. Turner believed that this was merely another example of George's willful disobedience and his wish to irritate his mother. No doubt Turner was partly right, but one can look at this incident from another angle. George's angry outbursts, his quarrels with his classmates, his inability to take pleasure in his schoolwork, all indicate that living with the Cheneys never erased his earliest emotional scars. If Sarah Turner had been able to see past George's provocative behavior, she might have been moved by how profoundly sad this event was. George was still trying to reach out to a mother who could not extend loving arms to him. She was removed from him, literally and figuratively. And from the other side of the door, a part of Mary may have wished to be with her son, but another part of her could not bear to be reminded of so much pain and anguish.[66]

By April 1856, it no longer mattered whether the door was locked or not. The Cheneys had decided to move to Minnesota and to take George with them; Mary would not see him again for almost a quarter of a century. Part of her may have never been reconciled to living apart from her son, but she was totally unprepared for this move and such a final separation. Current evidence unearthed by Smaus indicates that Mark Baker and Daniel Patterson conspired in having George placed in the custody of the Cheneys and in allowing him to be taken out of the state. It is hard to believe that at the time Mary was fully aware of the complicated legal maneuverings that wrested her son from her, but she may have suspected something, for in *Retrospection and Introspection* she said that "a plot was consummated for keeping us apart."[67]*

As it was, she immediately lapsed into a prolonged illness, and her health was fragile over the next several years, with Patterson having to spend a great deal of his time taking care of her. In May 1857, she noted in her scrapbook that she had had a poor night's sleep because she had been tortured by "memory *and wounded feelings*." Her spine was so inflamed and weakened that "the least mental emotion" caused her pain beyond words. She wondered how long she could bear it. A month later Martha Pilsbury wrote a letter to a family member wondering the same thing. Mary had been a virtual invalid for the past year and a half, with little hope for her recovery.[68]

Outside the immediate family, there was not much sympathy for Mary Patterson and her husband. As one old-timer told Georgine Milmine about Mary during these years, "Even good sensible people about everything else, to be carried away with *this* woman, will prove one of the rounds of 'witch-craft'—and if the managers of public affairs were on duty as in Salem 100 years ago, I'm sure she'd have the *same* treatment and *her* life taken upon the gallows." A nasty statement, and one all too easy to dismiss out of hand; yet it is worth examining for what it reveals about the villagers' perceptions of Mary and her husband.[69]

Even at a casual glance, Mary did not fit the popular stereotype of a witch. No matter how sick she seemed to get, no matter how withdrawn, she remained a remarkably attractive woman. Back in Sanbornton Bridge, Sarah Clement Kimball vividly recollected that Mary was "tall, slender, and exceedingly graceful." She had soft, silky, reddish-brown

---

* The circumstances surrounding Mrs. Patterson's relationship with her son and his eventual removal to Minnesota are highly complicated, to say the least. Her critics have cited this separation of mother and son as an example of what a self-centered, unstable person she was. Her supporters have stressed the deep love she felt for young George and her real inability to control events. As with so much else surrounding Mrs. Eddy's life, the "reality" is elusive. One might be safe in arguing that she loved her son, but because she was so susceptible to being upset by the emotional states of others—especially one as close to her as her son—she simply could not bear being with him for too long. Jewel Spangler Smaus uses recently discovered legal documents to build a case supporting Mrs. Eddy's contention that she wanted to keep George. We still lack Mrs. Eddy's full, explicit statements from the period, expressing what she felt about the whole affair. Her illnesses at this time, as I have suggested in the text, were, of course, related to the separation and eventual loss of her son. But her illnesses must also be seen as symbolic expressions covering a wide range of thoughts and feelings triggered by issues of separation and loss. On the legal documents, see Smaus's "An Important Historical Discovery," *Christian Science Journal* 101 (May 1983), pp. 284–88.

hair, which she wore up in ringlets. She also had striking blue-gray eyes. Sarah remembered her uncle saying that when he was a boy he used to sit in church thinking more about Mary and her good looks in the next pew than the stern words of the minister. Having an attractive widow in town may have set some men's eyes wandering, but it also set some tongues wagging when Dr. Richard Rust, a Methodist minister and a married man, was seen dropping by the Baker house quite frequently.[70]

Mary's beauty was not lost upon the people in the small villages that she called home before the outbreak of the Civil War. She was a striking woman, recalled Sarah Turner, and her gracious demeanor, along with the close attention she gave to her appearance in public, "made her a fascinating personage." But this fascination contained an ambivalence. In North Groton, Turner said, Mary carried herself with great dignity, and some of the townspeople thought she affected an air of superiority; consequently, they resented her. Addie Towns Arnold told a similar tale. Mary was always dressed impeccably, usually in black silk, and when she appeared in public, she carried herself "with such an air" that the Tilton people whispered that she "walked on her uppers." Back in North Groton, Daniel Patterson was not above irritating the villagers. One story had it that in purchasing a fifty-cent stagecoach ticket, Patterson would flash a large bill. To the poor farmers of this village, Patterson was being snooty.[71]*

The blind girl Myra Smith spent the years 1859–60 caring for a bedridden Mary Patterson. In reflecting upon these years, Smith thought that Mrs. Patterson's poor health contributed to her estrangement from the villagers. They were a hardy sort, she said, and they had little patience for Mrs. Patterson's delicate stomach and her languishing illnesses. Sarah Turner concurred with this assessment. Mrs. Patterson's invalidism, along with her "extreme nervousness," sometimes soured people toward her, and at times they simply did not know what to make of her. For instance, who could make sense of an episode when one day Mary became so ill that Patterson was terrified that she was going to die. He set off in the dead of winter to get the doctor, and when the two of

---

* In her elegant simplicity, Mary Patterson may have been demonstrating those middle-class values of dress that were practiced in the wider culture. As for Daniel Patterson, he always dressed the part of a dandy. When they appeared in public, the Pattersons must have stirred the envy and jealousy of their rustic neighbors. The role of dress in public is discussed by Karen Halttunen in her *Confidence Men and Painted Women: A Study of Middle-Class Culture in America, 1830–1870* (New Haven: Yale University Press, 1982), pp. 56–91. Daniel Patterson's dress habits are mentioned in Sibyl Wilbur, *The Life of Mary Baker Eddy* (Boston: Christian Science Publishing Society, 1941), p. 56. Class tensions in these small villages might have contributed to the catty gossip about Mary. On this issue, see Archives, Mrs. Addie Towns Arnold reminiscences.

them returned exhausted and chilled they found Mary sitting up and completely oblivious as to what all the fuss was about.[72]*

Myra Smith indicated that it was not always easy working in the Patterson home. Even if she could not see the Pattersons, Smith could hear their arguments, and Mrs. Patterson could be volatile. Before serving her a meal one day, Smith was asked to bring a jar of butter. Mrs. Patterson made some inquiry about it, and Smith either "sassed" her or gave a curt response. Before Smith could react, Mrs. Patterson slapped her. Then, just as quickly, Smith felt Mrs. Patterson's arms around her and heard her say, "These soft hands of mine could not hurt." In accounting for this unusual flash of anger, Smith attributed it to a lingering illness, which depleted Mrs. Patterson's strong reserves and caused her momentarily to become short-tempered. Mary probably would have agreed. As she once said about herself, "My temper is hasty but not sullen."[73]

One way to protect herself against her own anger and to shield herself from the tensions and hostilities emanating from others was to dress impeccably and to keep her home immaculate. Sarah Turner commented on Mary's pristine neatness and the fine quality of her attire, while Daniel Ridder was impressed that Mrs. Patterson kept her house "in the most perfect order."[74]

Mary Patterson's ill health kept her withdrawn from socializing in these New England villages, and so did her intellectual interests; she would sometimes employ her enriched vocabulary in her everyday talk, and this would leave a villager or two scratching his head and feeling a bit inferior.[75]

During these years we catch very few glimpses of Mary in the company of other adults. Her husband was with her when he was at home; her sister Abigail would stop by for a visit, and we hear of her talking to a neighbor now and then, but Myra Smith could not remember many callers or visitors. Mary was not completely isolated, however. If, perhaps out of mistrust, she kept her distance from many adults, she opened her heart to children. In 1911, a year after Mrs. Eddy's death, Elias F. Bailey remembered her in the North Groton days as openly affectionate with younger children, and noted that they in turn were very giving to her. Smith's sister recalled that when she was about ten years old in

---

* Among other things, this incident reveals that Mary was an effective externalizer of her internal conflicts. That is, once she externalized her conflicts, Daniel Patterson "caught" them; he became anxious and rushed for help. Freed from her tensions and anxiety, Mary then felt better. On the nature of this defense, see Jack Novick and Kerry Kelly, "Projection and Externalization," *Psychoanalytic Study of the Child* 25 (1970), pp. 69–93.

North Groton, Mary would gently pat her on the head and offer soothing words.[76]

Sarah G. Chard echoed these warm sentiments: Mrs. Patterson always welcomed small children into her home. Sarah and her little sister, Netti, used to go to the Patterson home to play when their mother went into the village. On those days when Mrs. Patterson was feeling well enough to sit up, she would take Netti on her lap, and, with Sarah standing by, would delight in engaging them in conversation. Sarah could not remember the content of their talks, but they must have been engrossing, because she and her sister could not wait to return.[77]

When we blend these various images of Mary Patterson into a composite picture, we can begin to understand why she might have been somewhat alienated from the villagers of New Hampshire. In many ways Mary did not conform to social expectations, and threatened social harmony. She was an intelligent woman seeking to make her mark in the literary world, while the rest of the townspeople were more concerned about the furrows in a field than the lines on a piece of paper. Mary was an attractive widow, maybe even a bit seductive. Though the men sneaking a peek at her might seem innocent enough, she posed a threat to some of the jealous, nervous women, who might have seen her as a danger to family stability. Her lingering illnesses, her inability to recover and resume her proper role as her husband's helpmate, and her failure to mother her own son while being open and generous to other children made Mary an even greater threat to traditional family stability and communal harmony.[78]

As the 1850s drew to a close, things were not going well for Mary and her husband. Daniel's dental practice was slipping from bad to worse, and rumor had it that he was seeing other women on his rounds. In the economically depressed years of the late 1850s, Martha Pilsbury, who held the mortgage on the Pattersons' North Groton house, concluded that she could no longer carry the Pattersons, and in 1859 she foreclosed on the mortgage. Within six months they were gone, but not before Daniel got into a brawl with a local family over some wood that he could not pay for. So Mary's five years in North Groton ended in a humiliating retreat; Daniel went ahead of her, and Abigail Tilton drove her to the boardinghouse in Rumney Station where Daniel had established temporary quarters. They eventually settled in a small house in Rumney village, which was tucked back in the hills. There Mary could continue to write her poetry, but little did she know that she would be drawn into the Civil War in a more direct, personal way.[79]

Early in 1862 Daniel Patterson made a colossal blunder. He had been commissioned by the governor of the state to transport funds raised in

New Hampshire to help Northern sympathizers in the South. On his way through Washington, he decided to take a look at the battlefield at Bull Run. He got too close a look; he was captured by the Rebels and marched off to prison. Mary was spurred into action. She stopped writing her poems and rifled off letters to anyone and everyone, including Albert's old mentor, Franklin Pierce, to see whether they could secure Patterson's release.[80]

Back on December 12, 1861, when Patterson was still with her, Mary had written a letter to a Mr. and Mrs. Taylor of Hill, New Hampshire, where Vail's Hydropathic Institute was located. If she decided to attend the institute, she wondered whether the Taylors might be able to board her. She felt stronger now than when she had asked them to board her last fall. Her husband was acquainted with Mr. Taylor and believed that their quiet family life would be just the thing for her. She would be no problem to feed, because her food was bland and simple. She ate nothing for breakfast except her Graham bread and a small helping of "thickened milk cold, in the shape of toast gravey." She ate only two meals a day, without meat, of course, and she dearly wished to board with them while her husband was absent from home attending to his dental practice.[81]

With Patterson in prison and her health continuing to falter, Mary decided to go to Vail's institute sometime in June 1862. This decision was probably more momentous than it looks; it was not a case of a frivolous woman flitting from one self-cure to the next. For nine years she had been practicing homeopathy; in fact, *Jahr's New Manual of Homeopathic Practice*, edited by A. Gerald Hull, lay right beside her Bible. Thus, when Mary opted to try the water cure, was this a signal that she had begun to question the efficacy of homeopathy? Or did it mean that she still believed in its curative powers but was willing to use the water cure as a supplement to her homeopathic practices? One thing is clear: by embracing the gentler principles of Samuel Hahnemann's homeopathy, Mary had turned her back on conventional medicine. This German physician, during the late eighteenth century, began to build a treatment system based partly on the healing powers of nature and two basic principles: the law of similars and the law of infinitesimals. The law of similars held that a small dose of the medicine produced the symptoms of a disease in one who was healthy. Supposedly, therefore, it eradicated the symptoms in a person who was sick. In other words, notes historian Catherine Albanese, "like healed like; a secret harmony inhabited the natural world, and its discovery would bring the end to illness." Hahnemann's second law, the law of infinitesimals, held that medicines are more efficacious the smaller the dose, "even as small as dilutions of one-millionth of a gram."[82]

In her autobiography, Mary Baker Eddy singled out homeopathy as a particularly important way station on the road to Christian Science. Over the long years when she had used Jahr's book, she had gotten "hints" from the many remedies she had employed. Finally, "one pervading secret" dawned upon her: "the less material medicine we have, and the more Mind, the better the work is done; a fact which seems to prove the Principle of Mind-healing."[83]

In her autobiography, Mrs. Eddy ascribed an importance to homeopathy that probably was not there at the time, at least not quite in the way she reconstructed it. This is not to deny that she was receiving "hints" from her experiences with it. This medical practice actually moved simultaneously in two directions: it was rooted in science, yet it encouraged a spiritual or metaphysical view of healing; indeed, Catherine Albanese has used the phrase "healing grace" when referring to homeopathy. According to the law of infinitesimals, the increasingly small doses had the greater effect of stimulating the body's "vital force" and thereby producing a cure. Hahnemann was certain that his medical treatments had the ability to act positively upon the hidden vital forces, and in a spiritual way. In his *Social Transformation of American Medicine*, Paul Starr has noted that followers of homeopathy "saw disease fundamentally as a matter of spirit," and with their close connections to both mesmerism and Swedenborgianism, practitioners of homeopathy were encouraged to draw close connections between the world of matter and the realm of the spirit.[84]

But if metaphysical thoughts could be stimulated by homeopathy, they were in a rudimentary state in Mary's mind in the years between 1853 and 1862. She was still far from her mature theology—that suffering was not sent by God and was not a part of the order of things, but had its origin in the human mentality. In fact, it could be argued that her thoughts were not well integrated in this period. Her daily reading of the Bible testified to an abiding religious faith fostered by Congregationalism. Some of her prose and poetry, laced with romanticism, spoke to a different—a mystical—spirituality. The rationality and asceticism that lay behind Graham's diet, even the science in which Hahnemann's homeopathy was rooted, may have been compatible to some degree with spiritual concerns, but Mary Patterson was not yet capable of integrating the meaning of science, matter, mind, and spirit.

Like many other health reforms in the first half of the nineteenth century, hydropathy argued that most sickness resulted from the individual's violation of natural laws. Just as the sinner who violated God's laws could expect to be punished, so ill health was the condign punishment for those who violated the laws of life. Good health, in these terms, became equated with salvation, poor health with sin and damnation. The water curists therefore claimed that the inner and outer self could be healed by the consumption and application of pure, soft water along with a special diet, exercise, and fresh air. Many—not all—water curists held out the promise that in conquering disease, man could attain perfection. Harriet N. Austin and James C. Jackson, two water curists, caught the flavor of this perfectionism when they wrote: "As Christian men and women, as well as advocates of a new Medical Philosophy, we insist that Sickness is no more necessary than Sin." In the words of one historian, the physiological reformers "recast sin into biological terms," and, one might add, in so doing they kept a strong tie to the Calvinist past. This was Mary's dilemma: she yearned for something new to provide inner and outer harmony, but she was still enmeshed in the past and could not let go.[85]

When Mary walked into Vail's institute, she was already dragging her feet. When they had considered the water cure as a possible treatment for her, Mary and her husband had been thinking about an alternative form of treatment. Phineas Parkhurst Quimby's cures in Portland, Maine, were becoming well known throughout New England, and in October of the previous year, Daniel Patterson had written to him, saying that Mary desperately needed the doctor's help. Shortly before leaving for Vail's, Mary sent a brief letter to Quimby. She informed him that for the past six years she had been stricken with "spinal inflammation and its train of sufferings—gastric and bilious." She further expressed her confidence in Quimby and confirmed her husband's plea that she needed to see him. Would he, could he, please come to see her at once?[86]

Quimby stayed in Portland; Mary went to Vail's. While she was there, for almost three months, a former patient of Vail who had since gone to Quimby came back to the water-cure institute extolling Quimby. Convinced that she had made a mistake in coming there, and feeling that her health had not improved, Mary again wrote Quimby in August 1862. When she entered the gates of the institute, she wrote that she was able to walk a half mile, but now she was so weak that she could only walk for a few minutes at a time. Even her faith in Quimby might not be enough to sustain her. She was "so excitable" that she might be able to keep herself alive until she got to him, but then she was afraid that there might not be a strong enough "foundation" for him to rebuild her health. She seemed to have only two choices left: to return to her friends at Sanbornton Bridge and die, or to go to Quimby and live. Accompanied by her oldest brother, Samuel, and his wife, Mary, in October 1862, she set off for Portland on another leg of her pilgrimage for physical and spiritual health.[87]

4

PHINEAS PARKHURST QUIMBY:
A PROPHET RAISED UP?

I will raise them up a Prophet from among their brethren,
like unto thee, and will put my words into his mouth; and he
shall speak unto them all that I shall command him.

Deuteronomy 18:18

DESPITE SOME MODEST ACCOMPLISHMENTS in her writing,
Mary Patterson, at forty-two, had to feel that life was passing her by
more rapidly than the wheels of her coach were carrying her to Portland.
From her youth on, Mary had been increasingly disenchanted with her
place in life, but her rebellious strivings had been subordinated to duty,
as one might expect of a woman in nineteenth-century America. In
joining her parents' Congregational Church, she had, to all outward
appearances, surrendered to its scriptural and ecclesiastical forms, and
on any given Sunday one would have been hard-pressed to distinguish
her from the bevy of women "feminizing" American religion.[1]

In Mary Patterson's case, however, external acceptance did not always
reflect internal acquiescence, and whether she was aware of it or not,
her ties to the institutional church were weakening. Despite its own rich
tradition in healing from the days of Christ's earliest ministry, the church
had generally ignored this part of its heritage and offered no succor to
Mary. Her prolonged illnesses had kept her from regular Sunday at-
tendance, and alone in her bedroom, often in great pain and suffering,
she read her Bible. We can only imagine how she read the Book without
the Congregational minister to impress his modified version of Calvinism
upon its verses.

Her suffering forced her to seek help from the various fads and health
movements that promised to heal her body and cure her soul. Each of
them provided some temporary relief, but the reemergence of her illnesses
left Mary feeling physically and spiritually unfit. Each setback renewed

the fear that she might never be healed, and in her darkest moments she was made aware that the specter of death was nearby. By late 1862, therefore, Mary was on a desperate pilgrimage. She had yet to meet Quimby, but she had already begun to idealize him.

Phineas Parkhurst Quimby. Just who was this man with the name that recalls a W. C. Fields character? "Park" Quimby was born in Lebanon, New Hampshire, in 1802. He was one of seven children, and his father, a blacksmith, had difficulty making ends meet. When he was a young boy, Quimby's family moved to Belfast, Maine, where, as with most lower-class people in rural New England, his schooling was piecemeal and erratic. Despite his lack of a formal education, or perhaps because of it, Quimby embodied one of the young country's most endearing traits: he was an inveterate tinkerer, actually a clockmaker of some repute, an inventor of a number of improvements for the band saw, and an experimenter with daguerreotypes. It was as though Ralph Waldo Emerson had Quimby in mind when he praised the natural, untutored mind in his essay "Self-Reliance":

> A sturdy lad from New Hampshire or Vermont, who in turn tries all the professions, who *teams it, farms it, peddles*, keeps a school, preaches, edits a newspaper, goes to Congress, buys a township, and so forth, in successive years, and always like a cat falls on his feet, is worth a hundred of these city dolls. He walks abreast with his days and feels no shame in not "studying a profession," for he does not postpone his life, but lives already. He has not one chance, but a hundred chances.[2]

Quimby's career was not as random or whimsical as it might seem. Take his interest in Louis Daguerre's mechanical invention. In 1836, several years before the introduction of the daguerreotype in America, Emerson talked about how one could gain spiritual insight through perceiving nature. In his oft-quoted passage from *Nature*, Emerson became a "transparent eyeball" that saw into nature and thereby attained a harmony with God. Emerson's transcendentalism and Daguerre's camera—there was a connection, perceptively noted by Richard Rudisill: "This thought of seeing beyond the surface of nature by keenly observing the surface was ideally the same concern for perception as the wish of the . . . [daguerreotypist] to reveal the inner character of his sitter by making a searching likness of his features."[3]

Quimby had his hands on an instrument with spiritual and psychological potential. To find a system that could reliably discern inner character from outward appearance, that could distinguish the true self from the false self—this was what engaged Quimby's curiosity. His restless imagination led him not only into daguerreotypy, but into a theory of mind that had close affinities to it.[4]

In 1838, Quimby attended a lecture by Charles Poyen, a Frenchman who was causing a stir with his lectures and demonstrations of mesmerism. "America's first full dose of animal magnetism came from the tongue" of Poyen, according to Robert Fuller, and Quimby lapped up everything he heard and saw, not only in this lecture but in a number of others as he followed Poyen around the lyceum circuit. In the late eighteenth century, Franz Anton Mesmer, a Viennese physician, claimed that he could heal people by means of an invisible energy that medical science could not see or measure. This energy, which circulated through the universe and the human body, he called animal magnetism. To be in tune with its currents was to be unified in mind, body, and spirit. Through such books as John Dods's *The Philosophy of Electrical Psychology* (1850) and Chauncy Townsend's *Facts in Mesmerism* (1844), mesmerism was transformed in its encounter with American culture from a medical cure to a psychoreligious cure of souls. In his widely read book, Townsend had listed six stages of development that lay along a continuum which eventually left the five senses behind and entered into an altered state of consciousness. In this deeper consciousness, people experienced waves of energy flowing through them, and they felt as if they were in direct communication with a transcendent reality. Once this mystical state was attained, they could use their power of magnetic healing to cure people. As Robert Fuller has noted, "In the mesmeric state, they learned that disease and even moral confusion were the unfortunate consequences of having fallen out of rapport with the invisible spiritual workings."[5]

In his travels on the lyceum circuit, Quimby discovered through trial and error that he was adept at contacting these energies within himself; hitching his mesmeric star to an impressionable young man named Lucius Burkmar, Quimby became famous throughout Maine for his demonstrations of the mind's mysterious powers. Quimby and Burkmar worked together from 1843 to 1847. As they thrilled wide-eyed villagers with their magical feats, they could be regarded as pure entertainment, or, more skeptically, as tricksters. It was also possible to take them very seriously as religious-medical practitioners who offered cures and healings that traditional doctors and ministers could not.

After Quimby gave a lecture about the mysterious connection between mind and matter, Burkmar joined him onstage, and in short order Quimby put him into a deep mesmeric sleep. Quimby invited members of the audience onstage, whereupon he turned control of Burkmar over to them. What transpired kept the villagers talking for weeks after the two showmen had left town.

While in his mesmeric trance, Burkmar apparently had the mental ability to travel to different locations and describe them in exact detail. During one performance, Burkmar was put in communication with a Mr. Buck, who "took" him to his house; Burkmar accurately described the furnishings, including a map that lay open on the floor. In hushed, amazed tones, Buck told the audience that moments before leaving the house to come to the performance, he had left the map on the floor exactly as Burkmar had described it.[6]

Burkmar's diagnosis of illness could be just as dumbfounding. One afternoon he "examined" a Mrs. Pillsbury, and his prognosis was dire: her brain was diseased; there was "a congestion. . . . and large clots of blood laid upon the brain and it would produce convulsions and fits." When Burkmar came out of his trance, Quimby told him that as he had been conveying this information to Mrs. Pillsbury, she had fallen into one of these very fits.[7]

Diagnoses of illness took place offstage as well; in homes and boardinghouses Quimby took an active role in the healings. In one town, Burkmar noted with awe and respect, Quimby produced "miracles." A Miss Harmond, who had been sick for thirteen years, presented herself before Quimby. The doctors had been stymied by her illness; they brushed it off as some form of "spinal complaint." Quimby "partially magnetized" this long-suffering woman and worked on her for half an hour. He was so successful in relieving her pains that she got up and walked around the room without anyone's aid. Quimby later called upon her again and "magnetized some water and it had the same effect as it did when he was working upon her."[8]

On another occasion Quimby and Burkmar went to visit a young boy, who, Burkmar guessed, was about ten years old. The lad was "very sensitive"—an ideal patient for Quimby's mental suggestion. Quimby "paralyzed" the boy's tongue and mentally stopped him from walking. Quimby had such complete mental control over him that he could "stop him when and where he pleased," wrote Burkmar, duly impressed. The next night, in front of a full house, Quimby brought the boy onstage and repeated the same feat. Not to be topped, Burkmar was "taken" to Havana, Cuba, by a sea captain; he described the harbor and the surrounding scenery, to the astonishment and delight of the audience.[9]

In some towns Quimby and Burkmar were well received and well paid. But sometimes their performance stirred the anxieties of staunch Protestants. Shouts of "fake" and "humbug" could be heard, and sometimes dark murmurings about animal magnetism drifted up. Once the two performers were threatened with violence during their act, but calmer heads prevailed, and early the next morning Quimby and Burkmar quietly made their exit.[10]

At some point after this hasty retreat, Quimby grew increasingly dubious about what was actually effecting the cures he demonstrated. He doubted that it had much to do with the herbal remedies or was totally located in the fluid energy. He also suspected that when Burkmar looked into a patient and described the condition of the organs, he was, in fact, only reading an opinion in the mind of the person, whether placed there by a doctor, a relative, or Burkmar himself. Quimby slowly reached the conclusion that the cure lay in the mind and not in the material remedies. Once this was clear to him, he left Burkmar and threw himself into a study of mental healing.

Recently Quimby's complete writings have been published in three lengthy volumes. The essays are not arranged chronologically, but they roughly cover the decade from the mid-1850s to the end of the Civil War. Quimby approached ideas the way he did his clocks and saws: he took a part from here, a piece from there, and through much tinkering eventually concocted his system of mind cure out of an intellectual hodgepodge of mesmerism, physiology, rudimentary psychology, and religion that he never neatly braided into a coherent intellectual system. At times his essays and his advice to patients focused sharply on the physiological aspects of disease, while in other instances he concentrated narrowly on the psychological aspects. In another letter or essay he might stress the religious roots of disease.

We should not be too hard on Quimby for his inconsistency. As a healer he was moving into new territory, coming on the scene at an opportune time; medicine and Protestantism had lost much of their explanatory power for an increasing number of people. A man who could present a synthesis—even a ragged one—would have a ready audience. As Catherine Albanese has said about Quimby, he "hammered out a confused—but still commanding—theology of healing, forming a charter document for American metaphysical religion." The crucial point is that no matter how intellectually muddled it might have been, Quimby's ideology had a compelling emotional coherence when applied to his patients.[11]

Quimby grew to understand that all disease had a psychosomatic root: imbalance and disharmony in the mind, caused by man's beliefs, and a belief in any disease, would create "a chemical change in the mind, and . . . a person will create a phenomenon corresponding to the symptoms." Therefore, people converted their mental torment into bodily illness. It stood to reason, then, that "there is a principle or inward man

that governs the outward man or body, and when these are at variance
or out of tune, disease is the effect, while by harmonizing them health
in the body is the result."[12]

Beliefs, however, were not the whole story for Quimby. He knew
from his earlier experiments with mesmerism that on a deeper, unobserved level magnetic fluids flowed through the system like a subterra-
nean stream. Beliefs that emanated from the outside world affected the
natural flow of this energic stream; they could either blend with the flow
and produce complete harmony and health, or they could disrupt the
flow, produce a chemical change, and thereby create disharmony and
illness. If the roots of illness lay in beliefs and their effects upon the
magnetic fluids, then a new method of healing was needed, a method
that somehow reached into the dark region of those fluids, where mind
and matter interacted to produce disease.

Everyone, Quimby argued, was vulnerable to the thoughts, feelings,
and opinions of others, whether openly or silently communicated. In
almost invisible and barely understood ways, our minds "act upon each
other more indifferently than we are taught to believe." By "indifferently" Quimby meant subconsciously. When he talked to a patient, the
patient understood his words, but Quimby was also communicating on
another, purely mental level. It was on this hidden level that he discovered the origins of disease, and it was this kind of unspoken communication that allowed Quimby to bypass the external self to reach the
inner self.[13]

Every person was a "book of himself," Quimby declared, in most
cases a "sealed book" whose pages were hidden even from the author.
So when Quimby sat by a patient, it was crucial that he understood
how to read those inner pages. His method would have to include a part
of himself that operated on the ordinary level of the senses as another
part listened to patients with what modern psychology calls the "third
ear." Quimby tried to explain the quality of this split self in an essay.
"I have two identities," he stated, "one in matter and the other out of
matter. One can be seen and felt by the natural man, and the other can
feel and see the sick man's identity," hidden from the patient's conscious
awareness. In this realm of the psyche, "their language is their feelings
which contain their trouble," said Quimby. And he did not hesitate to
tell his patients that "all their troubles are in this self or identity which
is not acknowledged."[14]

To one patient, a Mrs. H. Merrill, Quimby tried to explain that this
finely tuned instrument of his was a critical aspect of his ability to cure
disease. "When I first [sit] by you," Quimby wrote:

My desire to see you lights up my mind like a lamp; and as the light expands, my senses being attached to the light, each particle of light contains all the elements of the whole. So when the light is strong enough to see your light and dissipate your error and bring your light in your darkness or doubts, then I come in harmony with your light and dissipate your error and bring your light out of your darkness. Then I try to associate you with matter as a substance that is separate and apart from your light or senses.[15]

The light Quimby referred to was the power of clairvoyance, which revealed the disturbed part of a patient's inner self, enabling Quimby to provide his interpretation of the patient's disease. To the modern ear, it sounds as though Quimby was employing an inchoate form of psychology and an early form of the talking cure. Read his description of what transpired as he listened to a patient:

I then became a medium myself, but not like my subject. I retained my own consciousness and at the same time took the feelings of my patient. . . . I found that I had the power of not only feeling their aches and pains, but the state of their mind. I discovered that ideas took form and the patient was affected just according to the impression contained in the idea. For example, if a person lost a friend at sea the shock upon their nervous system would disturb the fluids of the body and create around them a vapor, and in that are all their ideas, right or wrong. This vapor or fluid contains the identity of the person.[16]

Quimby realized that his new powers of clairvoyance sounded much like the mesmerism he and Burkmar had practiced, and there were facets of this clairvoyance that were often as dramatic. Quimby thought that the body was "nothing but a dense shadow, condensed into what is called matter, or ignorance of God or Wisdom." If the body was not "real" in the everyday sense, and if it was encased in the darkness of belief, then reality lay elsewhere. For Quimby that elsewhere was in the mind, which he defined as a spiritual substance. If so, then the light of Quimby's Truth could transcend time and space; it could leave his body in Portland and enter the mind of a patient in another town. This transcendent sympathy in his clairvoyance, he said, "annihilates space," allowing him to produce cures even though he was not physically present.

"My senses can act upon a person at a distance without that person knowing it. This I know." In late December 1860, Quimby told a female patient that he could cure her even though he would not personally be with her. He allayed her anxieties by telling her, "You are as plain before my eyes as you were when I was talking to the shadow in Portland." He would come as a spiritual presence to cure her. "So you may expect me in a while in the evening," he assured her. "So keep on the lookout." She was to keep her lamp burning so that when "the Truth comes it shall not find you sleeping, but up straight, ready to receive the bridegroom."[17]

As he forged the link between the abstract concept of mind and the material basis in mesmerism, Quimby argued that there were two sciences; one rooted in the material world, the other anchored in the spiritual realm. In the former, beliefs and opinions held sway, while in the latter, Science ruled, which according to his definition was "something spiritual or a revelation from a higher state of being." The world of beliefs was limited, filled with bewildering change that resulted in personal fragmentation, disease, and death. The world of Science, in contrast, was infinite, always moving toward perfection.[18]

What had impeded the march toward perfection? What caused his patients to feel the inner disharmony that produced illness? Individual pathology—blaming the victim for his or her own misery—was an unsatisfactory answer for Quimby; rather, as he saw it, the diseases of his patients were symptomatic of a deep social malaise. Over his twenty-five-year career, which included thousands of patients, Quimby was swamped by myriad complaints, but he heard a common underlying theme: people felt insecure in their social world. It was as if the truths and certainties they had learned as children were no longer meaningful in their adult lives. And if their once-cherished values and ideals were shaky in the turmoil of the 1850s and 1860s, so were their attachments to formerly rock-solid institutions.[19]

In an influential essay, the historian John Higham has argued that after the romantic excess of the 1830s and 1840s, Northern society in the 1850s began to experience the transition from boundlessness to consolidation. As a broad, general pattern, this might have been true, but it was not the experience of Quimby's patients; they seemed to have trouble keeping themselves together. Whenever he sat by a patient, one of Quimby's tricks was to bring up the topics of "religion, politics and all ideas the discussion of which agitates society." He knew that these subjects would disturb his patients, because they "contain fear and excite the mind which by a false direction brings about the phenomenon called disease."[20]

Quimby's patients thus felt themselves unmoored, adrift in the uncharted seas of social change. As the strong undercurrents pulled them further and further from familiar landmarks, they learned not to trust the voices of cultural authority to guide them to safety. Quimby himself used this nautical metaphor to explain the alienation of his patients: "The wisdom of the world is like an ocean surrounded by inlets, harbors and false lights to decoy the traveller into the land." After the unsuspecting travelers had been seduced ashore, they were gulled into believing false doctrines. Once deceived, they no longer trusted these Sirens, these voices of authority. And once they experienced emotional detachment on a social level, it was not long before these feelings led to fears of abandonment and loss. A sick individual, Quimby observed sympathetically, was like a person in a mesmeric state who wanted to "return home having been carried away by false guides" and then found himself abandoned when he fell ill. These sick, lost souls reminded Quimby of a person cast out of his family's home "by the dissipation of his parents, driven from his own farm or house, where all his ties of earthly life are."[21]

Cast into an uncaring world, the sick were estranged from themselves and from others. This sense of alienation was so intense that the sick felt "as though no person could tell them how they feel." Quimby could, though, and it was one of the strengths of his healing. He was extremely sensitive to the plight of his patients; he was an empathic listener, a person his patients could trust not to lead them astray. The health of his patients, he once said, was "brought about by sympathy, and all persons who are sick are in need of this sympathy;" if this was not available to them, their alienation continued unchecked, and the fears of abandonment and loss were transformed into a heightened fear of death. "The fear of death," Quimby perceptively noted, "is the cause of nine-tenths of all disease."[22]

But just who implanted this fear in people and led Quimby's patients down the path to disease and death? As a close listener, Quimby had no trouble pinpointing where the blame lay; it rested squarely on the shoulders of doctors and ministers. At times Quimby muted his attack on the medical profession and granted it a modicum of respect. He thought that all doctors, no matter what kind of medicine they practiced, honestly believed that the remedies they prescribed had certain properties which produced certain benign effects in their patients. The homeopathic doctors, for example, believed their infinitesimals produced certain desired effects. But, Quimby countered, "all their medicine is of infinitely less importance than the opinions that accompany it."[23]

Quimby, however, was not about to let the doctors off this easily.

Whether he identified with his patients who came from small towns and had lower-class backgrounds, or with the dispossessed in general, an angry class-consciousness crept into his attack. The medical profession's diplomas, inscribed in Greek and Latin and granted by fancy schools, might look impressive, but this education did not increase a doctor's empathy for the common man. Just the opposite was true; they tailored their practice to the rich and neglected the poor. In a letter to an aspiring young physician, Quimby closed with this advice: "Be charitable to the poor. Keep the health of your patient in view, and if money comes, all well; but do not let that get the lead."[24]

Doctors might be duped; Quimby could forgive them that. What rankled him was when he sensed that their selfishness or ineptitude left the patient lost and adrift in the world. Any person traveling along the road of life was apt to be waylaid by "these blind guides" who lured the naïve and unsuspecting individual from his "father's house or health" and carried him off into the foreign land of belief. There they robbed the individual of his happiness, leaving him at the mercy of "strangers or physicians," who approached him pretending to be his friends, offering him "opium and drugs to soothe" the "wounded heart." When Quimby came upon this prostrate figure, the poor individual had been abandoned and left to die. Quimby, however, was the good Samaritan among healers. He picked up the fallen man and carried him "into an inn or happier state of mind."[25]

Recently Edward Shorter has written an intriguing book on the history of psychosomatic illness from Victorian times to the present. His complicated thesis involves cultural pressures and their impact on the doctor-patient relationship. Shorter discovered that as doctors changed their models of disease, their patients manifested physical symptoms to match the current model. Quimby clearly anticipated this insight. "Diseases," he declared, "are like fashions, and people are as apt to take a new disease as they are to fall in with any new fashion. Now if there was a law made to punish any person who should through any medical journal communicate to the people any new disease and its symptoms, it would put a stop to a great deal of sickness." In another essay, he sounded the same theme. Disease was a hoax perpetrated by the medical profession. Neuralgia was a common complaint of the day, but this was "giving way to a new invention called the spine disease. And there have been such improvements that this has almost lost its identity in the new inventions of human diseases." Surely, thought Quimby, there was not a respectable woman left who had not been "insulted by these quacks with the idea that she has this disease in some form or other."[26]

Quimby's sharpest words, however, were reserved for institutional religion. In one essay he exposed the history of religion as nothing more than one vast superstition laid upon another. The Bible had become so encrusted with false readings and interpretations, Quimby argued, that it was virtually useless as a guide unless one was ready to read it with fresh eyes. Institutional religion had to be yanked out by its roots. "My object," he declared boldly, "is the good of mankind, independent of all religious sects and creeds." What Quimby offered in their place was his method of healing, which, if understood correctly, lifted men and women from being passive victims of opinions and disease, and encouraged them to be free and self-governing. Quimby promised to make "man free and independent of all creeds and laws of man, and subject him to his own laws, he being free from the laws of sin, sickness, and death." Since he himself had already attained this kind of freedom, Quimby assured his readers that he could teach it to others.[27]

People often asked Quimby why he railed so strongly against religion but quoted Scriptures while he healed the sick. The answer was perhaps too obvious: Quimby was taking his cue from his patients, who often couched their complaints in religious terms. Many of his patients still struggled with the Calvinism they had inherited from their parents.

Quimby's mission was to free people from Calvinism's iron grip so that they could restore their health. He did this by asserting that Calvinism was a fabrication; it had nothing to do with truth. At one point he sounded like the philosopher Ludwig Feuerbach when he angrily denounced modern religion as a fiction, an invention of man to serve his own needs. In the summer of 1861, Quimby wrote to a Mrs. Emerson: "I have no confidence in this God of man's invention. He asks too much of man and never pays. He is too much like a man; in fact he is the embodiment of man's opinions." If man's beliefs distorted the true idea of God, they also obscured the true meaning of His Word. "One half of the diseases arise from a false belief in the Bible," Quimby flatly declared in an essay. The case he chose to illustrate his point is pertinent because in lambasting Calvinism as an outmoded, pernicious belief system, he spoke directly to the anxieties of a number of his patients, including Mary Patterson.[28]

A certain elderly lady came to him so badly crippled that she could barely walk on her crutches. She had lived this way for years; her only happiness came in reading and thinking over biblical passages. "She was a Calvinist Baptist," noted Quimby, "and by her belief she had imprisoned her senses (consciousness) in a creed so small and contracted that she could not stand upright or move ahead." When she turned to her

Bible to explain her suffering, she found no surcease from her pain. "Here in this tomb of Calvin her senses were laid, wrapt in her creed," Quimby solemnly observed.

When this suffering woman finally reached Quimby, he offered her a way to break the chains of Calvinism. He told her that her crippling disease arose from the way she read the Bible and from her attempts to reconcile the unreconcilable. She was emotionally paralyzed by such questions as: Why has God chosen to punish me? Do I deserve to be punished? How could a loving God punish so cruelly? "She thought upon religious subjects," said Quimby, "and not seeing the Scriptures clearly her mind became cloudy and stagnated." These false beliefs in turn revealed themselves in her body; her fluids became sluggish, causing her paralysis.[29]

Quimby knew that he had to change the fluids to restore the woman's circulation and health. To do this he attacked her false beliefs. There was, he was fond of pointing out, a fundamental difference between the true followers of Christ and those who believed in Calvinism. The latter relied heavily upon forms and ceremonies, while Christ opposed them. If her Calvinism had entombed her, he analogized, then it was as if she were dead, as if she were trapped in false forms. To bring her to life—to see the truth of healing—was to raise her from the dead. When Quimby showed her the truth by quoting the Bible on the resurrection of Christ and applying it to her situation, he smashed her faulty beliefs in Calvin's harsh, punishing God, and she was on the road to health.[30]

This elderly woman's case was hardly Quimby's last word on the stern, repressive God created by Calvinism. We supposedly respected and loved this God because we received everything from Him. But, Quimby objected, if He were responsible for everything man attributed to Him, then He would be a despicable tyrant. This was a harsh statement, especially during the Civil War when words like "slavery," "tyranny," and "freedom" were invested with intense moral overtones. Implicitly, Quimby was asking: Who would want to give up his or her freedom to be a slave to a God like that?

Quimby relished answering his own question. What he said next was eye-opening. "If we should look upon a parent as we are taught to look upon God, we should hate our very parents." When Quimby compared Calvin's omniscient, punishing God to a human father, the conclusion was evident: the children would reject the father as a tyrant. "Now all this talk about a God who reasons and makes bargains accompanied by rewards and punishments is so much like the natural man's wisdom that no one can help seeing that our Christian God is the embodiment of man's belief when man was far behind the present generation." In short, this God of Calvin was nothing more than an old belief, whose limitations could be overcome, and lead from disease and death to health and perfection. If a person accepted Quimby's science and wisdom, he or she would no longer have to fear the sting of death. It was this kind of confidence and assurance that made Quimby such an attractive figure to so many sick and troubled people.[31]

Like a number of other reformers of the age, Quimby brought an evangelical fervor to his work. He was convinced that he held the key to a new reality; his unfolding of the subconscious roots of illness had unlocked the secret of health that had eluded mankind for ages. His method, he once wrote to a clergyman, did not belong to any "man made or inherited wisdom"; it transcended that. The science he practiced "was taught eighteen hundred years ago, and has never had a place in the heart of man since, but is in the world, and the world knows it not."[32]

Quimby divorced his mind-healing theory and method from the contamination of history and all institutional religions, for they distorted and corrupted the message of Jesus. "What infidelity and hypocrisy there is in the nineteenth century," he fumed. "If any person can show me one single idea in any creed that Jesus ever subscribed to, I should like to see it." Evidently nobody was ever able to satisfy Quimby on these theological points, for he defiantly stated, "I do not believe in any God as taught me in my early days, neither do I believe in any religious belief or anything attributed to the Christian."[33]

Even more dramatically, in another essay on the meaning of Jesus' parables, he stated that Jesus abandoned all false religion and "worshipped God or Science." He gave His life for this science, and others could share in it if they forsook "their father or their old creeds and embrace[d] Christ or Science." This, and only this, he emphasized, was the true religion of Jesus. To be a genuine follower of Christ one had to renounce all religious forms and ceremonies. In a sense, then, Quimby leaped back over time and attached his healing to the primordial ideal of Jesus' healing ministry. And once he had securely attached himself and his ideas to this ideal, he jumped forward again into the nineteenth century convinced that he could dramatically change people's lives.[34]

In short, Quimby offered his patients a born-again experience. Disease, he asserted in an 1864 essay, was concocted by the ministers and taken over by the doctors. "The priests prophesied falsely and the doctors flourished by their lies," and for their own reasons people accepted these false doctrines. Now was the time to discard them; "I say," he practically shouted from the rooftops, "repent all, and be baptized in the Science that will wash away your sins and diseases with your belief."[35]

Quimby was not merely engaging in loud rhetoric; he was absolutely certain he knew what Jesus meant regarding life and death. This understanding was not derived from abstract theory; it came from experience, bubbling up from the deep well of spiritual feeling and intuition. "I have seen death myself and eternal life that he spoke of and can testify that I have passed from death unto life, as he taught his disciples."[36]

With statements like this, it is little wonder that his patients began to see Quimby as a Christ figure, and despite his disclaimers, he often encouraged this comparison. Sometimes Quimby made the connection indirectly, for as he read and reshaped the Bible to his own needs, it seemed as though he and Jesus were twins. In one essay, he talked about Jesus being baptized by John. After that experience, it was clear that Jesus (like Quimby) saw that the "priests and doctors were the cause of nine-tenths of man's misery." In another essay, Quimby asserted that Jesus (again, like Quimby) had to establish "a kingdom as the priests had done; theirs was based on opinions, his on science, so everything that they believed was only an opinion which his science could tear apart."[37]

In a number of instances, Quimby forged his link to Christ in unmistakable language. To one prospective patient, Quimby said, "When I take your feelings I am with you, not myself as a man, but this great truth which I call Christ or God." In one essay, Quimby was sharp and to the point: "This power, as you call it, I call Christ, acting through the man Quimby." Just as bluntly in another essay, he asserted that "Thus P. P. Q. is the medium of the truth to correct the errors of the world, just as Jesus was the medium of God or truth or Christ to convince man of his errors and lead him to Christ or health or truth."[38]

Quimby's similarities to Christ did not stop here. He considered his clairvoyance "perfect light," shared by only one other person in history: Christ. When Quimby used this special gift to illuminate the inner life of his patients and to lead them out of the darkness of their belief, then he was like Jesus, who had raised man "from the dead or error into the light of science." In a letter regarding a patient, Quimby returned to one of his favorite nautical metaphors. A certain woman yearned to have her health restored, but her barque floated on the rough sea of opinions and beliefs. As she lay moored on the sea, the "gale of disease" tossed her barque back and forth, and it was in danger of being swamped. But, Quimby promised, "if she can see me or my power walking on the water," saying to her aches and pains to be still, then the seas would be calmed, and she would get what she wanted, "her faith or cure."[39]

Quimby knew what it meant to challenge conventional wisdom and authority and to be attacked for his ideas. His brand of healing was also risky in another sense. Quimby once confessed in a letter to a patient that all of his patients felt "a sort of attachment to me," and as they became dependent upon him, it was impossible for him to avoid becoming, in turn, attached to them in some way, as he explained to another of his patients, a Mr. W. S. Atkins. It was hard, he admitted, not to get discouraged when one sat day in and day out listening to the problems of the sick. It was a "constant drain of a person's feelings," for the sick person would greatly affect him, and "he becomes identified with the suffering of his patients." There seemed to be no way to deflect these melancholy feelings and the weariness that came from this identification.[40]

The depressing stories were not the only kind that reached deeply into Quimby. Some cases touched so close to home that it was hard to know whether the issues and feelings came from within the patient or the doctor. As Quimby well understood, when he was with a patient for but a short time, "his feelings become mine." This occupational hazard was spelled out when Quimby observed:

> I have been so provoked when sitting by the sick, with the physician and in regard to certain classes of disease, that it was with the greatest difficulty I could keep my temper, and I had never seen the doctor or minister. But I always found that when I would get the patients clear from their opinions, they would express themselves in as strong terms as I had. I thought the fault might be with me, but I am now satisfied that I was only the scape-goat to carry off feelings they dared not lisp out, but could not tell why.[41]

In steering his ship through these treacherous waters, Quimby was anything but a passive navigator. He was like a ship's captain who, completely believing in his training and his nautical skills, was confident that he could bring his passengers through any storm. The captain's courage and confidence sustained his crew and ship; undoubtedly both would sink if the captain gave in to his fears. Thus, Quimby, like the fearless sea captain, asserted control over his patients and sometimes got into "sharp discussions" with them as he launched his attacks on their medical and religious beliefs.[42]

Quimby's healing method was something new, but one runs the risk of making him sound more modern than he really was. He did anticipate certain aspects of modern psychiatry, but in other ways he was locked into his own time. Like most nineteenth-century doctors, Quimby saw that his initial task was to assert his willpower over the patient until he or she was strong enough to act independently. Quimby's approach to his patients was psychotherapeutic, but it was neither modern psychiatry nor psychoanalysis. Quimby understood the existence of a subconscious mind, but he had no understanding of a dynamic unconscious. Thus, for Quimby, beliefs, even insanity, arose from the outside world and passed into the inside world of the patient. Once Quimby showed a patient that he or she had swallowed a false belief from the outside world, then he expected the patient to control his or her thoughts and emotions and extirpate the disease. Finally, while Quimby encouraged his patients to talk about their woes and how family relationships contributed to them, that was where it ended; the family history was not explored any further. Like his contemporaries, Quimby curbed introspection; he did not want his patients to dwell on their troubles; he wanted them to get rid of them.[43]

It is hard to imagine a modern doctor talking the way Quimby did. There were moments when Quimby's evangelical fervor seemed to get the better of him, and he thundered like any Old Testament patriarch trying to exorcise the evil out of man. "The devil," he warned ominously, "was a liar . . . and he is the father of all disease." The devil was, moreover, a malicious trickster. He put on the garb of ministers and hid his destructiveness behind the cloth and seemingly benign religious beliefs. The devil's kingdom was straight out of a Hieronymus Bosch painting; it was "in the air or out of sight," and was inhabited by grotesque people with false worldly beliefs. "It has all kinds of physicians and all kinds of diseases and they are spirits, prowling around seeking whom they may devour, and they have their agents through whom they communicate their will." Thus, when any problem in the world adversely affected man, one could count on the devil lurking nearby. For instance, if the devil wanted to destroy a man through disease, he would begin by telling him "about some idea that exists in the world or mind, for the mind is where the prince of darkness dwells."[44]

To bring light to this darkness, to reflect a true self, to give a patient a new picture of himself or herself; these were the parallels Quimby could draw to his earlier fascination with daguerreotypy. When Quimby opened himself to his patient's feelings, they were, so to speak, daguerreotyped on him. Once a seriously ill young woman came into Quimby's office escorted by her father. She seemed to be suffering from dropsy, a morbid accumulation of watery fluid in the serous cavities of the body's connective tissue. Quimby took her by the hand, and within a brief time she transported him from the fluid of her body to an ocean, where Quimby saw a brig being tossed in a gale. Standing on the bow of the boat was a man, who suddenly lost his balance and fell overboard.

In this case, Quimby drew a mental picture from the tone and feeling of the woman's words. Then, like a confident captain in the midst of an emotional squall, Quimby steered to where her fears lay. The man who fell overboard obviously was a loved one she had lost, and Quimby correctly sensed that this loss, which had happened five years before the onset of her disease, was directly related. He provided this interpretation convincingly to the patient, whereupon his words were "daguerreotyped" on her "receptive-plate." As the first rays of the sun broke up the early-morning darkness, the patient began to see herself and her illness in a new light. As she did, her confidence increased, hope replaced despair, and her new optimism was daguerreotyped to Quimby, who responded with a cheery enthusiasm of his own. Through this process of mutual daguerreotyping, the woman's dropsy was cured.[45]

Quimby's brimming self-confidence, his bottomless empathy, his forceful direction of a client in fighting disease, his ability to get his patients to reflect his thoughts and feelings, all suggest that the daguerreotype metaphor may be exchanged for a more modern one: the mirror or idealizing transference. Quimby actively encouraged his emotionally vulnerable patients to use him as a young child might use her mother, as a mirror to discover herself and to be reflected in the mother's (Quimby's) confidence and admiration. Or, his patients might idealize Quimby in order to experience themselves as part of him, feeling strong and good so long as this tie was maintained. Quimby felt this idealizing transference, knew it was there, even though he lacked a modern explanation of its dynamics. In a letter to a Mr. Capen, Quimby acknowledged that his cures depended "a great deal on the confidence of my patients" and in their belief that he had "a power."[46]

A woman, writing from Illinois in late 1860, explained what this "power" meant to her. She yearned to be with Quimby and to reexperience one of his "sittings." She groped to express exactly how she felt, but much as in her sessions with Quimby, she was unable to verbalize that "undefinable longing for something." She nevertheless marveled at Quimby's ability to see "the feelings *hidden within*." When she considered that Quimby had cured her and that he continued to cure hundreds of others, she knew he was somebody special. As far as she was concerned, he possessed "a knowledge far superior to any other person I have known or heard of." He had raised her from a long illness to a perfect health; Quimby surely was "the *nicest, best* man in the world."[47]

One man cured by Quimby addressed him in a letter as "My Preserver and Friend," while another lauded him as the good Samaritan, who,

like a protective parent, took his hand and opened his understanding to
the true meaning of disease. The cure was nothing short of a miracle,
and Quimby's fame was spreading. Some of his other patients echoed
these thoughts of Quimby as a miracle worker, and for some his health
cures were just short of Christ's raising Lazarus from the dead.[48]

As this last analogy attests and as we have previously seen, many of
Quimby's patients saw his healing power in expressly spiritual terms.
Any sick person longed for "his Messiah or Saviour to come and save
him," Quimby said. Lost in the cloud of their belief, trapped within
themselves as if in a prison, "starving for the bread of life," and ready
to die, patients latched on to Quimby because his voice of wisdom broke
up the cloud, unlocked the prison door, and fed them the bread of life.
"My wisdom," he said immodestly, "is the Science or the Saviour."[49]

Quimby, as previously noted, believed that his mind-healing method
divulged what caused this spiritual sickness and his "Wisdom" explained
it to the patient. In a circular that he distributed to the sick while he
was in Portland, Quimby said that his practice was unlike any medical
practice. He sat by the sick, listened to them, told them what caused
their disease, "and my explanation is the cure." However, Quimby was
only partly right in his understanding of how his cures worked. Today
we would point out that the cure was in the transference, not the
interpretation.[50]

There is little doubt that in his practice Quimby encouraged an early
mother-child transference relationship. He often argued not only that
illnesses were to be found in the deep recesses of the person, but that
they were put there in childhood. In a letter to a patient named Mrs.
Norcross, Quimby wrote, "Your mother probably changed the fluids of
your body, when an infant or at any early age, and some circumstance
located it in your leg." In another instance, Quimby tied the diseases
and complaints of his patients more tightly to the parent-child relationship. When he sat by the sick he found them "either like a child or a
person in belief. If they have no ideas that come within their senses they
are like one affected by surrounding circumstances, as a child whose
parents are fighting is frightened and perhaps killed by the parents' evil
acts."[51]

These last few letters again reflect Quimby's radical side, the one he
revealed in his attacks on cultural authorities. Not only was he at war
with the doctors and ministers, he was ready to take on the most sacred
institution in Victorian America: the family. It was self-evident that a
child was deeply influenced by his or her parents, who in turn were
influenced by the prevailing opinions of the day. Quimby was once called

to a home to attend a sick little girl. He found her lying on a chaise in a stupor; she had been in this listless condition for more than a year. Her worried parents had previously consulted a doctor, and, accepting his diagnosis, they told Quimby that not only did their girl have water on the brain but she was going mad as a result. After two or three visits, Quimby concluded that the parents were wrong. There was no water on the brain; "the child's insensibility was caused by her parents' belief in it." Having said this to the parents, Quimby proceeded to bring the child out of her stupor, and eventually he restored her to health. In this case, it was evident to Quimby that "the parents had communicated their belief, which they had derived from the doctor, to the child and were making her an idiot." Quimby thus offered his patients an escape from their personal and cultural pasts. He would save them from mental and emotional abuse, even when it came from well-intentioned parents and others.[52]

In letters to his patients, Quimby comfortably used the metaphor of a nurturing mother, only this time he was providing malnourished children with the right food. To a woman in New Hampshire he wrote that every word of his was like yeast. As she took his words in and digested them like food, they "came in contact with the food of your old bread or belief." To another patient, Mrs. Ware, Quimby advised that if she wanted to restore her health, she first had to turn to God and then to Quimby himself. To help her overcome her problems with digesting her food, Quimby urged her to be quiet, to think of his soothing advice. As his words entered her, they would "reverse the action from your head, and you will feel it passing out of your stomach."[53]

Quimby stressed this kind of maternal identification because it accurately reflected the kind of healing he practiced. A strong, competent man in touch with his nurturing side, Quimby, with his strength and compassion, must have been a welcome sight to male and female patients who had previously tried a number of cures and remedies without success. And in an age when many doctors dismissed women's illnesses as hysteria, Quimby's compassion and genuine concern about their emotional and physical states surely was one reason many women sought him out and believed in him deeply.

In the mid-1850s, Catharine Beecher wrote a small book, *Letters to the People on Health and Happiness*, in which she concluded that most women were neither healthy nor happy. Quimby took up the same issues in an essay in which he tried to account for why women were sicker than men. For Quimby part of the answer lay in the period's dominant ideology, with its separation of spheres and its cult of domesticity. Spending their time in their homes, women, he surmised, "have nothing to employ themselves about so they sit down and talk over their aches and pains, and in this way they make themselves sick." At this point, a doctor might have become perturbed and dismissed a woman's complaint of illness, but Quimby did not, for he knew that this was not the whole story.[54]

Everyone assumed that women had more intuition than men, and while the wider culture used this to relegate women to the home (the reason and logic needed in the competitive marketplace were male attributes), Quimby saw a particular strength in feminine traits. Everyone, he assumed, knew that women were more introspective than men: "they want to see more, they have more curiosity than men." So when women felt sick, they had a natural curiosity "to analyze their suffering . . . and they have a fear of coming under the law of disease," thus putting themselves at the mercy of the male doctors. However, if a woman proved intractable, if her disease could not readily be categorized and controlled by the male doctors, then she would be labeled "nervous, spleeny or hypochondriacal and receive no sympathy from anyone." Furthermore, no matter how debilitating or painful the illness was, no matter how humiliated or angry a woman might become at being dismissed by a male doctor, many of them refused to give up the illness. In his primitive way, Quimby had recognized what is today called the secondary gains of an illness; even when women realized that they had nothing to thank men for regarding their illnesses, "they hold on to it sometimes with great tenacity." When a man like Quimby came along and offered to free them from the prison they had unwittingly helped male doctors to construct, some women accepted his greater wisdom with joy and relief. Other women, however, were "so wedded to their opinions of disease" that they felt too anxious to let go of the old and embrace the new.[55]

In the realm of gender roles and expectations, then, Quimby was no less radical than he was in challenging the role of doctors and ministers. He took the cultural stereotype regarding gender and turned it on its head:

> Women have more endurance and more patience to in-
> vestigate any new science than man. And their wisdom is
> not of this world, but of that higher power called Science.
> When they give their idea to man, he then eats or under-
> stands, and then goes to work to form the idea that has
> been given to him by the woman. It has always been the

case that all spiritual wisdom has been received through the female. . . . As men's minds are more brutal and less scientific or spiritual, they never believe till they can see with the natural man's eyes.[56]

Quimby believed that God had created woman with a greater intuitive wisdom than man, with "more of that superior substance" needed to receive God's message. This special substance was "pure love," and while man's creative power might draw upon it, his creativity was more comfortable in the secular world. But, said Quimby, if Science were put into the soul of a woman, it would remain pure; it would separate the woman from matter and elevate her above animal life. A woman was thus better equipped to become a teacher of his spiritual science, which controlled all matter and which clearly differentiated the learning of this world from the wisdom of God. As a moral teacher, "the woman is the one who gives all the impressions to the child."[57]

So, if Quimby offered himself to his clients as an idealized, strong, yet nurturing figure, who empathized with the plight of women and saw spiritual strengths in them, who urged his patients to break the personal and social chains that kept them in misery, then no wonder Mary Patterson had idealized him before she came to Portland, and no wonder she began to feel better the moment she stepped into his waiting room in October 1862.[58]

Over the next three weeks Mary's health improved dramatically. The way Quimby treated her in their "sittings" is lost to history. Apparently he believed that women were more open to spiritual interpretations of disease, or perhaps that they saw their illnesses primarily in spiritual terms; whatever the reason, Quimby tended to introduce more biblical parables and analogies into his treatment of women than he did for men. We can only guess, however, whether he relied exclusively on this technique with Mary. Nevertheless, her health did improve, and she joined the legions of Quimby's patients who sang his praises. After a week's treatment she waxed ecstatic in a poem she submitted to the *Portland Evening Courier*. Quimby was the "sage profound," "the self-taught man walking in wisdom's ways," who had ascended heights not accounted for in the books of man. His intuitive wisdom had the power to cure all illness.[59]

By November, Mary had published an article in the *Evening Courier* extolling Quimby even more lavishly. Her opening line cast restraint to the winds. "When our Shakespeare decided that 'there were more things in this world than were dreamed of in your philosophy,' " she genuinely wondered whether the great bard might not have "had a foreknowledge of P. P. Quimby." She compared Quimby to some of the greatest philosophical and scientific minds of the ages, and used herself as an example to demonstrate his power. Three weeks earlier she had set out for Portland in a state of "mental and physical depression," and those close to her had all but given up hope of her recovery. In less than a week with Quimby, she had regained her strength and was now able to ascend the more than 180 steps to the dome of the City Hall. There was no stopping her now; she was "improving *ad infinitum.*"

Mary then sketched a brief analysis of Quimby's healing power. His teachings about clairvoyance and about the correspondence between spirit and matter left him open to charges that he was a spiritualist. Mary leaped to his defense. His healing works were the result "of superior wisdom, which can demonstrate a science not understood" by the everyday world and conventional methods. Nor did his healing have anything to do with animal magnetism. Mary confessed that in the past she had employed both electromagnetism and animal magnetism, and they had provided temporary relief from her miseries, but she had never succeeded in fully conquering her ailments. Quimby, however, stressed to her that disease was an independent entity; hence, "I could not be wiser than my teacher. But now I can see dimly at first . . . the great principle which underlies Dr. Quimby's faith and works; and just in proportion to my light perception of truth is my recovery."

This truth, that disease and pain are to be found in belief, if correctly understood transformed "the currents of the system," and the body functioned harmoniously. As taught and practiced by Quimby, this core truth was scientific and capable of demonstration. At present, Mary confessed, she was still invested too much in error and false belief to demonstrate it. Lest the paper's readers miss the point, Mary emphasized that Quimby's healing was "a very spiritual doctrine"; its truth would stand forever.[60]

The day after this laudatory article was published, a rival newspaper, the *Portland Advertiser*, mocked Mary's adulation of Quimby and took her to task for suggesting that his so-called superior wisdom might be compared to the healings of Jesus Christ. Quimby and Christ? What could possibly be next, the *Advertiser* hooted. The paper's sharp words stung Mary, and she dashed off a quick retort in the *Courier*. She did not retreat from her praise of Quimby. Despite the gibes of disbelievers, he stood upon a high plane of wisdom and truth. No man had ever uttered the truth the way Quimby had, and no man had healed as effectively as Quimby since the days of Christ. Could not one clearly see that he was "identified with truth, and is not this the Christ which is in him?" Much like Christ, Quimby had the power to roll away "the stone from the sepulchre of error, and health is the resurrection."[61]

Despite her belief in Quimby and his cure, Mary had to deal with nagging questions: Could Quimby truly be a savior and restore her health? Had she at last reached the end of her pilgrimage? Time would tell.

5

ISSUES FROM DEATH:
SALVATION THROUGH FEAR
AND TREMBLING

He that is our God is the God of salvation; and unto God
the Lord belong the issues from death.

Psalms 68:20

AFTER HER TEMPORARY RECOVERY in October, Mary remained in Portland for almost three months, staying close to Quimby and his teachings. George Quimby, who was his father's secretary, recalled years later that Mary Patterson had more than a passing interest in his father's ideas. Mary and Phineas spent considerable time huddled together mulling over his theories of health and healing. As Mary was learning at her master's knee, her husband, Daniel, made good an escape from a Southern prison, and by December he had joined her in Portland. By the new year they had returned to Sanbornton Bridge, where they stayed with Abigail and her family. Patterson attempted to revive his dental practice some hundred miles away in the bustling town of Lynn, Massachusetts, but to little avail. It did not seem to matter whether he was in the backwoods or the city; Daniel Patterson was not successful, and he and his wife continued to drift further apart.[1]

The return of her husband and her homecoming unnerved Mary, and she relapsed into her assorted ills and complaints. In January 1863, she wrote to Quimby, saying she had not been well for several days. She had a recurring pain and soreness in the stomach that also affected her spine. Eating aggravated her condition. When she arrived at her sister's house, she tried to eat regular food, but felt so emotionally drained (partly because of the long journey) that the old maladies, the very ones she thought she had conquered, began to reemerge in all their former strength. She felt that she did not have the energy to fight off the old beliefs of illness. What she wanted more than anything else was for

Quimby to provide his *occasional* aid," to come to her in his clairvoyant state and "remove this pain."[2]

The return of her old symptoms did not jar Mary's faith in Quimby. She even encouraged her sister Abigail to send her son, Albert, to Portland for treatment of his drinking and smoking habits. After a brief treatment by Quimby, Albert seemed to master his nasty habits, but as soon as he returned home his recidivism was inevitable. In early March 1863, Mary wrote to Quimby, alarmed by Albert's backsliding. In the same letter she informed her mentor that her own health had not really improved, but this was not the most upsetting thing to her. She had been trying to help Albert, and while employing Quimby's techniques she had discovered one of the hazards of the trade that the master knew well. Ever since she had been attending to Albert and his craving for cigarettes, she had begun to feel the same urge in herself. "Do pray rid me of this feeling," she implored Quimby. He might have smiled at a neophyte's attempts to keep a proper emotional distance from the unconscious desires and conflicts of a patient, but something more serious was transpiring between Mary and her nephew. As she experienced Albert's distasteful habits within herself, Mary's vulnerability to those early traumas and her deeply buried feelings threatened to resurface.[3]

Over the next several months, the power of Quimby's mind was not enough to cure Mary, and by the summer of 1863 she was on her way back to Portland. By late fall she had become a regular contributor to the Portland newspapers with her verse and prose pieces. She wrote a column for the *Portland Daily Press* called "Way-side Thoughts"; at least in one part of her life she was productive.

As we saw earlier, when her husband was captured by Southern troops, Mary responded with a flurry of letter writing. This subsided when she realized that no politician could get him released. After Daniel's escape, the war, of course, did not stop, but it is very difficult to determine what its effect was upon Mary.

The onset of the Civil War propelled white middle-class women into unprecedented public activity. Two weeks after the first shot was fired, they formed thousands of aid societies to provide the armies with clothing, food, and medical supplies. They plunged into work with the Sanitary Commission; they wrote petitions against slavery; they spent endless hours in their small-town auxiliaries organizing benevolence on the home front. Mary Patterson, as we noted earlier, was never a part of this wider network of women, and she did not participate in it this time around, either. This kept her a step or two removed from feeling immediately involved in the war effort, and from the effects of the war itself.[4]

The historian Philip Paludan has pointed out that in the mid-nine-teenth century Americans were no strangers to death; infant mortality was not an abstraction, nor was the sudden death of family members. But while they were able to construct social rituals and meanings around deaths that occurred as part of the normal course of life, Americans were not psychologically prepared for the slaughter of war. "The war brought death into the foreground of life. Newspapers, personal letters, word of mouth, brought home to every community the growing moun-tains of dead that the war was exacting." And, Paludan perceptively notes, there seemed no adequate way to mourn fathers and sons killed far from home.[5]

Since life had taught Mary Patterson the psychological horrors of annihilation and death, the posted reports of the dead and wounded must have been exceptionally painful for her, perhaps even contributing to her illnesses. In late December 1863, as she reflected on the meaning of the Christmas holiday, the family hearth, and the absent young men dying on the battlefields, she wrote one of her most heartfelt poems, "Christmas Day," which appeared in the *Portland Daily Press*. It was not a time of gifts and good cheer; it was a time when sons were separated from mothers, a time when "Blank despair, or trembling joy" filled the hearts of loved ones. In the poem's third stanza, Mary expressed as directly as she ever would the terrible reality of the war. She describes a mother "mourning at the threshold of a lonely household door." Her bittersweet memories hark back to when her child was young and she combed his golden locks. Her son, now lying mortally wounded at the front, his "bright locks blood-stained," yearns for the loving gaze of his mother.[6]

Mary did not linger on the dark side of the war for long. Rather than focus on its horrors, Mary chose to describe it as a noble duty. She wrote articles defending liberty and democracy while at the same time excoriating the "hydra-headed" Copperheads. When the governor of New Hampshire called for an enlistment of soldiers, Mary responded with a poem calling for sacrifice, duty, and honor. Declaring that it was better to die nobly than in shame, she encouraged men to enlist. She was fully supportive of the President, "our faithful Abraham," and she hoped that he would continue "to blend justice with victory" in dealing with the rebellious states.[7]

While writing for the paper, Mary boarded with Daniel Patterson's brothers in Saco, Maine, near Portland. From one letter during this time it is evident that though she was now physically closer to Quimby, her ill health dogged her steps. Her side ached, her head ached, and she had great difficulty falling asleep. There were times when her head hurt so badly that the rattling of pots and pans from the kitchen under her room jangled her nerves and worsened the pain. In the throes of such anguish and despair, she nostalgically yearned to see her son again. She even cried out for her husband.[8]

During the winter of 1863–64, Mary spent hours with Quimby, sitting in on his cases, discussing them with him, and retiring at night to write her notes. Although she continued to find her strength drained by her own recurring illnesses, she gave two spirited lectures in Portland that explained and extolled her mentor's work. Late in March 1864, Mary went to visit Mary Ann Jarvis of Warren, Maine, who had also been a patient of Quimby's. Miss Jarvis was an asthmatic who felt that she had made some gains under Quimby's direct care, but she feared a relapse once she returned home. Sure enough, upon returning she collapsed and immediately sent an urgent letter to Mary to come to her rescue.[9]

For Mary the two-day coach trip to her friend's house was grueling. But Mary's physical discomfort was nothing compared to the emotional jostling she was to experience during her stay with Mary Jarvis. Just as Mary had idealized Quimby and had become deeply attached to him, so Jarvis idealized her friend Mary. Lying submerged beneath the surface of this idealization, however, were the unconscious conflicts that would eventually put a strain on their relationship.

Just how dependent Jarvis was upon Mary was revealed in a letter that Mary wrote to Quimby shortly after arriving in Warren. Jarvis had expected Mary to arrive two days earlier, and when she did not, she broke into tears. Jarvis became so desperate that, feeling like an abandoned child, she was convinced that Mary was lost or was never going to come. When Mary finally got there, she found Jarvis in "a peculiar condition": she had great difficulty breathing because of the easterly wind. From her experiences with Quimby, Mary knew that the causes lay elsewhere. As she sat next to the suffering Jarvis, she tried to correct the erroneous belief. Shortly Jarvis's breathing became less labored; much to Mary's surprise, her friend was able to cough up phlegm easily and had not been bothered by a wracking cough until recently. While Mary may have effected a temporary cure, momentarily stepping into Quimby's shoes as a healer, she knew that she was a novice compared to him. Quimby the Master: just as his mind could control disease, so it could control the disturbing wind and the waves.

But an ill wind stirred by Mary soon undermined Jarvis's fragile condition and made for rough sailing for both of them. Mrs. Sarah Crosby, another friend and also a former patient of Quimby, had written Mary in Warren asking her when she might return for a visit. Mary made the gaffe of reading this letter to Jarvis. Partway through the letter she intuitively realized that something was wrong. Jarvis was depressed. As Mary said to Quimby, she had not exercised good judgment in reading the letter to her friend. Certainly a part of her knew the depressed feelings that arise when someone close leaves. Whether they were aware of it or not, Mary and Jarvis's relationship had the earmarks of a parent-child relationship. Already extremely sensitive to being left, Jarvis was now told that Mary, her idealized parent, was on the verge of abandoning her for another. Mary, for her part, had a life filled with overwhelming losses, and sometimes it was hard not to repeat them with others; perhaps this was what her intuition whispered to her as she read the letter.

Jarvis broke into prolonged crying, and even Mary's promise not to leave until her friend felt better failed to quiet the sobs or dry the tears. When Mary sat next to her, Jarvis seemed very anxious. Eventually this highly charged atmosphere began to undermine Mary, and it became difficult for her to tell where the anxiety was coming from. Was it in Jarvis? In herself? Or was it now in both? This was too much for Mary, and she begged Quimby for his guidance and for one of his clairvoyant visits to help her get some sleep and to "relieve the confined state of the bowels."

As long as she was with her friend, Mary was both physically and emotionally constricted. The distress and anxiety seemed unending to her. In this same long letter to Quimby, she began to mistrust her own capacities to help her friend and herself. As her confidence waned, Mary leaned more heavily on Quimby, even wondering, "What could I do without *you?*" She felt weaker that spring than she had at the same time the year before, when she had had trouble chewing and could not eat enough food. In her weakened condition, the same problem plagued her. She would like to take charge of the problem herself so that she would not have to visit Quimby again and be so dependent upon him. But where was her support to come from? It would have been nice to think that she could count on Daniel, she sighed wistfully, "but! but! but!" Only one thing was certain in her marriage to Patterson: their life together never came close to her ideal picture. Here the tone of Mary's letter became angry and rebellious. She did not respect people who sought material wealth at the expense of genuine spiritual growth. She would never sacrifice the one for the other.[10]

Over the next two months, Mary's stay with Mary Ann Jarvis lengthened into an emotional nightmare. She grew increasingly vulnerable to Jarvis's illnesses, and as she deteriorated, she pleaded more insistently for Quimby's help. She had enough spunk to give two lectures defending Quimby from the townspeople's accusations that he was a spiritualist. Most of her time, however, was absorbed in Jarvis. By mid-April a break in the heavy clouds that hung over the two women prompted a relieved Mary to write Quimby. Amazingly, Jarvis had shown improvement; no doubt her restored spirits were the result of one of Quimby's clairvoyant house calls. Mary questioned him: was it true that he had "called away" Jarvis's thoughts from her? It had to be so. As Jarvis improved, the atmosphere in the home lightened, and so did Mary's spirits. In this more cheerful mood, Mary felt safe and strong enough to ask Quimby to return Jarvis's potentially disturbing thoughts to her (Mary) so that she could again try to help her.[11]

A little more than a week later, Mary had lost her emotional equilibrium and suffered accordingly. She again yearned for an ideal home and marriage. She knew which steps she needed to take with her still afflicted friend, but she invariably stumbled. She could not help feeling the "old temptations" reasserting themselves in her body when she found herself being sucked into Jarvis's emotional vortex. She knew from Quimby what the spiritual truth was, but she simply was not strong enough to implement it.

In the final paragraphs of this letter to Quimby, the feelings and conflicts stirred by her relationship with Jarvis were clearly taking their toll on Mary. As she weakened, her anger toward Jarvis spilled out, though some of it was surely intended for Quimby. She had given up so much for him; she had believed so deeply in his truth. But now her recurring illnesses and her emotional entanglement with Jarvis chipped away at her idealization of Quimby. Could Quimby the savior be a failed God? It was possible, but Mary could not accept what this implied for her; what was left of the letter reaffirmed Quimby and his doctrines. She repeated his words and phrases much as a small child would repeat her parents' when she was alone and afraid.

Instead of faulting Quimby and his beliefs, Mary laid the blame for her current failures at her own doorstep. She thought she must practice his scientific healing perfectly in order to help herself and others. Obviously, she had fallen far short of this perfection, and her failure had hindered her work with Mary Ann Jarvis. No matter how much the outside community attacked and belittled, she vowed to Quimby that she would carry on his work.[12]

By May things had gone from bad to worse; it was as if she were living in a chamber of horrors. As she took in the "heat" of Jarvis's fears, Mary's spine began to hurt again. In her weakened condition, the terror unleashed by her friend's suffering invaded Mary. Within a few days she was shaken by a deep, hacking cough, and she began to cough up blood. Her breathing sounded labored and asthmatic. Her sleep was at best fitful, and as she lay there sick and exhausted, Mary's belief that

Quimby's spirit could travel over distance was transformed into a hallucination. After one particularly difficult night, Mary finally dozed off, only to awaken early in the morning, convinced that she heard someone calling her name. When she opened her eyes, she saw Quimby. Just that quickly her physical ailments began to vanish, thanks to "the help of the Lord (Quimby)."

With her health temporarily restored one more time, Mary's praise of Quimby knew no bounds. Was he not the perfect man? she questioned rhetorically. In the full flush of her idealization of him, Quimby was invincible. With his clairvoyant powers, even the devil did not stand a chance with Quimby. And Mary needed to borrow some of Quimby's strength. It had fallen to her to bear the sins of Mary Ann Jarvis, but Quimby had interceded to rescue her, although, as Mary hurriedly noted, there had been a moment in her deepest despair when she had wondered whether Quimby had forsaken her. But that was past. For now she hoped that he might occasionally make a clairvoyant call on her so that she might enjoy some relief for her constipation and get a good night's sleep.[13]

By the end of May, Quimby's spiritual visits had failed, and Mary was no closer to the perfection she desired. Her final letter to Quimby from the Jarvis home contained familiar laments. Again she yearned for Quimby to come to her at night to relieve her spinal pain. This time she resolved to go to Portland to put herself under his direct care. Her friend Sarah Crosby had urged Mary to join her in Albion, Maine, but Mary did not travel there immediately. Daniel Patterson had opened an office and was running ads in the Lynn paper. As she had written to Quimby, she yearned for the ideal home and marriage, so back to Lynn she went, but again she was disappointed.[14]

In July 1864, she wrote Quimby saying that her husband was sick with erysipelas, and she complained that he laughed at her when she tried to help him with Quimby's methods. Mary had done everything she could for Patterson. She herself was not feeling well enough to move back to Portland, and she felt dispirited. She again implored Quimby to transmit his spiritual aid to her husband. Her own emotional suffering continued, for there appeared to be no end to life's hardships: although Patterson's dental practice brought in a few coins to the family coffer, his eye began to wander again. Perhaps for these reasons Mary chose to travel to the home of Sarah Crosby.[15]

Mary had met Sarah Crosby earlier in 1864 in Portland when both were patients of Quimby. Mary had once described Crosby to Quimby as one of the few people with whom she felt a close affinity. Mrs. Crosby lived in a roomy farmhouse with her husband's family and spent much of her time as the "too yielding" wife and mother, clearly subordinate to tough old Grandmother Crosby. The Crosbys were ardent believers in spiritualism.

Sarah Crosby wrote years later that she and Mary were "two lone women" who spent hours in close emotional touch. These two friends could not have avoided arousing powerful feelings in each other. Crosby had to live day in and day out with a strong-willed mother-in-law. Mary also knew what it meant to be tied emotionally to a maternal figure, and no doubt Crosby and Mary reenacted the struggles of a mother-daughter relationship. This, then, was the setting for an episode that has been open to various interpretations, depending upon whether one is a supporter or a critic of Mrs. Eddy.[16]

According to Sarah Crosby's memory of the incident, one day she and Mary were seated at opposite ends of a table when suddenly Mary leaned back in her chair, gave a shiver, closed her eyes, and began to talk in a deep masculine voice. The voice identified itself as that of Albert Baker, Mary's long-dead brother; he said that he had been trying to control his sister for many days, and warned Crosby that she was becoming too attached to Mary and placing too much confidence in her. On another occasion Mary went into an altered state of consciousness, and through her Albert's spirit again spoke to Crosby. He told her that if she would look under the cushion of a certain chair, she would discover important notes from him. One note advised her to trust in Quimby's methods; the other offered spiritual encouragement.[17]

While her critics have gleefully discredited Mrs. Eddy for her involvement in this spiritualistic episode, Robert Peel has forcefully argued that she had already openly denounced spiritualism, so her episodes with Sarah Crosby were not what they appeared to be. She was not an active participant in the trances, argues Peel. Mary was fully in charge of herself—playing a role, as it were, using the trances to show Crosby what a sham they really were. Caught up in the moment, Crosby took them seriously.[18]

These events invite another interpretation, however. As we have seen, Mary was lugging heavy emotional burdens by the time she arrived at the Crosby home. Not too many months earlier she had been through a number of harrowing scenes with Mary Ann Jarvis. She also had to deal with the strains of her faltering marriage. More important, her recurrent illnesses were troubling reminders that she had not attained the perfection Quimby's doctrines promised. Despite some temporary gains from Quimby's healing techniques, her psychic wounds from her

early overwhelmings had not been healed, opening up a wide range of
strong, conflicting feelings. While the dependency (mother-daughter)
issues stirred up by Sarah Crosby no doubt touched upon Mary's relationship with her own mother, they also resonated strongly with her
more current relationship with Quimby. Given the spiritualist atmosphere in the Crosby home, Sarah Crosby's volatile emotions, Mary's
own unsettled emotional state, Mary's tendency to identify so closely
with external conflicts that she had trouble separating what came from
inside and what came from without, and Mary's (and Quimby's) affinity
with some aspects of spiritualism, one can understand how Mary might
have temporarily relaxed her strong reservations and fallen into spiritualist episodes.*

Shortly after the last trance, Mary regained her emotional equilibrium.
In a letter to Crosby, Mary told her flatly that "P. Quimby of Portland
has the spiritual truth of disease. You must imbibe it to be healed."
Once disentangled from the emotional thicket with Crosby, Mary was
able to understand better the nature of the conflicts. Although Crosby
continued to think of Mary as important for her physical and emotional
health, Mary tried to tell her that she was not. The two of them had to
separate, said Mary, for the sake of Crosby's improvement. "You will
miss me at first," she acknowledged, but after a time Crosby would feel
better about their separation, and she would be able to devote her time
to herself and her children.[19]

By late fall, reconciled one more time, Mary and Daniel Patterson
were living in Lynn. She continued to write for the *Lynn Weekly Reporter*, while Patterson's dental practice limped along. They joined the
Linwood Lodge of Good Templars, a temperance group and social organization; in time she was selected as Exalted Mistress of the Legion
of Honor, the women's auxiliary. By April 1865, her health had again
declined so badly that she visited Quimby and received temporary relief.
As soon as she returned home, however, she was thrown back into the
usual muddle. Daniel Patterson continued his amorous asides with other
women, and Mary felt abandoned and destitute.[20]

---

* Mrs. Eddy's flirtation with spiritualism never developed into a full-blown romance.
Over time she became adamantly opposed to it. Her firmest statement on its defects
can be found in *Science and Health with Key to the Scriptures* (Boston: First Church
of Christ, Scientist, 1934), pp. 70–99. Her opposition to spiritualism is spelled out in
Stephen Gottschalk, *The Emergence of Christian Science in American Religious Life*
(Berkeley: University of California Press, 1978), pp. 141–43. Christian Science's ambiguous link to spiritualism is noted by Anne Braude, *Radical Spirits: Spiritualism and
Women's Rights in Nineteenth-Century America* (Boston: Beacon Press, 1989),
pp. 182–89.

In late July she wrote Quimby a desperate letter, anguish spilling out of each line. She had just received a piece of information so emotionally wrenching that the first thing she thought of doing was "*to go to you like the Mother of old.*" She had been told that her son was desperately ill in Minnesota, that he had been on his way home to see her, but that he had been too weak to travel any farther. As sick as she was, she vowed to go in search of her son, even if she did not know the route. She begged Quimby to intercede with his spiritual telepathy and cure her son, or at least make him better until he could be found and brought to Quimby. Then, in a moment of deep despair, Mary sensed that it would be useless for her to set out on this journey, for it was now too late. Although she did not spell out directly what she meant by this, Mary seemed to be intimating that her son had died. Clearly, Mary was deeply distressed. As she finished her letter to Quimby, she cried out that she really did not know what she had meant by these last words.[21]

It is highly doubtful that Mary was literally referring to her son George in this letter, because he was nowhere near Minnesota. What comes through Mary's written words, however, is her overwhelming sense of isolation, abandonment, and anxiety about death. It is as if she had identified with a child's lonely quest to find his mother, but instead of a happy reunion, the sick, abandoned child was left to die. And just as she fantasized that her son was on his way to her, so she wished to return to her "Mother of old."

This wish would never be fulfilled, for at the moment she sought Quimby's help, his health was rapidly declining. To make things worse, her father was also in poor health. Her world was becoming increasingly unstable; Mary was on edge. In early September she lashed out at her sister Martha. In a brief, acerbic letter she accused Martha of talking behind her back to another woman, and she was furious that others continued to accuse her "of the most diabolical lies." We do not know what caused this flare-up with her sister, but Mary's sense of well-being was even more critically undermined on October 6, 1865, when Mark Baker died. Three months later, on January 16, 1866, Phineas Parkhurst Quimby also died. Mary could not have been more alone.[22]

Six days later Mary wrote a poem eulogizing Quimby, and on February 14 it was printed in the *Lynn Reporter*. The title alone—"Lines on the Death of P. P. Quimby, Who Healed with the Truth that Christ Taught in Contradistinction of all Isms"—reflects how significant he had been to her and how much she missed him. Cast adrift as she was, and feeling the loss of so many important people in her life, Mary's pilgrimage now seemed at a dead end. On Thursday, February 1, 1866,

Mary was making her way along the icy streets of Lynn, headed to a
Good Templars meeting. Many years later, in an interview with one of
her Christian Science students, Mrs. Eddy indicated that she had been
carrying a heavy emotional cross. Up to that point, she told Fannie
Pierce, her life "had been of the saddest history" that one could imagine.
What happened on that February evening was described in a matter-of-
fact blurb in the *Lynn Reporter*:

> Mrs. Mary M. Patterson, of Swampscott, fell upon the
> ice near the corner of Market and Oxford Streets, on
> Thursday evening, and was severely injured. She was
> taken up in an insensible condition and carried to the
> residence of S. M. Bubier, Esq., near by, where she was
> kindly cared for during the night. Dr. Cushing, who was
> called, found her injuries to be internal, and of a very
> serious nature, including spasms and intense suffering. She
> was removed to her home in Swampscott yesterday after-
> noon, though in a very critical condition.[23]

It is worth repeating this bland newspaper report in full, because it was
probably the last time the facts were directly and simply presented. While
everyone agrees that Mary Patterson fell, there is heated disagreement
as to the meaning of the event and what occurred over the next four or
five days. For Mary Patterson this fall on the ice was a turning point in
her life; for Christian Scientists it has become the founding moment. It
might be advantageous to sidestep the swirl of controversy created by
her supporters and detractors and keep our eye focused on what this
fall meant to Mary.

   Her fall was both literal and figurative. Although she was not consciously aware of it, her journey through life had prepared her for this
slip on the ice. For many of her more than forty years she had struggled
to come to terms with the punishing God of her parents' Calvinism. As
her ordeals with her father revealed, no matter how much she resented
this stern, patriarchal God, part of her was attached to Him through
her father and mother. When she internalized this part of her parents
and their culture, a part of her self became the object of this God; that
is, lying within her was a hated, helpless, vulnerable self. Somehow she
had to reconcile this punishing God of the Old Testament with the loving
and protective God of the New Testament, both of which she and her
contemporaries needed. And somehow she had to integrate the harsh,
punitive aspects of herself with the loving, caring ones.

   Mary's Graham diet, her study and practice of homeopathy, and her brief encounter with hydropathy forged special links between the mind and body, between matter and spirit. Each of these disciplines, with its optimistic belief in progress and perfection, sought, in the words of Robert Fuller, to "narrow the great gulf that Calvinism had posited between a stern, wrathful God and His weak, depraved creation." But none of them ever quite succeeded in this, and none closed the fissure within Mary. Self-discipline and willpower, the weapons of ascetic Protestantism, never provided the kind of victory Mary so desperately needed, and with each setback she had to wrestle with her agonizing doubts and her Calvinistic guilt over her disobedience to divine law.[24]

These inner struggles absorbed much of Mary's energy, and they weakened her emotional ties to traditional institutions, especially the Congregational Church. She was becoming detached in other ways as well. Though she had had a close friend or two in adolescence and later, and though she was active in the Good Templars, much of Mary's adult life was spent outside the mainstream, outside the broad network of women's reform groups that mushroomed during the nineteenth century. Life's experiences had taught Mary that she was not like everyone else. Indeed, Mary was alone even when she was living with others. Her illnesses turned her inward to her private world of fantasy and imagination, which were relatively unchecked by the usual daily exchanges with the outside world. Her imagination focused on her pressing need for health and wholeness, and this led her to seek perfection in a more metaphysical vein. We first saw this romantic/transcendental side in her poetry; then it was expressed in her interest in homeopathy, spiritualism, and, importantly, in her daily reading of the Bible.[25]

Then Quimby entered her life. He had a practical, scientific side—within the nineteenth century's broad definition of science—which he balanced with his spiritual/mystical side, shaped by his encounters with mesmerism, Swedenborgianism, and Christianity. Here at last, or so Mary wished, was the whole package: a practical asceticism, yet freed from the crippling restraints of Calvinism; a material theory of the body and mind blended into a higher spiritual reality. Where Calvinism had failed to close the gap between God and man, Quimby had succeeded, and his theory allowed women an active role in healing. He was a cultural maverick, and once Mary idealized him and his work, it furthered her own detachment from traditional institutions and roles. With his success in healing and his dazzling displays of intuitional powers, Quimby was Mary's savior.[26]

As a child might slip her small hand into the large one of a wise, caring parent, Mary had placed her trust in Quimby. Before his death she struggled to keep her trust and her idealization of him from falling apart. It is sadly ironic that two key men in her life—Mark Baker, with his religious truth built around a Calvinistic fatalism, and Phineas P. Quimby, with his healing truth built around an inventive view of the mind-body relationship—died within months of each other. Mark had failed her spiritual needs, and Quimby could not fulfill them, either. In her elegy, Mary continued to extol Quimby as the man "who hath made us whole." But this sentiment reflected wish more than reality.

When Quimby's healing methods failed to mend Mary's soul, her old fears of annihilation and death were at first like a gentle surf, posing no threat. They continued to gain force, however, beginning to resemble a tidal wave. No doubt Mary was injured in her fall, and as she lay in bed she was convinced, as she once told the Unitarian minister Frank L. Phalen, that she was virtually a helpless invalid facing a bleak future. At one point she read the expressions, tones, and words of the doctor and her friends to mean that she was dying. Whether they actually whispered such dire words to each other, or whether Mary's thoughts and feelings shaped what she thought she saw and heard, is almost beside the point: she believed that she was at death's doorstep. When they had all quietly tiptoed from the room and she lay alone in great pain, seemingly abandoned, her hopes collapsed.[27]

As the shadows gathered around her, and as she plunged deeper into herself, Mary's eyes searched the Bible for meaning. In the dim light her eyes rested on one of the healings of Jesus, and it contributed to her profound spiritual transformation. In February 1866, however, Mary was far from understanding the meaning of her experience. In the interview with Reverend Phalen, Mrs. Eddy told him that she had tried everything to improve her health, but nothing had really worked. As she slipped slowly but inexorably into the depths of despair, she was certain that her death was imminent.[28]

In short, after the failures and the deaths of Quimby and her father, and the conflicting feelings aroused in her by these events, Mary was emotionally drained. In this fragile state, her current reality began to take on the texture of her younger years, when she had been overwhelmed by the specter of abandonment and death. This time, however, as she told Phalen, she felt a sudden surge; an inspiration "possessed her" to throw herself on God's mercy.[29]

Rather than being passively overwhelmed by the old fears, Mary was transformed: an old self, the one that depended upon parents, authoritative figures, external powers, was dying. If she was to survive at all, a new self—more spiritual, elevated, and intact—had to dominate. She could be attached to God but not to man, to the Word but not to the bodies of others. Or, as Robert Peel aptly describes this special moment, she had a vision in which "she saw all being as spiritual, divine, immortal, wholly good. There was no room for fear or pain or death, no room for the limits that men define as matter."[30]*

In some ways this religious experience was Mary Patterson's ultimate act of creativity. She, of course, never would have expressed it this way. This makes the experience sound too much as if it were a human product, that she instead of God shaped its meaning. She always saw herself as a passive recipient of God's active intervention and His healing truth. God's creative hand had shaped this experience, not hers. In recounting this event for one of her students a quarter century later, Mrs. Eddy said that when the attending doctor, who had given up on her, asked her how she had been healed, she replied that it felt to her to be "all a thing or state of my mental consciousness," but not in any conventional physiological or psychological sense. She meant that something spiritual had touched and transformed her. But this realm of mental consciousness is vast and complex. While still respecting the spiritual nature of her feelings and experience, one might argue that the inspiration came partly from within Mary instead of wholly outside from God. In this sense, she was active and creative, and perhaps the best way to understand this point is by way of analogy.[31]

In both her poetry and her religious experience, Mary created a special place for herself, a transitional space (to use Winnicott's term) in which her imaginative life could be expressed not just in the realm of fantasy but in the social world. She used words—her poems—as the link to the outside world, as the transitional object that allowed her to interact with and manage reality. In her religious experience her image of God was psychologically woven from aspects of her self and her interactions with the important people from all stages of her life, her parents and Quimby among them. This process was labyrinthine in its complexity, but there

---

* Mary's conversion experience, while unique to her, had much in common with the conversion experiences of other nineteenth-century women. Like other women, Mary moved from defeat to victory, from submission to empowerment, from death to life. Unlike a number of other women, however, neither before nor after her experience was Mary consumed by a sense of sin. Whatever anger and rebellion she might have felt were muted by the way she had dealt with these feelings previously in her life. If anything seems to separate Mary's experience from other women's, it is that she faced particularly strong fears associated with the meaning of one's death, both literally and psychologically. Even after her recovery from the fall, Mary never saw death as a grand metaphor for the passage from a sinful life to a new one. On women's conversion experiences, see Virginia Lieson Brereton, *From Sin to Salvation: Stories of Women's Conversions, 1800 to the Present* (Bloomington: Indiana University Press, 1991), pp. 3–39.

was one more important part in this image to make it what Paul Pruyser has called a "transcendent object." Building upon Winnicott's concept of the transitional object, Pruyser argues for a special kind of religious object. "Transcendent objects are beyond the ordinary division made between a fantasy image produced by and lodged in someone's mind and the perceptual image produced by actual entities in the world that impinge upon the sense organs." Pruyser goes on to say that "another reason the word *transcendent* is appropriate is that illusionistic objects have a touch of the sacred and tend to be charged with symbolic surplus values." One might add, Mary's relationship to God occurred in a special transcendent sphere that allowed her to be withdrawn into it and attached to reality simultaneously.[32]

A sense of this special place and her special relationship to God was conveyed to a friend some two years after the fall. Mary suggested that the friend open her Bible to Luke 9 and read it closely if she really wanted to understand what kind of change Mary had undergone. She was now first and foremost a spiritual self, and this had significant implications. She had previously been dependent upon others; now she was fully sustained by God. Adam Dickey, Mrs. Eddy's secretary, once talked about her unique relationship with her followers. People who followed a great leader usually believed that they knew and understood the person whom they admired. In Mrs. Eddy's case, few people, if any, could say with confidence that they knew her.[33]

To one of her followers in the 1890s, Mrs. Eddy tried to explain the particular kind of relationship she had with people in which they might feel close to her but she felt removed from them. She made it sound as if there were two separate and distinct Mrs. Eddys. The Mrs. Eddy who was a woman with ordinary strengths and weaknesses could relate to people and be, as she phrased it, "pliant as wax." The Mrs. Eddy who was a spiritual leader in touch with God and His reality was rock-firm and immovable. When she was in this spiritual realm not only was she impregnable, she was so far removed from ordinary mortals that no one could really see her or understand her. Julia Bartlett, one of Mrs. Eddy's most dedicated followers, confirmed this last point. There were times when Mrs. Eddy was so far advanced in Truth, "so far above the world," that she felt absolutely alone in it. During these moments Mrs. Eddy cherished the hope that someday her students might progress to the point at which she could share with them what she saw.[34]

Attachment to others in the personal sense would always be a potential source of despair and anger, bad feelings, and a sense of deep unworthiness, helplessness, and vulnerability. Insofar as she continued to become involved with people after her healing experience, all this in fact happened. She would sometimes have difficulty keeping the personal and impersonal senses separate, and she would have trouble discriminating between her own bad feelings and those of others, as we shall see in the chapters ahead.

When Mary emerged from her religious experience, she claimed years later, the Bible became her special text, and it answered her questions as to how she was healed. "The Scriptures had a new meaning, a new tongue"; their true spiritual meaning became evident to her for the first time. Mary's new relationship to God and His Word led her to see the world through new eyes, and in her trusting relationship with Him, she had a new ideal to measure herself by. Spiritual self-certainty meant self-discipline and self-containment, inner resolve, concentration, fortitude; in time it would also mean the ability in her elevated state to help others to be cured where and in the way she had been or wished to have been cured: in the Mind. The healing experience was to her religious, and we must acknowledge the authenticity of the religious expression, for that was in and of her culture. It would be a serious error to disregard it, for as it was once said of Mrs. Eddy by one of her students, when one discussed religion he had to mention Mrs. Eddy in the same breath; "in a most essential and vital sense" the two were inseparable.[35]

In the many years left to her after her fall and recovery, Mrs. Eddy continued to struggle with physical disability and emotional stress. Some days and some months were darker than others; her bouts with illness were persistent reminders that even though she had experienced the allness of God in her healing experience, the perfection it implied was not a gift once given. While the spiritual meaning of the healing she experienced after the fall would unfold gradually over the years, and in time its full meaning would become clearer to her, there can be little doubt that the healing did not end her suffering in one fell swoop.

Though the healing event would have a momentous impact upon the direction of Mrs. Eddy's life, her emotional conflicts were never completely subsumed under or sublimated into the spiritual realm. Her healing experience in that winter of 1866 was not the first or the last step in a creative illness, as it has been described by Henri Ellenberger. Nor does this event quite fit into the pattern of the mourning-liberation process about which the psychoanalyst George Pollock has written so extensively. On the one hand, it helped to consolidate certain elements in Mrs. Eddy's personality that would propel her along a new path, that of a religious leader. On the other hand, the event did not silence the warring forces within her. Her emotional conflicts would continue to surface in the ensuing years. Paradoxically, then, the healing would lead to growth and progress, but her inner personal self would never be completely healed.[36]*

In sum, Mary Patterson was not miraculously transformed in an instant; the slate of her previous forty-five years was not wiped clean. The next forty-five years were to be just as trying and difficult, perhaps even more so. Despite the gains and emotional strength that resulted from her fall on the ice, the residues from her earlier conflicts remained. When she finally got out of bed and reentered society, Mary would have to deal with rebuff and hostility from a world that could revive older conflicts and issues. Only this time Mary had her relationship with God and her faith to guide her.†

* While George Pollock's work is informative and may open a number of doors for historians, Mrs. Eddy cannot be fit snugly into his framework. One might argue, in fact, that instead of becoming engaged in the mourning process and ultimately integrating the many meanings of her separation and loss experiences, including the deaths of her brother Albert, her parents, and Quimby, Mrs. Eddy circumvented the usual process in her religious experience. I have benefited from Peter Homans's discussion of the loss of attachments to community (and its symbols) and the creative responses that such a loss can engender. See his *The Ability to Mourn: Disillusionment and the Social Origins of Psychoanalysis* (Chicago: University of Chicago Press, 1989).

† After she became a religious leader, this split between the personal and impersonal senses would mark Mrs. Eddy's relationships. The impersonal self was united with God; in this sense she was spiritually integrated. The personal self, however, remained vulnerable, and it is in this realm that one can observe the problems and conflicts that have been commonly associated with narcissistic issues. In this context, see Otto F. Kernberg, "Normal Narcissism in Middle Age" and "Pathological Narcissism in Middle Age," in his *Internal World and External Reality: Object Relations Theory Applied* (New York: Jason Aronson, 1980), pp. 121–34; 134–53.

6

HER WORDS WERE NOW WRITTEN

Oh that my words were now written!
oh that they were printed in a book!
Job 19:23

FOR THE PRECEDING SEVERAL DECADES women had been pushing beyond the private spaces of the home to the open areas of public life, where they were finding new careers for themselves. Within the religious realm alone, capable, hardworking women were doing more than filling the pews of churches. Some became influential as ministers' wives, some became ministers in their own right with their own churches. Others sought missionary work or became important laypeople within their congregations. Women were doing men's work even if they did not receive men's pay. Yet despite these gains, and even within the so-called feminine sphere of religion, women had to tread lightly because they came up so quickly against hostility, fear, and deeply ingrained cultural stereotypes regarding women perceived as stepping outside their proper roles.[1]

Middle-class women who chose to break from the routine of domesticity and enter the world of reform often had the support of a women's network. Mary did not. Even if she had had this kind of support, she would have had trouble adjusting, especially considering the change she underwent. In her initial attempts to deal with the new, then, Mary initially tried to reestablish familiar landmarks for herself. In February 1866, she sent an urgent letter to Julius Dresser, one of Quimby's foremost disciples, pleading with him to take the place of the fallen master. She told Dresser about her fall on the ice and about her regaining consciousness only to find herself the helpless invalid she had been before being aided by Quimby. She implored Dresser to fill the vacuum that

Quimby's death had created, certain that he could become as effective as Quimby had been. When she had taken her first weakened steps after her fall, she had given the lie to the doctor's prognosis that she would never walk again, yet she confessed to Dresser that she was now quite anxious. "The nervous heat" of her friends was beginning to adversely affect her again despite her best efforts to combat it; "the terrible spinal affection" which had caused her so much suffering in the past was again crippling her spirit. Under different circumstances, Mary thought, she might have the capacity to be a healer in her own right. For now she felt she was getting worse, and she begged Dresser to take her as a patient.[2]*

Three weeks later, Dresser replied. He told her that he was sorry to hear that she was suffering so, but he had no inclination to assume Quimby's mantle. He let Mary know that he could never fill Quimby's shoes; nobody could. After all, how could "an infant do a strong man's work?" This might not have been what Mary wanted to hear; nevertheless, these last words must have leaped from the page. With no idealized Quimby to guide her, and with Dresser refusing to assume the role, Mary remained, ill and anxious, at the side of her husband.[3]

Over the next several months, they bounced from boardinghouse to boardinghouse; in August 1866 their marriage finally collapsed. Although they did not divorce until 1873, Daniel moved out altogether, and Mary was now alone. In September, the *Lynn Reporter* published a poem appropriately titled "I'm Sitting Alone." In it Mary fabricated idealized versions of the past in order to assuage the pain of the present and so keep hope alive for a better future. As she sketched "in light the heavens of my youth" with its "starry hopes," Mary reexplored her familiar themes of a lost ideal, loneliness, and flickering hope. In the

---

* As Walter Conn points out, "at the heart of the Christian Gospel is the call to a radical conversion, a change not simply of degree, but of basic *direction*, a fundamental reorientation of the total self, a personal revolution." In her healing experience, Mary heard that call, but as she discovered, change, especially radical change, is highly disruptive and difficult to assimilate. Even in the structured setting of psychoanalytic treatment, change is arduous. As Peter Marris notes, it is "slow, painful and difficult for an adult to reconstruct a radically different way of seeing life" because we feel "immediately threatened if our basic assumptions and emotional attachments are challenged." This threat is not imaginary; it is real, "for these attachments are the principles of regularity on which our ability to predict our own behavior and the behavior of others depends." As Marris clearly indicates, without the inner assurance of continuity, it is hard for anyone to interpret events, and it is equally difficult to explore what lies ahead with any confidence. Conn, *Christian Conversion: A Developmental Interpretation of Autonomy and Surrender* (New York: Paulist Press, 1986), p. 17; Peter Marris, *Loss and Change* (New York: Pantheon, 1974), pp. 9–10.

last stanza she cries out, "I'm weeping alone that the vision's fled," and she yearns for integration and harmony.[4]

A month earlier, at the dedication of a local temperance hall, Mary had written the dedicatory hymn, and one of the verses the audience sang that day expressed not only conventional biblical wisdom but also, perhaps, something that was beginning to stir in Mary herself:

> *And she, first at the cross,*
> *First at the tomb, who waits—*
> Woman—*will watch to cleanse from dross*
> *The cause she elevates.*[5]

Over the next three years Mary moved from one boardinghouse to another, sometimes finding kindness and sympathy, sometimes falling into arguments and disputes. At times she was in the company of spiritualists, and it was rumored that she participated in more than one séance. In the late fall of 1866, she was staying with the George Clark family, whose doors were reputedly open to spiritualists. There she met Hiram S. Crafts, a spiritualist and one of Lynn's many shoemakers. In the course of their many conversations, he became intrigued with her rudimentary theories of healing.[6]*

Mary eventually moved to the Crafts' house in East Stoughton. By the end of 1866 she was instructing Hiram in the art of healing and weaning him away from spiritualism. By April 1867 he had proved an able enough student, so when Mrs. Patterson and the Crafts moved to Taunton, he set up his own practice as a healer. James Ingham and Alanson Wentworth would later testify to Mrs. Patterson's healing of them in this period. These healings were a beginning for Mary, as she attempted to construct a context in which her emerging ideas and evolving practices would make sense and be meaningful.[7]

By the end of July 1867, Mary had been called back to Sanbornton Bridge, where her niece Ellen Pilsbury lay desperately ill. Mary cured her niece, but her sister Abigail was not there to witness it. In a letter a few days later, in fact, a disapproving Abigail voiced her apprehension over Mary's actions. She was tired of dealing with Mary's "unjust distracted conduct," she wrote to Martha Pilsbury, and she wished Mary would stop meddling in the lives of others. She told Martha that no

---

* According to Alfred Farlow, shortly after her healing experience, Mary became aware that when she held similar thoughts regarding the maladies of her neighbors (the same that she had experienced in her healing), they, too, were able to be healed. It was through this trial-and-error method that she learned to give "mental treatment." Archives, Farlow, "Historical Facts concerning Mary Baker Eddy and Christian Science."

good would come of the commotion Mary had stirred up by her intervention with Ellen. Even so, Abigail hoped she might be wrong and that
Ellen's restored health might redound to Mary's benefit.[8]*

From this time on, the ties that bound Mary and Abigail became
increasingly tenuous. Another family tie was severed when George Sullivan Baker, now blind and ill, refused Mary's efforts to help him. Within
a few months he died. Mary put her thoughts and feelings into words.
She wrote "Alone" on August 13, 1867, in one of the verses expressing
her anger and resentment at Abigail's rejection:

> I've sought the home my childhood gave—
> A moment's shelter from the wave—
> Then those when sick, whose pain I bore,
> A Sister! drove me from the door,
> O weary heart, O tired sigh,
> So wronged to live—alone I'd die!

However, Mary did not resign herself to rejection, abandonment, and
death, for now within herself she found the seeds of hope in a loving
God.[9]

By late 1867, Mary was living with the Nathaniel Websters in Amesbury, Massachusetts; she would spend the next ten months with them.
Well known in the community as a spiritualist, Mrs. Webster opened
her large home to other spiritualists and a variety of afflicted souls who
sought her mediumistic treatment. Mrs. Glover, as Mary Patterson now
called herself, moved right in, had a room of her own, and used Mrs.
Webster's séance room as a study. There, as she sat at Mrs. Webster's
"spiritual desk," Mary poured long hours into the writing of what is
now known as her Genesis manuscript.[10]

Before her first edition of *Science and Health* appeared in 1875, she
said that back in the late 1860s she had been working on a project that
she had never published.

Mary Glover's project of reinterpreting the Bible, especially the Book
of Genesis, was not out of the ordinary in the decades after the Civil
War. While the conflict between religion and science in the nineteenth
century belongs to the wider shifting cultural patterns in Victorian America, and while historians may disagree over the severity of that conflict,
Frederick Gregory is surely safe in saying that "After Darwin the relation
between God, man, and nature could never again be as clear as once it
had been." In the midst of these impassioned squabbles and debates,

---

* Ellen suffered from enteritis, and the doctor considered her case hopeless. Her Aunt
Mary cured her within five days.

the Book of Genesis became a familiar battleground for a number of scholars trying to harmonize science and Scripture, particularly the accounts of the Creation and the Flood. In a recent essay on geologists and interpreters of Genesis in the nineteenth century, James R. Moore has argued that Genesis may be viewed as "a prime piece of ideological property and as a strategic territory" for explaining the existing arrangements of nature and society, and, one might add, the self. Where Moore primarily focuses on the use of the text by cultural elites to buttress their cultural authority and preserve their roles as "keepers of the cosmology of an industrial and imperial social order," Mary chose to reinterpret Genesis for more personal reasons, which were hardly conservative. What had been revealed to her—"the existing arrangements of nature and society"—was radically different from anything she had previously known. She wanted to open others' eyes to this spiritual reality; what better place to begin than in a total rewriting and redefining of the reality in Genesis.[11]

Mary Glover's Genesis manuscript is a difficult, sometimes intimidating document. In her attempts to express the spiritual reality she had glimpsed, her language took on many forms. Romantic, poetic phrases dissolve into streams of consciousness that appear as close to the primary process as one can imagine. In many instances, her reinterpretation of the fifty chapters that comprise the Book of Genesis is closely related to the particular chapter and verse in question. In other instances, however, where a verse has triggered a set of private associations and feelings, the verse seems to have no direct bearing on her interpretation. We are unfortunately given no clue as to what spurred the associations and prompted her thinking. Unlike her earlier poetry, in which she used conventional forms and content as a reassuring structure, there are moments in the Genesis manuscript when Mrs. Glover seems barely restrained by conventions, intellectually and emotionally dashing first in one direction and then in another in her efforts to recapture the essence of her experience.

Making one's way through the Genesis manuscript, one can quickly lose one's bearings, and for good reason: the needle on Mrs. Glover's intellectual compass seems to have spun and pointed in all directions simultaneously. The needle rested temporarily on a primitive past as she sought to recapture the purity of Christianity's "first times." But then the needle would jiggle and jump to the present; not resting there for long, it spun in the direction of the future. Thus, one can find elements from the past sitting alongside those from the present. When she tried to glue them into a synthesis, they formed something new, something different. The manuscript is thus radically old and radically new; it is a part of its time and culture, but in many ways its spiritual concerns transcend the limits of that time and place.[12]*

There are passages in the manuscript when Mrs. Glover seemed to be grappling with her profound healing experience, trying to shape it and give it meaning. Her interpretation of Genesis 14:10 is suffused with intense emotion and rings out with the anguish of her own experiences as she plunged deeply within herself only to rise from the depths. The pits that we stumble into are created by man's hands; they symbolize "the mouths of error gaping to be heard and believed." Those people fortunate enough to escape from "the slime pits" fled to the mountains whose very peaks stretched toward "the spiritual senses," toward the "life giving atmosphere of truth," toward the domain of God.

In her interpretation of Genesis 26:4, it is evident that she experienced her healing as a rebirth, as an "offspring of Faith" which would provide a greater awareness "of Wisdom in the spiritual senses." In the next verse she embroidered upon this thought as she described what it was like to be a child who had discovered a new parent and a new self. "The seed of faith," she wrote confidently, would soon find "scientific happiness" because it separates itself from matter and "*trusts* outside of that which is seen, heard, or felt by the personal senses." This letting go of erroneous belief, of giving up the old self, was the moment when faith linked a person to God; it was the moment when one was reborn as a little child in order to grasp the spiritual meaning of God and the reality that existed outside the realm of matter.

After reading the full manuscript, one is impressed by the real struggle Mrs. Glover was having in putting the meaning of her experience into words. Her interpretation of Joseph leaving home in Genesis 44:28 obviously struck a chord in her, for she, too, was leaving a home, the Calvinistic "home" of her parents and New England culture. When Joseph left his home, he was leaving "Theology," the old encrusted church dogma that clouded one's eyes to spiritual truth. No one, she

* The American quest to restore the primordium is brilliantly described by Theodore Dwight Bozeman, *To Live Ancient Lives: The Primitivist Dimension in Puritanism* (Chapel Hill: University of North Carolina Press, 1988). On p. 355, Bozeman includes Mary Baker Eddy among those who were influenced by this quest to recover and restore a primitive ideal. She was so influenced, but unlike the Puritans whom Bozeman describes, a more modern definition of progress had entered her vocabulary. She looked forward as well as backward. Two other books that contain valuable information on these issues are Richard T. Hughes and C. Leonard Allen, *Illusions of Innocence: Protestant Primitivism in America, 1630–1875* (Chicago: University of Chicago Press, 1988); Richard T. Hughes, ed., *The American Quest for the Primitive Church* (Urbana: University of Illinois Press, 1988). Unfortunately, neither book contains a section on Mary Baker Eddy and Christian Science.

wrote, has the ability to "comprehend the visions of truth seen by the spiritual senses" until that dogma is cast aside.

Mrs. Glover was trying to find new meanings for old words; her definitions and usage are not consistent throughout the manuscript. "Love" and "Wisdom," for example, would eventually become synonyms for God's attributes in Mrs. Glover's lexicon, but in the Genesis manuscript their meanings are fluid. She had not yet established her idea of an all-encompassing Father-Mother God, so some of her terms are more specifically gender-related. "Love" was often used to denote a feminine attribute; "Wisdom" was masculine and resided in God the Father. Yet she was already hinting that she was trying to forge some kind of spiritual synthesis of the traditional meanings of "masculine" and "feminine" when she discussed the creation of Adam and Eve, and declared that in the origin of things, they, representing Wisdom and Love, were united.

Despite her muddled exposition, there were some things that Mrs. Glover was absolutely clear about, even in this early stage as she sought to redefine the meaning of illness in the nineteenth century and to reconstruct the meaning of the sacred in an increasingly secular, scientific world. In sharply drawn dichotomies, she separated the spiritual world of truth, wisdom, and love from the illusionary world of matter, belief, and error. The former promised health and harmony; the latter offered sickness, disease, and death. She was also certain that this inchoate Science of hers could be taught, but never through belief or knowledge gained from the senses, as she pointed out in her reworking of Genesis 43:2. One could teach it only by understanding it in a scientific, spiritual way. "Science requires a demonstration for its proof," she averred. "A man teaching the science of truth, which is all the Christianity there ever was or ever can be, will demonstrate that truth in his work."[13]

In writing and rewriting her interpretations of the early chapters of Genesis, Mrs. Glover would occasionally flip over a page and jot down some random thoughts. In one spot she commented on spiritual healing. This form of healing was new to Mrs. Glover; from the few times she had demonstrated it on her niece and others, she believed that its truth would be startling to other people as well. As new as it might have felt to her, however, this method of healing was old; its roots were to be found in the practice and in the death and resurrection of Christ. He had demonstrated through His healing of the sick and dying that man could overcome evil with good and that one could achieve "infinite perfectness." But man's creeds, rituals, and institutional churches tended to obscure the purity of the Science; it was ignored and neglected, and eventually the disciples stopped preaching and healing. As a result, its simple but powerful meaning had been lost through the ages, but now it was time to restore it by challenging all the false beliefs and opinions that had for centuries swirled about man, confusing him and threatening to sweep him off his feet. "Yes," she vowed, "we must learn the truth which walks above these changing currents even at the risk of being called fanatical and transcendental."[14]*

At the moment when Mrs. Glover was linking her new spiritual truth to the ideal of Christ, which is timeless, she was simultaneously disengaging herself from much of the past. Although one foot might have been outside history, another was learning to walk in it. On the back pages of the manuscript, Mrs. Glover mused that the world had survived without her brand of "transcendentalism." Indeed it had; but, she argued, the world had also been content with the stagecoach and the sailboat as modes of transportation until the genius of Robert Fulton discovered the principle that made steam a blessing to mankind. And if Fulton could successfully harness the new energies of his generation and put them into a new form to meet the growing needs of the people, then what was to hold someone back from doing the same thing in religion? Nothing. In words that she would later drop from her vocabulary when speaking about Christ, Mrs. Glover said that when He healed the sick, it was through his particular "matter form or electricity."

While her use of the word "science" in this instance clearly reflected the mid- to late-nineteenth-century faith that science and technology would lead to a better world, it also had other roots and other meanings. Recently one scholar has rightly argued that Mrs. Eddy's use of the term "science" was firmly anchored in her Puritan/Calvinist past, especially to Jonathan Edwards and his modifications of Puritan doctrine. But we need not stop there, for she was also influenced by the Enlightenment and the sweeping power of the "Baconian philosophy," though her theology would eventually break sharply from them. Like many other Americans in the post–Civil War decades, Mrs. Glover was in quest of certainty, for an authentic experience, for "the real thing." Her quest

---

* In her creative synthesis, Mrs. Eddy closed a gap that was widening in her time. Sudhir Kakar has spoken about this gap in general terms. "The real line of cleavage, cutting across cultures and historical eras," he said, "seems to be between those whose ideological orientation is more toward the biomedical paradigm of the illness, who strictly insist on empiricism and rational therapeutics and whose self-image is close to that of a technician, and others whose paradigm of illness is metaphysical, psychological or social, who accord a great recognition to *arationality* in their therapeutics, and who see themselves (and are seen by others) as nearer to the priest." See Kakar's *Shamans, Mystics and Doctors: A Psychological Inquiry into India and Its Healing Traditions* (New York: Alfred A. Knopf, 1983), p. 31.

took her into the spiritual realm, where she tried to braid the order, discipline, and certainty of science with the expressive truths of religion. Of course, she was not alone in this venture. For many Protestants, as one historian notes, "the veracity of the Bible justified the notion that biblical theology was no less a 'science' than astronomy or biology." Indeed, in the words of the nineteenth-century biblical scholar Charles Hodge, "the Bible is to the theologian what nature is to the man of science. It is his storehouse of facts." Asa Mahan of Oberlin College made the same connection; the Bible was "a scientific treatise" on morality.[15]

Stephen Gottschalk is certainly correct when he comments that Mrs. Eddy's use of the term "science" was "clearly congruent with its general use in late nineteenth century thought, in which science was a prestige-laden word connoting the ideas of authority, universality and infallibility." Carrying this idea a step further, Catherine Albanese has clearly spelled out what science meant to Mrs. Eddy once she attached it to her theology. "For Mary Baker Eddy and her followers, it meant the laws by which God governed the universe, but it also connoted the methods, or rules, used for Christian Science 'demonstration' and the certainty with which these rules could be applied. In other words, the assertion was that Christian Science healings, like scientific experiments, were repeatable procedures. They could be counted on, so long as one had studied and practiced correctly."[16]*

When Mrs. Glover declared in her manuscript that all sickness, pain, and death were to be found in the universe of matter and belief, and that the doctors and ministers created all the suffering, we can hear the faint strains of Quimby's attack on the established medical and religious practices of the day. The faint strains became even louder in her interpretation of Genesis 40:2, when Mrs. Glover seemed to ignore the content of the verse and launched into an attack on current medical practices. The doctor who prescribed diet and exercise to cure the sick, and the patient who pinned his or her hopes for recovery upon these false beliefs, silently colluded to make the patient even sicker. God never intended this. No law derived from the Principle, which controlled matter, ever relied upon matter to preserve truth. Hence, the physician's law—the law of matter—was false and erroneous.

In her rewriting of a number of verses, Mrs. Glover employed an

---

* In the Genesis manuscript, Mrs. Eddy sometimes capitalized the word "Science," and she seemed to be pointing toward her mature theology. More frequently, though, she used a small "s," and in those instances the word loses its precise meaning. This is clearly an indication that the meaning of the concept was not yet firmly established in her own mind.

imagery that seemed to place her somewhere between the Puritan sen-
sibilities of Jonathan Edwards and the romantic effusions of Emerson.
In her description of the act of Creation, rocks became "primeval rep-
resentatives" of a basic principle, while grass stood for "the tender
verdure of instant intelligence." Herbs, "wild" and "luxuriant," were
the representation of intelligence, and as for the delicate flowers, they
were "ideas of spiritual love." The tall trees stretching toward the skies
appeared to her as "aspirations after Wisdom," and their limbs bore
"the fruit of progress."

In her interpretation of Genesis 1:1, Mrs. Glover brought her poetic
imagination to a description of the origin of life. In one version of this
verse, she wrote that "the body of God was earth," and thus it represented the "idea of God." Heaven was "the atmosphere" of truth and
principle, and it found its symbolic expression in the sky. As for man,
he was symbolically divided along similar lines: his brain was the symbol
of the higher atmosphere, while his body corresponded to the material
realm. For Mrs. Glover the correspondence between heaven and earth,
God and man, brain and body meant that the truth as a principle was
divided from the "idea of truth"; the former was placed in the higher
region of the brain, while "the basal region represented the ideas of
earth in animalty."[17]

Despite the bank of ideas that she inherited from her culture, and
despite her use of some of Quimby's words in the Genesis manuscript,
one senses that Mary Glover was continually struggling to find a language of her own that might open the eyes and soul to the spiritual
reality that she had glimpsed.

While she groped in the Genesis manuscript for the right words to
convey her new understanding about reality, she had more success in
explaining herself during the late 1860s in encounters with others. The
Charles Winslows of Lynn, friends of Mrs. Glover, and Mrs. Winslow's
nephew, Charles Allen Taber, often met with Mary in the Winslow home.
Although she was unaware of it at the time, her experiences with them
were like a dress rehearsal for the big show that lay ahead. To get the
world to see her truth, she would have to change the minds of people
and alter the ways in which they had constructed reality. She would
have to persuade them to accept her particular definition of reality.[18]

Years later, when he was an old man, Taber described what it was
like to be in the same room with her as she warmed to the task of
explaining her new theories. After several meetings, Taber began to sense
that Mary was something special. There was an aura about her; she
seemed to fill the room with her presence, and her ideas were compelling.
Taber's aunt and wife were devoted church members, and both were

familiar with Scripture, but Mrs. Glover "led us toward an understanding of the Bible" which none of them had ever contemplated.

At one point, Taber had to confess to Mrs. Glover that she was reading more into the Bible than they were ready to accept. After a few more sessions, she offered Taber and his wife a manuscript, encouraging them to read it and share their thoughts about it. Pockmarked with deletions and interlineations, the manuscript was rough going for Charles Taber, and he soon gave up trying to make sense of it. His rejection was a foreshadowing—and a restrained one at that—of the way some people would reject Mrs. Glover's ideas, for one reason or another. Yet there was a glimmer of hope for Mrs. Glover, because Mrs. Taber, though strongly attached to her own church and its doctrines, became engrossed in the manuscript, and on a number of occasions read excerpts to her husband. Then, with real insight, he understood Mrs. Glover's struggle. The corrections and changes in her manuscript suggested that she was trying to find the right words to shape a spiritual truth she had grasped. Her mind and heart—her entire being—had absorbed certain Christian ideas that a traditional reading of the Bible and traditional Protestant theology could not adequately explain. It seemed evident to Taber that Mrs. Glover was trying to express ideas and thoughts regarding the basic teachings of Christ which dealt with the ability to control "our physical systems, and perhaps . . . the physical systems of others." At that time, however, she had formulated these ideas only in a rudimentary way.[19]

Early in the summer of 1868, while she was still working to shape her thoughts, Mary decided that it was time to advertise for students, and on July 4th the following notice appeared in the *Banner of Light*, Boston's leading spiritualist newspaper:

> Any person desiring to learn how to heal the sick can receive of the undersigned instruction that will enable them to commence healing on a principle of science with a success far beyond any of the present modes. No medicine, electricity, physiology or hygiene required for unparalleled success in the most difficult cases. No pay required unless this skill is obtained.
>
> Address Mrs. Mary B. Glover, Amesbury,
> Mass., Box 61.

On the hot day in July when her advertisement first appeared, Mrs. Mary B. Glover was a long way from being Mary Baker Eddy, the renowned leader of Christian Science. The modern reader is struck by the way her promises of curing the sick are lost on a page full of similar

promises from health faddists and mind curists of all stripes. Certainly
the "principle of science" did not convey the religious implications of
her cure; and people did not flock to her door.

For a while it probably seemed to her that she might not have a door
that anyone could find. Apparently the Websters' grandchildren came
from New York each summer to vacation at the Amesbury house. As a
result, Mrs. Glover and other boarders were unceremoniously expelled
from their rooms. One of the other evacuees was nineteen-year-old Richard Kennedy, who in a few short years would play an important role
in Mrs. Glover's life. With the aid of another ousted boarder, Mrs.
Glover made her way down the street to the home of Miss Sarah Bagley,
a seamstress with spiritualist leanings. For the next three months Mrs.
Glover engaged both Bagley and young Kennedy in discussions of the
Bible and her manuscripts. Despite progress in her writing, not all was
going well. She had little money, and some of her old symptoms returned
to slow her efforts. As a result, she accepted an invitation to live with
the Alanson Wentworth family in Stoughton, Massachusetts. Her departure from Sarah Bagley's home was so sudden that Bagley was not
sure where Mary had gone until she got a letter in early September.[20]

Despite the abruptness of the parting, Mary and Sarah Bagley remained friends, and they kept in touch by letter. Loneliness often seized
Mary; she prized Bagley's friendship and fondly recalled the happy times
they had shared, sewing, reading, and talking. Her relationship with
Bagley was remarkable for its openness, unlike the interactions she had
with other people. The Winslows had asked Mary to stay with them
over the winter, but she wanted none of that. She hated the false fronts
and hypocrisy she found among the so-called better sort. Part of Mary's
frustration with society might have stemmed from being a once-
widowed, now separated, single woman in polite Victorian society. As
she explained to Bagley, she had to suffer many hardships because of
her "anomalous position" as a married woman who was not living with
her husband. Without a husband, moreover, it was extremely difficult
for a woman to transact any kind of business, and if someone owed her
money, what power did she have to collect it?[21]

If Mary chafed under society's restrictions, she apparently did not
share this side of herself with the Wentworths. Through the eyes of two
of the children, seventeen-year-old Charles and his thirteen-year-old sister, Lucy, we have perhaps the clearest picture of Mrs. Glover in the
days and months after her advertisement appeared. Lucy's portrait was
lean and stark. Mrs. Glover was "a lonely woman" who had seen hard
days and was well past the prime of life. Her sparse wardrobe included
a few morning dresses, with a black-and-white-plaid one for variation,

and she took meticulous care of them. But no matter what she wore, thought Lucy, Mrs. Glover seemed to carry herself with a certain aplomb. Lucy felt that Mrs. Glover's shoulders might have been a bit broad for her small waist, and outside of this Mrs. Glover did not seem to have any distinguishing physical characteristics, except for her eyes, which were gray with a distant look. They were "very expressive," and when Mrs. Glover got excited or agitated they seemed to be darker than they actually were.

While she lived with the Wentworths, Mary worked long hours each day on her Genesis manuscript and an early version of another manuscript, "The Science of Man." Sealing herself in her room, Mary would write and write until she was ready for the company of the children. Then she would allow Lucy, Charles, and sometimes one of Charles's friends into the room. In the evening she might play games with the children or read to them. At such moments she sloughed off her weariness and became childlike, throwing herself into the fun. No wonder the children found her fascinating. But all was not fun and games. There were times—Lucy used the word "often"—when Mrs. Glover seemed deeply discouraged and her anguish was written in the lines of her face. In these dark moments, it took all of Lucy's "childhood ingenuity and affection" to lift Mrs. Glover's spirits.[22]

During this time Mary wrote a letter to a friend in Rumney that supports young Lucy's perception that her spirits were often depressed. In one paragraph, Mary wrote that she had been devoting most of her time to the Genesis manuscript and a work she called the "Science of Soul." Besides this, she had been trying to cover expenses by doing some teaching, and she was exhausted. She wearily confessed that at times she had lost her zest for life and felt it might be easier to surrender to death.[23]

Charles Wentworth remembered the long hours Mrs. Glover spent behind her locked door buried in her writing. He found her complicated and hard to figure out. There were times when she would come from behind the closed door and share her new ideas with the family. In some instances heated controversies broke out. When Mrs. Glover felt that she was in the right, there was no budging her. She wanted no truck with wrongdoing or evil, Charles observed respectfully, and her rebukes could be stern. Her "moral strength was unusual," Charles continued, yet her basic nature was as sanguine as a child's.[24]

Looking over Mary Glover's life during the four years or so after her fall on the ice, and reading what the Wentworth children had to say, one might conclude that little had changed in her day-to-day living. Yet Mary has left us with clues that lead us to conclude that she was a profoundly altered woman. In random thoughts scribbled on the backs of the Genesis pages, Mary, as noted earlier, compared herself to the great inventor Robert Fulton. Her only source for the Science of man was the Bible, but Science was not to be found in the usual interpretations, the common beliefs, and the accepted opinions regarding the Scriptures. Rather, the truth would come from Mary and her writing; her words, freighted with the spiritual truth of God and Jesus, would be the equal of any great inventor's project, even Fulton's. Apparently, long before anyone else was willing to recognize her greatness or to acknowledge the importance of her discovery, Mary had claimed those exalted prerogatives for her mission. God had communicated His reality to her; now it was her task and duty to share it with the world.

Nourished by God, Mary had the strength to devote endless hours to her writing, and this single-mindedness was another indication of an inner transformation. Like the Apostle Paul, she had been called to do great work. In her case, she had been called to write and to communicate the word of God, which she did with unswerving devotion.

In an address to the National Christian Scientist Association in Chicago in 1888, Mrs. Eddy conveyed the uniqueness of her relationship to God and her work: Christian Science was her "only ideal," and it was impossible to separate an individual from his or her ideal. If either she or her ideal were ever "misunderstood or maligned," the attack on one "eclipses the other with the shadow cast by this error."[25]*

---

* Pinchas Noy's ideas on creativity are highly instructive in terms of understanding Mrs. Eddy's feeling of uniqueness. In "Originality and Creativity," in *The Annual of Psychoanalysis*, 12/13 (New York: International Universities Press, 1985), pp. 440–41, he notes:

> The motive for creativity is always a self-centered one. In fact, because creativity is a compound activity driven by various motives, such as the strive [sic] for perfection, the quest for originality, the search for aesthetic form, and the need for articulation, we have to speak about "motives" in the plural. Each of these motives has its origin in one of the major developmental struggles of the self, or, in other words, each of the various component activities of creativity is related to one of the major needs of the developing self. The specific need to which originality is related is the need of the self for individuation, the need to develop a sense of self experience as something unique, separated, and different from all the other objects. This struggle for individuation is one of the major developmental tasks of early childhood and continues to occupy every person for his entire life.

7

BEHOLD A MOTHER IN ISRAEL

The inhabitants of the villages ceased, they ceased in Israel,
until that I Deborah arose, that I arose a mother in Israel.

Judges 5:7

IF ONE WERE to measure success or failure by the number of lambs this shepherdess, Mrs. Eddy, had gathered into her Christian Science flock, she would have to be counted a failure in the 1870s and early 1880s. Numbers alone, of course, do not tell the whole story. Septimus Hanna, an important figure in the Christian Science movement, recalled the first time he met Mary Baker Eddy. He was immediately impressed by her dignity and bearing; she had an indescribable quality that he had never seen in anyone else. To him she appeared "tall and stately," when actually she was only "of medium height." For Gilbert Carpenter, this was an everyday experience in the year he was at Pleasant View, Mrs. Eddy's Concord home. Mrs. Eddy was not a tall woman, but every time he encountered her walking down the hall, she seemed to be "at least seven feet tall." Carpenter knew that his mind's eye was playing tricks on him. His perception came from "the spiritual height of her thought."[1]

In this portrait of Mrs. Eddy, I do not follow a strict chronology. After her final separation from Daniel Patterson, she used the name Glover, until her marriage to Asa Gilbert Eddy in January 1877. (In the ensuing pages, therefore, some reminiscences refer to her as Mrs. Glover and some as Mrs. Eddy.)

Whether she was conducting a discouragingly small class of three in the early years of the movement or leading an overflowing class in the later years, Mrs. Eddy had lost none of the physical attractiveness that characterized her youth. As late as 1898 Emma Shipman commented upon Mrs. Eddy's dignity, beauty, and poise as she stood before her students.[2]

Clearly Mrs. Eddy's most riveting feature was her eyes, and they seemed to glow even brighter with the passing of time. Samuel Putnam Bancroft seemed mesmerized by them; he remembered them as "large and deep-set, dark blue and piercing." They seemed to look right through one into the distance; similarly, when a person looked into them, he seemed to be looking beyond the ordinary.[3]

Mrs. Eddy indeed claimed more than ordinary vision. In a letter to Septimus Hanna, she made it eminently clear that she had a special power, almost a sixth sense, that allowed her to discern the "thoughts, motives, and purposes" of the human mind. "This mind-reading," she flatly declared, was God's gift to her. Mrs. Eddy's ability to read unspoken thoughts was confirmed by Bliss Knapp. In one incident, a student named Mrs. Helen Nixon came to Mrs. Eddy's house and was shown into a room to wait for her leader. Mrs. Nixon looked out a window and saw a drunken man across the street. She began to ponder the subjective and objective meaning of reality. Was the drunken condition really outside in the man, or had her feelings and perception created it? At the very moment she puzzled over this, Mrs. Eddy entered the room unobserved and, without hesitating, answered Mrs. Nixon's unspoken question. The inebriation was not in her thought; it was out there in the stranger.[4]

James Henry Wiggin, a former Unitarian minister, was hired by Mrs. Eddy in 1885 to help her bring out the sixteenth edition of *Science and Health*; he did such a good job that he eventually became the editor of *The Christian Science Journal* during the late 1880s. After Mrs. Eddy asked Wiggin to join her class, he, too, observed her intuition. Not only was she "glowingly earnest" when she presented her ideas to her students, wrote Wiggin, but her choice of words was always precise. A person might not always agree with her statements, but he would still be impressed with the force and conviction of her beliefs. Even when totally absorbed in what she was saying, Mrs. Eddy had the uncanny ability to read the faces of her students; she immediately knew how her teachings were being received, and she was quick to detect a student's deviation from them. Once she sensed this, she did not hesitate to expose the student's misunderstanding. In Wiggin's estimation, Mrs. Eddy was "a natural class-leader."[5]

Jennie Sawyer, who did splendid work for Christian Science throughout her long career, recalled a special aura, a religious glow that seemed to suffuse Mrs. Eddy's whole being. Her "face would become actually radiant with the spiritual uplift," and one could tell that her words were inspired by God, as though it were God speaking through her. Mrs. Eddy spoke with such intimacy, recalled Abigail Thompson, that it communicated her vision "vividly to one's consciousness." A spellbound listener experienced Mrs. Eddy's teaching much as the disciples did Christ's sermons.[6]

Even one of Mrs. Eddy's harshest critics, Georgine Milmine, speaks of her effectiveness and power as a teacher. In her interviews with a number of Mrs. Eddy's former students, many of whom had later become disaffected, Milmine concluded that several still believed that they had gotten something from Mrs. Eddy that could not be measured in concrete terms. "They speak of a certain spiritual or emotional exaltation," Milmine wrote, "which she was able to impart in her classroom; a feeling so strong that it was like the birth of a new understanding and seemed to open to them a new heaven and a new earth."[7]

Grace Choate Huse once recalled that Mrs. Glover had many sides to her personality. Depending upon the context and the situation, she could be "patient and loving, serious and instructive, [or] amusing and playful." J. Henry Jones reminisced long after Mrs. Eddy had died that she had a sharp wit and a keen sense of humor. When she heard an amusing story, she relished repeating it. She once confessed that a good laugh often loosened the grip "of troubling thoughts and feelings." Still, Mrs. Eddy was a serious woman on a serious mission. Part of this gravity was reflected in her demand for discipline and order. "We must have a system," she emphasized. Their cause could not progress in a slapdash manner. All tasks had to be done "decently" and with efficiency and order.[8]*

One indelible impression Emma Shipman had of Mrs. Eddy was the exacting attention she gave to details. Nothing seemed to get by her, whether in the supervision of her house or in the direction of her movement. "She watched, she prayed," and she worked harder than anyone Shipman had ever met. To her work Mrs. Eddy brought the qualities of "order, neatness, accuracy and dispatch." J. Henry Jones once noted that Mrs. Eddy had little patience for sloppiness of any kind; fastidiousness marked all aspects of her life, and she expected no less from her followers. She spelled out the reasons for this kind of discipline in *Retrospection and Introspection*:

---

* After her religious transformation Mrs. Eddy's personal reasons for self-control would remain, but something new was added: she could now use her demands for exactness and order in the service of her mission. For mention of self-control in terms of religious self-transcendence, see Walter Conn, *Christian Conversion: A Developmental Interpretation of Autonomy and Surrender* (New York: Paulist Press, 1986), p. 113.

I had learned that thought must be spiritualized, in order
to apprehend Spirit. It must become honest, unselfish, and
pure, in order to have the least understanding of God in
divine Science. The first must become last. Our reliance
upon material things must be transferred to a perception
of and dependence on spiritual things. For Spirit to be
supreme in demonstration, it must be supreme in our
affections, and we must be clad with divine power. Purity,
self-renunciation, faith, and understanding must reduce
all things real to their own mental denomination.[9]*

Armed with these qualities, the follower was ready to take the most
important walk of his or her life.

The journey down the Christian Science path into the radically new
yet old spiritual reality was a precarious one for Mrs. Eddy's students;
diversions lurked everywhere. Jesus' life had been one of obedience and
sacrifice, and Mrs. Eddy demanded this of herself and her students.
"Obedience is the offspring of Love," she once said, and in turn Love
was the governing Principle of all unity. It was the foundation of all
correct thought and action; it fulfilled God's law. Obedience to the divine
Principle demonstrated Truth; therefore, to avoid error man's will had
to be made obedient to divine will. A student could not afford to be
caught napping, but always had to be ready to do God's work. Disobedience, no matter how small and apparently insignificant, meant defeat, a surrender to the false, material senses, to an assertion of man's
will, to selfish pursuits, and to secular temptations. Mrs. Eddy did not
mince her words: "Insubordination to the law of Love even in the least,
or strict obedience thereto, tests and discriminates between the real and
unreal Scientist."[10]

Even though Mrs. Glover personified loving-kindness, she could also
be quite "stern and unyielding" when it came to her doctrines and the
direction of her movement. If her followers took a detour from Science's
straight and narrow path—for example, confusing her doctrines with
spiritualism, which she hotly attacked in the "science of man" and in

---

* The rapid changes in the late nineteenth century also produced a rage for order throughout much of American culture. As Miles Orvell points out, "the abundance of products
  in the marketplace created the necessity, embraced enthusiastically, of imposing system
  and order on a scale previously unknown. (One sees this tendency not only in the realm
  of practical aesthetics and business, but in the sciences and social sciences too, encom-
  passing everything from Mendeleyev's periodic table of the chemical elements, to Melville Dewey's decimal system. . . .)." Orvell, *The Real Thing: Imitation and Authenticity
  in American Culture, 1880–1940* (Chapel Hill: University of North Carolina Press,
  1989), p. 43.

her first edition of *Science and Health*—her strong rebukes could get
them back into line in a hurry. Sometimes her scoldings were so stinging
that they temporarily left the dazed student feeling angry, hurt, guilty,
and humiliated.[11]

These reprimands were a point of tension in the movement almost
from the first day. A number of students who left the movement later
criticized Mrs. Eddy for her un-Christian verbal attacks. Judging by the
number of times Mrs. Eddy explained the meaning of her rebukes and
how poorly her students understood her reasons for administering them,
it is important for us to see them from her perspective.

God could not be judged by human standards. He expressed His pity
"in modes above the human. His chastisements are the manifestations
of Love." As a spiritual leader, Mrs. Eddy saw her scoldings as emulating
the kind of love that God had for man. Her harsh words and tone were
meant to jolt her students back into a true spirituality. Irving Tomlinson,
who worked with Mrs. Eddy in the early part of the twentieth century,
recalled that on one lovely winter morning he was called into Mrs. Eddy's
study. She was seated in her accustomed chair; a Bible lay open in her
lap. In the course of their chat, Mrs. Eddy said that whenever Jesus
praised or commended his students, he also reminded them what the
consequences were of failure. Scripture was her authority, and she referred directly to Hebrews 12:6–8:

> For whom the Lord loveth he chasteneth, and scourgeth
> every son whom he receiveth. If ye endure chastening,
> God dealeth with you as sons; for what son is he whom
> the father chasteneth not?
> But if ye be without chastisement, whereof all are par-
> takers, then are ye bastards, and not sons.

This, according to Mrs. Eddy, justified "the punishment and chastisement of others for their own sake." She concluded by telling Tomlinson
that those who could not accept her rebukes were not, according to
Scripture, sons, because they were not "the legitimate offspring of
Truth." Those who accepted her chastisements lived "in the spirit, not
in the senses."[12]*

Mrs. Eddy's assertion of selfless love in her chastisements was a difficult concept for her followers to grasp, for it was an impossible ideal.
A selfless love was God's love for man; it was totally caring, giving, and

---

* Thomas Simmons, *The Unseen Shore: Memories of a Christian Science Childhood*
(Boston: Beacon Press, 1991), contains many examples of how his Christian Science
parents' interpretation of God's all-loving power masked aspects of cruelty and rigid
authority.

protecting. By loving us this way, God provided a model for man's love in that, as Stanley Leavy has put it, "Human fulfillment is never adequate when it is only fulfillment of the self: the other who cares, or the others who care, are the guarantors of our personal fulfillment." The flaw, of course, is that we are human, which means that we cannot emulate the wholeness and perfection of God's love. As a result, says Leavy, ordinary human love is qualified and contingent: "I love you only if you love me. This is no longer the *imago dei*."[13]*

In a similar vein, it was certain that Mrs. Eddy's followers would fall short of the ideal moral standards she set. No matter what kind of conversion experience a person has undergone, moral ideas do not exist in a pure realm, even if they are temporarily experienced that way. For the sake of argument, we can admit that there are those exceptional people who are through and through moral in the sense that their love and respect for themselves flow from a deep wellspring within and touch their relationships with others. These people exude an inner strength and quietness; their declamations of moral and ethical principles are not noisy; their insistence on Christian love is not forced and demanding. Indeed, when we encounter such a person, we know that we are in the presence of a *gentle*man or *gentle*woman.

Once moral ideas get into the hands—and minds—of ordinary mortals, however, they are contaminated by human strengths and weaknesses. Moral ideas, in fact, are like Herman Melville's confidence man; they come dressed in many guises. They can be tricksters, seducing the self and others. For instance, they can be used as a defense to help master sexual and aggressive feelings that an individual finds too threatening, while concurrently they can be used to gratify those very feelings and wishes.

Moral ideas can also be used as a means to deny or overcome experiences of loss, humiliation, and helplessness; and sometimes in the garb of moral righteousness one can make others feel what one dislikes in oneself. Moral ideas can be used to loosen the tight grip of trauma, for as psychoanalyst Ernest Kafka notes, "moral obligations can be used to magically enhance the sense of power by assisting in the denial of past calamities and by practically modifying expected future distress." Finally, moral ideas can help a person modify his or her moods and self-

---

* Thomas Simmons also indicates that moral commands to be perfect can cripple the self, not improve it. "Like the other Christian Science children I played with, I struggled to be 'perfect'—intelligent and well-behaved and free from illness—and when I failed, I took this as evidence that I was unworthy of the perfect, finished world that Christian Science offered me." *The Unseen Shore*, p. 52.

perceptions, and they can aid in the continuing task of adapting to social reality. Given the complexity of moral ideas and their multiple uses, and given the difficulty of achieving a selfless love, we can well understand why Mrs. Eddy's followers questioned the sincerity of her love in her punishments, and we can also understand how even Mrs. Eddy herself might have difficulty living by the high moral ideas she held out for herself and others. Nevertheless, she kept her eye on this high standard and expected others to do so as well.[14]

Many of Mrs. Eddy's students not only admired her but also became attached to her as an ideal, maternal figure. Samuel Bancroft recalled in the early days of the movement that she shared with her small band of adherents "the loving-kindness of a mother." Early in 1872, when a temporary strain developed between Mrs. Glover and Bancroft, she wrote to him tenderly asking him to come to her and explain why he was upset with her. She had assumed from what he had once said that he regarded her "as an adopted sort of mother." Similarly, George Barry of Lynn, who would one day cut his ties to the movement, was a young, deeply devoted follower. Mrs. Glover's instruction was like a rebirth for Barry, and he felt so attached that he became the first pupil to ask permission to call her Mother.[15]

By the early 1880s, one can find Mrs. Eddy's correspondence sprinkled with references to her followers as children and to herself as Mother. Julia Bartlett, for example, had been orphaned by the time she reached her sixteenth birthday, and over the next twenty years or so she suffered from a number of afflictions. In the spring of 1880, she heard about Christian Science, came to Boston, and was promptly healed. Not long after this, Mrs. Eddy wrote her a letter with the salutation "My dear Student and 'own child,' " and ended it by offering Bartlett her love as her "Affectionate Teacher and Mother." In a letter to Ellen Clark, who was in the same class with Julia Bartlett, Mrs. Eddy admitted that the more she saw of Bartlett the more she grew to love her as if she were her own child. And she did not limit her maternal love to Bartlett, for later in the letter she extended it to Ellen Clark and to all of her students as they grew spiritually.[16]

Richard Kennedy was the first important student to emerge in the fledgling movement. This was the same young man who had paid Mrs. Glover several visits when she resided in Stoughton. He had studied with her then, and it did not take him long to charm her with his boyish good looks and his enthusiasm for her ideas. At some point she and Kennedy decided to enter into a partnership; he would do the healing, for he seemed to have real talent, while she would do the teaching and writing. In February 1870, they signed an agreement. In the early spring they moved to Lynn, where they eventually found rooms on the second floor of a boardinghouse.

Within a brief period Kennedy's office was filled with patients, and his reputation as a healer spread. It seemed, indeed, as if his hands had magic in them. While he was healing his patients with spectacular results, Mrs. Glover, quietly working in the background, was touched by him. Kennedy seemed to be the person she had been looking for, a man who could carry her ideas into the world. In a letter to Sarah Bagley, she gushed about Kennedy's "glorious nature" and his "noble soul." In the not too distant future she would have to face the fact that he fell short of glorious, that he was less than noble. For the time being, however, Kennedy could do no wrong, and he was an important contributor to her first classes.[17]

From Samuel Bancroft's account of the early days in the movement, we learn that before the studying commenced Kennedy would rub each pupil's head and solar plexus in order to acquaint them with the physical aspects of healing. Kennedy told them that these were the most sensitive parts of the body; this gentle stimulation would prepare them for Mrs. Glover's spiritual lessons. While this may have sounded good in theory, the inevitable question was asked: How could she teach that the body was an illusion and yet encourage Kennedy's manipulations?[18]

Bancroft believed that this laying on of hands was a mistake, a vestige from Mrs. Glover's days with Quimby. That may well be, but there were other reasons for it as well. In reading "Questions and Answers in Moral Science," the manuscript she used with Bancroft's class, we can see that she tried to bring this aspect of healing within the religious framework she was developing. Mrs. Glover was not completely convinced of the value of the practice, but saw the virtue of rubbing in the effect it had on the patient. If the patient thought that the rubbing helped to get rid of a belief, which was located in the brain anyway, then it might be all right to employ this method. One had to be careful with this practice, however, and Mrs. Glover warned her students not to focus their thoughts on the body or regard touching as the healing agent; the patient must always be aware of the spiritual power, the power of Soul. It was this Principle that established harmony and well-being. Even if Mrs. Glover did not wholeheartedly support this aspect of healing, Bancroft was right about one thing: touching in healing was a serious mistake, and it would come to cause her a great deal of anguish.[19]

It was in the spring of 1871, or perhaps a year later, that Mrs. Glover wrote Sarah Bagley a letter saying that Bagley would undoubtedly be pleased with her crop of students. She informed Bagley that "no mischief-making" was permitted among the students, that she never listened to the complaints and gossip, and that they never tried to undermine her authority. These were, she noted proudly, "the cardinal points of our *social fraternity.*"[20]

This may have been more of a wishful thought than a reality. Certainly a handful of students struggled to do good work, but ugly dissension was brewing within the social fraternity. A twenty-five-year-old named Wallace W. Wright came through Mrs. Glover's third class and was then sent to Knoxville, Tennessee, where Mrs. Daniel Spofford had already set up a practice. Whatever spiritual sense Wright took south with him soon gave way to the personal in his relationship with the Spoffords and Mrs. Glover, and he succeeded in doing just what Mary told Sarah Bagley a student should not do.

Initially Wright seemed successful in his practice. Soon, however, he locked horns with Mrs. Spofford and undermined the efforts of the movement in Knoxville. As their conflict bubbled over, it spilled into the lap of Mrs. Glover. In an exchange of letters with her in August 1871, a bitter, disillusioned Wright not only insisted that his tuition money be refunded but also demanded recompense for his time and effort. He insinuated that Mrs. Glover's favored student, Kennedy, had had an affair with Mrs. Spofford. In her reply, Mrs. Glover tried to remain calm and above the conflict, but Wright was unrelenting in his attack. He returned to Lynn in a rage, and in January 1872 he made his animosity public by putting it into the pages of the *Lynn Transcript*.

Just what Mrs. Glover and her infant movement needed—a public brawl! And it got nasty. It is difficult to know what motivated Wright; ostensibly it was a matter of money and broken promises (the money issue would entangle Mrs. Glover several times over the years), but the depth of his anger and his wish to hurt Mrs. Glover in public, to humiliate her as he somehow felt she had humiliated him, suggests that other forces were at work. We do not know how much it cost him, in another sense, to join the movement. His father was a Universalist minister; some of Mrs. Glover's students had a hard time separating from their traditional churches, and it must have been especially difficult for a minister's son. In Knoxville, Wright appeared to get into a competitive struggle with Mrs. Spofford; this was one of the first signs that Christian Science teachers would become jealous of each other's success and attempt to meddle with one another's students. Once Mrs. Glover sided with Mrs. Spofford, Wright became incensed, and whatever admiration he had for

Mrs. Glover, whatever ideal image of her as a chosen religious leader he had constructed, collapsed. The love and affection he might have felt for her was now replaced by a vengeful anger.

The charges that Wright made in the newspaper were ones that Mrs. Glover would have to face many times in the next thirty and more years. After claiming that Christian Science would destroy the fabric of the family, Wright attacked the movement at its vulnerable point, what some people called its radical idealism. Christian Science taught, Wright charged, that man was a delusion; in fact, everything that God created in the material world was a delusion. Mrs. Glover's manuscript claimed that "sickness or sensation in matter is not a reality, but is an illusion"; Wright might have understood this in spiritual terms at one point, but now he mocked such thinking. "Are cancers, tumors, tubercles . . . ," he asked in words dripping with angry sarcasm, "the result of the *imagination*? Are broken bones, gun-shot wounds, unintentional poisons, *imaginary*? Do dogs imagine they are mad?"

In this article Wright was just warming to the task at hand. He continued to use Mrs. Glover's own writings against her. Farther down the column, he again assailed her for her beliefs regarding material reality, and his personal anger was at best thinly veiled when he asked, "Will she permit her jugular vein to be severed, to test whether blood is necessary in order that she may live?" The Christian Science he once believed in and practiced was now "vain deceptive humbuggery," and he could barely contain his glee in denouncing it.[21]

In one last article in the *Transcript*, Wright challenged Mrs. Glover to demonstrate publicly all that she claimed Christian Science could do. This began to sound like Christ and the temptations in the wilderness, and for Mrs. Glover it must have felt that way. Wright listed five demands and declared that if she failed to exhibit her powers, then she and her movement were failures. His first two demands were for Mrs. Glover to demonstrate her Christlike qualities; she was to restore the dead to life and walk on water "without the aid of artificial means." She had said that she could do this; so let her prove it. His third demand sounded more like a request for Houdini: she was to live a day without air, or, if she did not want to do that, then she could try twenty-four days without food and water. Wright's fourth and final demands were minor miracles. He wanted Mrs. Glover to restore sight in an eye whose optic nerve had been severed, and he called on her to heal a broken bone without material means.[22]

Though Wright was doing his best to belittle her in public, and had broken a promise not to disclose her writings publicly, Mrs. Glover defended herself ably in a number of replies in the *Transcript*, and in a letter to Sarah Bagley she did not seem unduly disturbed by his attacks. She obviously took some comfort when a number of her students sent a letter of support to the *Transcript* in February 1872.[23]

During the late 1870s and early 1880s, Mrs. Eddy must have felt at times as if she were bouncing from one crisis to the next. In 1879 she wrote to Clara Choate, one of her ablest students, about the bickering and strife that continued to impede the growth of the movement. Thinking about the halcyon days of the movement's early years—"before mesmerism began in our ranks seven years ago"—Mrs. Eddy fondly recalled that she and her students had shared affection and love for each other; no discordant note had marred this harmony. We might dismiss this reverie as an obvious distortion, but Samuel Bancroft shared a similar remembrance. In the early 1870s, he said, "We were a happy company, not withstanding our loss of numbers and the ridicule and contempt with which we were sometimes regarded."[24]

These expressions of nostalgia, as human as they are, could not hide the fact that the Christian Science movement, even in its earliest days, was faced with tension and conflict, as one might well expect of any movement. Despite Bancroft's and Sawyer's feelings about their earliest experiences in the movement, the strife seemed to spread in the 1880s.

8

SOMETHING FEARFUL THIS WAY COMES

*Be not afraid of sudden fear, neither of the desolation of the
wicked, when it cometh.*

Proverbs 3:25

MANY NASTY CONFLICTS have an unforeseen benefit. The affair
with Wallace Wright proved helpful in at least one way: his charges of
mesmerism pushed Mrs. Glover to rethink her use of touching in curing
patients. She chose to stop doing it and urged Richard Kennedy to do
the same. Underneath his charm and healing prowess, she began to
realize other forces were at play; his rubbing may have produced temporary cures, but it also stimulated a dependence upon him rather than
upon her spiritual truth. Mrs. Glover had seen this sort of thing with
Quimby. When she tried to curb Kennedy's touching, their relationship
became strained. Their partnership continued for a number of months
after the Wright fiasco, but ultimately, in May 1872, it dissolved.

This disaffection did not sit lightly with Mrs. Glover; it left her feeling
emotionally fragile. About this time she wrote to Bancroft, bemoaning
the fact that she felt separated from the secure truth of her teachings
and was being pulled into the "grosser abyss of folly and hate." The
truth was that she was exhausted by the "malice" of her students. She
had given so much of herself to them, loved and praised them, but now
evidently her love was unrequited. As a result, she was losing her health
and happiness; she felt as if she were on the verge of falling into a "dark
labyrinth." Were her students, she wondered, on this same shaky
ground?

One student in particular upset her. It pained to her to think how
much of herself she had invested in Kennedy's work, and how much of
her spiritual understanding she had shared with this "wicked boy."

Apparently it had all been for nothing. Kennedy even mentioned to Susie Oliver, the married daughter of one of Mrs. Glover's Quaker friends, that she suffered so much from the inept work of her bad students that if he failed her in any way it would probably kill her. Mrs. Glover was not about to give Kennedy that satisfaction, but as she said to Bancroft, she was worried that Kennedy's shenanigans might "ruin [her] sweet disposition!"[1]

As this letter clearly reveals, Mrs. Glover's feelings toward Kennedy had changed: she was left deeply grieved and angry. Yet she pushed on. Over the next two years Mrs. Glover devoted her prodigious energies to writing *Science and Health* and directing the activities of her few students in the field. From 1872 to 1875, she held no more classes, though Bancroft reflected that despite the loss of some students and the contempt they faced in the outside world, they had not lost faith in their cause.[2]

When her first edition of *Science and Health* was published in 1875, the last chapter, "Healing the Sick," contained a lengthy warning against the evils of mesmerism. While some of her other students might have been susceptible to its influences, she surely was talking about Richard Kennedy, though she did not name him outright. Some outsiders might have been jarred by the intensity of her opening paragraph. Those who chose personal fame and reward, or were eager for popularity at the expense of conscience and truth, defamed those who practiced healing the right way. In a battle with such "error," no quarter was to be expected and none was to be given. "You attack with intent to kill," she wrote dramatically, "and the wounded or cornered beast bites you if he can." One way this "beast" retaliated was to get others to condemn you and thereby undermine your confidence and influence.

This was clearly no mere falling-out over methods of healing; for Mrs. Glover this was a spiritual life-and-death struggle. As nobly strong as Kennedy had been in her idealization of him, he eventually became ignobly powerful. His mesmeric practice had the power to subvert her whole movement before it got established. To an extent she was right. Put her spiritual methods in the wrong hands and they became a se-duction instead of a healing. Quimby had always run this risk; now Kennedy was doing the same; and all the while the public associated his name with Mrs. Glover's.

"Filled with revenge and evil passions," she wrote passionately, the mental malpractitioner relied upon all kinds of mental and physical manipulation (the rubbing of a patient's head) to control the patient, virtually absorbing the mind of a patient into his. This mode of seduction was but a stepping-stone to wider mischief. By controlling the mind of a single individual, the malpractitioner was well on his way to controlling the mind of a community in order to inflate himself or to injure others. Unfortunately, others could not detect this mental manipulation; patients controlled by the malpractitioner's will did as he commanded and acted like hypnotized subjects carrying out his evil plans, all the while believing him honest and moral.

Mrs. Glover assured her readers that these mental zombies were not the figment of her overactive imagination; they existed and they were "the victims of mal-practice." While there was a valuable lesson to be learned from uncovering such machinations, it was better to keep one's eye on what constituted genuine healing and to practice it honestly.[3]

In the spring of 1875, when she moved into a permanent residence at 8 Broad Street in Lynn, it seemed as if Mrs. Glover was ready to settle down in more ways than one. The past few years had amply provided her with heartaches and problems. Her troubles with Kennedy might have occupied a disproportionate amount of her time and energy, but her well-intentioned students also demanded her attention and guidance. The number of letters she sent daily into the field, urging, prodding, rebuking, and praising, is impressive. When we consider that she was writing occasional pieces for the local papers during the same twenty-four hours, then we begin to appreciate not only her productivity, but also how depleting this round-the-clock activity became. To Eldridge J. Smith of Philadelphia she wrote a letter in late November 1876 that at once expressed her weariness, her hope, and her continued faith in what she was doing. Smith had little idea of what awesome burdens and responsibilities rested on her shoulders.[4]

Samuel Bancroft had more than a faint conception of the burdens Mrs. Glover bore. He observed firsthand how inordinately devoted she was to her work. It absorbed so much of her energy that she became "very sensitive to any seeming neglect" coming from her students. She "suffered deeply," said Bancroft, when it seemed to her that she had been abandoned by those students for whom she had sacrificed so much. When Mrs. Glover received kind words and supportive letters from her students, she gratefully acknowledged them; nevertheless, one could also hear a familiar plaint from her lips: when she suffered for the Cause, they did not support her; they "disgrace my efforts," she said, by their failures, or, even worse, by becoming mesmerists and turning against her.[5]

As she poured her energies into her writing and into the day-to-day governing of her movement, she occasionally felt not only drained but emotionally vulnerable. Earlier we heard from a number of her followers about her communion with God and the continuing revelations of His truth. While these experiences were spiritually fulfilling and enhanced her image in the eyes of her followers, the ascension to these spiritual heights left Mrs. Glover feeling alone, even empty, in her human relationships. Communicating her growing understanding of Christian Science absorbed all of Mrs. Glover's creative efforts, contributing to her feeling of separation and estrangement from others.

In these moments of loneliness, particularly when she was surrounded by the failures of her wayward students, by annoying snags in her writing and publication, and by serious defections within the movement, the accumulated stress was emotionally depleting. Such moments of depletion, noted Heinz Kohut, can be "frightening experiences which repeat those overwhelming anxious moments of early life when the child felt alone, abandoned, unsupported."[6]

She wrote to a friend in Rumney shortly after a period in which she had been so absorbed in her work that when she came up for air, it seemed she had been out of touch with her friend forever. However, this lack of communication could not erase the fond memories of her friend's family that she had stored in her "lonely heart." After sharing a pleasant reverie with her friend, Mrs. Glover told her that within the past year she had sent a copy of "Science of Soul" to the press and had reworked the Book of Genesis. These efforts had exhausted her to the point where she had "lost [her] love of life completely" and felt sometimes like dying.[7]

After the break with Kennedy, other students came and went, but none seemed more promising in the mid-1870s than Daniel Harrison Spofford. His wife had studied with Mrs. Glover in 1870; we have already seen that she succumbed to Kennedy's charms. In the spring of 1875, while he was taking the course, Spofford sent a letter to his teacher, telling her that he was fully aware of the awesome responsibilities they had as her students. At one point he said to her that he hoped he might be worthy enough to give her the "living water which you must desire to drink." Over the next year he more than quenched Mrs. Glover's spiritual thirst. After Spofford had produced a number of eye-opening cures, Mrs. Glover was convinced that she had found a student to replace Kennedy and to carry her work into the world.[8]

The first edition of *Science and Health* was published in 1875; Mrs. Glover's hopes and expectations were brought up short when within half a year of its publication only two hundred or so copies out of a thousand had been sold. Despite an encouraging review from the *Boston Investigator*, which seemed receptive to her purer, more spiritual form of Christianity, and a few other good notices, it was evident that the general public had ignored the book and that few infirm souls had taken up her spiritual healing. Of course, there were critical reviews, some scoffing at her radical idealism. They were willing to allow that the mind can affect the body, but not to grant the differences between illusion and reality that she saw.[9]

With this generally cool reception of her book, and with her movement seemingly at a standstill, Spofford was a godsend. In her correspondence with him, one finds a couple of lines, like glimmering nuggets, that suggest Mrs. Glover tended to elevate Spofford and his work. On October 1, 1876, she was once more distraught by setbacks and the incessant demands of her students, but she did not include Spofford in her exasperated lament. In this same letter she expressed confidence that Spofford was carrying her message to the world and would not be a burden to her. She was overjoyed to know that at last she had "one living student" after so many years of "struggle, toil, and defeat." He was not in a position now to understand what all of this meant, but he would in the future when "the whole labor" was left in his hands.[10]

Three weeks later, as her revised version of *Science and Health* was about to be published, she wrote Spofford another letter sharing her fears and hopes about the book, which, as she phrased it, was about to go out "like Noah's dove" over the rough waters of doubt, cynicism, and entrenched dogmatism. With God's guidance, her book might find dry ground. She urged Spofford to continue with his work. He had no inkling of his true abilities in her religious science; she reminded him to keep the ideal of Christ before him and to count less on his own gifts, to rely on God instead of the self.[11]

As the above letter indicates, in her ark of safety, in her religious sphere, which was segregated from the everyday struggles for power, Mrs. Glover and her students were equal in Christ and in spirit. Like the animals on the ark, none was better than the other. Along with this equality came a sense of empowerment that was nurtured in this sphere and could be exercised outside it (as the individual remained secure within it). Authority could be exercised if one measured one's stature by Christ as, one might add, Mrs. Glover had done, and as she exhorted Spofford to do.

Earlier that July, Mrs. Glover had been having trouble feeling good about anything. She wrote to her cousin Hattie that she had recently had a "violent seizure" because she had been "in the atmosphere of the sick" far too long. In this weakened state, she collapsed, and one of her new students, Asa Gilbert Eddy, was quickly summoned. When he entered the room, he found Mrs. Glover lying unconscious. Without a moment's hesitation, he attended to her and broke the spell. Mrs. Glover confessed to Hattie that she was "astonished" at his healing skills, his calmness, and his fortitude. Until that moment when he had spiritually restored her health, she had never seen what his true character was; he was "so tender and yet so controlling." It was hard to believe, but she had fallen in love with him.[12]

Some ten years younger than Mrs. Glover, Gilbert Eddy had grown up on a farm in Londonderry, Vermont. There seemed to be nothing very distinguished about his father; he was a Vermont farmer working hard to keep his seven children fed and clothed. The farmer's wife, Betsy, however, was anything but conventional. According to one of Gilbert Eddy's old classmates, "The children were reared in a manner somewhat out of the ordinary." As soon as they were old enough to attend school, Betsy Eddy would send them off in the morning and then spend much of her day driving around the roads and paths of the countryside. Gilbert, so it seemed, was his mother's favorite son; he would often accompany her on her drives and wind the quills on her loom when she was in the mood to spin or weave. Later Gilbert became an accomplished tailor.[13]*

Like most rural children in the nineteenth century, Gilbert was an indifferent student and did not progress far in his education. He left home in 1860 and, after several jobs in various factories, made his way to the Boston area as a drummer for the Singer Sewing Machine Company. Though somewhat taciturn and withdrawn at times, he possessed great personal warmth. Mary Godfrey, as a young girl living in Lynn near Mrs. Glover at 8 Broad Street, remembered Gilbert Eddy for his kindness. As a child she was shy and did not open up to new people readily, but she was immediately drawn to Gilbert because of his fondness for children. He was always kind to her, and in his own quiet way was "a jolly playmate." His pleasant smile and gentle eyes made it hard to imagine that he could hurt anyone. Mary also recalled that Gilbert was a spiritual man, but he was often ill. Seeking to restore his health, Gilbert was attracted to a number of fads, including spiritualism. His quest for health eventually led him to Mrs. Glover.[14]

As she became more attracted to this man who had shown such tenderness and strength in helping her, Mrs. Glover placed more confidence in him. When she transferred some of Spofford's patients to Eddy, her relationship with Spofford began to sour; then it turned bitter.

---

* Betsy was odd in other ways as well. She and the family had no special church affiliation. She put little stock in doctors, and whenever the children got sick, she relied on folk remedies. She summoned Lucy Cook, also known as "Sleeping Lucy," who, in a self-induced trance, was able to diagnose disease and prescribe a remedy. Georgine Milmine, *The Life of Mary Baker G. Eddy and the History of Christian Science* (New York: Doubleday, Page & Co., 1909), p. 170; Ernest Sutherland Bates and John V. Dittemore, *Mary Baker Eddy: The Truth and the Tradition* (New York: Alfred A. Knopf, 1932), pp. 118–24.

In late December 1876, she sent Spofford a letter placing one of her recent relapses at his doorstep. His mind had caused her suffering; if he did not desist, it would kill her. She implored him to turn his harmful thoughts elsewhere and tried to assuage his fears that someone was trying to separate him from her.[15]

A few days later Gilbert Eddy proposed marriage to her. That night she had a dream, which she related to Emma Shipman years later. She saw herself standing on the edge of a vast, flowing field of wheat. To all appearances, nothing seemed unfriendly or threatening about this fertile field, and initially she felt secure in crossing it. But then she sensed that somewhere underneath lurked "dark, swinish forms" whose aggressive "uprooting instincts" were ruining all that was worthwhile. Mary was paralyzed with fear. She then saw Gilbert on the other side of the field; he offered her support and encouragement, telling her that he would help her cross.[16]

The themes in this dark dream bear striking similarities to an eye-opening story that Mrs. Eddy told Clara Shannon many years later about what prompted her to marry Gilbert. Just before he asked her to marry him, she was living in Lynn, and one day she had to go into Boston to see her publisher. She was forced to cut her trip short and return by early afternoon because she was being followed by several men. During the evening, a number of these men rang the doorbell to harass her; the police were called to watch the house. Understandably, these mysterious events frightened her. To make matters worse, the harassment continued to the point where friends and supporters refused to stay with her. At this low point, when Mary felt paralyzed with fear and abandoned by her friends and followers, Gilbert interceded, urging her to marry him so that he could protect her.[17]

It is highly doubtful that these terrifying events actually happened; rather, the ominous men, like the "dark, swinish forms" in her dream, are symbolic expressions of the anxieties that threatened to overwhelm her. As we have seen, she freighted day-to-day events with deep moral and religious significance. The usual problems in running an organization—followers misinterpreting her directions, snags in the publication of her writings, missed appointments—were anything but petty to her. She needed Gilbert's help to shield her from the assaults that prevented her from doing God's work.

And help her he did. On January 1, 1877, Mary Baker Glover took the name that the world would come to know her by: Mary Baker Eddy. In March of that year she wrote to a student saying that her marriage to Gilbert was "a union of affection and . . . high purposes." It was not, she wrote pointedly, "a sexual union," and her husband totally agreed with this.

Gilbert Eddy's devotion to her was "most ideal," said Clara Choate in a 1914 interview. He anticipated her every wish, though they might disagree on how to implement her plans. He helped students establish their practices and offered them guidance. If her writings were to be sold or finances accounted for, Gilbert took charge. Just as important, he was a model Scientist: Mrs. Eddy obeyed God; Gilbert Eddy obeyed his wife's every instruction.[18]

After her marriage to Gilbert, Mary's dream seemed to come true. A number of "dark, swinish forms" would loom to block her progress during the late 1870s and early 1880s, making it appear for a while that she would never be able to cross that field. George Barry, one of her early and most loyal students, had deeply admired Mrs. Glover and had worked hard for her. A brief poem he wrote expressed the love and devotion he felt for his "mother mine" and the "unextinguishable debt" he owed her.

When Mrs. Glover married Gilbert, Barry obviously felt displaced in her affections. He lashed out at her as his love eroded into hate. In early 1877 he sought compensation for his "unextinguishable debt"; he sued Mrs. Eddy over certain financial considerations. So much for loyalty, and so much for the faithful son who was the first to call Mrs. Eddy Mother.[19]

Such defections and attacks by once-idealized students, while not common, occurred with more frequency than Mrs. Eddy would have liked. Daniel Spofford relished attacking Mrs. Eddy whenever he could, and he figured in several lawsuits against her. Edward J. Arens, an ambitious, smooth-talking young man, captured Mrs. Eddy's ardent interest. After Arens built up a thriving practice, she praised him in glowing terms to another student. But it did not take him long to become something more slippery than spiritual, and he brought disrepute and ridicule to Mrs. Eddy's movement in two 1878 court proceedings. The first, charging Spofford with harmful mesmerism, caused the local papers to mock the case as a revival of the witchcraft trials. The other case concerned the bizarre (and unproven) charges that Arens and Gilbert Eddy had conspired to kill Spofford.[20]

Burdened by these developments, Mrs. Eddy seemed on the verge of collapse. The depth of her suffering was exposed in the spring of 1878, between the two trials. In the parlor of Mrs. Eddy's residence at 8 Broad Street, Lynn, she was joined by a number of her students in a regular meeting of the Christian Scientist Association. After the opening exercises, Samuel Bancroft, the oldest student present, asked whether it was possible to say that they were "perfect, holy, or infallible now?" Mrs. Eddy rose from her chair to proclaim dramatically, "I am infallible, I am infallible now, *we* are infallible now."

The silence that followed her declaration was deafening. Her students were stunned; this was incomprehensible, for it contradicted all of her previous teachings. Once he found his tongue, Bancroft began to argue with her; if this statement was truly believed it would cripple the growth of Christian Science and undermine its text, *Science and Health*. In pressing his point, Bancroft became heated, but it was evident that he was beginning to convince some of the other students that Mrs. Eddy had erred. Mrs. Eddy's statement contradicted everything she had previously said about perfection. In *Science and Health*, she was quite clear about the attainment of perfection as an evolutionary process. "In the midst of imperfection," she wrote, "perfection is seen and acknowledged only by degrees. The ages must slowly work up to perfection." And a bit later in the book, she declared, "God requires perfection, but not until the battle between Spirit and flesh is fought and the victory won. To stop eating, drinking, or being clothed materially before the spiritual facts of existence are gained step by step, is not legitimate. . . . Imperfect mortals grasp the ultimate of spiritual perfection slowly."[21]

Given these statements, we can well understand Bancroft's puzzlement and shock. What did she mean by saying she was infallible? Perhaps she meant that as Christian Scientists they reflected God's idea, and in this sense they mirrored His perfection. If this were true, Mrs. Eddy could be seen as trying to raise their flagging spirits. But this is not how her students heard her; if they had understood her words on this level, they would not have been so stunned by her statement.

Standing outside the stormy feelings aroused in that room, we can see that Mrs. Eddy's declaration reflected the emotional strain she was under as her troubles mounted. To keep herself intact, she unconsciously fused aspects of her personal self, her elevated spiritual self, and the love of God into a self that temporarily experienced immediate perfection. It was the security and absolute certainty of this ideal state that she then conveyed to her bewildered followers.

Despite her setbacks and defeats, Mrs. Eddy's recuperative powers were amazing. And she would need all the strength she could muster, for within three years she faced her first major defection of students. On the evening of October 26, 1881, at a meeting of the Christian Scientist Association, Mrs. Eddy was presented with the resignation of eight of her most trusted students. The following declaration was read aloud:

> We, the undersigned, while we acknowledge and appre-
> ciate the understanding of Truth imparted to us by our
> Teacher, Mrs. Mary B. G. Eddy, led by Divine Intelligence
> to perceive with sorrow that departure from the straight
> and narrow road (which alone leads to growth of Christ-
> like virtues) made manifest by frequent ebullitions of tem-
> per, love of money, and the appearance of hypocrisy,
> *cannot* longer submit to such Leadership; therefore, with-
> out aught of hatred, revenge, or petty spite in our hearts,
> from a sense of duty alone, to her, the Cause, and our-
> selves, do most respectfully withdraw our names from the
> Christian Science Association and Church of Christ
> (Scientist).[22]

Mrs. Eddy sat speechless, stunned. She then rose and went into another room. What transpired next comes from the reminiscences of Julia Bart-lett, who was in Salem when the news of the bombshell hit. She im-mediately rushed to 8 Broad Street to be by her teacher's side. Some other students who had remained with Mrs. Eddy told Bartlett that just before Bartlett got there Mrs. Eddy had completely withdrawn into herself. Suddenly, she arose from her chair as if the gloom had lifted. Standing in the middle of the room, she seemed to be changed and transfixed, "with a far-away look" as if she were perceiving things that the human eye could not see. She began to talk, uttering prophecies of the rewards that would accrue to the faithful. Those who had abandoned her were doomed to a condign punishment. Her prophecies had the ring of Scripture, and some of the students jotted down her words as best they could:

> Is this humiliation, the humility the oppressor would heap
> upon me! O, the exaltation of Spirit! I have made thee
> ruler over many things. Height upon height! Holiness!
> Unquenchable light! Divine Being! The Womanhood of
> God! Well done, good and faithful, enter thou into the
> joy of thy Lord.
>
> One woe is passed, and behold, another cometh
> quickly; and so a sign shall be given thee. Sufficient unto
> the day is the evil thereof. Woe, woe unto my people! The
> furnace is heated, the dross will be destroyed.
>
> And the false prophet that is among you shall deceive
> if possible the very elect, and he shall lead them into
> forbidden paths. And their feet shall bleed upon the jagged
> rocks. And the briars shall tear the rags from them. For

they are not clothed with a garment of righteousness.

And I will give to thee, daughter of Zion, a new heritage
and a new people.

Her ways shall be ways of pleasantness and ways of
peace.[23]

When she was finished speaking, Mrs. Eddy lowered her hand and
declared, "Why, I haven't any body." Then it was as if she returned to
the reality of the people around her. Her students, filled with reverential
awe, were overcome by what they had just witnessed; one knelt by the
couch in tears. This was the scene that greeted Bartlett when she walked
into the room. For the next three days Mrs. Eddy shared further revelations, and for her students, Bartlett wrote, it was as if they "were on
the Mount."[24]

From the depths of humiliation, shame, and defeat, she had risen to
the most exalted heights: "The Womanhood of God." In this empyrean
realm, Mrs. Eddy had an unobstructed view; she became a prophet
predicting the doom of those who had abandoned and betrayed her.
Even as the false prophets were destroyed, she, a "daughter of Zion,"
would come in their place, bringing with her the promise of "a new
heritage and a new people."

With her recovery from this devastating blow, Mrs. Eddy rebounded.
In April 1882, she and Gilbert established their home in Boston at 569
Columbus Avenue, which also served as the headquarters of their new
Massachusetts Metaphysical College, which Mrs. Eddy had founded the
previous year to provide instruction for her students and to gain wider
notice for her movement. Within a month she had begun to teach a new
class. Things seemed once more to be improving.

The fearful struggles of the years just past, however, had taken their
toll on Gilbert. If he had been her shield against the outside world, he
had been severely tested. By May his health was declining, and several
times he was driven to bed with severe chest pains. Dr. Rufus K. Noyes
examined Gilbert and made a diagnosis of organic heart disease. The
prognosis was not good. Mrs. Eddy knew that her husband was in
desperate straits, but her diagnosis was considerably different: Gilbert
was the victim of malicious mesmerism. She treated him several times
when he had his attacks, but to no avail; he died in his sleep on June
2, 1882.

His death could not have come at a worse time, because she did not
have the luxury of withdrawing immediately and totally into her grief.
She and her movement faced a serious challenge: given her Christian
Science beliefs about material reality and death, how could she possibly

explain the death of her husband? Mrs. Eddy did not wait for the barrage of snide attacks; she took the offensive. Firm in her conviction that Christian Science had not failed, she wrote Edward Arens's father-in-law, Benjamin Atkinson, a brief but powerful letter pinpointing the cause of her husband's death. She did not waste time on pleasantries; grief, anger, and anxiety coursed through the lines of her letter. She asserted the power to see why Gilbert died, and she had no doubt that Arens and his "cooperators" had mentally caused his death.

Gilbert's death, she continued, was the last in a long line of Arens's assaults on Mrs. Eddy and her movement. She and her husband had sacrificed and given much to him, but their kindness was cruelly repaid by Arens's fraud. He tried to take her money, even claimed part of her writings as his own, and finally, as if this were not enough, "in cold blood with malice aforethought," he took Gilbert. At the end of the letter an overwrought Mrs. Eddy told Atkinson that within half an hour after he had learned that Gilbert was dead, Arens had attacked her, but to no avail.[25]

Her letter to Atkinson was not enough; Mrs. Eddy needed to inform a wider audience about the perils of malicious mesmerism and, in effect, quickly repair any damage to Christian Science's reputation. She summoned a reporter from the Boston *Globe* and essentially repeated her story, though she omitted Arens's name. When the autopsy she ordered on Gilbert's body confirmed the verdict of degenerative heart disease, she refused to recognize this finding and immediately called a press conference to voice her convictions about the real cause—the mental cause—of her husband's death.

Mrs. Eddy was convinced that Gilbert had been poisoned in a special way, not in the way reporters and the public generally understood the term "poison." She had to explain what she meant when she said that it was "not material poison but mesmeric poison" that had taken Gilbert's life. Her husband had been in fine health and rarely complained about any illness. Just before he died, however, he cried out several times for relief from the mental poison that was causing him great pain. It was a well-known fact, Mrs. Eddy asserted to the assemblage of reporters, "that by constantly dwelling upon any subject in thought finally comes the poison of the belief through the whole system." She had, in fact, "seen mesmerists, merely by a glance or a motion, make an arm or a leg of a subject stiff, and then relax it again or give pain and relieve it again."

Earlier Mrs. Eddy had faced public disbelief and ridicule over the claims and counterclaims about mental influences in the "witchcraft trial" with Spofford, but this time she was not going to overlook it; too much was at stake for both herself and her movement. She had never known "a more self-possessed man" than Gilbert, she told the Boston *Post* reporter. Gilbert had told the attending doctor that he was strong enough to handle the case himself, and had even hinted himself that the etiology of his disease did not lie in the heart but in a poison that was spreading throughout his body.

As fate would have it, circumstances had kept Mrs. Eddy from turning her full attention to her husband's case. He continually reassured her that he was strong enough, so, absorbed as she was in business affairs, she did not become aware of how serious things were until it was too late. She had cured worse cases than his, but she had been called in before things had degenerated so badly. One of her students, "a malpractitioner," reportedly said that Arens would hound them forever. Obviously, she pointed out, "he has already reached my husband." Beyond all doubt, Gilbert had been given doses of mesmeric poisoning, which had not been countered early enough. Had Christian Science been applied in time, Gilbert would have been saved. Her firmness in this conviction provided Mrs. Eddy some comfort. God reigned supreme over all error, she declared emphatically, and this knowledge comforted her.[26]

Still, whatever solace she could find in her relationship with God, she remained torn by grief. By early July it was evident that she needed to escape Boston in order to grieve and to regain her strength. With two trusted students, Arthur Buswell and Alice Sibley, Mrs. Eddy traveled to Buswell's old house in Vermont, where she began her painful recovery. On July 16, she wrote Clara Choate a letter that gives us a glimpse of her state of mind. She desperately missed Gilbert. She yearned to recapture the sense of wholeness she had experienced in her healing of 1866, where she could overcome the material world by living in the spiritual realm with God. She voiced this wish to Choate when she said that she was trying "to sever all the cords" that attached her to people or to "things material."[27]

Toward the end of July, she began to recover. In a letter to one student she expressed the wish that she might be her old self again, even for just a year, so that she could regain a secure footing, but she still had lingering doubts that she would be able to do this. By the early fall of 1882, Mrs. Eddy had taken tentative steps back into the world. To Eldridge Smith she wrote in October that she felt "like an innocent child" who viewed society expectantly but fearfully because she no longer had Gilbert to lean on. She rested comfortably, however, in knowing that her Christian Science would sustain her, that she had climbed higher spiritual heights than anyone, and that she was drawing closer to God than ever before.[28]

Though Mrs. Eddy was slowly preparing herself to accept new challenges, her fears of mesmerism remained undiminished. With varying degrees of intensity, the iniquitousness of mesmerism occupied a significant role in her thinking during the 1880s as she was confronted by litigious ex-students, defections within the movement, and simple bunglings by her remaining devoted few.

Samuel Bancroft, that sharp observer of the early years of the movement, recalled that from 1870 to 1882 Mrs. Eddy asked him and many other students to fight what became known in the movement as malicious animal magnetism. Because there were times when she seemed absolutely preoccupied by it, Bancroft ranked it the "most vulnerable feature" of Mrs. Eddy's personality. In his opinion it was her "bête noire," and she seemingly feared it more than Christian Science's mortal enemies of sin, sickness, and death.

As Bancroft saw it, there was a crucial difference between malicious animal magnetism and sickness; the former was a kind of "premeditated wickedness," while the latter was simply a "false belief" which was comparatively easy to combat. Admittedly, said Bancroft, Mrs. Eddy did not draw this kind of fine distinction in her teachings, "excepting between Truth and error, Mind and matter, the Soul of man and personal sense." She had no fear when she combated sickness, and she was understanding with those who made honest mistakes in their healing. But she "suffered intensely" when she believed that her work was being hindered by malpractitioners, those turncoats with whom she had once shared her knowledge of healing. What really upset her was to think that she had placed "a dangerous weapon" in their hands which they were using against her and her loyal students.[29]

Since Richard Kennedy's departure in 1872, Mrs. Eddy had become keenly aware of the problem of mesmerism, especially of malicious animal magnetism, through the actions and failures of her students and ex-students. In 1878, when Spofford and Mrs. Eddy became embroiled in the court cases that threatened to drain what little cash resources she had and trained the harsh glare of the public light upon her and her movement, she fought back with her disclosure and indictment of destructive mesmerism. In an early edition of *Science and Health*, she wrote that a mesmerist, or mental practitioner, had the ability to influence and control the minds of others. Once he had gained this power, he could control the body. Even if one disease might be healed by this "dangerous doctor," another would be induced. There is little doubt that Mrs. Eddy was thinking of Spofford when she said, "Mesmerism is practiced through manipulation—and without it." Since *Science and Health* had first gone to press, it had become increasingly evident that another kind of "mesmeric outlaw" existed, one who did not touch the body but who nevertheless "sullenly attempted to avenge himself on certain individuals." This new mental invader had lost his morals; his "silent malpractice" was "criminal in the extreme."[30]

The thoughts of the mesmerist were more insidious and harmful than the ordinary crimes that were visible to the eye. When evil thoughts, or lustful wishes, or malicious purposes flowed from one mind and entered another, they could cause untold misery to an individual and a group, unless Truth intervened. In the throes of her open conflict with Spofford in the fall of 1878, Mrs. Eddy wrote him a letter, urging him to stop his sinful ways and get back on the right path. She told him that her rebukes were intended to destroy the malignant error; they were not intended to be ad hominem attacks. His "silent arguments," which he was so obviously employing with others in order to undermine her, had, in fact, just the opposite of their intended effect. Truth, she vowed, had elevated her former self and allowed her to know who was employing this mental argument, what was being said, and when. Knowing this, she was safe from his mental attacks.[31]

During the late 1870s, when she often felt under siege, Mrs. Eddy wrote her students asking them to turn their thoughts away from her, because she often felt their mental conflicts in her body. At times, convinced that Spofford was behind all the turmoil, she urged her followers and others to combat him mentally. In the midst of her 1878 court case against him for malicious mesmerism, Mrs. Eddy sent a hurried note to Samuel Bancroft urging him to take up Spofford mentally at four in the morning, then at four in the afternoon, and again at nine that evening. If Bancroft did his mental work the way she asked, Spofford could not undermine her students by making them sick or by diverting them from her and her Truth.[32]

Mrs. Eddy was convinced that during these hours Spofford would most likely be turning his mind against her and the movement. By asking Bancroft to take up Spofford mentally, she meant that he should pray about Spofford's kind of mental malpractice, to see it for what it was and to know its powerlessness. Through prayer Bancroft would yield his human will to the divine Will which was free of evil; in so doing, he would be able to counter Spofford's evil.

In the third edition of *Science and Health* (1881), Mrs. Eddy's chapter "Demonology" clearly spelled out how this malicious mental practice had come close to crippling her movement and how obsessed she was by it. She rehashed the court cases of 1878, printing brief excerpts from the trials to illustrate this demonic mesmerism at work. She named the principal players or, at times, thinly veiled their identities by referring to Dr. S (Spofford) or, in an earlier incident, to W (Wright). The activities of these men, as well as Dr. K (Kennedy) and others during recent years, had convinced her that history was unfolding mesmerism's wickedness. "The warp and woof of crime hidden in the dark recesses of mortal thought are weaving webs so complicated and subtle" that they could seduce and entrap without warning. While Edward Arens and others would get their share of blame, Richard Kennedy's influence was to be feared the most. She was obviously referring to him when, in the early paragraphs of the chapter, she spoke about an "unwise young man" who had tampered with the true metaphysical method and had "subverted his mental power apparently for the purposes of tyranny." This student's unbridled ambition and his lack of morals led him down one path: the despotic subjugation of others.

Kennedy had kept this part of himself concealed from Mrs. Eddy and his patients. "Through unsurpassed secretiveness, he wore the mask of innocence and youth." But his appearances were deceiving, as she so painfully discovered. He was a "marvelous plotter, dark and designing . . . and we half shut our eyes to avoid the pain of discovery." When they could no longer deny what was before their eyes, they could see the full extent of his evil. He had seduced some of his female patients and split their families apart. This mental practitioner stirred the passions and appetites, induced disease and suffering, reactivated old problems, and caused mental anguish. At the end of her chapter, Mrs. Eddy held out a warning to her readers: Mesmerism (or malicious animal magnetism) was an evil stalking the land, and even if the courts in their rational wisdom could not see it, it existed nonetheless. This form of mental murder was just as real as the shooting or stabbing of a person, and she, for one, was not going to stop combating it just because others would not or could not see it.[33]

Because she had invested so much in Kennedy in the early 1870s, when her movement was so young and trying to gain a foothold, his betrayal of her ideal (and ideals) was especially damaging. It was as if the person she had loved, trusted, and depended upon most had forsaken her. This was an insult that Mrs. Eddy could neither forgive nor forget. Throughout the coming decades, her thoughts and feelings about Kennedy lay submerged in shallow waters, but surfaced whenever she encountered similar crises and conflicts.

In 1881, several years after the court trials and during the same year that her eight students defected, Mrs. Eddy had a series of dreams that were dutifully transcribed by Calvin Frye, her trustworthy factotum. One fragment of a dream shows the feelings of humiliation, powerlessness, and dreadful emptiness that Kennedy could induce in her.

In a dream that Frye recorded in February 1883, Mrs. Eddy said that she saw Kennedy, who had become quite prosperous and was surrounded by admiring friends. Also standing there, in obvious contrast to Kennedy's well-fed success, was Mrs. Eddy, "a mere skeleton wasted away with consumption." Kennedy turned to her and presumably all the eyes of the group fastened on her as he said, "You have done this." At that terse comment, Kennedy and his friends broke into laughter.[34*]

Sometimes Mrs. Eddy would share her dreams with her classes, using them in a didactic way. Kennedy kept popping up in them over the years, and as late as 1892 he and mesmerism were the subject of a long dream. As in the brief description above, Kennedy and malicious animal magnetism had the power to enfeeble her and cripple her movement. Some have snickered that this was merely a manifestation of witchcraft, while others have pointed to the suspicions, conspiratorial charges, and projected fantasies as evidence that Mrs. Eddy and her Christian Science followers were submerged in a murky swamp of paranoid delusions. Whatever one wishes to believe, there can be no doubt that the tension was palpable, as the November 15, 1883, entry in Calvin Frye's diary graphically reveals. "Mrs. Eddy has had a belief of difficulty of breathing for the last two days," he noted. On the morning of the fifteenth, around four o'clock, she urgently summoned him to help her. Frye did his best, but after ten minutes or so Mrs. Eddy gasped that he was only making things worse. Afterward, she told Frye that she could not arise from the bed to speak to him because of "the suffocating sense it produced." Around nine-thirty in the morning Mrs. Eddy discovered that "the mesmerists were arguing to her inflammation and paralysis of spinal nerve to produce paralysis of muscles of lungs and heart so to prevent breathing." Apparently she only felt relief when she and Frye "took up Kennedy & Arens to break their attempt to make her suffer."[35]

When we read Luther Marston, a Christian Scientist who early broke away from the movement, about this period in the everyday world of the Massachusetts Metaphysical College, it may seem as if we have ventured into a harrowing world. Two-thirds of Mrs. Eddy's lectures, he claimed, were specifically related to the subject of mesmerism. She taught her students that the mesmerists had "secret service men and women" in their employ, who watched every movement of Mrs. Eddy and her students. When they left her residence, they could be certain

---

* These dreams were transcribed by Calvin Frye, and Gilbert Carpenter provided his interpretation. As far back as 1872, when Mrs. Glover and Kennedy parted ways, she wrote a letter in which she voiced her alarm about Kennedy's double-dealing. She was convinced that he had entered into a conspiracy with Wallace Wright, and they were out to do her harm. Archives, 5664, letter to Mr. Fred O. Ellis, dated May 27, 1872.

that these spies were following them. Mrs. Eddy also believed that the United States Post Office was so enveloped in mesmerism that loyal Christian Science students had to mail their letters secretly. Georgine Milmine claimed that Mrs. Eddy's terror of mesmerism knew no bounds. When she wrote letters, Mrs. Eddy had one of her students take them to a remote part of town and deposit them in a mailbox. Moreover, she was convinced that "the mesmerists kept her under continual espionage, and she seldom went out of the house alone."[36]

By the time Bancroft joined her in the early 1870s, Mrs. Eddy's thinking about mesmerism first and foremost had a religious base, and her model was the life of Jesus. "The cross is the central emblem of human history," Mrs. Eddy wrote in *Unity of Good*. Jesus fully understood suffering, but it did not arise out of his sins; rather, as the Scriptures tell us, he bore our sins in his body on the cross. Therefore, concluded Mrs. Eddy, Jesus' suffering must have stemmed from "the mentality of others; since all suffering comes from mind, not from matter, and there could be no sin or suffering in the Mind which is God." Every true Christian Scientist drank from His cup of sorrows; they, too, knew what it meant to suffer in the flesh and "from the mentality which opposes the law of Spirit."

The prophets and apostles also suffered from the thoughts of others, Mrs. Eddy continued, because "their conscious being was not fully exempt from physicality and the sense of sin." Jesus' suffering on the cross, however, promised a new life, a triumph over "all mortal mentality." This victory did not come free of cost, as Christ's suffering demonstrated. And, just as important, there was a close affinity between the uniqueness of Christ's suffering and His spiritual sensitivity, which was far more developed than that of His disciples or any ordinary man's. On one of His journeys with His students, Jesus knew their thoughts by reading them scientifically, Mrs. Eddy wrote in *Science and Health*. In a similar manner He *read* disease and effected cures. Emulating Christ in this ability to heal, Christian Science allowed a person to *read* the mind, "but not as a clairvoyant"; it gave a person the power to "heal through Mind, but not as a mesmerist."[37]

It was precisely in this realm that the mesmerist exhibited his power, because through his control of another's mind he had the ability to pervert the healing power of Christ. If one looked at the destructive expressions of mesmerism from her religious and moral perspective, then Mrs. Eddy's alarms seemed to make sense. Robert Peel has emphasized the rationality in her stance against mesmerism, especially in her dire warnings about malicious animal magnetism. Indeed, when she sounded the tocsin against a person's malicious use of his will to manipulate and control others, she was, according to Peel, well within the range of normality. Moreover, Peel goes on to say:

> As Christian Scientists see it, this kind of subtle psychological manipulation of others' thinking is the antithesis of yielding to the divine Mind and letting God's will be done. It is a form of mental mal-practice, hypnotic in action and rooted in self-will. Where used as a conscious, calculated technique it may lead finally to what Eddy called moral idiocy. But she drew a clear distinction between its malicious form and what she described as merely ignorant animal magnetism.
>
> The remedy for all such attacks . . . was to let the pure sunlight of Truth and Love shine down on the situation and disclose the dark corners of thought to be swept clean. But the malice of the carnal mind that Paul defined as enmity against God was not to be destroyed by shutting one's eyes to its 'mad antics.' "[38]

Peel is a strong corrective to Marston and Milmine, and he is right as far as he goes. The story, however, is more convoluted. Mrs. Eddy's beliefs and fears about mesmerism emerged from an intricate web of relationships and experiences, thoughts, and feelings that stretched from childhood to Quimby and back again. However, we must yet account for the times when Mrs. Eddy's emotional responses to subversion of herself and her movement seemed excessive and her alarms exceptionally shrill. And this leads us back to her particular way of seeing and experiencing reality.

One may argue that Mrs. Eddy was acutely sensitive to a form of interpersonal interaction that is largely unconscious, and a process that is far more common than we like to admit. In any institution—a family, a school, a business, or a religious organization—the words that flow on the surface to communicate goals and aspirations, the ideals and well-being of the individual and the group, may be subverted simultaneously by an undercurrent that not only contradicts the overt message, but covertly hurts the very people it is supposed to help. Mrs. Eddy had carried this way of knowing into the metaphors and symbols of her poetry, eventually into her relationship with God, and finally into her religious doctrines. The subtle and harmful psychological manipulation of others through mental suggestion (which is what she meant by malicious animal magnetism) was particularly odious to her because it separated a person from God's Truth. The stakes were high. As Samuel Bancroft told us earlier, there was no compromising with this kind of mental manipulation of others, for it violated the principle of spiritual autonomy. When it came to mesmerism in any of its forms, Mrs. Eddy sharply drew the line between "Truth and error, Mind and matter, the Soul of man and personal sense."

Mrs. Eddy saw her spiritual sense as fundamentally different from Ralph Waldo Emerson's cosmic pantheism, but on a purely descriptive level she and Emerson seemed to have something in common. By reading Emerson closely for just a moment, perhaps we can begin to unwrap the other layers in this special form of communication that the two of them apparently shared though their basic philosophies were miles apart. Emerson caught something of the flavor of this intuitive, expressive way of relating to the world in his famous essay "Nature," when he joyfully proclaimed: "The greatest delight which the fields and woods minister is the suggestion of an occult relation between man and vegetable. I am not alone and unacknowledged. They nod to me, and I to them."[39]

This occult relation reflected the romantic's way of "knowing" reality, and both Emerson and Thoreau had the ability to express this preverbal form of communication in intellectual terms. Beneath the surface of their sophisticated language, we hear a flow of sounds that triggers some of our earliest memories of communication. That is, the romantic's way of comprehending reality has close affinities with the early maternal relationship, where unconscious expressions and feelings often find a pathway between mother and child by the look in the eye, the tension in the lines of the face and forehead, the tone of the voice or cry, the touch of the hands. This quasitelepathic mode of communication does not stay fixed at this early stage; to the contrary, aspects of it can be found at all stages of life, as the commonly accepted term "body language" testifies.*

---

* The important point here is that this mode of communication could be experienced by Mrs. Eddy and her students on different developmental levels. I am not arguing for psychological uniformity. In fact, just the opposite is true; there is a wide diversity within this phenomenon. Rather than my paraphrasing Walter Joffe and Joseph Sandler, it is worth quoting them extensively, for what they say is germane. As they note:

> If we apply the idea of persistence to processes of identification and projection in the older child or adult, we can postulate that there will always be a momentary persistence of the primary state of confusion, however fleeting, whenever an object is perceived or its representation recalled. What happens then is that the boundaries between self and object *become imposed* by a definite act of inhibiting and of boundary-setting. It is as if the ego says, "This is I and that is he." This is a very different idea from that of a static ego boundary or self-boundary which remains once it has been created. What develops . . . is the ego function of *disidentifying*, a mental act of distinguishing between self and object which has to be repeated over and over again; and the function of disidentifying makes use of structures we call boundaries. The persistence of this genetically earlier primary confusion in normal experience is evident when we think of the way in which we move and tense our bodies when we watch ice skaters, or see a Western. We must all surely have

With Mrs. Eddy's uncanny ability to experience the feelings, moods, and thoughts of others, there were some real gains to be derived from this way of relating. The truly sensitive mother can empathize with her child; she can know what the child feels inside (by "reading" him or her), and she can then respond in the child's best interests. In her spiritual realm, in her impersonal sense, this is how Mother Eddy wished to be with her children: her students.

On one occasion, in a brief essay, Mrs. Eddy declared that unless a person was keenly alert to the "modes of mental malpractice," he ran the risk of being lulled into mistaking its insidious thoughts for his own. If this happened, he would journey down the wrong path of life without ever knowing it. When Mrs. Eddy sounded this warning, she was speaking as a religious leader, not only about an obstacle to spiritual healing but also about a danger in the process of interpersonal healing. Mrs. Eddy's warning has more than a faint ring of familiarity to the psychoanalyst, who understands that in the interaction with patients—especially in transference-countertransference and in experiences with projective identification—unspoken, unconscious wishes and feelings can pass from the patient to the analyst and back again. With a sharpened awareness of his or her own internal experiences and of those perceived in the patient, the analyst can enhance his or her insight into, and experience with, the patient.[40]

The analyst, of course, expects the patient to place, transfer, or project unwanted wishes, thoughts, and fantasies onto the analyst, and sometimes the analyst is not immune to responding to the patient by what has been stirred up inside himself or herself. This is a hard, sometimes risky game. Mrs. Eddy and her students, playing their variation of it, were not safe from its pitfalls. Even the prophets and apostles, Mrs. Eddy reminded us, were "not fully exempt from physicality and the

---

had the experience of righting ourselves when we see someone slip or stumble. In these everyday experiences there is a persistence of the primary confusion between self and object; this may more readily occur in states of relaxation or of intense concentration in which the bringing into play of boundary-setting may temporarily be suspended or delayed. . . . The persistence of this genetically early state . . . must surely provide the basis for feelings of empathy, for aesthetic appreciation, for forms of transference and counter-transference in analysis. . . . And in connection with what we call secondary identification and projection, we would suggest that the bridge to these processes is the persisting momentary state of primary confusion or primary identification which occurs before the process of "sorting out" or "disidentifying" occurs.

Sandler and Joffe quoted in Joseph Sandler, "The Concept of Projective Identification," in Joseph Sandler, ed., *Projection, Identification, and Projective Identification* (Madison, Conn.: International Universities Press, 1987), pp. 25–26.

sense of sin." In this realm of the personal sense, she and her students were exposed to some of the emotional conflicts and problems that arose from their experiences and their relationships.

In certain circumstances this mode of relating would enable Mrs. Eddy to assess people accurately and to sense the direction her movement should take. In other instances, however, when she felt under heavy stress, when she felt unrelenting pressure building from within and without, this way of knowing the world could lead to excessive fears of malicious animal magnetism.

The late 1870s and early 1880s, the years Marston and Milmine refer to, were particularly trying for Mrs. Eddy and the movement; a number of strands from her personal life interwove with elements of the culture to produce her heightened sensitivity to what she called malicious animal magnetism. As a neophyte leader, she was faced with an unsympathetic outside world, a world that did not easily accept women who, for whatever reason, appeared assertive and aggressive—women, that is, who overstepped the prescribed boundaries. Mrs. Eddy needed to marshal her assertive side in order to function as a religious leader and promote her cause. Unlike an aggressive, assertive man, however, she could not count on the support and toleration of the wider culture. This lack of wider support might cause anyone to question the legitimacy of his or her assertiveness; it must have been an especially difficult issue for Mrs. Eddy.

When the unrelenting attacks from within and without became unbearable, Mrs. Eddy was confronted with her most intense form of alienation: she feared that she might be separated from God. If this ever came to pass, the self that had been carefully constructed and pieced together in her conversion experience would begin to fragment and she would be thrown back into the horrors of death. Under such pressure, Mrs. Eddy's strengths—her demands for discipline and order, her perception of the world in clear-cut moral terms, and her ability to find meaning beneath the surface—*temporarily* collapsed and coalesced into the fear of an outside malignant force: malicious animal magnetism. In these tense moments and in these episodes, Mrs. Eddy's thoughts and actions seemed to be colored by the characteristics usually associated with paranoia.[41]

In Mrs. Eddy's world, one governed by a unique set of rules, the fears of mesmerism made sense; they were not paranoid delusions but legitimate perceptions of reality. This was vividly described in the notes Martha Bogue took while a member of Mrs. Eddy's Primary and Normal classes in 1888 and 1889. In one lesson, Mrs. Eddy discoursed on the meaning of "mortal mind" and "animal magnetism." The air in the room crackled with electricity as Mrs. Eddy addressed these sensitive issues. Animal magnetism was especially threatening when it was not confined to material expression. This unchained aspect of man's mind was "the red dragon of Revelation." And, Mrs. Eddy noted prophetically, the time was near, no, it was already here, when people could murder, steal, or poison without having to travel physically. Now they could send their thoughts through mental suggestion. The times were ominous, she noted in apocalyptic tones. Hell had never been so apparent nor crime so cleverly hidden as today.[42]

In another lecture, Mrs. Eddy told Martha Bogue's class that animal magnetism was often very difficult to detect because it had an admixture of good and evil in it. Here was how a person might detect evil embedded in what was ostensibly good: Anything that had both characteristics and could be used either way had to be the opposite of God, who was totally good. As in the Garden of Eden, the snake coiled around the tree was "the animal magnetism of now," she insisted. The snake had to be recognized for what it really was, a betrayer and seducer, a Judas. And, Mrs. Eddy warned, the Judases of today were far more iniquitous than the one with whom Jesus had to contend, because the crafty ones today did not "betray themselves." Thus, it was paramount for Christian Scientists to meet this evil of animal magnetism and defeat it.[43]

In the examples from Martha Bogue's class notes, the key issue is how Mrs. Eddy intended her students to hear her message and how they actually heard it. We can imagine that in times when the movement was not felt to be under heavy attack, Mrs. Eddy's words on animal magnetism were meant to be taken as rich symbols and metaphors that helped structure the meaning of what they were doing, why they were doing it, and why they were so sorely tried by obstacles placed in their path. But again, under unremitting tension and strain, anyone—including Mrs. Eddy and her students—might temporarily regress in thinking and behavior by translating the metaphors and symbols as concrete realities.[44]

If we take Mrs. Eddy and her world seriously, then we must admit that even from our bird's-eye view atop our late-twentieth-century perch, we cannot say with confidence which speech of Mrs. Eddy's or which episode might be considered "normal" and which might represent a slide into paranoia. There is no doubt, however, that this kind of shift could, and did, happen to Christian Science students. Mary Collson, for one, had a harrowing experience with it. As we shall see in Chapter 10, she came to Christian Science with her own needs and expectations. She was a capable practitioner in Evansville, Indiana, in 1905, but her career was filled with ups and downs. By 1914, she had her name withdrawn from the church rolls; she later returned, only to withdraw for good in 1932. For our purposes, what is interesting about Mary Collson is the way she responded to the movement's emphasis on malicious animal magnetism.

An independent, liberal thinker, Collson at first was highly skeptical about malicious animal magnetism when the concept was taught to her by Alfred Farlow, an important and influential Christian Scientist. According to Collson, in one of his first classes Farlow gave a vigorous lecture on this topic. To Collson, Farlow was too vivid and graphic; she voiced her reservations by complaining that this was by far the worst kind of evil she had ever encountered. "You have talked this thing up until I am . . . actually getting scared," she said to Farlow. During the first week of class, she and Farlow argued so much on this topic that she almost quit the movement then and there.[45]

Collson stayed, but she did not wholly accept the Church's teachings on mental malpractice: "I resolved to do the best I could to keep the teachings I liked in the foreground and let them shy the bogies off," she said. As she would learn, however, the bogey of malicious animal magnetism was not easily ignored or deflected. As so often happened within the movement, Collson got caught up in personal conflicts with other Christian Scientists. The hostility, the jealousy, the resentment and anger that these conflicts engendered first in Evansville, then in Boston, undermined her initial confidence. As she wavered, she could no longer dismiss malicious animal magnetism so cavalierly. With each crisis her emotional reserves were drained, and she increasingly saw malicious magnetism not as an abstraction but as a real evil.[46]

Collson took a year's leave from the rigors of working in the field, but she found little relief from the mental strain; for a number of reasons—some stemming from her personal problems and some from Farlow's actions—her intense anger and her equally intense fears centered on Farlow. In New York, the external upheaval in the movement and her own inner turmoil threw her into the maw of animal magnetism. As she later put it, "The monotonous repetition of statements which I employed to ward off the evil influences of my teacher soon put me into a state of superstitious anticipation . . . exceeding anything I had previously experienced."[47]

What Collson was about to experience was harrowing; the only thing close to it was the mental breakdowns she had suffered before coming into Christian Science. She was consumed by her fears of malicious animal magnetism; in this state of mind she got on a subway one morning to go to her office. Suddenly she felt as if she could not breathe. At the first stop, she got off, transferred to a bus, but could not breathe any easier. As the bus approached her stop, Collson grew increasingly anxious about having to go to work. It was as if she were paralyzed; she could not get off the bus. She stayed on until it ran its route again, but she could not budge. She continued riding the bus for hours; every time she saw her office building, she felt as if she were glued to her seat. At this point, the story is best told in Collson's own words:

> I said the Lord's Prayer and the "scientific statement of being" over and over. I repeated the "definition of God" and everything else I could think of as statements of Truth with power to exorcise animal magnetism. I declared that this experience was unreal, that it was a dream, and I repeated these declarations until, as in a dream, the bus began to appear to be floating along, rather than rolling over the pavement. It was almost like a phantom bus, and with the Ancient Mariner I could easily have said that Death and Life-in-Death were casting dice for my soul.[48]

As it turned out, Collson did not have another mental breakdown. She got a grip on reality, and when she clarified in her own mind what had caused her to fall under the spell of malicious animal magnetism, she wrote the Mother Church asking that her name be dropped from the rolls. While she was a person of considerable talents, her previous experiences with emotional stress indicate that she was highly vulnerable to the kinds of strains and fears engendered by a preoccupation with malicious animal magnetism. Her experiences with it throw into bold relief the way this unseen mental force could be taken in and expressed on a number of emotional levels by an individual. Depending on the person and the circumstances, malicious animal magnetism could be dealt with realistically or, in moments of severe emotional crisis, could become his or her worst nightmare.

Fortunately, Mary Collson did not remain on a regressed level; she pulled herself out of the emotional chaos. More important for Christian Science, if and when Mrs. Eddy had these kinds of episodes, she, too, pulled herself up from the regressed level. In the late 1880s, just when it seemed that Mrs. Eddy was being personally overwhelmed by the forces of animal magnetism, and when the editor of *The Christian Science Journal* was publishing hair-raising accounts of mental suggestion, Mrs. Eddy pulled back and began to curb this growing excess in her movement. In 1890 she wrote in the *Journal* that all talk of malicious animal magnetism had better cease until Scientists "understand clearly how to handle error,—until they are not in danger of dwarfing their growth in love, by falling into this lamentable practice in their attempts to meet it."[49]

Before we move on, a few final words must be said about mesmerism, animal magnetism, and malicious animal magnetism. The belief in their harmful power served a number of functions. In one sense the fears surrounding these mental powers functioned much like the Puritan's jeremiad, a dire warning that held out the promise of greater spiritual renewal. One could receive a gentle nudge urging spiritual self-improvement, or one could receive a forceful push inveighing against evil. Also, like the Puritans, Mrs. Eddy and her Christian Science followers could use these beliefs as a way of confirming their special mission to the world and promoting a sense of solidarity. Somewhat paradoxically, however, at times Mrs. Eddy and some of her students could use these same beliefs in such a way as to increase tension and conflict within the group. There are no simple answers or solutions here; the issues get just as complicated when we examine some of Mrs. Eddy's relationships in more detail.[50]*

* The paranoid features in Mrs. Eddy's fears of malicious animal magnetism can be placed in an even wider social context. When reality is perceived as highly unstable, then we would expect to see manifestations of paranoid thinking on collective and institutional levels. Historians have located a paranoid style in American politics that has erupted from time to time. For example, see Richard Hofstadter, *The Paranoid Style of American Politics* (New York: Alfred A. Knopf, 1965); David Brion Davis, ed., *The Fear of Conspiracy: Images of Un-American Subversion from the Revolution to the Present* (Ithaca, N.Y.: Cornell University Press, 1971). Certainly in the late nineteenth century Mrs. Eddy and her Christian Scientists were not alone in feeling threatened by an outside world in flux. The historian John Kasson has recently explored how the traditional signs of middle-class Victorians were rendered indecipherable by the pace of change in their increasingly problematical social world, and how Americans became vulnerable to the wiles of confidence men, tricksters, and dissemblers of all sorts. These anxious middle-class Victorians thus set about constructing new signs so that they might be able to probe beneath deceptive appearances in order to read the city, others, and themselves. Clear readings of these "texts" would establish a sense of coherence and order in an emerging modern society. John F. Kasson, *Rudeness and Civility: Manners in Nineteenth-Century Urban America* (New York: Hill & Wang, 1990), p. 94. Ch. 3, "Reading the City: The Semiotics of Everyday Life," pp. 70–111, is enlightening. Also see Karen Halttunen, *Confidence Men and Painted Women: A Study of Middle-Class Culture in America, 1830–1870* (New Haven: Yale University Press, 1982), pp. 153–90.

9

PLEASANT VIEW:
TO RULE HER OWN HOUSE

For if a man know not how to rule his own house, how shall he take care of the church of God?

1 Timothy 3:5

IN MANY RESPECTS the late 1870s and the following decade were productive years for Mrs. Eddy, no matter how often malicious animal magnetism vexed her. She gained a firmer social toehold when in April 1879 she formed the Church of Christ, Scientist. It was centered in Boston, and she was its president. In January 1881, she established the Massachusetts Metaphysical College. The school's curriculum included Christian Science doctrines and healing methods. Again, she was trying to give her teachings a firmer structure and more respectability in the community. Mrs. Eddy now carried the title Professor of Obstetrics, Metaphysics, and Christian Science, and her graduates took away a diploma from a state-chartered school.[1]

In the spring of 1883 she brought out the first issue of *The Journal of Christian Science*, and by February 1886 she had published the sixteenth edition of *Science and Health* and formed the National Christian Scientist Association. These achievements become all the more impressive when one remembers how much energy she had to devote to the minutiae of daily affairs and the continuing conflicts.

By the late 1880s she had to protect her young movement from critics and others who linked Christian Science with the New Thought movement. Early in 1887 Julius Dresser delivered a lecture at the Church of Divine Unity in Boston, titled "The True History of Mental Science," which extolled Quimby and relegated Mrs. Eddy to the status of one of his copiers. As if she did not have enough problems, she was thrust back into the old battles of who had taken what from whom. A year later

Mrs. Eddy had to contend with another embarrassing defection of students; Ursula N. Gestefeld, a once-trusted student, published her own interpretation of Christian Science, presenting Mrs. Eddy with yet another significant challenge. One should not be surprised to learn that the turbulent years of 1887 and 1888 brought a renewed emphasis on the question of animal magnetism, which now became commonly known among Scientists as malicious animal magnetism (M.A.M.). A monthly column, "Animal Magnetism," in *The Christian Science Journal* was ample testimony to the degree of insecurity the subject evoked in the movement as a whole.[2]

During this decade Mrs. Eddy's two sisters died, Martha in 1884 and the strong-willed Abigail two years later. Mrs. Eddy had had virtually no contact with them for the previous twenty years, so their passing probably did not touch her very deeply. They were from the family of her past; Mother Eddy was now more invested in the family of her present and future, her Christian Science students. Her children, the good Lord knew, needed their mother's watchful eye and firm hand. For every student who took a step forward in his or her healing practice and brought credit to the teachings of Christian Science, there seemed to be two or three who faltered. Mrs. Eddy not only had to expend a great deal of time and energy in keeping well-intentioned students in line but faced serious challenges to her role as leader and teacher. The endless upheaval taxed her health, and at one point she feared that her movement would not outlive her.

In the midst of all this turmoil, she stunned her followers by legally adopting Ebenezer J. Foster. This was a fast rise for a man who had been in the Christian Science movement slightly more than a year. Foster Eddy had graduated from the Hahnemann Medical College in Philadelphia. He then became a successful homeopathist in Waterbury, Vermont, but in 1887, at the age of forty, he grew intrigued with Christian Science after witnessing a number of healings. In that same year, he closed his practice and entered one of Mrs. Eddy's classes.

Foster was a kind man and an eager learner. These attributes quickly caught Mrs. Eddy's eye, but they were not the only qualities she saw in him. His medical degree attracted her; it lent the movement a prestige and respectability which it sorely needed. More personally, Foster was roughly the same age as her long-departed son, George; one can begin to understand why Mrs. Eddy favored this new student, even seeing him as her possible successor.[3]

Whatever doubts other followers of Mrs. Eddy may have had about Foster's new preeminence, they could all agree that the movement was changing. In a July 1888 article in the *Journal*, she alluded to the dissension that had continued to plague the advance of Christian Science, and then announced that she would be "gradually withdrawing from active membership in the Christian Science Association." This slow withdrawal was accelerated when Mrs. Eddy resigned the pastorate on May 28, 1889.[4]

In that same month, reeling from the many conflicts and changes that beset her Christian Science movement, Mrs. Eddy, left Boston for Concord, New Hampshire, where she could enjoy the relative quiet of Concord's tree-lined streets. Here she made other monumental decisions regarding the future of her church. In the fall of 1889, Mrs. Eddy dissolved the formal organization of her association and the Metaphysical College, and, at some subsequent date, the National Christian Scientist Association.

In 1892, Mrs. Eddy settled permanently in the magnificent surroundings of Pleasant View. For the next fifteen years she would use this tranquil setting in Concord to shape and reshape the structure of her religious movement. In many respects, the move to Concord and Pleasant View was an emotional retreat, but it was not a defeated withdrawal into the countryside. Concord was, in a way, a spatial metaphor: a medium-sized town, it was somewhere between the quiet New England villages of the past and the bustling cities of the future. It was close enough to Boston that she could keep on top of events, and through the mails she could monitor the progress of her movement as it slowly—in fits and starts—spread throughout the land and into foreign countries.

The back veranda of her Pleasant View, where she often liked to pace while in a reflective mood, faced the hills that arched to her childhood home in Bow. As her wistful memories drifted back to those quieter times, she found a sense of warmth and strength in them (especially in many fond memories of her mother). They also helped prepare her for the day she would leave Pleasant View for Chestnut Hill, outside Boston, as she constantly probed new directions and shaped the future of her Christian Science movement.[5]

No matter how idyllic and restful Pleasant View might have looked from the outside, with its sloping hills, resplendent gardens, lush orchards, and gentle reflecting pond, the view inside was markedly different. Indoors there was a sense of intense purpose, discipline, and order that was reflected in the staid Victorian decor. Mother Eddy ran a very strict religious household; her daily routine would probably have drawn a smile of recognition from Ben Franklin himself. In his *Autobiography*, Franklin devised a daily schedule accounting for each hour's activity from morning to night. By monitoring himself through critical self-examination, Franklin hoped to achieve moral perfection.[6]

As she sought to achieve spiritual perfection, Mrs. Eddy's daily schedule was no less demanding. From the reminiscences of Gilbert Carpenter, who came to Pleasant View in 1905 and served as Mrs. Eddy's personal secretary for a year, and of Adelaide Still, who was Mrs. Eddy's maid from 1907 to 1910, we can piece together a rough facsimile of Pleasant View's daily routine:

> 7:30 a.m.—breakfast
> 8:30–9:00 a.m.—secretaries begin to sort mail
> 9:00–10:00 a.m.—first watch hour
> 9:00–10:00 a.m.—Mrs. Eddy tours downstairs rooms
> 10:00 a.m.–noon—mail sorted and delivered to Mrs. Eddy, who begins her correspondence
> noon–1:00 p.m.—dinner
> 1:00–2:00 (or 2:30) p.m.—Mrs. Eddy's daily drive
> 2:30–3:00 p.m.—Mrs. Eddy's rest period
> 3:00–4:00 p.m.—second watch hour
> 3:00–6:00 p.m.—Mrs. Eddy works on her letters and church business
> 6:00–7:00 p.m.—supper
> 7:00–8:00 p.m.—period of quiet conversation
> 8:00–9:00 p.m.—third watch hour; Mrs. Eddy goes to porch and sits on swing
> 9:00 p.m.—Mrs. Eddy prepares to retire[7]

A quick glance at this schedule confirms Adelaide Still's comment that Mrs. Eddy preserved the habits of her New England background, but it does not begin to reveal what made the routine at Pleasant View different from that in any other upper-middle-class Victorian home.

In her home, Mrs. Eddy expected everything to be orderly and neat. Still noted that Mrs. Eddy was especially sensitive about her own appearance. "Her hair and clothes were always in perfect order," she said. During the first two or three weeks that she was on the job as her maid, Still remembered that Mrs. Eddy would occasionally make her open the hat box so that she might see for herself whether or not Still had folded the bonnet strings correctly. When she went on her drives, Mrs. Eddy did not want her appearance marred. She usually wore white kid gloves; to make sure that the gloves were not soiled by dust on the banister as she walked down the stairs, Mrs. Eddy put a pair of white woolen gloves over them. She would hand these to a maid when she reached the hall.

This meticulousness extended to all activities at Pleasant View. When Mrs. Eddy took her morning stroll through the downstairs rooms, she was quick to tell a housekeeper if a piece of furniture was out of place

or a curtain needed straightening. Promptness was expected; lateness
was not tolerated. There were no bells at mealtime; the food was put
on the table with the expectation that everyone would be in his or her
proper seat at the correct time.

All the workers went out of their way to make sure that nothing
disrupted Mrs. Eddy's routine. The moment Mrs. Eddy left on her afternoon drive, her three maids quickly and efficiently cleaned her study so
that she could devote her full energies to her work when she got back.
Moreover, when Mrs. Eddy conducted her daily excursion through the
downstairs rooms, the help avoided entering a room while she was there
so as not to disturb her.[8]

Even by late-nineteenth-century standards, one can see that Mrs.
Eddy's demands for discipline and order were excessive. It is easy for
us today to pass judgment on Mrs. Eddy for her rigidity and her readiness
to chastise an unsuspecting worker. What is more difficult is to understand all of this from Mrs. Eddy's and her workers' perspectives. To
help us in this understanding, we can turn to the thoughts of Gilbert
Carpenter. He was devoted to Mrs. Eddy and quick to see how others
might misjudge her actions. He knew that her demands for perfect order,
her daily rituals and routines, could be seen as excessively rigid, and
that one could begin to build on this a case for Mrs. Eddy's emotional
instability.

For Carpenter, however, the mere hint of a personal element in any
of Mrs. Eddy's actions made for a gross distortion. Her demands for
discipline and order were never a reflection of her own fears and fastidiousness. He once stressed that Pleasant View was the only place
where each and every activity was intended "to restore spiritual
thinking." This meant that every task, no matter how trivial, was
freighted with spiritual meaning.[9]

Even cooking a meal gained extraordinary significance at Pleasant
View. Mrs. Eddy felt the lack of a "demonstration" (evidence that actions
were being guided by God rather than being controlled by human
belief) with her food more keenly than anything else, said Carpenter,
because she found it essential to be "nourished spiritually." As a pre-
cautionary measure, the cook often prepared two dinners. One was
called the *in-case* meal; the cook held it back in the kitchen just in case
Mrs. Eddy thought the first dinner not seasoned with the right spiritual
condiments.[10]

Again, Carpenter was sensitive to the way this pickiness might sound
to outsiders or even to Christian Scientists who were not in tune with
Mrs. Eddy; he did not hesitate to interpret it in what he considered the
right frame of reference. For Carpenter the only way to understand Mrs.

Eddy was to know that she lived in Mind and drew her strength from spiritual sources. For her, therefore, all outward effects were external symbols of an internal mental state. If, as was believed in Christian Science, mind was causation, then behind every effect lay a mental cause. The symbol and how one read it determined the meaning of reality.[11]

With her spiritual-intuitive powers, Mrs. Eddy was the only one who knew how to read the symbols—the everyday acts and occurrences— in her home. Thus, argued Carpenter, the simple, ordinary things at Pleasant View, even the smallest details that escaped everyone else's notice, were "symbols having divine implications." If all life was to be directed to God, then even the insignificant and ordinary items like chairs and carpets became an "expression of spiritual thought" in total harmony with God. A chair placed slightly off center or a dirty carpet meant only one thing: a mind out of tune with God.[12]

As we know, when Mrs. Eddy read the symbols of everyday life at Pleasant View, she was very sensitive to what she perceived as harmful mental influence; its very presence threatened to undermine her spiritual equilibrium. From their experiences with Mrs. Eddy, her workers knew that their leader could be thrown off balance; indeed, they had ample opportunity to see what happened when Mrs. Eddy momentarily lost contact with the spiritual life that flowed from God. When this occurred without apparent cause, her actions and behavior led some students to suspect that the frustration, disappointment, and anger came from within her and that her behavior had fallen short of her professed spiritual ideals. When things reached this point, it is interesting to see how some of her students justified Mrs. Eddy's behavior and how their trust in her was not violated.

Even when a student carried out one of her assignments with all the best intentions, genuinely believing that the act was good, Mrs. Eddy's superior spiritual wisdom intuited the underlying mental error. Once she detected it and read the symbolic act for what it was, the student received a rebuke to shake him or her out of spiritual complacency. Often, however, Mrs. Eddy's students were baffled when she looked at what they had done and saw errors, while they looked at the same act and saw none. Indeed, it seemed at times to her workers that on the surface things were running smoothly at Pleasant View. To everyone but Mrs. Eddy, that is; her deeper vision saw something no one else could. "A negative state of mind" was creeping over her unaware students just at the moment when all seemed well, Carpenter explained. It was as if Mrs. Eddy were a spiritual barometer; the day might be sunny, but Mrs. Eddy broke up the harmony in the home by creating "an artificial storm." She summoned her students and verbally shook them with scoldings until everyone in the house seemed tense and agitated.[13]

Carpenter was the first to admit that when Mrs. Eddy felt secure within herself, when she was able to keep her thought in the elevated spiritual realm, the students' lack of demonstration in the home did not rile her. According to Carpenter, when she reprimanded them for failing to demonstrate properly, it was a signal that error was trying "to rob her of her spiritual thought." To the untrained eye, therefore, it might look as if Mrs. Eddy were scolding a student because she felt insecure within herself; it might even seem that the rebuke had no direct relationship to what the student had or had not done. If a person listened carefully, he or she might overhear whisperings about this problem on days when Mrs. Eddy unleashed volleys of censures. Indeed, the nature and meaning of her upbraidings posed an issue that would not die either at Pleasant View or within the wider Christian Science movement. Time and again Carpenter returned to the topic in his sprawling manuscript, clearly a sign of just how much misunderstanding Mrs. Eddy's chastisements created within the movement, and just how anxious Carpenter was to put this issue in a good light.[14]

Carpenter admitted that one way error or malicious animal magnetism attempted to undermine Mrs. Eddy was to make her consciously aware of "a personal vulnerability," which then triggered her associations to "black times of the past." Did this mean that at least a part of Mrs. Eddy rebuked her students out of her own personal failings? Nothing could have been further from the truth, Carpenter argued. Mrs. Eddy's disturbances never arose from emotional disturbances. With her great spiritual sensitivity, she was always responding to error that originated in the outer world; the attacks came from outside, never inside. When her students were blissfully ignorant of an unseen danger (a danger that she saw coming), it was all Mrs. Eddy needed for one of her crisp chidings.[15]

Adelaide Still saw another reason for the apparent incongruities in Mrs. Eddy's actions: her states of consciousness ran a wider gamut than the ordinary person's. Even though Mrs. Eddy had ascended the highest spiritual peak, this did not mean her footing was always secure; like anyone else, she could not escape the emotional pull of life's experiences. Admittedly, Mrs. Eddy was far more vulnerable to mental thought than the ordinary mortal was. Pleasant View, for example, had no telephone because Mrs. Eddy did not want any interruption of her spiritual thought. She knew, wrote Carpenter, that the phone could be misused to commit "mental murder." Through the phone's electrical wires, a mental thought could penetrate the walls of Pleasant View and contaminate the atmosphere. Another example of her hypersensitivity to mental thought lay in her belief that once her students left Pleasant View, their thoughts could continue to affect her. The reasoning went something like this: since Mrs. Eddy rarely departed from her strict routine, she was convinced that students who had left her service were able to tell what she was doing at each moment of the day. If they happened to focus their thinking on Pleasant View, this "mental murder" could "enter into the mental activity of Mrs. Eddy's life" almost as if the students were still there.[16]

As powerful as she was spiritually, Mrs. Eddy gave the appearance of being vulnerable, and Carpenter had a ready explanation for this. From his perspective, a person could not separate Mrs. Eddy's weakness from her strength, because her endurance was not like anyone else's. If an ordinary person's spiritual faith was shaken, he or she still had a core part of the self to turn to for comfort and reassurance. Mrs. Eddy, however, had renounced the material self—the human part called Mary—and surrendered herself so completely to the spiritual part that without the support of Divine Mind she temporarily felt empty and abandoned when she sensed that that support was cut off. Every time Mrs. Eddy sensed that she was on the verge of being separated from her spiritual thought, she was thrust into a life-and-death struggle because her spirituality was her whole life.[17]

Clearly, then, when the daily flow of spiritual life was diminished in any way, Mrs. Eddy felt herself in real danger. No wonder that she believed that any attempt to disrupt this spiritual flow by exposing her to mortal belief or animal magnetism was nothing less than an attempt to kill her. These attacks usually came when Mrs. Eddy "was suffering under some claim" or her spiritual equilibrium was thrown off kilter. In her darkest moments, when it seemed she might succumb to mental assaults, Mrs. Eddy leaned on her students, using them much as she would a practitioner. During the evening a student would be summoned to Mrs. Eddy's bedroom to "give her an audible treatment." After she recovered, and had regained her spiritual balance, Mrs. Eddy gave clear warnings that any more help would be a sign of animal magnetism.[18]

Evidently, what Mrs. Eddy really feared was that when she was not securely anchored in the spiritual realm, and her students were mentally asleep, she would be exposed to potentially life-threatening mental attacks. Carpenter witnessed how devastating these attacks on Mrs. Eddy could be, and like Adelaide Still he saw that mental error particularly undermined Mrs. Eddy's spiritual poise, especially when it touched old personal issues. Mrs. Eddy herself once admitted that when her thoughts were in tune with God, and as far as she knew they always were except when she was *"wrung with grief,"* then she could benefit everyone, friends and enemies alike.[19]

John Salchow, one of her hardest-working, most devoted helpers at Pleasant View, confirmed this in a story he repeated, having heard it from one of the other household workers. One day Mrs. Eddy noticed a small spider crawling on her dress. She became very agitated and called the maid to remove the spider immediately. After she regained her composure, she smiled sweetly and said, "That was not the Founder of Christian Science. That was Mary." Salchow, without adducing other anecdotes, recalled that "the human sense of things cropped out in similar little incidents," and Mrs. Eddy would speak of herself in both the spiritual and personal senses.[20]

What Mrs. Eddy's maid and other students had witnessed from time to time could be potentially damaging to Mrs. Eddy and a real test of a student's faith, for if she could be influenced by her personal past, then her rebukes might emanate from this source, and her critics might be right in calling her a querulous old lady. How were loyal students to understand these two sides of their leader?

Carpenter knew that he could not be heavyhanded on this issue; he had to handle it delicately. To begin with, one had to accept the fact that Mrs. Eddy had two sides: a side that had remained attached to her personal history, and a side that had separated from it, thus allowing her to ascend the highest spiritual peaks. But, Carpenter argued, one had to see these two sides of Mrs. Eddy as totally distinct; it was never Mrs. Eddy as Mary who contributed to her spiritual leadership. When she was in her spiritual realm, she was governed by the spirit of God; this was what made her a powerful spiritual force. Therefore, an accurate appraisal of Mrs. Eddy must begin with the realization that her spirituality did not come through perfecting any personal attributes; it came through the qualities she reflected from God.

Mrs. Eddy was the first to condemn her personal side if she sensed that it interfered with spiritual work. When, for any reason, she failed to reflect His spirit, "she had nothing," Carpenter reiterated. No student could ever know the pain Mrs. Eddy felt when she momentarily lost her closeness to God, because no other person, save Jesus, had attained the spiritual heights she had. Yet the students had no greater honor or privilege than to see Mrs. Eddy when she seemed utterly helpless and weak, said Carpenter. For this was actually her way of showing them the strength and harmony one had when one reflected God, as well as the overpowering anguish one felt when one lost that reflection, even temporarily. The way Carpenter saw it, these moments of deep suffering on Mrs. Eddy's part were morally instructive because she was suffering to show her students what happened when the spiritual meaning of life was lost.[21]

According to Carpenter, the kind of help Mrs. Eddy really needed was to be reassured in a dark hour (times when mental disturbance loosened her spiritual grip on God's hand) that, because she had faithfully established for herself a true sense of God, and because she had always leaned on Him, her God would now sustain her. It was crucial, therefore, for Mrs. Eddy's most trusted students to do everything in their power to protect their leader from all pernicious mental influences. In a metaphysical sense, Carpenter said, the students at Pleasant View were like "food tasters" for Mrs. Eddy. Their task was to detect through their spiritual sensitivity whether or not the food served to her was "impregnated with the goodness of God and not the poison of human thinking." If the students did their job of protecting Mrs. Eddy, she could devote her undivided attention to her calling. Knowing this, we are in a better position to understand why three "watch periods" played a significant part in the daily routine at Pleasant View.[22]

To say that the watches were significant does not capture just how important they were to Mrs. Eddy and her sense of spiritual and emotional well-being. Not only did Pleasant View have three scheduled watches, but, on top of this, her students were expected to do this mental work on their own time. Carpenter, for instance, had the midnight-to-1:00 a.m. shift. During the watch periods, according to Mrs. Eddy's instructions, her mental workers were to sit quietly in their rooms, to watch and pray in order to shield her and her work from mental contamination, and to reestablish the spiritual presence of God in the home. Her inspiration for this kind of mental work came from the Bible, particularly Matthew 26:40, where it is stated, "And he cometh unto the disciples, and findeth them asleep, and saith unto Peter, What, could ye not watch with me one hour?" and similarly in Mark 14:37: "And he cometh, and findeth them sleeping, and saith unto Peter, Simon, sleepest thou? couldest not thou watch one hour?"[23]

Mrs. Eddy usually wrote out her watch instructions and had Calvin Frye take them to each mental worker. Many of her instructions were thoughts and suggestions, one or two lines long, that left it up to the mental worker to fill in the spaces with his or her own prayer and work. Some of her instructions were like mental pep talks, reaffirming the basic principles of Christian Science and rearming her workers in spiritual truth. In one set of instructions she urged her mental workers that the first thing they were to do was call on God to deliver them from temptation and to help them keep alert. Once they were awakened to the potential evil in the world, then they were ready to do their tasks "not as a dreamy hashish eater," but as clearheaded Christians who knew absolutely the difference between right and wrong.[24]

One of the more unusual aspects of these watch periods was Mrs. Eddy's weather watches. These were not happenstance; Laura Sargent, one of Mrs. Eddy's closest and ablest students, spent much of her watch time devoted to the weather. In one of her watch instructions Mrs. Eddy jotted down these succinct instructions: The weather was controlled by Love; "no electricity of mortal mind." Since Divine Mind governed all, it could not be a part of the harsh and destructive elements in nature. What did Mrs. Eddy mean by this? Did mind control matter? Was this nothing more than magical thinking?[25]

Magic had nothing to do with it, according to Mrs. Eddy. In reality, weather was the atmosphere or reflection of the Divine Mind (God). God governed the weather, and since God was total love and harmony, it was impossible for Him to be in the angry winds, the destructive lightning, or the frightening thunder. Clara Shannon, who joined Mrs. Eddy's household in 1894 and served loyally for about nine years, recalled that at Pleasant View, control over the weather, especially over storms, was treated just the same as control over anything else in the material world. After a long drought, for instance, Mrs. Eddy turned her attention to it, and after much prayer, rain fell from a cloudless sky.

Shannon remembered another time when she saw dark clouds moving in the direction of Pleasant View. Mrs. Eddy had instructed her that whenever she saw a storm approaching, she was to let Mrs. Eddy know immediately. When Shannon informed her, Mrs. Eddy went to the back veranda; by that time the ominous clouds had moved over the house. Mrs. Eddy quickly went to the front vestibule and looked out, whereupon she returned to the veranda and blurted, "The children in Boston!" Upon hearing this, Shannon ran downstairs, threw open the front door, and looked up into the dark sky, where she saw an uncanny sight. In the heavy black clouds that hung over the house, it looked as if a black sea had parted, with the clouds beginning to separate and move in opposite directions.

When Shannon rushed back upstairs and told Mrs. Eddy what she had just seen, Mrs. Eddy replied, "Clouds? What clouds?" Puzzled, Shannon looked again and saw the clouds dissolving, and Mrs. Eddy quietly said that no clouds could ever obscure God's face, nothing could ever come between them and the light of God's Truth. The cloudless sky, the calm day; this was God's weather. As Shannon listened to these words, she saw that Mrs. Eddy's face was in rapture; she realized that Mrs. Eddy was not seeing clouds but "realizing the Truth."[26]

The weather was an important test for a Christian Science student because the elements represented a clear example of mortal mind's control. The Bible, said Carpenter, spoke much about the weather and man's ability to control it. An ideal day, full of sunshine, with a clear blue sky and no humidity; this was a day that reflected the Divine Mind. If he regained control over the turbulent storms, "the threatening weather of belief," man would no longer be tossed about by the winds of change or be attacked by "those dreaded elements" which derived their power through man's fears. Thus, in her demonstrations against the elements, and by urging her students to control them, Mrs. Eddy was showing her students how to be a part of the larger scheme "of spiritual existence and living."

There was one more aspect of Mrs. Eddy's need for weather watches; for Carpenter it might have been the most important. It seemed to him that the fluctuations in Concord's weather were ominous only as they directly impinged upon Mrs. Eddy's sense of well-being. When she traced the effect of rough or threatening weather to its cause, she discovered "aggressive action" emanating from mortal thought, and this was being expressed in the turbulent weather conditions. Understanding this, Carpenter took up the weather knowing that he was really protecting Mrs. Eddy's spiritual thought "from the consolidation of mortal fear" which was directed at her. As soon as Mrs. Eddy regained her spiritual composure, as soon, that is, as her "thought was quieted and became harmonious," Carpenter saw the weather return to normal.[27]

No matter what the weather portended, many of Mrs. Eddy's watch instructions sounded like spiritual air alerts warning her household about an impending attack from malicious animal magnetism in all of its mental forms. In the late 1890s, as we have seen, she moved to curb the movement's intense preoccupation with this malevolent mental force in the pages of *The Christian Science Journal*. But while this was done publicly, privately malicious animal magnetism continued to be a vibrant issue at Pleasant View. The following examples of her watch instructions capture the flavor of this ever-present concern:

> Watch: Malicious Animal Magnetism "rages": a Christian Scientist must be firm and counteract this "secret influence" with his or her own strong mental work.
> Watch: An unconscious mind does not exist. The mind is totally conscious. All thoughts are under your control; no mental poison can contaminate your mind.
> Watch: Malicious Animal Magnetism has no inherent ability to create a law that would allow it to mentally

poison the body. No credence can be given to a "mentality" that can "hypnotically" administer poison to the
body.

Watch: You have the power to heal the sick and no mortal
mind can make a person suffer. There is no suffering
in the mind "from any argument of poison." God, not
mortal mind, is the one and only power.

Watch: There is no material reality, and there is no "poi-
sonous thought or mind." Forms of mental malpractice
by mental malpractitioners can not attack your mind.
"There is no mind to transfer or be transferred, tele-
graphed or transmitted. . . ."

Watch: Animal Magnetism can neither create harmful
new beliefs in a person nor can it revive destructive old
beliefs because in the Divine Mind beliefs do not exist.
Knowing this, a person becomes impervious to the wiles
of Animal Magnetism.

Watch: Arsenic and opiates have no effect on anyone at
Pleasant View, and no one can be seduced into believing
that either has any effect. True spiritual love guides all
affairs in this house; "there are no evil suggestions, no
hypnotism, theosophy, no electro-magnetism."[28]

The modern reader might be puzzled by Mrs. Eddy's unusual use of
such ordinary words as "poison" and "electricity." They indicate that
she had constructed a new meaning of reality in her Christian Science;
her words would point the way and open the doors to this spiritual
realm. So Mrs. Eddy took old words like "arsenic," "opium," "hashish," "poison," and "electricity" as vivid metaphors, as emotionally
charged abstractions that pointed to a real menace: malicious animal
magnetism.[29]

During his year at Pleasant View, said Carpenter, animal magnetism
proved a subject of unending interest. But, of course, there was more
to life at Pleasant View than this. Viewed through the eyes of an outsider,
Mrs. Eddy's strict schedule, her insistence upon discipline and order,
and her need for watches and severe rebukes might have made one
wonder how anyone could have survived in this oppressive atmosphere.
That is precisely the point: Mrs. Eddy's workers never felt life at Pleasant
View oppressive. Demanding? Yes. Frustrating? Yes, at times. Demor-
alizing? Yes, temporarily, whenever they were out of harmony with her
spiritual demands. But oppressive, as if they were living under some
authoritarian regime? No. Mrs. Eddy's students considered it a privilege

and honor to serve her; when they received the call, most of them knew how strenuous the mental work would be. Overall, they saw the justice in her strict means of working toward her spiritual goal. Mrs. Eddy was unyielding in her spiritual demands; she practiced what today might be called tough love. As a result, life at Pleasant View was spiritually challenging and fulfilling.[30]

One winter's day in 1892 an outsider walked onto the grounds of Pleasant View. The forty-two-year-old James Gilman arrived carrying art supplies and a reputation as a competent landscape painter. In the mid-1870s he was a popular art instructor at the Goddard Seminary of the Universalist Church. He had read his Emerson and had more than a passing acquaintance with another transcendentalist poet, Jones Very. As he traveled the New Hampshire country roads, Gilman admired the romantic powers of nature, an appreciation he tried to convey to his students in a small booklet with a long, imposing title, *Instruction in Pictorial Art for the Home Student with Illustrations Adapted to the Requirements of Instructions.* The romantic strains of Emerson and Very could be heard in Gilman's advice to young would-be artists, who were encouraged to study nature closely, "persistently, devotedly, and lovingly" in order to improve their "self-culture." Nature was "the soundest educator"; it heightened one's powers of observation.[31]

In his walks across New Hampshire, Gilman would stop to sketch a scene that arrested his eye. He often found an appreciative audience for his work among the affluent farmers and townspeople. He was welcomed into homes as someone who could capture on canvas the face of a loved one or a family's much-cherished farm. For his services he received room, board, and modest payment. Gilman's steps along these country roads, writes Adele Dawson, "can be traced by the pictures he left behind on the walls of prosperous farm houses."[32]

Gilman's travels and his need for work eventually led him to the doorstep of Pleasant View. After appraising the man and his work, Mrs. Eddy's photographer, S. A. Bowers, hired Gilman to do several sketches of her home with the intention of presenting the drawings and some interior photographs to Mrs. Eddy as a gift. Gilman's commission, however, was not as serendipitous as it might appear. At several times in his life he had fallen ill, and by all accounts he had suffered from bouts of depression. It is not clear whether one of these depressed episodes prompted him to turn to Mrs. Eddy's writings in 1884; nevertheless, as he expressed it, he felt compelled to travel to Concord.[33]

We are fortunate that Gilman obeyed his instincts, because in the year or so that he was associated with Mrs. Eddy, he kept a diary of his experiences with her. Part of the diary is composed of letters to Miss

Carrie Huse, which may or may not have been sent. Whether they were or not, the diary served as a psychological outlet for Gilman, and the thoughts and feelings he jotted down regarding his exchanges with Mrs. Eddy have a freshness and directness that many other sources lack. Therefore, we will first look at Mrs. Eddy's dealings with Gilman and then shift our attention to her relationships with some of her followers.[34]

Late in December 1892, as he was making a preliminary sketch of the back of Pleasant View, Gilman espied an object that fully tested his artist's eye and piqued his romantic imagination. His words have the ring of an introduction to a Gothic novel. As his eye darted back and forth from the sketch pad to the upper veranda, he suddenly glimpsed a dark-clad figure pacing back and forth. Fifteen or twenty minutes later, Gilman finished his sketching, and as he walked by the veranda, a closer look at "this decisively active figure in black" gave him the eerie feeling that he had seen an apparition like this only in his dreams. His eye was drawn to the unusual garb of the pacing figure. The size and shape of the bonnet seemed to throw the figure out of proportion; it almost appeared as if the figure were a child instead of a woman. The black dress, coupled with the agitated walking, suggested to Gilman's artistic imagination that he was observing a woman in deep sorrow.

At first, Gilman did not seem to realize that the object of his attention was Mary Baker Eddy. Through a close study of her writings, he felt that he had come to know her intimately, for her healing thought had lifted him more than once out of depression. When he first met the corporeal embodiment of this dreamlike figure several days later, Mrs. Eddy chuckled over this episode. Gilman let it be known that when he had first observed her, he had intuitively known that she must be wrestling with "the darkness of materiality," the enemy with whom she so often bravely struggled. Whether or not he was aware of it, Gilman said the right thing at the right time. Earlier in the fall, along with twelve of her most trusted students, Mrs. Eddy had formally organized the Mother Church. This was the rebirth of Mother Eddy's child, and she was rightfully worried about its growth and development.[35]

Mrs. Eddy was obviously moved by Gilman's remark. She turned from him, moved deliberately to the window, and gazed wistfully upon the gently rolling lawn. Gilman was afraid at first that he had offended her, but when she came back to him she confessed that she loved the beauty of nature and was pleased to find similar qualities in people. Gilman then asked her: Was it one of nature's laws that we advanced by impulses, like the lapping waves of the sea, or was it perhaps more like the gentle ebbing and flowing of the tides? There was a pause; then Mrs. Eddy leaned toward him and said rapturously that that was the way it was when we were dragged down by material thought, but in the spiritual realm there was no ebbing; there was no inertia. Everything was uplifting, tireless action.

In this refreshed spirit she shared with him some reminiscences of how she happened to come to Pleasant View. She even gave him a brief tour of her room. In the course of their conversation Mrs. Eddy intimated that far too often people tended to worship her personally rather than love her "as God's reflection *or child*." Maybe Gilman's ears were alerted to this remark about her spiritual innocence, for he noted in his diary that her animation revealed a quality that he had not expected to see in this admirable but demanding woman: she was childlike. This quality engaged Gilman's romantic imagination, and he would note it several times in his diary during the year and a half he was in Concord.[36]

Early in 1893 Mrs. Eddy had written a poem titled *Christ and Christmas*, and she wanted Gilman to illustrate the slim book. Honored, he accepted her assignment with enthusiasm. Poor Gilman. He might have had some set notions of what constituted good art, and his reading in transcendentalism might have given him a romantic's feel for a reality lying behind conventional forms, but there was nothing to prepare him for the emotionally draining experience of finding the correct visual symbol to convey Mrs. Eddy's spiritual message.

If Gilman's intuition had been a bit sharper, he might have sensed some of the difficulty that lay ahead. In a conversation in early January 1893, she told him that she had a natural aptitude for expressing man's beautiful and noble qualities. This thought then guided her into a reverie about her childhood. Early in life, she said, she had shown a natural talent for poetry, music, and drawing. Her precocious talent was such that her friends and relatives fully expected that one day she would win acclaim. Unforeseen events, however, worked against her; sometimes an illness sidetracked her, at other times a different adversity crippled her chances to reach her goal.

Young Mary Baker might have been an artist manqué, but as she exclaimed joyously to Gilman, in the writing of *Science and Health* her thwarted talents had found fruition. All of her youthful aspirations and hopes were not lost; in a sense they had been lying dormant, waiting to be reawakened. God had been severely testing her through the years until He allowed her creativity to burst forth in her religious writings.

In the course of her nostalgic musing about youthful ideals lost and recovered, Mrs. Eddy told Gilman about a small portrait of her that had been made sometime in her early years. To her it was an especially beautiful, accurate representation of the way she used to look "in her girlhood and early womanhood days." This portrait had mysteriously disappeared. Its loss saddened her. Gilman, listening intently, failed to see that this story might have an indirect connection to his own assignment.

Years later Mrs. Eddy sent a letter to another student, Emma McLauthlin, that bears directly on Gilman's assignment. She had no picture of herself that came close to pleasing her, she wrote. A "far-off gaze— the absent from the body look" came over her when she was suffused with the rapture that comes from seeing higher spiritual truths; that was what she had wanted an artist to capture, and so far none had. And as she would later tell another student, Carol Norton, the whole *Christ and Christmas* project was inspired from first to last. God had guided her pen more clearly than when he had guided her hand in the writing of *Science and Health*.[37]

Gilman would soon discover that Mrs. Eddy's hopes and aspirations for this book would complicate his task. On the one hand, he was being asked to capture spiritual beauty in artistic language. On the other hand, in the personal sense, Mrs. Eddy yearned for an ideal self that, like the early portrait, seemed irretrievably lost under the stress of running her movement. So, at least on one level, Gilman was being asked to recover and restore the image of an idealized self that had been damaged and lost. We have seen that it was not always easy for her to keep the spiritual and personal sides of herself separated. A troublesome reality could trigger her "grief" and bring these two selves closer together than she liked. As it turned out, it did not take long for an incident to occur that really hurt her.

In early January, several weeks before she asked Gilman to work on the book with her, Gilman found himself an unwitting pawn in a game between Foster Eddy and his adoptive mother. Mrs. Eddy had been so impressed with Gilman's sensitivity that she offered him a place in her next class of select students, if and when it met. Foster Eddy, however, had ambitions of his own; he wanted his students to be regarded on a par with hers within the movement. With this in mind, he went behind his mother's back by taking Gilman into a January 1893 class that he taught in Boston. Gilman assumed that Foster Eddy was doing this with his mother's approval.

When Mrs. Eddy discovered that Foster had transgressed her authority, it was more than just another burden to her. It was one more sign that Foster was turning out to be a wayward son, and his ill-conceived actions were hurting the growth of Christian Science. Gilman told Mrs. Eddy that Foster was initially a forceful teacher, but in the later lessons was far less persuasive. This piece of information confirmed Mrs. Eddy's worst fears; her adopted son was not living up to her hopes.

She was, to put it mildly, annoyed. But she still had that other child of hers, Christian Science, to worry about.

She hoped that the *Christ and Christmas* book would present Christian Science's spiritual ideal to the rest of the world. This was a big task; she would be intimately involved in each of the eleven pictures that would illustrate the book. This close supervision would, of course, tax her emotionally. It would test her ability to manage her personal "grief" and keep her spiritual side in ascendance.

Emotionally, Mrs. Eddy had invested a great deal in the project; indeed, it is evident that she identified closely with the woman in the pictures. In a sketch illustrating "Christian Science Healing," she thought the man looked "just as if he was determined I should not heal him." For the sketching of "Truth *versus* Error," she offered to remove her shoe and hose so that Gilman could capture the bare foot which was revealed beneath the woman's long garment. And for a sketch of "Seeking and Finding," Mrs. Eddy posed for him so that he would know exactly how she wanted to be drawn.[38]

In mid-March, as she and Gilman discussed how to represent visually a number of the poem's verses, Mrs. Eddy impressed Gilman with the fact that she wanted him to bring out "the thought of spiritual Motherhood." In particular, she seemed to emphasize the need for Gilman to illustrate the spiritual basis of Love and Truth "in the most perfect form of feminine youthful beauty." In some of the illustrations, apropos of the title, Gilman would have to depict the Virgin Mary and the infant Christ, a theme that must have triggered a wide range of associations for Mrs. Eddy. On the spiritual level, there were two Marys—Mary and the Christ child, and Mother Mary and the infant Christian Science—and both Marys could reflect "the most perfect form of feminine youthful beauty."

Alongside the spiritual connotations, however, lay other associations. The mother and child possibly represented the Christian Science organization that she had dismantled a few years previously in the midst of continuing conflict and strife. And this was not the first child of hers to prove disappointing. Her identifications, though, were more complicated than this, for not only did she identify with the maternal figure, but part of her also identified with the infant and the cherubs as idealized aspects of herself. The child's comforting relationship with the mother would, in an ideal way, repeat her own experience of parental reward, as if the child were her own parent. It was critical for Mrs. Eddy to keep these ideal images intact, for they kept her anchored in the material world, and they maintained her emotional balance. Needless to say, Gilman would be hard-pressed to paint this ideal spiritual relationship, for if he failed to do so in Mrs. Eddy's eyes, the less than perfect mother-and-child relationship might be exposed, and things could really become unhinged.

As early as March 30, 1893, Gilman had a brief encounter with Mrs. Eddy's inability to contain her worries and conflicts. He received a special delivery letter from Pleasant View instructing him to see Mrs. Eddy that evening. When he arrived, Mrs. Eddy confronted him, questioning whether anyone else knew that he had come. She charged that "a shadow of hatred and envy" accompanied him whenever he came to Pleasant View. Gilman must have been both anxious and confused at this accusation, but he breathed a sigh of relief when Mrs. Eddy caught herself and said that she was probably wrong. No, it was not Gilman. The real problem lay with a Mrs. O., who had recently come to Pleasant View, and it had been discovered that she had taken one of Foster Eddy's classes in February. With this, Mrs. Eddy proceeded to unburden herself, telling Gilman freely about the many sorrows she had to bear because her students were not teaching the way she had instructed them. They —and no doubt she was referring directly though not exclusively to Foster—were putting themselves and the letter of the law above true spirituality. She then asked Gilman a question: Who did Jesus say were His true disciples? Gilman replied: Those who kept His commandments. Mrs. Eddy nodded her approval, adding that the students who genuinely loved her obeyed her, and were thus protected from "the toils of the evil one."

Working closely with Mrs. Eddy on the book's illustrations, Gilman found it virtually impossible to obey her explicit instructions, especially when she told him they came from divine inspiration. While he was laboring over a sketch of "Christmas Morn," Mrs. Eddy wrote Gilman that she had been divinely inspired to change the sixth verse, and consequently the figures and landscape in the sketch would also have to be changed. She charged him to muster his skill as an artist so that he could depict her Christian Science story, "the new story of Christ." If he did as she wished, the world would feel the full healing impact of her religion. She warned him to follow exactly the suggestions God had given her; he was not to add or subtract from them in any way.[39]

As we have seen, even the best of Mrs. Eddy's students at Pleasant View could not avoid deviating from her spiritual demands. And like those students, Gilman could not duck the rebukes hurled in his direction. On several occasions her dissatisfaction sent him into the depths of depression. The only way he could climb out of it was to decide that Mrs. Eddy's judgment was right: his personal sense had intruded into the picture and had inadvertently altered the spiritual essence of the objects.

Once Gilman became convinced that the fault lay within himself, he could marvel at Mrs. Eddy's uncanny ability to discern the error and sin buried in mortal thought, even though it might be camouflaged by good intentions and ostensibly good results. Thus, where Gilman might have thought that his illustrations were technically among the best he had ever done, Mrs. Eddy, like an all-knowing mother looking into and through the eyes of her young child, knew the motives and thoughts behind the apparently good artwork. His own self-regard was involved, for at the very moment he was supposedly depicting God's glory, he was really puffing himself. Once she confronted him with this, it did not take Gilman long to feel guilty and sink into gloom.

As long as Gilman could continue believing that Mrs. Eddy's sharp attacks came from her impersonal, spiritual sense and were not directed at him personally, he could believe that God was behind her reprimands. Gilman shared this insight with Mrs. Eddy, and she beamed with pleasure when he told her that God was speaking through her without her full awareness. It was not simply a lack of self-regard and self-control that made her appear "unjust or ungenerous or unkind or impatient," said Gilman, but her need to obey God strictly in all that she said and did. Of course, Gilman could not always see this spiritual side of Mrs. Eddy at work, especially when he was being scolded by her.

In late November 1893, Mrs. Eddy asked Gilman to paint a portrait of her but cautioned him not to tell a soul. She was convinced that Gilman was too impressionable; if he mentioned the picture to anyone, then that person's opinions would erase her instructions to him and ruin the picture. Mrs. Eddy was right, to a degree. Gilman had a volatile, romantic side; he was highly malleable and moody. What she did not see was that she, too, was susceptible to the emotional atmosphere around her. One must question, therefore, whether the impetus for this secrecy about the painting came from an objective assessment of Gilman or from her subjective needs. For a while, she debated within herself whether or not the portrait was a good idea. One day she canceled the commission, but then abruptly renewed it. Whatever the sources of her ambivalence, it appears that she handed part of them to Gilman, for she told him that she had temporarily canceled the portrait in order to bring him to a higher level of obedience.

About a week before Christmas Mrs. Eddy had already received some good reviews for the *Christ and Christmas* book, and she was in a talkative mood. She chatted with Gilman about her early days of healing before she had written *Science and Health*, and revealed that while she was healing the sick and dying, she knew that it was obedience to God that gave us the true sense of "perfection and harmony" and how to achieve it. If only others could see what she had seen, they, too, could accomplish such works in the spirit of Truth. Because the vision of her students was not as clear as hers, however, she constantly had to remind them about this kind of obedience. When she chastised them, they often turned on her "with their darkness," adding greatly to her burdens. She constantly had to monitor this because their darkness could affect her thought and she could "reflect it upon them again." She vowed to Gilman that she never asked her students to do anything that she had not suffered through herself.

Oh, she exclaimed intensely but wearily to Gilman, it was not the passing years that had changed her brown hair to white. No, it was the suffering from the harmful, dark thoughts of her followers, who turned on her because she obeyed the Truth for their benefit. The roots of this suffering seemingly were buried deep in her past, because when she contemplated the meaning of suffering, her thoughts drifted to a childhood incident involving her mother. She immediately shared this memory with Gilman. But before we examine it, we need to be reminded that somewhere behind Mrs. Eddy's idealization of her mother lay the "real" Abigail, warts and all. There is no reason to doubt that Abigail was a woman of strength and virtue, one to be recalled with fondness. One may argue, however, that the exaggeration of her endearing qualities arose out of a confluence of Mrs. Eddy's current and past needs regarding love (the love of oneself, the love from others, the love of God), and they served an integrative purpose for her. With that said, let us turn to Mrs. Eddy's important recollection.[40]

She recalled that one day when she was a very little girl, she had "troubled and teased" her mother, who was busy at the spinning wheel, until Abigail's patience had reached its limits, drawing from her "unwillingly a quick and incisive retribution." Her mother reached out, snatched her hand, and placed it in the flies while the wheel was still spinning. Frightened by the suddenness of this punishment, Mary drew back in tears. After a while she quietly returned to her mother's side, reached up, and put her arms lovingly around her mother's neck. This act of atonement and reconciliation was prompted by young Mary's realization that she had been at fault. Her actions had irritated her mother and drawn her anger. So the moral blame did not rest on the shoulders of the mother; the fault lay with the daughter. After all was said and done, Mary pitied her mother because she had blatantly provoked her, causing her to punish Mary for her own good.

What is noteworthy about this ordinary event is that Mrs. Eddy remembered it with such clarity after so many years. With hindsight, we can see that variations of it, like invisible threads, wove their way through her life's history. There was the time when her idealization of Phineas Quimby was crumbling and she blamed (punished) herself for her troubles with her sickly friend Mary Ann Jarvis rather than strike out at Quimby for his failures. There was the episode when Mrs. Eddy slapped the disobedient servant Myra Smith, only to put her arms around her and say that her gentle hands could never hurt anyone. And if we listen closely enough to Mrs. Eddy's vignette, we can hear the faint echoes of her Calvinistic struggles with obedience and submission to authority, and the dire results of disobedience.[41]

Despite Mrs. Eddy's clear memory of this brief exchange with her mother, we do not know exactly what drove her to provoke her parent. We do know that she instigated the action with persistent teasing. One may argue that she was asking to be controlled, perhaps even looking to be punished, but young Mary seemed totally unprepared for what actually transpired. Instead of the expected response from a usually patient and loving mother, Mary, without any warning, felt herself being grabbed and her fingers thrust into her mother's machine. Stung by the banging of the spinning wheel, a startled Mary withdrew in tears.

We do not hear in Mrs. Eddy's recollection any mention of her mother's providing comfort or expressing remorse. Rather, we have the picture of a young girl, seemingly overwhelmed, humiliated, and abandoned by the very one she cared about the most, trying to come to terms with the frightening event. Given the circumstances, she did the best she could; she turned a passive event into an active, purposeful one. The rage and desire for revenge that she undoubtedly felt toward her mother were suppressed and transformed into their opposite: pity, through which she completely exonerated her mother and accepted the punishment as an expression of her mother's love.

On one level, a cultural explanation can be offered for Mary's emotional gymnastics whereby rage changed into pity. Mary was raised in a Calvinistic home where, despite the differences in the temperaments of the parents, immediate obedience was expected from the children. It was, furthermore, a home where the Bible occupied a prominent place and where God's punishments were the model for the discipline of children. As Philip Greven has painfully made clear, the Book of Proverbs —not to mention other parts of the Bible—has provided all the justification some adults need to inflict corporal punishment on their children. "Chasten thy son while there is hope, and let not thy soul spare for his crying"; "The rod and reproof give wisdom; but a child left to himself bringeth his mother to shame"; these are but two of the many examples one can choose to justify corporal punishment.[42]

But as Greven points out, this is only part of the story. In some families the aggression, pain, and anger are denied and transformed into love. In one account in Greven's book, the Reverend David Wilkerson and his sister Ruth were beaten by their father with his monogrammed razor strap. As soon as their father was done, the children were expected to ask his forgiveness and that of their Father in heaven. In Ruth Wilkerson's recollection, "Our rebellious spirits were humbled even more when we were told to put our arms around Dad's neck and say, if we *could* in our grief, 'I love you, Daddy. Forgive me for disobeying.' Then Dad would tell us, 'I love you too, but now we must ask God to help you overcome your stubbornness.'" Greven concludes this recollection with some words of his own that deeply resonate with Mrs. Eddy's incident: "Love and pain, rebellion and submission, disobedience, punishment, and forgiveness thus were intertwined in a powerful mixture of opposing feelings and experiences."[43]

Mary's response to her mother's punishment might have been culturally derived, in part an identification with her parents' Calvinistic expectations for obedience and submission. But as Greven suggests, these punishments have ways of seeping into the deep recesses of a person's emotional life, where they lie attached to overpowering feelings. In Mary's case, she kept her inner lions and tigers leashed; her change of feelings and reversal of roles helped her protect herself and her mother from her rage. Not incidentally, these psychological maneuvers also sheltered Mary's idealization of her mother, thus permitting Mary to maintain an identification with her.

Even though Mrs. Eddy told Gilman of this childhood memory for obvious didactic purposes—he, like the child Mary, was to accept the severe reproofs because they led to a higher good, and Mrs. Eddy, like her mother, was busy doing important work, only to be interrupted by a disobedient child—the remembered event also reveals that Mrs. Eddy, without being fully aware of it, was like the punishing side of her mother. She, too, used her position as Mother as a justification; she could express the anger and rationalize it so that its hypocrisy never had to be publicly acknowledged, particularly when others sensed that her anger emanated from her personal self. Perhaps this helps explain why Mrs. Eddy was often irritated and baffled by students who took her rebukes personally.

The memory also indicates that when Mrs. Eddy felt swamped by the day-to-day running of the movement, when problems accumulated and triggered her "grief," then she found it very hard to keep the personal feelings out of her rebukes, no matter how many assurances she gave that they were spiritual. And, like her mother, she would hope that the subject of her attack could see the goodness in it anyway.

This memory does not sit isolated from Mrs. Eddy's other childhood recollections. When we attach it to two others that she fondly told and retold in later years, we can better appreciate why she responded to mounting turmoil the way she did. According to her own reminiscences, Mrs. Eddy had not only known what it meant to be severely reprimanded by her mother, but she had also felt what it was like to be special, to be different, to be a chosen one.

In a talk with Clara Shannon, Mrs. Eddy once explained why it was such a struggle for her to establish her Christian Science principles. "The reason was prenatal," she said. One day about four and a half months before Mary was born, Mrs. Eddy's mother went into the attic to get some wool for her knitting. She was suddenly overcome by the belief that she was "filled with the Holy Ghost." At that very moment, she felt her baby stir within her, and this movement simultaneously stirred guilt in her for thinking that she "could have dominion." This sin—the idea that she had been chosen by God to bring forth His child—deeply troubled Abigail, so she confessed to Sarah Gault, a pious neighbor with whom she often met to pray and to discuss religious matters. Gault comforted her by saying that this was a legitimate experience justified by the first chapter of Genesis, in which it is written that man was created in God's image and given dominion over the Creation.[44]

In another instance, Mrs. Eddy fondly told a number of trusted students about the time when, as a child, she heard voices. She claimed that when she was eight years old, and for about a year thereafter, she repeatedly heard a voice calling her name. She thought it might be her mother, but when she inquired, her mother had no idea what she was talking about. One day, when a cousin was visiting, she, too, heard a voice, but when they ran to Mary's mother, she once more denied calling Mary. Later Mary overheard her cousin confirming to Abigail that someone had called Mary's name. That night, before Mary went to sleep, her mother read to her the scriptural narrative in which Samuel hears the voice of God. Abigail told her that the next time the voice called out she should emulate Samuel and ask God to speak. But when the voice came once more, Mary was afraid and did not answer. Afterward she cried, asking God to forgive her and resolving to do as her mother had asked should the voice ever come again. The voice did return; Mary answered, and experienced the sensation of being "gently lifted up." This religious experience was never repeated, at least not "to the material senses."[45]

One might argue cynically that these two recollections were nothing more than fabrications to enhance Mrs. Eddy's spiritual authority. The Baker family correspondence in fact fails to offer any corroborating evidence that both her mother and God had marked her as a chosen one. As the youngest child in the family, she may have had favored status, but this hardly accounts for the sense of uniqueness contained in her reminiscences.[46]*

Yet these memories should not be summarily dismissed, for Mrs. Eddy was using them in a highly creative way. She was shaping her personal myth; that is, she was constructing a spiritual pattern for her life that provided coherence and stability. But she was doing this for reasons other than self-glorification: it was for Christian Science. After hearing the story of Abigail's pregnancy, Clara Shannon concluded that this prenatal experience had laid the basis for Mary, who had been chosen like Christ to reveal God's message to the world so that man could have mastery over sin, sickness, and death. In a sense, this mythic story of origins was also Mrs. Eddy's way of explaining her divided nature, the Mary of the flesh and the Mary of the spirit. As she said to Shannon, this telling event accounted for the difficulties and hardships she had to endure when she tried to explain to the rest of the world the differences between the meaning of flesh and spirit, error and Truth.[47]

These memories also conveyed an emotional actuality that was far more important than any historical truth. The episode in which the voice called out to Mary suggests that Abigail might have encouraged her young daughter to believe that there were alternative ways of knowing reality. Both memories endow the young Mary with a sense of uniqueness. Despite the lack of supporting evidence independent of the cousin's recollection, this is not a complete fabrication. We remember that Abigail had a tendency to idealize all her children, not just Mary. Mary's own

---

* Mrs. Eddy's recollections centered on her mother for a number of reasons. In idealizing her mother and this part of her past, Mrs. Eddy provided a sense of inner continuity for herself. She also used this idealized image of her mother in an interesting way. By identifying with the idealized aspects of her mother, Mrs. Eddy could share in these qualities and thus reinforce her current position as Mother Eddy. As I have tried to indicate in the text, Mrs. Eddy's recollections are not simply an indulgence in nostalgia. They are complex phenomena and not open to simple interpretations. While the focus is on Mrs. Eddy's relationship to her mother, I am by no means suggesting that this is the sole source of Mrs. Eddy's problems. Any historical event has a plurality of causes, and these memories are no exception. They are probably drawn from a number of events in her life, many of which are remote and inaccessible to the historian. What I am arguing is that these memories, no matter what their "real" source, allow us to tease out certain patterns of Mrs. Eddy's behavior; her strengths, her vulnerabilities, and her responses to setbacks. On these issues, see Samuel Novey, *The Second Look: The Reconstruction of Personal History in Psychiatry and Psychoanalysis* (Baltimore: Johns Hopkins University Press, 1968), pp. 41–58.

childhood needs and wishes—we must never forget her anxiety regarding death—influenced the tone and feeling of her own experience (the hearing of the voice) and the family legend (that Abigail was carrying a special child). Thus, when we place these two childhood memories alongside the one Mrs. Eddy related to Gilman—in which her mother imposed a quick, severe punishment—another picture comes into focus. Young Mary's sense of being exalted and chosen could, with sudden abruptness, dissolve into feelings of worthlessness.*

As I have said, Mrs. Eddy's identifications with her mother were spun into a delicate, complex web. Not only did she identify with aspects of the chosen and punished child who failed to live up to her mother's demands, but she also identified with aspects of the idealized yet punishing mother who meted out swift castigation for failing to live up to those high standards. Again, what is so difficult for the historian is to know when Mrs. Eddy was predominantly acting from her spiritual self and when her rebukes reflected her more personal concerns.†

---

* The psychoanalyst Harold P. Blum states that an infantile ego ideal may be either in conflict or in "concert with an archaic punitive superego." While the more familiar sadistic superego is often associated with excessive parental ideals and unreachable perfectionist demands, "high ideals may be paradoxically paired with expectations and impossible, premature demands may lead to further parental assault and criticism of the child." There were times when Mrs. Eddy seemed to embody this kind of conflict. But this is not to argue that she always acted on this level. Blum, "The Maternal Ego Ideal and the Regulation of Maternal Qualities," in Stanley I. Greenspan and George H. Pollock, eds., *The Course of Life: Psychoanalytic Contributions Toward Understanding Personality Development*, vol. 3 (Adelphi, Md.: National Institute of Mental Health, 1981), p. 110.

† Since we do not have access to Mrs. Eddy's earliest experiences with her mother, we must necessarily, but cautiously, move into the realm of conjecture. These three memories indirectly suggest that Mrs. Eddy's fight against the intrusive nature of her father's Calvinism also had other meanings, which were largely hidden from her. If Abigail's high spiritual ideals and her demands for obedience to those ideals took precedence over her empathic response to her young daughter, and if she projected these demands onto Mary, then the young Mary had no choice but to comply. And this might be one factor contributing to Mary's struggle throughout her life to be perfect in the eyes of others, to reshape herself in order to gain self-acceptance and recognition from others, to be effective, and to maintain a sense of self-control.

Moreover, if, for reasons already noted, Mary and her mother had a strong symbiotic tie that made separation extremely difficult; if Mary, because of this strong emotional bond, had difficulty acknowledging and confirming a separate bodily and emotional self from her mother's, then these factors might have contributed to her choosing the Graham diet. Finally, these factors might help to explain why she experienced external stimuli as impingements—a feeling that her body, indeed her self, was easily invaded, influenced, and overwhelmed by external forces, especially by important people and events. A fine article on many of these issues is David W. Kreuger, "The 'Parent Loss' of Empathic Failures and the Model Symbolic Restitution of Eating Disorders," in David R. Dietrich and Peter C. Shabad, eds., *The Problem of Loss and Mourning: Psychoanalytic Perspectives* (Madison, Conn.: International Universities Press, 1989), pp. 213–30.

The historian's problem is more of an intellectual one; for Gilman it was deeply emotional. In the late summer of 1893 he faced a severe test. During the previous months Mrs. Eddy's reprimands and her cold withdrawals from him had taken their toll, and he slipped in and out of depressive moods. As for Mrs. Eddy herself, she was obviously under great strain. In conversations with Gilman, she let him know that animal magnetism was continually fouling her best efforts. She had to contend with disobedient students like her own adopted son; she was involved in putting Christian Science's best foot forward at the World's Columbian Exposition in Chicago; Madame Blavatsky's Theosophy continued to be a thorn in her side, and she was making important changes of personnel in her new church organization that ruffled feathers and stirred up backbiting among her students. Animal magnetism was on the loose. The heated struggles on the outside produced the anger that inflamed her mind and body, and her agitated feelings sometimes added weight to her scoldings of Gilman.

All of this activity would be onerous for any leader, and it was doubly difficult for Mrs. Eddy, who was then in her early seventies. She expressed her sense of loneliness and depletion to Gilman one day early in July 1893. Mrs. Eddy was in a pensive mood, deep in thought while she gazed out her window upon a flower that was growing by itself in the garden. She clearly saw something of herself in that flower. She, like it, stood alone with God, and just as someone might come along and cut the flower and remove it from nature's garden, so people were trying to sever her tie to God's Truth. How much she would have given, she sighed wearily, to be able to talk with someone who had more spiritual knowledge than she did, but that was not to be for the spiritual pathfinder, the discoverer, "the pioneer." She not only felt alone, but as she explained to Gilman, in the early days of her healing the sick, she had been so poor she had sometimes wondered why God had not provided for her needs. With hindsight, she could now see that God had been testing her for better things.

There were times in the present, however, when it probably felt to Mrs. Eddy that God never let up in His testing of her. On August 3rd, she complained to Gilman that some of her students in the West (probably meaning Chicago) had caused her some trouble. She said that malicious animal magnetism had been spreading across the land trying its best to "precipitate evil" and laying the blame at the doorstep of Christian Science, but she was steadfastly resisting it. Gilman did not quite comprehend. Not being understood, feeling that Gilman was not emotionally in tune with her, left Mrs. Eddy all the more empty and alone, and she lashed out at him: He was not dumb, was he? Surely he knew the meaning of words, did he not? She did not know how she could make it any clearer to him.

Five days later nothing was very plain to Gilman, because he became embroiled in an exhaustive controversy with her. This brief incident appears straightforward at first, but the closer one looks the more it begins to have the texture of Akira Kurosawa's *Rashomon*: depending on one's point of view, the event looks different, feels different, and has a different meaning. What looks relatively simple and uncomplicated at first glance is thus anything but that.

Earlier, when Gilman had finished his illustrations of the cherubic figures, Mrs. Eddy had warmly given her approval, which meant that Gilman was successfully capturing the spiritual qualities she wanted. In *Science and Health*, Mrs. Eddy gave an indication of what these spiritual qualities were. Angels were "pure thoughts" and "exalted thoughts" "winged with Truth and Love." Moreover, they were "messages of the true idea of divinity flowing into humanity. These upward-soaring thoughts never lead mortals toward self or sin, but guide them to the principle of all good."[48]

Mrs. Eddy wanted Gilman to invest this kind of spiritual abstraction in his drawings of the cherubs. Shortly after giving her initial approval, however, Mrs. Eddy abruptly changed her mind and claimed that his representations were inadequate. Gilman protested. He had barely changed the figures; moreover, she had approved them. Mrs. Eddy refused to budge. No, she had never approved them; Gilman was clearly mistaken; she had never seen them before. Moreover, she could never have approved the "personality thing" that was now so clearly evident in the figures of the children. She censured Gilman for being in a deep sleep; he needed to be shaken out of it, but he seemed to be getting worse as each day passed. He was becoming as bad as the rest of her disobedient students.

In the course of her upbraiding, Mrs. Eddy pointedly asked him: Was not Principle absolute in its power and unvarying rightness? Of course it was. Then why did Gilman not follow it and eradicate the animal magnetism that was infecting his artwork? Before adjourning, Mrs. Eddy fired one more salvo at the bewildered Gilman, telling him that he ought to be seeking God's strength and wisdom every hour of the day. She had urged him to do so more than once, but evidently he was headstrong and paid no attention to her. The result was that "animal magnetism has its own way at the Concord publishing office and we get nothing done but worthless work." Gilman was speechless and livid.

From one angle we can understand Mrs. Eddy's distress. Her aesthetic eye was focused on the spiritual perfection embedded in her description of the angels, a quality Gilman's figures were supposed to symbolize. Gilman's preliminary sketches had approached that spiritual ideal, but then he had altered them, putting in more of his artistic concerns. Thus, Mrs. Eddy's criticism emanated from her spiritual side.

If we stand slightly to one side of Mrs. Eddy and look at the drawings, the event takes on a different shading. We know that Pleasant View was not a secluded spiritual hideaway. Mrs. Eddy kept abreast of outside reality and of what was transpiring in her movement. As usual there were problems—the Concord publishing office, among others—and they upset her, for once again spiritual truth was being thwarted. As her frustration mounted, she began to view Gilman's work—the very same work she had approved a short time earlier—through different eyes. It was true that he had added to the figures, but it was also true that her view of things had changed. The children in the picture, the children in her movement, and her own adopted son, had lost their spirituality; animal magnetism had done its dirty work; the mind was not pure. No matter how hard Mother Eddy had tried to teach them the Truth, they ignored her and disobeyed her, much as she had disobeyed her own mother when she was a little girl. By blaming Gilman, by making him the source of bad feelings and engaging him in a quarrel, she could reenact the script of an old play, only this time instead of being overwhelmed she would master the situation.

From where Gilman stood, things were going from bad to worse. We can appreciate his dilemma if we examine a metaphor Mrs. Eddy was fond of using to convey her sense of what being a reflection of God meant. In *Science and Health*, she wrote that when a person looked into a mirror, he saw his own reflection. When the person spoke, the image of the lips in the mirror moved in perfect synchronization. Now, she analogized, compare the man looking at his image in the mirror to man standing before God. For the sake of argument, we shall call the mirror "divine Science," the man "reflection." The man reflected in this Christian Science mirror was not corporeal; he was spiritual, for he reflected the spirituality of God. And when Christian Scientists accepted this spiritual reflection and not the corporeal one as the true image of man, then this "true likeness and reflection" would be manifested everywhere.[49]

Mrs. Eddy had marched Gilman to the mirror and was telling him to look. What she wanted him to see was just how far he had failed to capture the true spiritual image of Christian Science and how far his own image was from reflecting the divine Principle. When Gilman looked into the mirror, however, he saw not just his own image, but his stern mother's standing right beside him. He blinked. Could his eyes be deceiving him? Was her image the one that was flawed? Was she the one who was failing to subordinate her personal sense to the ideal image of Science? Was she the one who failed to reflect Truth and Love?[50]

For Gilman, it was as if a heavy mist had begun to lift and slowly the shadowy image before him was taking clear shape. There it was; he could not avoid it: the source of the trouble was Mrs. Eddy. By being so adamant and unreasonable, by doing the very things she complained about most loudly, she was "the cause of most of the seeming magnetism." With further reflection, Gilman came to believe that Mrs. Eddy was the one who lacked the Christian virtues and true Christian spirit that she demanded from others.

The shock of this recognition was almost too much for Gilman. He admired Mrs. Eddy and her teachings; he believed in her, though he had not formally become a Christian Scientist. But once his idealization of her was shattered, his anger was unsheathed and she diminished further in his estimation. Gilman's anguish was considerable. It was almost as though a young child's trust in his mother had been betrayed, and he was now filled with suspicion and doubt. At this point, and in this frame of mind, Gilman saw her the way Gilbert Carpenter feared some might: her spirituality was hollow; her rebukes reflected her own personal problems, which she externalized onto others.

Gilman was wrestling with his conscience when, some twenty minutes later, Mrs. Eddy returned to the room where he was working. He tried to placate her, but she insisted that he wake up from his spiritual lethargy. She strongly impressed upon him that he must guide his thoughts and actions by the "perfection of absolute Science." Gilman argued that her ideal of the spiritual was admirable, but it was impossible to convey it the way she wanted. Some concessions had to be made to the limitations of the artist and the material senses, otherwise how would anyone be able to read spiritual symbols? Furthermore, since he had not yet begun to approach her standard of perfection, he had to take the intermediate steps first; there was simply no way to skip them.

Mrs. Eddy had a ready reply. Had she not also taken the intermediate position? Was she also not imperfect? Gilman remained mute, but he wanted to say to her, "Yes, I hear you. You say you are not perfect, but whenever you instruct me about the sketches, you seem to demand perfection."

He was still seething when Mrs. Eddy cordially asked him to stay for lunch that day. This must have been confusing for him. From Mrs. Eddy's perspective there was nothing to be confused about. Her rebukes always flowed from her spiritual core as she exhorted her students to be more spiritual in their own lives. Her love and anger were not separated; they were intertwined in her scoldings. When she had made her point, her love was there immediately; in fact, it had never been absent.

Mrs. Eddy might have felt better about things after scolding him, but Gilman was still wary, for he was not wholly convinced that her anger was a manifestation of her love. It must have felt to him that somehow she had emptied her angry feelings into him, and once rid of them, she felt good about herself again. Harboring these kinds of feelings, Gilman did not want to stay for lunch or, as he put it, "to stay under her eye." To him it seemed as though she were asking for a total surrender, a mortification of the self that felt like a death to him. This was too much to ask of anyone. The more Gilman contemplated it, the more it seemed to him that Mrs. Eddy was seeking his "complete subjection" to her will, that in effect he should become her "abject slave." If so, then he would be forced to accept whatever she said as the absolute truth, and if he disagreed with her, then he would be accused of being unfaithful.

Gilman ultimately resolved his doubts about Mrs. Eddy in a manner reminiscent of the way the young Mary Baker resolved her reproof by her mother. Gilman accepted her version (and vision) of reality: her ability to know the mental states of others made her acutely sensitive to the fact that the ideal beauty inherent in God's goodness was being besmirched. When placed in this light, Mrs. Eddy experienced material thought, which was laced with sin and error, as an offense to her own "pure sense of Spirit." Thus Gilman merited her scoldings.

Gilman did stay for lunch that day. Between bites of food Mrs. Eddy fed him stories about what had happened to those formerly prominent Christian Science students who had persistently disobeyed her. They had all fallen on hard times from the day they broke away from her teachings and the movement. Edward Arens was in an insane asylum; another follower was destitute and abused by the man for whom she had left her husband; a third defector had left the country to practice her false healing methods. The message was eminently clear: once Mother Eddy's children disobeyed her, they were abandoned to their own desperate fates unless they saw the error of their ways and reconciled with her. And Mrs. Eddy was the final judge in these matters because, as Gilman put it, she was hypersensitive to error of any kind. She was able to feel its vibrations, even though "its outward form" was not there to verify it.

Gilman had his own run-in with the hidden, insidious power of malicious animal magnetism. The publishing house had apparently bungled the reproductions of the *Christ and Christmas* pictures that she had sent, a mishap that irritated Mrs. Eddy no end. She was convinced that malicious animal magnetism was working to keep this book from being published. But what else could one expect? *Science and Health* and *Retrospection and Introspection* had faced similar opposition. The way Mrs. Eddy explained it to Gilman, this malicious mind worked in unseen ways to defeat her purposes. Ordinary cause-and-effect relationships did not hold in these instances. The presses would break down or a worker would get sick. Fifteen workers were, in fact, out at one time with one illness or another, and they could not continue the work until the Christian Scientists undertook the job to heal them in the Christian Science way.

Mrs. Eddy was not fooled; she knew what lay behind the breakdown of the presses and the illnesses of the workers: in a word, it was Theosophy. If this puzzled Gilman, he did not record it in his diary; instead, he faithfully jotted down Mrs. Eddy's reasoning. Theosophy was the outward form the enemy was now assuming. Theosophists were concentrating their energies against Christian Science, their arch-foe. She added that she could tell him stories about Theosophy that would curl his hair, but she would spare him that. All she would say was that Theosophy expressed itself "in the form of electricity, but it [had] no power."

If a mental storm was brewing in Mrs. Eddy, this time it was matched by the threatening weather outside. Perhaps Gilman sensed the connection, because his next statement in his diary seems a non sequitur. Instead of responding promptly to Mrs. Eddy, he took the time to write that the storm outside was frightfully violent, galelike winds shook the house, rain pelted the windowpanes. A romantic artist like Gilman could not have asked for a more apt metaphor for the inner storm in Mrs. Eddy, so he took the opportunity to say to her that nature seemed very upset and angry this morning. Mrs. Eddy gave him a knowing look and replied that that was the way it looked for the moment, but God would pacify the storm.

Gilman, as it turned out, was asked to help calm the storm. Mrs. Eddy had a mission for him; he was to be her secret courier. God had told her that her child, the book, had to be hidden from its enemies. As a result, Gilman had to be ready to leave for Gardner, Massachusetts, the following Monday morning. She had already arranged for her son "Benny" to meet Gilman there, and she had concocted an elaborate scheme to make sure that the pictures were not waylaid or altered. Gilman was to help the man with the reproductions, making sure that he did the work correctly. But, she cautioned, Gilman was not to say for whom the work was being done. This mission was a deadly serious business to Mrs. Eddy, a conviction she tried to impress upon Gilman.

The way things eventually turned out, Gilman might have saved himself a trip. In January 1894, Mrs. Eddy withdrew publication of *Christ and Christmas* (she reissued it in December 1897, and it has been in print ever since) when she discovered that some of her students were hurting the cause of Christian Science and themselves by their misuse of the book. As she wrote to Augusta Stetson, she never intended the book to be used for healing purposes. The poem was fine, but the pictures were only to be looked at and then forgotten. Some students apparently saw her spiritual likeness in some of the pictures, and they tried to heal from them. That, she claimed, was something she had never intended. She also insisted that the pictures were "types, not realities." At the same time Mrs. Eddy canceled the portrait that she had requested of Gilman. Laura Sargent, for one, was relieved when this project was brought to a halt, for while it was under way, the house was in turmoil from Mrs. Eddy's conflicting moods.[51]

Gilman fades from the story at this point, but we should not lose sight of what transpired in his brief but close working relationship with Mrs. Eddy. At times it was exhilarating and rewarding when she gently prodded him and encouraged his efforts with her approval. There were even light moments when they could enjoy a laugh or two. When he was in tune with her spiritual requests and her personal needs, nothing could have been better. Gilman found out over time, however, that it was not a simple thing to stay in step with her. When he could not do so, emotional upheaval ensued. Gilman's previous experiences with depression and his wide fluctuations in self-esteem made him a ready target for what was pitched his way. His emotional tumult with Mrs. Eddy, in some respects, then, casts in bold relief what a number of her students encountered in their interactions and correspondence with her. It is to some of their stories that we now turn.

Children of Light and Day

Ye are all the children of light, and the children of the day:
we are not of the night, nor of darkness.

I Thessalonians 5:5

IT IS ALWAYS RISKY to generalize about the ties that bind any leader
to his or her followers. Sometimes it seems the better part of wisdom
to say, "Of course she had charisma," and let it go at that. But the
reality surrounding Mrs. Eddy and her leadership is much more complex.
For one thing, thousands of people were healed through her writings;
Mrs. Eddy never had direct contact with them. Even some of her students
who became prominent in the movement were first healed by other
students before they met the woman behind the words. If Mrs. Eddy
was charismatic—and as we have seen, she certainly had a number of
compelling traits usually associated with charisma—she was an oddly
different leader.

Any relationship between two people is like a rich tapestry with many
threads—both seen and unseen—interwoven into a seamless whole, but
Mrs. Eddy used two dominant threads to tie herself to her students: a
need to idealize and the spiritual metaphor of a mother and child. As
long as Mrs. Eddy and her students treated the familial relationship as
a spiritual metaphor, and as long as the idealization was kept within
bounds, then things could progress smoothly. If, however, the threads
of personal wishes and demands were woven into the metaphor and the
idealization, or if the idealization remained in the spiritual realm but
became inflated, then conflict usually arose.*

---

* In this chapter and the following two, the letters between Mrs. Eddy and her followers,
the reminiscences, and other data indicated to me that the issues of narcissism, ideals,
and the ego ideal played a key part in determining the strengths and weaknesses in

While this mother-and-child metaphor cropped up frequently throughout her voluminous correspondence, Mrs. Eddy used it in a particularly rich way in *The Christian Science Journal*. In an 1889 article, she tried to define for her readers what her role as a leader was and just how difficult it was for people living in a secular world to understand the spiritual tie that bound a religious leader to her followers. To know Mrs. Eddy, a person would have to relinquish her human aspect and accept her as divinely inspired. People who focused too sharply on her human side were blind to her true spiritual self. In the spiritual sense, she was a mother of almost four thousand Christian Science children, each of whom had advanced spiritually to approximately the age of six, with very few progressing beyond that point. Her best children ran their own households efficiently and were never a burden on their mother, but "the envious and malicious ones" clearly did not love their mother and were a drain on her. They willfully disobeyed her not only by meddling in her household but by returning to their own homes and setting up their own interpretation of Christian Science.

What was a mother to do with such disobedient children? A mother's love, Mrs. Eddy lamented, could do only so much to encourage peace within a family. Some of the children were frisky, thinking they were ready to run freely without their mother's guidance. Near the end of the article, however, Mrs. Eddy noted reassuringly that once her children concentrated on completing their spiritual tasks the way they had been taught, harmony would be restored to the family.[1]

Mrs. Eddy never doubted for a moment that the tension in her Christian Science family arose not from the actions of the parent but from the disobedience of the children. She was also asserting in this *Journal*

---

these relationships. Some of the psychoanalytic material I have found most useful is Roy Schafer, "Ideals, the Ego Ideal, and the Ideal Self," in Robert R. Holt, ed., *Motives and Thought: Psychoanalytic Essays in Memory of David Rapaport, Psychological Issues*, Monograph 18/19 (New York: International Universities Press, 1967), pp. 131–74; Joseph Sandler, Alex Holder, and Dale Meers, "Ego Ideal and Ideal Self," in Joseph Sandler, ed., *From Safety to Superego: Selected Papers of Joseph Sandler* (New York: Guilford Press, 1987), pp. 73–89; Walter G. Joffe and Joseph Sandler, "On Disorders of Narcissism," ibid., pp. 180–90; Helen H. Tartakoff, "The Normal Personality in Our Culture and the Nobel Prize Complex," in Rudolph M. Loewenstein, ed., *Psychoanalysis—A General Psychology: Essays in Honor of Heinz Hartmann* (New York: International Universities Press, 1966), pp. 222–49; Peter Blos, "The Genealogy of the Ego Ideal," in his *The Adolescent Passage: Developmental Issues* (New York: International Universities Press, 1979), pp. 319–69; Arnold Rothstein, *The Narcissistic Pursuit of Perfection* (New York: International Universities Press, 1980); Annie Reich, "Pathologic Forms of Self-Esteem Regulation," in *Annie Reich: Psychoanalytic Contributions* (New York: International Universities Press, 1973), pp. 288–311. Finally, see the strong collection of essays in Arnold P. Morrison, ed., *Essential Papers on Narcissism* (New York: New York University Press, 1986).

article that her authority as mother was derived from her spiritual qualities and not from her personal characteristics. Her children still had much to learn. Spiritually, there was a wide generation gap between this mother and her offspring. Her momentous healing experience might have left Mrs. Eddy feeling like a small child before the loving allness of God. While she stood ready to obey God as a young child would obey a loving parent, this experience also elevated her in the eyes of her followers. Mrs. Eddy was not just any religious leader. She embodied the highest spiritual ideals. In their own faltering ways, her students aspired to reach the heights she had already climbed, and it looked sometimes as if Mrs. Eddy, the ideal they wished to emulate, had already been to the mountaintop while they were on their first leg of the trek up the steep slope.

Among Mrs. Eddy's followers, Julia Field-King knew well what this gap was and just how difficult it was to reach the heights, to measure up to the ideal. In the summer of 1889, feeling stressed by a number of troubling issues, she wrote to Mrs. Eddy seeking understanding and comfort. She looked to Mrs. Eddy not as one who had replaced the Father in heaven, but as one who had been appointed by God to be their "divinely Commissioned Mother." Several years later, when Mrs. Eddy asked her to edit *The Christian Science Journal*, Mrs. Field-King had doubts that she could do the job. As she put it, she was on the lowest rung of the spiritual ladder; Mrs. Eddy stood on the highest. Indeed, Mrs. Eddy seemed so elevated and so far removed from Field-King's position that it must have seemed to her that she was looking at her leader through the wrong end of the binoculars.[2]

Mrs. Eddy had occasion to remind her students of the gap between them. To one student she wrote that only God could understand why she had to scold her students. They were, after all, mere children when it came to understanding spiritual truth. The older they got, the more they grew spiritually, the more she as their mother found reason to love them and to scold them severely for their errors. While each new endeavor was a step in spiritual growth for the student, it was an old and tried effort for her, and she knew exactly how it would all end.[3]

As much as Mrs. Eddy may have wished to have her students see her in a homogeneous, spiritual way—she was a vessel of God; He spoke through her; her students could gain direct access to His Truth through her teachings and writings—she had actually created something more diverse. Not only had she established a spiritual and psychological space for herself in Christian Science, but she was also beginning to create a special niche in the culture for herself and her followers. To borrow Winnicott's term one more time, she became for her students a transitional object. In this sense, just as one could never argue that all children who invest their teddy bears and blankets with special significance relate to the objects in exactly the same way, one cannot argue that Mrs. Eddy's followers related to her in exactly the same way. People were attracted to Christian Science for many reasons; Mrs. Eddy had unknowingly provided multiple ways for her students to identify with her and multiple ways for them to use Christian Science.[4]

Mary Collson's decision to become a Christian Scientist is a case in point. From Chapter 8 we remember her frightful experiences with malicious animal magnetism. Before coming to Christian Science, Collson was a woman of considerable intellectual strengths, but as her sympathetic biographer, Cynthia Grant Tucker, reveals, she had difficulty overcoming an emotionally distant father and a series of childhood illnesses. The Unitarian Church played a key role in Collson's life; it helped to shape her intellectual interests, and it fostered her inchoate feminism. After attending Iowa State University and Meadville Theological Seminary, Collson became a Unitarian minister in Iowa.

Collson's external accomplishments, however, masked a fragile sense of self-worth, and eventually the strains of being a female minister in a male world took their toll. She suffered a breakdown. When she recovered, she went to Chicago, where she joined the staff of Jane Addams's Hull House as a juvenile probation officer. It was one thing for an idealistic young reformer to see the horrible effects of poverty in a Jacob Riis photograph; it was another to walk slum streets and witness the devastating effects of poverty on lower-class families. The stress of this job led to another emotional breakdown; this time Collson sought out a Christian Science practitioner.

The need for physical and mental health was clearly an overriding reason for Collson's decision to become a Christian Scientist, but it was far from the sole reason. In many respects she saw in Christian Science what she wanted to see; she was drawn to it for a number of reasons that would have raised Mrs. Eddy's eyebrows. As a girl Collson had been attracted to Emersonian transcendentalism; she thought she recognized this same idealism and mystical strain in Christian Science doctrines. Moreover, her strong attachment to a church, to her feminism, and to her reform impulse made an activist church led by a woman very appealing. Finally, Collson's practical side was drawn to the scientific bent in Christian Science, with its promise of healing and of bringing order to a world that was increasingly unmanageable. Whether Mary Collson understood Mrs. Eddy and Christian Science correctly is beside the point. Her decision to embrace Christian Science and eventually become a practitioner was based on a tangled skein of motives.[5]

Janet Coleman, who had a successful career as a teacher and practitioner and who was asked to help organize the First Church of Christ, Scientist in 1892, attended the Chicago Convention in 1888 and heard Mrs. Eddy deliver two addresses. On the first day Mrs. Eddy spoke to a gathering of her students. The confidence of her manner and the conviction of her words gave Coleman the impression of inordinate power; indeed, Mrs. Eddy seemed "more like a man." The next day Mrs. Eddy addressed a wider audience; many were moved and even healed. On this occasion, and in her role as a strong but compassionate healer, Mrs. Eddy came across as gentler, and nurturing, "more . . . [like] a woman."[6]

Coleman was not the only student to observe these qualities. Septimus Hanna, whom we will meet shortly, said that in the course of a single interview with Mrs. Eddy, she had the ability to change her demeanor many times. When talking about current events or everyday happenings, Mrs. Eddy appeared "youthful and sprightly almost to girlishness." This engaging feminine side, however, faded the moment she began to discourse on Christian Science or religious topics. At such times her words carried a spiritual weight, a masculine assertiveness; there was nothing feminine about Mrs. Eddy's eyes or countenance; her eyes seemed to grow larger and darker as she became enraptured by what she was saying. Hanna marveled at the way in which her moods seemed to change her very being.[7]

Mrs. Eddy's students were able to identify with her by drawing on these gender-related qualities in varying ways. John Salchow, for one, identified more fully with Mrs. Eddy's maternal side. He fondly recalled that she was "more tender and compassionate" than a natural mother could have been. From her spiritual sense of mother love she had frequently given him revelations of truth and wisdom that had changed his life for the better. Salchow, who was Mrs. Eddy's devoted handyman at Pleasant View for a decade, thus used Mrs. Eddy as both a moral guide and a nurturing figure to carve a small niche for himself in the Christian Science movement.[8]

Other followers found these qualities in Mrs. Eddy, and something more. Her sense of mission—her healing and calling after her fall on the ice—infused her life with a sense of integrity and purpose that had simply not been there earlier. Some followers were attracted to this tough-minded, assertive side. She in turn had a place for them in her movement, because she needed equally dedicated people to carry her message to the wider world. For some competent, ambitious students who were willing to stay within her strict spiritual guidelines, Mrs. Eddy gave the opportunity to exercise authority. As critical as Georgine Milmine was of Mrs. Eddy, she recognized that one of the strongest parts

of Mrs. Eddy's leadership was her ability to draw out the best in many
of her students. Some of these students, Milmine said, "never worked
so well after they withdrew from her compelling leadership, and their
contact with her remained the most vivid and important event in their
lives. Out of her abundant energy and determination," she was able to
"steel many an irresolute will."⁹

Oconto, Wisconsin, was far from the hub of Boston and the center
of Christian Science, but the long arm of Mrs. Eddy's religion reached
out to Laura Sargent. She was healed in 1883 by a friend; shortly thereafter she purchased a copy of *Science and Health* and in 1884 attended
the only class Mrs. Eddy ever taught in Chicago. Sargent's letters to
Mrs. Eddy reveal a fervent yet solidly practical student. She praised Mrs.
Eddy, but she never became gushy or sentimental; most of her letters
have a down-to-earth quality. Sargent showed an inner toughness; she
knew what it was like to be a Christian Science pioneer. In early 1885,
she and a few others were trying to establish a Christian Science church
in Oconto. The local press and ministers greeted them with hostile attacks. Emotionally battered but undaunted, Sargent wrote to Mrs. Eddy
that she and the other students were starting to appreciate what it meant
to suffer for Christ's truth.¹⁰

If one of the central purposes of founding *The Christian Science
Journal* was to spread the practical truth of Christian Science to a wider
audience, Sargent told Mrs. Eddy that it also had a profound effect
within the movement. Isolated as they were from other Christian Scientists, Sargent and the others in the Oconto area eagerly looked forward
to the delivery of the *Journal*, because it connected them to a wider
network of Scientists, supported their sense of community, and but-
tressed their faith. Sargent worked tirelessly for Christian Science and
wanted to make sure that whatever she did to foster its growth was in
accordance with Mrs. Eddy's plans. Sargent's initiative and obedience
did not go unrecognized or unappreciated. Mrs. Eddy wrote that Sargent's wonderful letters refreshed her.¹¹

In the spring of 1886 Mrs. Eddy made her first real demand upon
Sargent; her talents were needed in St. Paul, Minnesota. Sargent faced
a predicament that many women confront today: what about her husband? Understandably, Sargent was afraid to broach the subject with
him. Nevertheless, she felt so strongly about her Christian Science faith,
and felt so empowered by her work, that if, as she anticipated, her
husband disapproved of her temporary move, she was determined to
defy him. On a Sunday, as she was trying to screw up her courage to
tell him, Sargent opened her Bible and her eyes fell on Luke 5:4, in
which Jesus said to Simon: "Launch out into the deep, and let down

your nets for a draught." Sargent went immediately to her husband and informed him of her intention to go to St. Paul.[12]

Much to her surprise, her husband gave his blessing; she did good work in St. Paul, and when it was finished she returned home. Within four years Sargent's unflagging work in the field, her skill, and her unflinching devotion to Mrs. Eddy's principles raised her high in her leader's estimation; by 1888 Mrs. Eddy asked Sargent to come to Boston. She promised Sargent that she would grow spiritually in her home, and, not incidentally, as a companion Sargent would be a tremendous comfort. As we shall see in the final chapter, the outside world saw Mrs. Eddy through a distorted, stereotypical lens: she was a petty tyrant, an authoritarian religious leader whose students were her spiritual slaves. If this was true, somebody forgot to tell Laura Sargent. She did not take Mrs. Eddy's request for her presence in Boston as a command; she felt free to say no. Mrs. Eddy wrote that she would wait; she knew that God would send Sargent to her when it was time.[13]

The time came two years later, and from 1890 until Mrs. Eddy's last days in 1910, Sargent was with her often. Writing Sargent's sister, Victoria, from Concord, New Hampshire, in 1891, Mrs. Eddy waxed ecstatic about Laura's joining her. She was deeply indebted to Laura's husband for allowing her to come to Concord and only wished Laura could stay with her permanently. She praised Laura to the skies; no one could have been kinder or more loving, and no one could have been more grateful than Mrs. Eddy, who had felt the pangs of loneliness without a female companion. In her long, loving service to her leader, Laura Sargent was asked to stretch herself, to take on new duties even though she might lack experience. On one occasion Mrs. Eddy asked Sargent to do the household bookkeeping. Sargent demurred, offering the excuse that she had never done this before. Mrs. Eddy quickly rebutted that God wore many hats, and one of them was a businessman's. He ran the universe as efficiently as the sharpest of businessmen, and, she reminded Sargent, she reflected this aspect of God. In short, Mrs. Eddy was asking Sargent to trust God; He would make her more competent than she ever realized. Thus encouraged, Sargent successfully balanced the household books.[14]

In this instance and many others, Sargent learned to trust Mrs. Eddy's spiritual wisdom. Her demands might at first seem excessive; her rebukes might sometimes drive Sargent to tears, but Sargent learned that they led to spiritual growth and increased competence. Moreover, Sargent learned to put her trials and tribulations into their proper perspective. As she wrote to another student, Mrs. Eddy's natural position as their leader demanded respect and gratitude. No matter how much a student might have felt he or she had sacrificed in the name of the cause, it never approached what Mrs. Eddy had sacrificed and endured for them and mankind.[15]

Laura Lathrop also came from the Midwest, and after being healed in 1885, she went to Boston, where she had several classes with Mrs. Eddy. Lathrop was then sent by Mrs. Eddy to New York City, becoming an early worker in that busy, competitive field. She worked and practiced there for twenty-six years, helping to establish the First Church of Christ, Scientist, and then the Second Church of Christ, Scientist. When the Board of Education was established in 1899, Lathrop became one of its officers.

By this criterion, Lathrop was a Christian Science success story, a model for other women. But this brief list of accomplishments does not begin to capture how radically Lathrop was changed once she embraced Christian Science. When she went to Chicago to be healed in 1885, she was passive, dependent, and weak. For much of the past twenty years she had been an invalid. In the fall of 1884, she had written Mrs. Eddy a sad letter telling her that in August her husband had suddenly died, leaving her with fifteen dollars and two young children. With remarkable frankness, Lathrop said that at forty-one she had been suffering from a host of ailments ranging from menopausal symptoms to mental exhaustion.[16]

These changes and setbacks, her recurring invalidism, and her duties as a wife and mother deprived Lathrop of a secret lifelong dream. She had always entertained the fantasy of becoming a renowned conversationalist, something along the lines of Madame de Staël. But this ambition never became a reality until she turned to Christian Science. As it turned out, Lathrop's healing not only restored her health but also allowed her to express her active, assertive side by channeling it into her spiritual work.[17]

Restored in body and spirit, Lathrop threw herself into her New York work. It was exhausting. In the early spring of 1887, Lathrop responded to a letter in which she felt Mrs. Eddy was criticizing her for not doing more to advance Christian Science. Part of the problem stemmed from Lathrop's feeling inadequate to the challenge. Mrs. Eddy had asked her to establish a Christian Science Institute in New York, but Lathrop had reminded her in an 1886 letter that until Lathrop had come into Christian Science, she had been virtually helpless, barely able to do the shopping for her family, and completely without business sense.[18]

Laura Sargent could have told Laura Lathrop a thing or two about this kind of excuse. Mrs. Eddy refused to accept it, keeping after Lathrop to accept this responsibility. In a reply to Mrs. Eddy's proddings, Lathrop said that she knew that she must be a disappointment to Mrs. Eddy because she had not yet established a Bible class or organized an Association, and taught comparatively few students. But, Lathrop protested, she hardly had any breathing room in her daily schedule. She began treating patients at 8:15 in the morning, usually giving about twenty treatments before she had to be at the church. Then she grabbed a quick lunch, barely taking the time to digest it before hurrying off to see bedridden or "partially helpless" people scattered across the city. When she finally got back to her office, she saw half a dozen or more patients before supper at 6:30. By that hour, she was on the verge of exhaustion and welcomed even a moment's rest.[19]

There were few moments of rest for Lathrop in New York. Augusta Stetson, a powerful and beguiling Christian Science teacher, kept the Christian Science pot boiling in the city, and Lathrop could not keep herself out of the hot water. We will encounter Mrs. Stetson in Chapter 12; it is enough to note here that Lathrop did not come out of these frays unscathed. She had her trying moments in the late 1880s, which merited her share of dressings-down from Mrs. Eddy. But she accepted them. In the summer of 1901, after receiving a strong scolding, Lathrop wrote Mrs. Eddy expressing herself in words reminiscent of young Mary Baker's to her mother: if Lathrop had been doing her job properly, Mrs. Eddy would not have been forced to remind her what her duties were. Lathrop asked for Mrs. Eddy's forgiveness; she knew that she was slow to open her eyes to Truth. If Mrs. Eddy only knew how gladly Lathrop accepted her rebukes, she would reprove her more often. Mrs. Eddy had done everything for her a mother could, and the thanks Lathrop gave her was to let her loving mother down. Lathrop's heart ached for Mrs. Eddy when she thought that she was not living up to her standards.[20]

By the late 1890s, Lathrop had matured in her role as a Christian Science leader. Her letters to Mrs. Eddy are more self-assured and less conflicted. In June 1898, she wrote Mrs. Eddy about the church she was building in New York. When we remember the frail, sickly woman who came to Christian Science unable to balance a checkbook, this letter is truly remarkable. Could this be the same Laura Lathrop? She sounds like an astute businesswoman, telling Mrs. Eddy how the plot of ground has been measured, how much money she has already raised, how she will allocate the funds, and how much debt she will be carrying. Many years later, Lathrop discovered some letters dealing with the building of the Second Church. Lathrop reread them and then wrote to Mrs. Eddy, expressing her gratitude for her guidance and direction. No mother was as firm yet gentle in guiding the unsteady feet of her small child, who was just learning to take her first tentative steps.[21]

Lathrop eventually demonstrated a confidence and initiative that Mrs. Eddy wished her other students had. In the fall of 1897, Lathrop wrote to Mrs. Eddy informing her that in the summer she and her son, John, had been conducting church services. No other student had yet done this; moreover, Lathrop had not received Mrs. Eddy's prior approval. Lathrop knew that this was grounds for rebuke, but it was not forthcoming. Instead, Mrs. Eddy praised her. By holding church services through the summer, Lathrop had set a fine example for other Christian Science students. Mrs. Eddy thought services should be established in all the other churches, but she did not want this change to come through her dictum. She would have preferred her other students to do as Lathrop had done: listen to the voice of God and be governed by it.[22]

Lathrop shared more than church business with Mrs. Eddy. In times of personal crisis, she could turn to her as a mother, as a womanly figure who understood the pain in another woman's heart. In 1899 she needed to lean on Mrs. Eddy for emotional strength because of her daughter's marital problems. In September of that year Mrs. Eddy wrote Lathrop a letter that was apparently addressed to this trying issue. Mrs. Eddy reminded Lathrop that she had more suffering in her life than Lathrop could imagine. If Lathrop could feel, even for a moment, how alone and desolate Mrs. Eddy was in this harsh wilderness of a world, or how many trials she endured, then Lathrop might not feel as bad as she did. Anyway, Mrs. Eddy would never think of asking Lathrop or any other student to bear such burdens. And she and Lathrop had something to be thankful for: John, Lathrop's son and Mrs. Eddy's beloved disciple.[23]

John Carroll Lathrop was the apple of two mothers' eyes. In 1886 he went to New York with his mother; nine years later he joined the Mother Church. After taking a Primary Class with his mother, he became a Christian Science practitioner in 1896; two years later he took a class from Mrs. Eddy. John was a strong right arm for his mother, and it is evident that he deeply impressed Mrs. Eddy. In December 1898, she wrote John and his mother a letter praising their efforts, and said to Laura that she should feel blessed to have a son like John and to know that God had rewarded her for being such a good mother.[24]

Two days later Laura Lathrop responded to this letter with one full of motherly pride. What Mrs. Eddy glimpsed in John briefly in her class, Lathrop saw every day in his work in New York, and she was more than willing to extol his virtues to Mrs. Eddy. Everything he did was exemplary. He was wise beyond his years and had a wonderful ability to work with people. In every way, Lathrop wrote, he was Mother Eddy's son, but Lathrop would like to hang on to him just a little longer. She needed John to stay with her until the Second Church was built, paid for, and dedicated, but after that she was willing to send him to Pleasant View. His rightful place was by Mrs. Eddy's side; he was made to do God's work. Years ago she had seen the Christ-spirit manifested in Mother Eddy, just as she had seen it in John. Laura was willing to make the ultimate maternal sacrifice: to give up her son to the woman and the religion she loved.[25]

Mrs. Eddy's call would come five years later, in 1903, when she asked John to join her staff at Pleasant View. Intermittently over five years, he served her faithfully, sometimes as her corresponding secretary. What Laura Lathrop was willing to surrender to Mrs. Eddy in theory was harder to do in fact, and not in the ways one might expect. We can all understand how difficult it might be for a mother to surrender her son to another woman; indeed, Mrs. Eddy had had this painful experience in her own life with her son, George. But this is not what bothered Lathrop, for she sincerely meant it when she professed to see the religious significance in Mrs. Eddy's call. What Lathrop was not prepared for was the jealousy aroused in her when she thought that John was closer to Mother Eddy than she was.

In June 1903, she confessed in a letter to Mrs. Eddy that she was hurt that she had never been called to serve at Pleasant View, while her son had. She even entertained the thought that Mother Eddy did not love her, at least not as much as she loved John and some of the other students. Lathrop placed the blame on herself. Something in her must have prevented her from being invited by Mrs. Eddy. In a moment of honest self-appraisal, Lathrop said that on an unconscious level, she had undoubtedly resented the fact that she had not been called to Mrs. Eddy's side, whereas John, a relative neophyte, had. It was now evident to Lathrop that it was not Mrs. Eddy who had kept her away from Pleasant View, but rather her own festering jealousy and hurt feelings. Mrs. Eddy had always loved Lathrop, but Lathrop had not unequivocally loved her, though she'd thought she had. It was evident to Lathrop that she should have trusted Mrs. Eddy more fully, and that unconsciously she was separating herself from John. By the time Lathrop concluded this letter, she had reconciled herself to John's move and reaffirmed her love for Mrs. Eddy.[26]

Other Christian Science students gained as much autonomy as Laura Lathrop exercised. When Septimus J. Hanna and his wife, Camilla, immediately captured Mrs. Eddy's respect, she opened doors for them which they gladly walked through. Septimus Hanna had come to Christian Science after seeing it restore his wife's health. After four years of investigating its doctrines, Hanna gave up his law career for one in Christian Science. His good work in the field did not escape Mrs. Eddy's eye. Once she decided to remove Julia Field-King as editor of the *Journal*, Hanna was the logical replacement. Supported by Camilla, who was an assistant editor, he did a good job of keeping his ambition within Mrs. Eddy's close guidelines. Mrs. Eddy, as one can well imagine, was grateful for his professional expertise, and she was unstinting in her praise of his steady, devoted work in Christian Science.[27]

Though Hanna exercised his judgment and initiative as the *Journal*'s editor, he tried not to lose sight of his proper role in Mrs. Eddy's army. He was a subaltern and fully expected to obey her orders implicitly. All the members of this spiritual army were under divine orders, and as the general, Mrs. Eddy was their interpreter. All Hanna needed was "to discern her wish to know what my orders are." Hanna was never more discerning than in the April and May 1894 issues of the *Journal*, in which he published an article interpreting the Ten Commandments from a Christian Science perspective. Hanna was a devout student of the Bible, but he knew that a theological article like this had to be submitted to Mrs. Eddy for her approval before it was published. As it turned out, Hanna could not have been more in tune with Mrs. Eddy's thoughts on this subject than if he had copied one of her articles word for word.

Mrs. Eddy praised his article, calling it an excellent piece of writing. Four years previously, she had marked the verses of the Sermon on the Mount and how they corresponded to the Ten Commandments. She had shared this interpretation with another student, but she had never gotten around to shaping her ideas for publication. Hanna had captured her precise meaning, and she was thankful that he had saved her the trouble of writing it herself.

For his outstanding work as editor, Hanna was rewarded in 1894 by being named pastor of the Mother Church. Naturally, he had some hesitations about holding two important, time-consuming jobs simultaneously. In March of that year, Mrs. Eddy wrote him a supportive letter that both prodded him and encouraged him to believe that he had more ability than he realized. She agreed that these two jobs held in one hand made a big responsibility. But she had faith in him. More important, God's goodness and power would be his safeguard. "The physical question is overcome the same as the moral," she exhorted. "*Your strength* is omnipotence." Now it was up to him to shore up his strength in Christian Science, to know without hesitation what he believed in, and to comprehend the meaning of spiritual "omnipotence" as fully as he could. If he did this, he would be invulnerable.[28]

Over his long service to Mrs. Eddy and Christian Science, Hanna would find that it was not so easy to follow explicit orders and to keep his personal sense out of things. Mrs. Eddy's stinging reprimands hurt.

In the end, however, they did not devastate him, for if at first he could not see her love behind them, in time he did.

Equally devoted to Mrs. Eddy, Camilla Hanna was a sensitive reader of Mrs. Eddy's spirituality. When Mrs. Eddy was seeking direction and guidance from God, her genuine humility and selflessness were evident. Over the years, God's messages to their leader at times proved downright frustrating to some of her followers when she, after listening to God's counsel, shifted course. Rather than allow personal frustration to get in the way, Camilla Hanna believed that Mrs. Eddy's decisions were based on a higher authority. She and others had witnessed Mrs. Eddy's tacking back and forth, seeking the right wind while all the while listening to God's voice guiding her. Mrs. Eddy was "groping to find her way," said Camilla, much as she had done in the past in order to convey higher spiritual truths to her students. And with breathless admiration Camilla noted that when God's answer came to Mrs. Eddy, she spoke with firmness and resolution; nothing could alter her opinion.

Camilla also saw Mrs. Eddy's suffering in religious terms. Her mental and bodily suffering were not the signs of weakness and did not undermine the truth of her Christian Science teachings. To the contrary, Mrs. Eddy's suffering was spiritual in nature and ultimately led to higher truths. Not only that, her suffering was not long-lasting; it was sharp but temporary and could be the prelude to action. Camilla told a story about the laying of the cornerstone for the Mother Church in May 1894. Much difficulty had attended the making of this momentous event, so for Camilla it was a moment of quiet pride and celebration. They were late in getting the *Journal* out; an article of Mrs. Eddy's needed to be added, so Camilla traveled to Pleasant View. As she stepped into the library, she took Mrs. Eddy's hand and exclaimed joyously that the cornerstone had been laid that day. Mrs. Eddy acknowledged it, but instead of looking pleased at this important step in her church's growth, she looked as if the stone had been placed on her shoulders, as if she were carrying the weight of the world. Circles ringed her eyes; they looked drawn and black. She looked bent, weakened to the point of breaking. Camilla quietly told Mrs. Eddy why she was there. Mrs. Eddy replied that she was too weary to read the article, and asked Camilla to read it to her.

As Camilla read, Mrs. Eddy listened raptly and commented that it was wonderful, almost as if she had never heard it before. Camilla agreed and went so far to say that it was one of the best things Mrs. Eddy had ever written. Mrs. Eddy's reply was a quick and assertive "No"; *Science and Health* was the most wonderful work she had ever written. She sprang to her feet and beckoned Camilla upstairs, where she had something even better than the article. All evidence of weariness was gone; she was sprightly and alert. Apparently her statement about *Science and Health* had triggered the association to her recent writing, and that had restored her vitality. During their long association with Mrs. Eddy, the Hannas witnessed this kind of suffering and recovery many times. Seemingly mired in weariness, Mrs. Eddy would be struck by "the flash recognition of Truth" and would be immediately restored.[29]

In her correspondence with the Hannas, we do not hear Mrs. Eddy becoming engaged in the emotionally destructive conflicts that, as we shall see, characterized her relationships with other strong students. While she may have had occasion to scold the Hannas for their lapses, she also praised and encouraged them. In one troubled moment, she told them that they had the inner strength to overcome the problem. The turmoil of the world tended to enervate the good Christian Science worker, but she knew that the Hannas were true spiritual workers who did not weary.[30]

Caroline Noyes came to Christian Science in the early 1880s, attending Mrs. Eddy's Primary Class in 1884 and her Normal Class the following year. In Chicago, Noyes helped set up the Illinois Christian Science Institute, and she played a part in establishing the first Christian Science Church in Chicago. Her relationship with Mrs. Eddy remained relatively tranquil over many years. She had no inkling in the beginning what a difficult task it would be to walk the narrow spiritual path Mrs. Eddy had set out for her students.

Noyes's career illustrates that establishing a sense of autonomy did not come easily. A steady, continuing introspection, a constant self-monitoring; these were essential for spiritual growth, even for the best of Mrs. Eddy's students. And, as we have noted, this was something Mrs. Eddy always encouraged.[31]

A July 1887 letter to Mrs. Eddy depicts Noyes in the throes of deep introspection; ever since Christmas she had been wrestling with herself to control personal ambition. For many of Mrs. Eddy's promising students, as we have seen, this was an occupational hazard. In effecting a spiritual cure or in becoming an instructor, it was sometimes hard to remember that one was reflecting God's Truth. It was often tempting instead to think that one's own charms, empathy, or power made one an effective healer and teacher. Noyes, to her dismay, found it nearly impossible to resist this temptation. While she ardently desired to place Truth and the welfare of others ahead of her own needs, she sensed that while her conscious motives had been above reproach, she had also been "pursuing something of a selfish purpose unconsciously." Knowing that she was sinning, she realized that she had to change. In words that must have been a joy to Mrs. Eddy in the troubled days of 1887, Noyes concluded that if any student allowed personal ambition to creep into his or her work, then the work was automatically corrupted. Whatever it was, it was not Christian Science. If anything, it was probably will-power or mind cure.[32]

Noyes's periods of critical self-examination did not end in 1887. In early 1891, she informed Mrs. Eddy that even the "perfect letter of Christian Science," as it found expression in *Science and Health* and the Bible, could be twisted by a person's conscious and subconscious wishes and feelings. When this happened, Mrs. Eddy's message was perverted and dissension was fostered in the movement. Noyes thus felt compelled to demonstrate her real fear that she might be practicing the letter of Christian Science instead of its spirit. Throughout her correspondence with Mrs. Eddy, Noyes's letters indicate that some weeks were better than others as she strove to improve herself spiritually. She was deter-mined, however, not to let setbacks deter her progress in Christian Science.[33]

Her determination aside, like all other Christian Science students and teachers, Noyes was not immune to the malefic power of malicious animal magnetism. In September 1893 she wrote Mrs. Eddy a letter detailing her fight against it. She knew that malicious animal magne-tism might be everywhere. It potentially lay in every act, even the best-intentioned ones. One could not deny that malicious animal magnetism and personal ambition went hand in glove. In the early 1890s, Noyes wrote to Mrs. Eddy that she could not honestly tell herself that she was free from any pride or ambition to preach. She well knew that if any Christian Scientist assumed the pulpit for self-centered reasons, then malicious animal magnetism would be filling the position instead of the true Christian Science spirit. A year later Noyes was still absorbed in the same struggles. In a June 1894 letter she confessed to Mrs. Eddy that she had been trying to master her self-aggrandizing impulses for the past three years, and she had been fairly successful in thwarting the lure of power and popularity. In this same letter she added that she had been just as successful in working against the "claim of sensuality for four or five years."[34]

Noyes seemed to have the knack of saying the right thing at the right time to Mrs. Eddy. Whenever she was chastised, she took it in the right spirit, even thanking Mrs. Eddy for setting her and her husband on the right path. After some fourteen to fifteen years' service, Noyes wanted Mrs. Eddy to know that she appreciated what Mrs. Eddy's writings and instructions had done for her and her husband. Both of them knew that Mrs. Eddy's work reflected God; Noyes had learned to accept her leader's spiritual authority, never to question her directives no matter how difficult they might be to understand. God's ways were not always scrutable at first, either. In fact, if Christ spoke from "the Father God," then Mrs. Eddy spoke from "the Mother God which is Divine Love." In some ways, Noyes thought, Mrs. Eddy's work was like Jesus', but in another way it was greater because it came at a later age and fulfilled His teachings and promises.[35]

Caroline's praise in this letter was honest and direct, and her thoughts about malicious animal magnetism and personal ambition were not calculating; she was not telling Mrs. Eddy what she thought she wanted to hear. Her concerns over these issues arose from the conflicts she and her husband encountered in Chicago. This bustling Midwestern city was important to the growth of Christian Science, but it was wracked by competition and strife between those who remained loyal to Mrs. Eddy and those who had parted company with her. Some of Mrs. Eddy's former students were stirring up their own gusts in the Windy City. Joseph Adams, after washing out of the movement, established a monthly called *The Chicago Christian Scientist* in June 1887. Emma Hopkins had started her own College of Christian Science in Chicago, and Mary Plunkett, another apostate, was busy setting up institutions in the Midwest. One other student, Ursula Gestefeld, quickly went off the track in Chicago and even became a member of the Theosophical Society. By 1888 she had published a book that explained her own version of Christian Science.

Caroline Noyes not only had to contend with some of these outsiders and pretenders, but had to deal with some of Mrs. Eddy's other loyal students. She got caught up in the jealousies over who was teaching whom and who had the most students. As she once admitted, she worked well against foes of the Church, but when her foes worked through her so-called friends to attack her, then her "worst difficulties" manifested themselves because it was hard to distinguish true friends from dissemblers.[36]

Rumors of Noyes's personal ambition filtered back to Mrs. Eddy; when Noyes got wind of this gossip, she was deeply distressed. Some of the whisperings against her no doubt stemmed from her run-ins (which are not clearly spelled out in the correspondence) with George Day. Day had once been a voice to reckon with in Chicago, but by the early 1890s his faith in Christian Science was wavering badly. He eventually broke with the movement, but not before causing great consternation among Mrs. Eddy's loyal followers. To Noyes all the rumors about her so-called ambition stemmed from "the Day affair" and were the result of malicious animal magnetism.[37]

Noyes went out of her way to impress Mrs. Eddy with this last point because she knew that over the previous year gossip and backbiting—two strategies of malicious animal magnetism—had cast her in the worst possible light in Mrs. Eddy's eyes. She had been told that Mrs. Eddy no longer trusted or approved of her. With such malevolence at work clearly trying to separate her from her mother, Noyes knew precisely where her hope and salvation lay: in the understanding and recognition that Mrs. Eddy was "the Daughter of God as Christ" who had come again in bodily form in order to reveal the "Motherhood of God" and to offer the hope of restoring man's complete, spiritual self. At this point in the letter, Noyes stepped back, perhaps a bit winded, and said that she was not quite sure why she was writing to Mrs. Eddy that morning except that she yearned to be standing on firm spiritual ground with the one who most completely reflected God in this world.[38]

Although this praise of Mrs. Eddy may sound cloying, it was as excessive as Noyes got in her long correspondence with her mentor. In the context of her other letters, Noyes's praise was sincere, and Mrs. Eddy recognized it as such. Mrs. Eddy never became as intensely involved with Noyes as she did with some of her other students, for Noyes engaged her on a more neutral level, and the letters from Mrs. Eddy reflect this neutrality. Mrs. Eddy rebuked her, but not devastatingly. She also praised her for her good work. In March 1887, she thanked Noyes for her expressions of "Christian sympathy," and in another instance she praised her for sagacious words, duly noted her "kind intentions," and assured her that she was more spiritually advanced than many other students.[39]

Alfred Farlow was another student who grew in stature in the movement. In 1886 he had written Mrs. Eddy of his express desire to study under her, and a year later he told her that Christian Science had completely transformed his life. In important ways it had. Farlow was born on a farm in Knoxville, Illinois, the oldest of eight children. He had had to work to help support the family. According to Mary Collson, one of his students, he told her that he had once hoped to be a lawyer, but the family's lack of money made that impossible. "But for Christian Science," he admitted, "my life would have been a flat failure."[40]

Within Christian Science, Farlow was not a failure; his wishes to be competent and autonomous were largely fulfilled. In 1887 Mrs. Eddy wrote to him affectionately that if he was hungry for the truth, then he should "come to the Mother nest and let me feed you." Unlike some of the other students whom we shall meet, Farlow never seemed to become personally entangled in this spiritual metaphor, and by keeping it on a spiritual plane, he could stay focused on his job. He did yeoman's work while he tilled the spiritual fields of Kansas City. While there in 1893, he wrote to Mrs. Eddy that God had blessed him with the ability to explain Christian Science truth clearly to new students. Farlow did show an ability to straddle the two spheres—Christian Science and the outside world—and make Mrs. Eddy's doctrines understandable to outsiders. This was no mean achievement.[41]

Today if one reads the 1890s *Christian Science Journal*, the words begin to blur as the dogma becomes tedious. With luck a reader will come across one of Farlow's essays or speeches. In an 1898 lecture delivered in Kansas City, Farlow creatively used simile, metaphor, and symbol to convey Mrs. Eddy's ideas in tightly woven arguments. His felicitous touch transformed abstruse Christian Science metaphysics into understandable concepts for the uninformed reader.

He must have been a good teacher, although Mary Collson would have hotly disagreed with this assessment. Despite Christian Science's many strengths and its appeal to "the hungry and needy ones," Farlow knew that they felt guilty when they so much as thought of forsaking the religion of their ancestors, much as a child in grade school might develop a crush on his teacher and not want to leave her at the end of the term. Yet to grow and mature, the student had to move on, no matter how sad or painful the progress to the next level.

Farlow recognized that a number of timid students feared growth and change because anger got mixed in with the sadness of separation. He tried to alleviate this anxiety by saying that the "venerable . . . and progressive" grandparents would have been among the first to embrace Christian Science. To cling to the church of one's childhood—the church of one's grandparents and parents—was tantamount to rejecting the wonders of electricity because the older generation had used pine knots or candles to light their houses. Once a person made the decision to leave the past of his childhood church for the future of Christian Science, he would not feel anxiety over the loss, because in his new church he would find the welcoming arms of a new and different kind of parent. Farlow said that Christian Scientists sought Mrs. Eddy's counsel much as a child sought the advice of his mother. Because of "her peculiar relationship to us" in their spiritual work, they had grown accustomed to calling her Mother.[42]

Farlow's talents as a teacher and defender of the faith did not escape Mrs. Eddy's notice, and she encouraged his growth. Early in 1899, she wrote him that "Mother wants you to come to her in Boston." She needed him and the cause needed him; indeed, he must hearken to his mother's call because he had established one of the best records in her more than thirty years' experience. In 1901 Mrs. Eddy wrote Farlow an engaging letter in which she borrowed metaphors from the culture's wider preoccupation with physical fitness and sports. While her brand of muscular Christianity may indicate that in old age she kept abreast of social developments as closely as she had when she pasted articles into her scrapbooks decades earlier, she did not employ this language very often, so it is a bit odd but refreshing to hear these terms coming from the silver-haired leader of the Christian Scientists.[43]

She told Farlow that although he had a way to go to conquer belief, spiritual exercise would make him that much stronger. Muscles, so the physiologists said, were strengthened by regular exercise; the muscles were like "mortal thoughts," and if Farlow trained his thoughts the way a boxer trained his body, he would be in spiritual shape to fend off the attacks on Christian Science. She urged Farlow to keep his spirits up. When she was attacked in print, he must respond with every bit of "the muscle and nerve of the Divine Mind." She, for that matter, needed a strong human hand to hold hers up, just as Moses had. And Farlow had done well in learning how to handle the press. When he learned to master malicious animal magnetism more effectively, he would be able to do even more on her behalf.[44]

If Alfred Farlow was a shining star in the Christian Science firmament, Edward Kimball was a blazing meteor. A prosperous manufacturer in Chicago, Kimball was associated with the First Church of Christ, Scientist, and in 1894 was elected its First Reader. He would also serve on the Board of Lectureship, and in 1899 he was one of the first teachers appointed to the Board of Education. Like Farlow, Kimball carried himself with a genuine Christian humility. In describing him, Bliss Knapp, whose parents were among the early students in the movement and who himself was a prominent figure in Christian Science, said that Kimball combined "a penetrating intellect with great kindliness." He had a keen power of analysis and argued with a forceful logic. In many ways Kimball combined the heart and the intellect to become a highly respected figure in the Christian Science movement.[45]

Kimball was drawn to Christian Science because of congestion, stomach distress, and a vaguely defined nervous disorder. After being introduced to Christian Science, and after reading *Science and Health*, Kimball yearned to study with Mrs. Eddy, which he did with his wife, Kate, in March 1888 (by 1899 he had taken two more classes with her). By 1890 he had retired from the business world to devote himself to Christian Science. Within a short time he established himself as the leading Christian Science figure in the city. Over the years Kimball would hold a number of positions of trust and importance in the movement. He was placed in charge of the Christian Science exhibit at the World's

Columbian Exposition in 1893. He was elected to the Board of Lectureship and delivered cogent lectures for more than nine years. In 1898 Mrs. Eddy had her copyrights transferred to Kimball; in 1899 he was designated the official teacher of the Christian Science Board of Education and conducted several classes in Boston. In 1901 Mrs. Eddy trusted him to represent her in all matters relating to the noisy and messy lawsuit with her former student, Josephine Curtis Woodbury.[46]

In the course of his long correspondence with Mrs. Eddy, Kimball was remarkably frank. He and Mrs. Eddy would not see eye to eye on every issue, but their disputes never became destructive. While Kimball might not always have intuited Mrs. Eddy's reasons for a course of action, he did understand her, and to the best of his ability he avoided the flare-ups that sometimes consumed her and other students. During the early to mid-1890s, Kimball's letters to Mrs. Eddy are filled with matters of church organization and what he and others might do to spread the cause. His notes and letters to Mrs. Eddy do not brim over with flattery; they do not try to draw her into emotional squabbles; they do not burden her with his woes.

What ambition Kimball had was kept well subordinated to the needs of Mrs. Eddy and the greater good of Christian Science. In late February 1893, for instance, he asked Mrs. Eddy whether he should begin teaching a formal class, and in the same breath, he voiced his doubts about the request. As he saw it, formal teaching was antithetical to the spirit of primitive Christianity that imbued Christian Science. Instead of bringing people together, the position of a teacher established artificial distinctions among a community of believers and led to "much mischief."[47]

Kimball did his best to steer clear of the power struggles that continually wracked the movement, but was unable to entirely avoid disputes with Mrs. Eddy. The 1893 World's Columbian Exposition would draw people to Chicago from all points of the compass. Mrs. Eddy had chosen not to attend, but her students would participate in four activities at the exposition: an exhibit of literature in the Publishers' Department; an exhibit of Mrs. Eddy's publications in the Woman's Department; a Christian Science "Congress," which was "an adjourned meeting" of the National Christian Scientist Association; and the World's Parliament of Religions.

In the early stages of the exposition, Mrs. Eddy was asked by one of her students what she thought of the whole event. She replied that it was "a political movement to consolidate and unify error." The way events would turn out, she should have obeyed her instincts. Initially it seemed as if her students had pulled off a coup in Chicago. The *Chicago Inter-Ocean* wrote a glowing report of a meeting of Scientists. A couple of days later, Septimus Hanna read an address by Mrs. Eddy to the Parliament of Religions. Mrs. Eddy had given a great deal of time to compiling from her previous writings the talk presented in her name. Kimball knew this, so he reassured her that Hanna's performance had been outstanding and had been favorably received. "In the warfare against false theology and demonology," they were now working from a stronger position, he wrote enthusiastically.[48]

This euphoria did not last long. In a letter to Mrs. Eddy, Hanna let her know that he, Foster Eddy, and Kimball had decided that the newspapers should have a copy of her speech. Along with the body of the speech they sent an addendum clarifying that the speech had been read by Hanna. The newspapers printed the speech as though it were Hanna's. How could such a mistake have been made? For Hanna the answer to this question was obvious: malicious animal magnetism had again thwarted the best efforts of Mrs. Eddy by trying to diminish her influence and prop up someone else in her place.[49]

Mrs. Eddy was far more disturbed over this glaring mistake than Hanna was. She may have understood that Kimball and Hanna were not using the Parliament as personal stepping-stones, but she was deeply distressed to see that Christian Science participation in the Parliament was marked by the kind of denominational pride and self-aggrandizement that undercut its Christian purposes. The handling of this talk was significant to her Church, and it had been botched. She therefore moved quickly to prevent her address from being published in the Parliament book.

Hanna and Kimball were dumbfounded. To them Mrs. Eddy seemed to be blowing a minor mistake totally out of proportion. Hanna, upset and angry, wrote her to this effect in a long letter in late September 1893, in which he said that if she had taken the time to cool down, she might not have requested the withdrawal of her speech from the book; nor, on reflection, would she have written a letter to the publishers throwing the whole responsibility for the mistake upon her students. She was, apparently, accusing her loyal students of seeking their own ends rather than serving hers. Hanna was stung by this "unjust and cruel" accusation, and he could not make himself believe that it came from Mrs. Eddy's lips. He and Kimball had done their best to carry out her instructions; to be castigated as "disobedient and over-ambitious" was unjust.[50]

Kimball was equally distressed. As Mrs. Eddy's complimentary letters abruptly changed to stinging remonstrances, Kimball replied with as much equanimity as he could muster. In a September 1893 letter, he tried to reason with her, politely telling Mrs. Eddy to calm down.[51]

Calm down? Take this mistake in stride? Not likely. Mrs. Eddy was outraged, and she let Kimball know it. Evidently Kimball had no idea what he was doing. Ever since the newspapers had taken "the heart of my works into their jaws" and devoured her true intent, an evil had been unleashed threatening the very foundation of the cause. Christian Science's enemies were now trying to confuse and mislead the public by having her speech, "that pearl," published in the Parliament book.[52]

Kimball replied to these verbal lashings. He was sorry that everything that he now said or did was "evidence of evil." From her state of mind it was clear that no matter what he said, it would only aggravate matters. Yet he thought she should know that no student of hers was more loyal or dedicated. She might be angry about the speech, but he knew that he had not acted out of selfish motives.[53]

A day later Kimball sent Mrs. Eddy another letter, addressing her charge that the enemy was working to get a distorted version of her address into the book. Kimball told her that all the uproar was simply not emotionally worth it to him, so he had given up his efforts to get the speech published. He assured her that with a bit more effort the Christian Scientist Association could do a better job of monitoring which writings of hers got into the press and which did not. He wished she would be more precise when she urged him to stop "the mental cyclone in Chicago" or be prepared to meet the consequences. He had already suffered enough in this ordeal, but he really had no idea what she meant. Most of the students were oblivious to the situation and seemed quite calm. He saw no external signs of any commotion "among the out-siders."[54]

Kimball was in a predicament. He still loved and respected Mrs. Eddy, so he muted his anger and chose his words carefully. Indirectly, however, he was suggesting that Mrs. Eddy had overreacted. The "mental cyclone" was not in him, and it was not in Chicago. It was in her.

Kimball was doing his best not to get swept up by this emotional cyclone, but Mrs. Eddy would not let things settle down. She wrote to Caroline Noyes in early October 1893 demanding that she end all her efforts to get the speech into the Parliament book. "The dose is *too great*," Mrs. Eddy cautioned, "the chemicalization" would do irrepar-able damage. Such fiascoes as this always reminded her why God kept her from publishing her works as fully and freely as some of her students wanted. She urged Noyes, who was a member of the Board of Directors of the First Church, to take this letter to the other students in Chicago, read it to them, convince Kimball to drop the whole issue, and leave her address out of it.[55]

When Noyes took Mrs. Eddy's letter to Kimball, he was incensed and felt compelled to defend himself. He wrote Mrs. Eddy that once all the facts were known about the Parliament, about who was responsible and who was truly obedient to her, he would be judged right. Then he could willingly accept and endure her "chastisement of Love." But he did not appreciate the way Mrs. Eddy had involved other students in this affair. He was hard-pressed to see how it was "any part of humility or decent manhood" to submit to Mrs. Noyes's criticism or any other student's when they were probably motivated by jealousy. If Mrs. Eddy could not keep him on the right path, then surely it made no sense to have another student speak in her place. Kimball assured Mrs. Eddy that she was mistaken about him. He was not willfully stubborn; he had no intention of being disobedient, and he certainly was not rebellious.[56]

What had happened? The existing letters from Mrs. Eddy do not hint at anything on the surface that could have agitated Kimball so. In fact, it seems to an outside reader that the brouhaha was subsiding, that all the principals were about to get back to their Christian Science business. Why, then, did Kimball react so strongly, and why did it seem his self-respect was at stake when Mrs. Eddy's directions were read to him? There is always the chance that Caroline Noyes read to him another letter that has since been lost, but this does not seem likely. We really do not know from the existing correspondence what kind of working or social relationship Kimball had with Noyes. In the Chicago hierarchy, she was his superior; it is possible that he chafed at taking orders from a woman. Or perhaps he transferred any dislike of taking directions from Mrs. Eddy to Noyes, a safer target.*

For the past several years the atmosphere had been tense in Chicago as Christian Science teachers vied with one another not only for students but for Mrs. Eddy's favor. They sometimes acted like spiritual siblings fighting for their place in the family and for their mother's love and approval. We have already seen that Noyes tried to control her personal ambition, but she was not always successful. Perhaps the way she read Mrs. Eddy's letter to Kimball wounded him.

There is another possible explanation for the prolonged uproar. Chicago might have been in disarray, but things were not that stable in Concord, either, as James Gilman could have testified. No matter where she looked, Mrs. Eddy wrote to another student, her followers were not complying with her demands. She complained about the Christian Sci-

---

* At the time of the World's Columbian Exposition, Caroline Noyes was president of the Central Dispensary and the Board of Directors of the Church in Chicago. It was her responsibility to appoint a committee to deal with the exposition. She assigned Kimball to a position on this committee. Caroline D. Noyes, "Christian Science Notes," in *Miscellaneous Documents relating to Christian Science* (privately printed), p. 225.

entists in Concord, and about the Buswells not doing their part. She had Kimball and Hanna in mind, along with others who were letting her down, when she complained in the letter that she could not rely on her students to support her in her fight against evil. Not only did she feel misunderstood, but she felt that her students had abandoned her to deal with the agony of the fight alone. "I mourn," she lamented, and her students had not the foggiest notion why. God willing, her students would awaken from "this deep sleep of the carnal mind."[57]

Feelings of betrayal and abandonment, of humiliation and depletion, had overtaken Mrs. Eddy. Until she regained her spiritual equilibrium, no one was going to rest easy, especially Kimball, whom she used as a repository for her troubled wishes and feelings. Although Mrs. Eddy had been a spiritual leader for more than two decades and more people were being attracted to the Church, the movement was still relatively small and on shaky ground. This instability made the errors of her best students all the more galling. We have seen that Mrs. Eddy was an adept reader of her students' feelings and moods, and for some students there was an open conduit to her. Perhaps some of them felt that they could see beyond the mere word on the printed page; they could feel what she was feeling. If, underneath, Mother Eddy was becoming upset and anxious over a certain course of action, then as perceptive a student as Caroline Noyes could "pick it up" and deliver the message to another student.

For approximately the next two months, the letters passed each other on the way to Pleasant View and Chicago. Mrs. Eddy tried to explain to Kimball why the mishap in Chicago was a deep injury to the movement. Her enemies would do anything to distort the message of Christian Science. Kimball should have been alert to this kind of distortion. If he thought she wanted or needed publicity, he was mistaken; all she wanted was to do God's work. Thanks to mistakes like Kimball's, her task was never an easy one. She had suffered greatly, not because she thought her reputation might be sullied (for she had "quietly borne" insults for the cause since its inception), but because she feared that "God's cause" might be misunderstood, even "dishonored."[58]

In late October, Mrs. Eddy sent Kimball a long letter accusing the Chicago Church (and indirectly him) of not acknowledging her as Leader. Every time God had directed the course of Christian Science, Kimball had, she sharply noted, "taken issue with me from man's directions" to the extent that he changed or altered her intent. Who or what was guiding them? If it was God, then obey Him, but if it was man's selfish interest, then she would have nothing more to do with the whole mess. Listen to the voice of God, she urged Kimball; do not be seduced by the voice of man.[59]

This letter seemed to indicate that the gale sweeping down from Pleasant View had not quite subsided, but was beginning to diminish. Kimball had time to reconcile himself to the fact that even though he felt he had been loyal to Mrs. Eddy and obedient to her wishes, her wisdom was greater than his, and her reading of the affair had been correct: his unconscious personal motives had led him onto the path of disobedience. Kimball acknowledged her rebuke, but he still had reservations. It did not seem right for him to continue in his job in Chicago when he apparently did not understand enough about Christian Science and the pitfalls of error to see that he was working unconsciously to hurt Mrs. Eddy and the movement. The emotional strain, he added, was too much. He felt condemned by her and, because of their intense jealousy, hated "by the pioneers" in the movement. It seemed as though he had been "pushed upon a pedestal," then had teetered and fallen off. At this point, he felt bruised and battered. If he could do as he wished, he would drop the whole thing and "retire to obscurity."[60]

A week later, the storm returned to lash Kimball one last time. Caroline Noyes summoned him for the purpose of reading a letter she had received from Mrs. Eddy. Although Noyes did not show Kimball the letter, and Kimball did not fully disclose its contents in his reply, he once more was furious with both Noyes and Mrs. Eddy. He reminded Mrs. Eddy that she had entrusted him with carrying out her instructions for the speech. Since she had also explicitly told him not to divulge her thoughts to anyone, his lips had been sealed. But Mrs. Eddy had then turned around and told other students—namely Noyes—what Kimball was doing. This, Kimball declared, confused the others and started the gossip mill humming. Moreover, the letter, a personal slight to Kimball, undermined his position with the local Christian Science community. To him the letter was a clear indication of Mrs. Eddy's lack of confidence in him because it instructed Noyes to "undo some of [his] work," if it was not already too late for that. Once more, however, he assured Mrs. Eddy that he was willing to step down if she was not pleased with his work on her behalf.[61]

By early December the storm had spent itself. Noyes began to praise Kimball's efforts in a very difficult situation, and Mrs. Eddy, having regrouped, wrote to Noyes and her husband that "dear Mr. Kimball" had extricated himself from the situation "*wisely*" and assuredly deserved their thanks. She now hoped that the breach that had been opened among her students would heal and that they could recapture the "good feeling and bright prospects" that they had enjoyed before the World's Parliament of Religions.[62]

Kimball seemed to survive the upheaval relatively unscathed. By the middle of December he had received his copy of *Christ and Christmas*, and he felt compelled to write Mrs. Eddy. As it was revealed to Mrs. Eddy, Christian Science was the sole religion that explained all previous revelation, he wrote in an affirmative mood. Because Christian Science was unique, the wider public had to know it "in close identity with God's messenger." As for all the recent turmoil, he assured Mrs. Eddy that he had never believed that she had sought personal glory in the affair. Rather, he had acted to convince her that he knew the importance of her Christian Science message and the necessity of bringing it before an uneducated public. In the years ahead, Kimball would perform this service brilliantly for Mrs. Eddy. He would have some low moments; in particular, a real test of his character came in 1904 when Mrs. Eddy relieved him of some power. All things considered, though, Kimball's own inner balance and the strength of his religious beliefs helped make him an indispensable ally of Mrs. Eddy and her cause.[63]

In those days from September through December 1893, Kimball went through an emotional wringer that many Christian Science students experienced to some degree. What had begun as a minor gaffe, at least in the eyes of the student, was elevated by Mrs. Eddy into a major offense involving betrayal, selfishness, and disobedience. As Kimball suggested to Mrs. Eddy, part of the problem might have stemmed from misinformation sent to Pleasant View by disgruntled, jealous students. But this possibility does not fully explain Mrs. Eddy's willingness to believe that Kimball had disobeyed her.

As in her disagreements with the artist James Gilman over the *Christ and Christmas* project, a number of variables were involved. To Mrs. Eddy, her rebuke of Gilman was well deserved; because his own artistic interests had guided his hand in drawing the cherubs, he had lost sight of the spiritual beauty she was after. In 1893 this was not a new problem for Mrs. Eddy. Four years earlier, in a time of turmoil, she had written in exasperation that she had "never taught a student to handle evil" who had completely grasped her meaning and carried it "up to [her] ideal."[64]

When she felt that her ideal was not being met, when she felt that others were on the verge of separating her from God, Mrs. Eddy's "grief" could become unbearable. As she did with Gilman, she tended to externalize her troubling feelings. When her speech was published with Hanna credited as its author, the faux pas triggered a familiar scene. Throughout it all, Mrs. Eddy saw herself as innocent; God had been, and was, totally directing her thoughts and actions. Kimball might consciously have had good intentions, but unconsciously he had acted out of personal self-interest. Since she had been doing God's work, she felt morally justified in excoriating him. Kimball, at least initially, believed himself innocent of her charges. In defending himself, he even intimated that Mrs. Eddy was not a passive victim in all of this; it was not a simple matter of her students' failing her. It was as if an unacknowledged part of herself kept things stirred up no matter how much she complained in her letters about the disobedience of her students and the suffering she endured.

Whether Kimball knew it or not, his experience with Caroline Noyes and Mrs. Eddy was not an isolated one. Mrs. Eddy's correspondence is sprinkled with details concerning one student's remarks about another student, one student's injured feelings because of something Mrs. Eddy wrote to another student, and students' protests that they were loyal and obedient when, unknown to them, Mrs. Eddy was secretly giving instructions to others who opposed them. In the spring of 1888, for example, Mrs. Eddy had to defend herself from the accusation that she was encouraging discord. Some students had the impression, she wrote to Clara Choate, that Mrs. Eddy wanted articles printed attacking some of her students and that she had helped to foment quarrels in the ranks. These suspicions—need she say?—were absolutely false. She had tried to counsel peace. She did admit that there had been times when she had answered questions in letters and had said things to individuals about other individuals, but never with the intention of hurting anyone. She had always done it with the best interests of the students and the movement in mind; she had only wanted to impart the truth.[65]

Two years later, in 1890, Mrs. Eddy again defended herself against charges that somehow she was stirring up trouble among the students. Viewing her actions as morally justified, she believed that she was the misunderstood one. She felt morally compelled, she said in no uncertain terms, to inform one student about another's mistakes, but she did not do this to hurt anyone. Instead of heeding her moral lesson and trying to improve himself, the student distorted her words, "thus traducing the mother motive" and losing sight of the spiritual truth that lay in her lesson.[66]

In 1895 she complained to Choate that she had heard numerous rumors about what she had supposedly said and done, but there was virtually no substance to the malicious tongue-wagging. If she had learned anything from all this, it was to keep herself above the quarrels of her students. This was a resolution that she had repeated often in the 1880s and 1890s, but unfortunately she could not keep to it. In November 1896, she wrote to Julia Field-King, in the course of the letter stating that her golden rule was never to harm anyone, not even if that person was Richard Kennedy. Then she alluded to a student whom she had discussed with Field-King at Pleasant View. She had forgotten to remind Field-King not to repeat anything they had discussed. Now that she had the opportunity, she reminded her to "be sure and not bring up these dead carcasses." What she had told Field-King was confidential and for the greater good of the cause.[67]

Similar statements to other students could be stacked end upon end here, but one thing seems clear: despite her disavowals and her apparent wish for harmony among her students, Mrs. Eddy's hand sometimes kept things unsettled. In a slightly different context, Grace Choate Huse remembered that when she was a girl, Mrs. Eddy used to confide in her. When she told Grace about her many hardships, her revelations puzzled the girl. Why would this woman, this religious leader, be telling her these things? Grace thought it was a bit odd, "a matter of poor taste, if not misjudgment." Later Grace found reasons to justify Mrs. Eddy's disclosures, but her initial puzzlement was an appropriate reaction. After all, why should a woman who often appeared as a strong, self-possessed figure need to share her woes with a young child? Or with her own students?[68]

An answer, and the one her loyal students found acceptable, was that Mrs. Eddy embodied Christ's example of suffering. In her correspondence over several decades, Mrs. Eddy shared her miseries with her students, often telling them that they had no idea how deeply or how long she had suffered. Her intention was not to make her students feel sorry for her; Gilbert Carpenter has already explained to us the spiritual nature of Mrs. Eddy's suffering: she suffered for her students' mistakes, for their lapses, and for their human errors, which prevented God's Truth from being known.

When her suffering emanated predominantly from her spiritual side —when her personal side did not rub salt into the wounds—suffering took on its own meaning in Christian Science. Her complaints are so long and loud, and fill so much of the correspondence, that one begins to wonder how she held anyone in the movement. However, her litany of woes has such a consistent ring that after a while one begins to suspect that it was seen by the group as a ritual. This does not mean that Mrs. Eddy's suffering was feigned or was not deeply felt; it does imply that her suffering was used to draw the group more tightly together around her ideal. No one, least of all Mrs. Eddy's loyal followers, would have dismissed her suffering as an act, but like Camilla Hanna, they recognized that though she could languish in the depths of despair, in the blink of an eye she could spring into action. When she suffered, therefore, it was for the same reason that she administered rebukes: because her students had done something to impede God's Truth. She, like Christ, suffered for their sakes; her suffering was a reminder that they must correct their errors and reach for the ideal standards she had set forth in Christian Science. Once she felt assured that they were taking the steps to mend their ways, she would quickly recover.

Regarding her suffering and her chastisements, Mrs. Eddy once wrote a former Christian Science student and tried to explain the effect she had on some of her students. She admitted that some students who had not seen her for a while "chemicalize severely after calling on me." There was a difference between this chemicalization and animal magnetism, which she explained. In being chemicalized, a student would feel better after the ferment was over, while in the case of animal magnetism, a student would not recover so quickly and might even think that Mrs. Eddy had caused the suffering. But, she declared in no uncertain terms, she could not be the cause or the source of suffering. "The Truth may wound to heal," but heal it did.[69]*

It must have been very hard for Mrs. Eddy's students to know precisely when her castigations emanated from her spiritual self. Though she said she could not cause suffering, she could; Kimball and others told her so. What they felt was something Mrs. Eddy could not see in herself: it was sometimes easy to glide (unconsciously) into the personal sense, and when this occurred the reprimands and the suffering took on a different meaning. That is what befell Kimball in Chicago. What had looked, at first, like a minor mistake had been transformed into a major error of self-interest and disobedience. For his role in this error, Kimball was put through an emotional meat-grinder. When he was ground out the other end, he had experienced briefly a sense of being overwhelmed. This feeling had been passed to him by Mrs. Eddy. As the constant demands and errors of her students drained her, they began to feel like an assault, and sometimes these attacks came close to reviving the memories and feelings associated with past attacks and overwhelmings. Mrs. Eddy was not about to allow that to happen again, so she went on the offensive. Like the young Mary Baker who had her hand thrust into the spinning wheel by her mother, Kimball was learning from his spiritual mother

---

* "Chemicalize" has its own special meaning within Christian Science. In *Science and Health*, pp. 168–69, Mrs. Eddy defined the word in terms of a process in which the mind and body experience a change in belief from the material to the spiritual. Whenever a mental chemicalization produced an agitation of the symptoms, she saw "the mental signs" long before the patient felt them; thus she knew before the patient did that the danger was over. Also see her briefer definition on p. 401.

what it meant to be overwhelmed. And Kimball, much like young Mary Baker, submitted to the mother by apologizing to her, by accepting the guilt for his actions, and by putting his arms symbolically around her neck and reaffirming his love for his mother and her cause.[70]

While this psychological aspect was a part of Mrs. Eddy's rebukes, and while it sometimes informed the nature of her suffering, we should not forget that she did not see herself and her suffering in this light. Even when her students had glimpses that the personal self was involved, their overall belief in her spirituality, in the conviction that she had been chosen by God to bring His Truth to mankind, overrode their hurts and disappointments. Their love for Mother Eddy remained. Some, like Kimball, stood by her and carried her word to the rest of the world.

STRANGE CHILDREN

*Rid me, and deliver me from the hand of strange
children, whose mouth speaketh vanity, and their right
hand is a right hand of falsehood.*

Psalms 144:11

IN THE MORE THAN forty years before her fall and healing experience, Mrs. Eddy had known what it meant to be a passive, dependent woman. Society's expectations of women and her own illnesses had helped to ensure this, but so had her struggles with her father and her Congregational pastor, Reverend Corser, over the severity of their Calvinism. And her experiences with prejudices against an impoverished, widowed, and divorced woman made her sensitive to the plight of the outsider. Once Phineas Quimby's theories proved congenial to the aspirations of women, Mrs. Eddy saw a glimmer of hope for herself. After her fall, she began to build a spiritual sphere for herself in which she could begin to exercise an autonomy not granted to women in the outside world. In turn this meant that she could offer autonomy to other women within this sphere.

As Georgine Milmine noted, in the 1880s, Mrs. Eddy's church was still a "feeble society of less than fifty members, which had already been shattered by dissensions and quarrels." As Milmine went on to point out, however, the next eight years might have their hardships, but they would also be a time of explosive growth. The only way Milmine could account for the growth was to conclude that Mrs. Eddy's Christian Science was giving people something they wanted and presenting it to them in a clear, effective way.[1]

In 1882, as Mrs. Eddy was getting ready to go to Washington, D.C., on business, she asked Julia Bartlett to read a poem to the members of the Church, most of whom were women. If the poem is any indication,

Milmine was right when she said that Christian Science gave people something they wanted. Mrs. Eddy comes across as a positive, forceful leader, offering women the chance to become assertive, competent, and effective healers. In her imagery, they are like a church militant. The weak and the weary need not apply for a spot in this woman's army, at war against sin, disease, and death. Day and night, she avowed, "sisters labor on," and with the aid of "God's own science," they would emerge triumphant.[2]

One of the first women to gain prominence was Clara Choate. Sometime in 1877 she had an interview with Mrs. Eddy and came away from it enthralled, for this new woman seemed to be putting into words exactly what she had been feeling so deeply. On the way home, her awe of Mrs. Eddy inflated to the point that she was almost lifted off the ground. She had no doubt that Mrs. Eddy "walked and talked with God"; as soon as she got home she opened *Science and Health* and began reading. Later that night, she got a clearer insight into Mrs. Eddy's mission and the purpose of her great book.[3]

Choate's admiration for Mrs. Eddy was quickly enveloped in the mother-child metaphor. Still in her twenties, Choate wrote to Mrs. Eddy that she was awed by Mrs. Eddy's love, and sometimes felt unworthy of it. Like a wise, loving mother, Mrs. Eddy understood her in a way no one else could. Choate was also quick to confess that she was far from perfect. She was struggling to reach that selflessness that was demanded in healing. Compared to Mrs. Eddy, she was a spiritual beginner, a small child sitting at the foot of a great mother. Mrs. Eddy had set such a high ideal that when Choate felt overcome by "some trial or grief," she was jolted into seeing just how wide the gap was between her and the ideal. Like the apostle Peter when he walked on the wave, she wanted to cry out, "Save me, save me."[4]

Choate was saved, and she showed great promise as a student and a healer. In the dark days of the early 1880s, that was exactly what Mrs. Eddy needed. She was trying desperately to expand her handful of Christian Science followers into hundreds. With her movement—her spiritual child—struggling for its life, one can well understand why Mother Eddy would be ready to mirror the idealization of a gifted child. For a while Mrs. Eddy seemed unwavering in her admiration of Clara Choate. Then, however, forces were set loose that would eventually undermine their relationship.

In 1880 Mrs. Eddy and Gilbert Eddy left their Lynn residence for a summer's stay in Concord, New Hampshire. There she would have the peace and quiet to revise *Science and Health*. But one student, James C. Howard, who the following year would betray Mrs. Eddy, disturbed her by sharing with her his suspicions about Choate: she seemed far too interested in knowing where her leader had gone. The more he thought about it, the more evident it was that Choate coveted the office of president of the Christian Scientist Association. What was even worse for Howard was that at their last meeting Choate had inquired about his wife, and when he got home he found to his horror that within five minutes of her seemingly innocent inquiry, his wife had taken sick. Mrs. Eddy's response to Howard's alarms suggested that she no longer held the same idealized view of Choate, particularly when she told Howard that Choate had fallen prey to the mental suggestions of those two ominous foes, Richard Kennedy and Daniel Spofford.[5]

It is hard to tell from the existing documents whether or not Choate really aspired to be president of the Association. It is also very difficult to decide just whose unbridled ambition we are talking about, Choate's or Howard's. To begin with, Howard was not the most reliable, unbiased source. He had recently studied with Mrs. Eddy, and at the church services where Choate led the singing, he played the cornet. Beneath the surface of their musical harmony, however, lay mutual resentment and jealousy. While Choate may have sensed that he was a rival for her position within the church, Howard may have resented Choate's fast-growing reputation within the community of Christian Scientists.[6] We must also question whether Howard had Mrs. Eddy's best interests at heart. If he was the only one in the Boston group who knew where the Eddys had gone, he must have understood that she needed a rest from this kind of jealous bickering. It is, moreover, asking too much of us to believe that he did not know what effect the news of his wife's illness would have on Mrs. Eddy. Whatever his motivations were in seeking to foment trouble between Choate and Mrs. Eddy, it is evident that Howard could not contain his excitement and passed it on to the two women.

This was where Mrs. Eddy was right in her evaluation of her followers. At times they became envious of one another. As in any family, the jealous, angry children had their own ways of involving the parent in the squabble. What is interesting about this particular parent—Mrs. Eddy—is how she chose to respond to her children's narcissistic wounds. For some reason (she may have believed that Choate was ambitious; she may have wished to dispel the rumors that Choate was her favorite student), she accepted one child's (Howard's) version of the story and then diagnosed the other child (Choate) as being under the malicious spell of the movement's archenemies. It was one thing for Mrs. Eddy to believe this, but it was another thing for her to talk about one child that way to the other. Howard must have felt vindicated and may have had some trouble controlling his spiteful glee at having undermined Choate. In apparently taking sides this way, Mrs. Eddy was, inadvertently or not, playing one child off the other.

The barbed gossip did not stop with Howard's sharp pen. When the infamous eight bolted from the Christian Science ranks in October 1881, with Howard among them, Mrs. Eddy, obviously in great distress, fired off a letter to Choate. She feared that the defections might not stop at eight, and that at least one of her followers and "the *anti-Choate* party" were out to disgrace her. She had, furthermore, learned beyond any doubt that two key defectors had persuaded the others to leave by drawing Choate's name into it. Claiming that Mrs. Eddy was being manipulated by her favorite pupil, they had no recourse but to disavow Mrs. Eddy's leadership. Since mesmerism had gained control over her students' minds, she had not been their leader. These students refused to take her guiding hand, and, she snapped, she was "getting disgusted with such canting hypocrisy."[7]

Over the next two years, from 1881 through 1882, the letters only hint at a growing tension between Mrs. Eddy and Choate. As mesmerism continued to exact its fearful toll on Mrs. Eddy and the movement, she wrote to Choate complaining about the ingratitude of certain students. Early in February 1882, she wrote a brief letter from Washington, D.C. She was encouraged that her Christian Science teachings had stirred up some local interest; yet as she drew the letter to a close she told Choate, "The demons are at work here in *some respects*." They might be as determined as ever, but they could not stop her from fulfilling her tasks.

A little more than a month later she sent Choate another letter in which she marveled at what active women were accomplishing in the temperance movement. They were certainly more effective than men had ever been. All evidence pointed to the fact that this was "the period of *women*"; proudly carrying the banners of reform, they marched at the head of the parade. In their own moral endeavors, Christian Scientists could learn a thing or two from the suffragists, whose voices were being heard all over the country. If they wanted to emulate these dedicated reformers, then they had to be as tightly knit an organization. Within this unity, if each person did his or her assigned task, then Christian Science would easily withstand "the puny kicks of mesmerism." In the past, the demons of this foe had split their ranks by turning students against each other and against their leader. But each student would love Mrs. Eddy "instinctively" if it were not for her old nemesis, malicious animal magnetism.[8]

Mrs. Eddy warmly included Choate in the phalanx of women who were soon to transform the moral and religious landscape of America. But even as Mother Eddy addressed her daughter in affectionate terms, she admonished her, albeit without citing specific offenses. If the Christian Scientists were to be at the forefront of this grand reformation and were to become as well known and productive as the suffragists, then there could be no division in their ranks.

Mrs. Eddy may be forgiven for assuming that the suffragists had no breaches in their ranks. They must have looked good compared to her out-of-step, ragtag battalion. If Christian Scientists were unified, then the kicks of mesmerism would not hurt, but in the midst of so much disaffection and disunity, even a glancing strike felt like a body blow. The problem was that *some people*—and Choate could write her name in one of the blanks—were not doing the job that they were supposed to. Like the "old" young dragon, Richard Kennedy, *some people* had begun to aggrandize their power and position with the movement, and in so doing were turning loyal students against their leader.

In the best of times Mrs. Eddy's charges would have been serious enough, but in the early 1880s, her movement—her handful of followers—was fighting to stay alive. Even with Mrs. Eddy's unswerving devotion to her mission, an odds-maker might not have given the Christian Scientists much of a chance to survive. It is in this context that we must assess Mrs. Eddy's deteriorating relationship with Choate. Mrs. Eddy often felt as if malicious animal magnetism was coming at her from every direction. Rightly or wrongly, Choate's name had been tightly linked to the defection of prized students in 1881. Mrs. Eddy became increasingly sensitive to any deviation in Choate; in turn, Choate became ever more aware of her leader's changed attitude toward her, making her more guarded, suspicious, and defensive.

By 1883 the veil was lifted off the charges against Choate. It was still whispered among some students that Choate was their leader's favorite. Choate had built up a highly successful practice around Boston, and in August she asked Mrs. Eddy's permission to hold classes in Christian Science. Two months later something had gone terribly wrong. Mrs. Eddy requested her to take no more classes and to transfer her prospective students to the Massachusetts Metaphysical College. A quick exchange of letters in December sheds some light on what prompted Mrs. Eddy to take such strong steps.

In late December, in those chilly, dark days described earlier by Marston and Milmine when malicious animal magnetism seemed especially virulent, Mrs. Eddy sent an impassioned letter to Choate. Once again Mrs. Eddy seemed to be on the verge of collapsing under the weight of incessant discord. Ever since some of her students had fallen prey to

"demons in the shape of human forms," her life had been one of "drudg-
ery and *abuse*." Facing one shocking disclosure after another, Mrs. Eddy
began to reexperience feelings of isolation; she felt as if no one could
possibly comprehend the depth of her anguish. The last straw was the
wicked rumor circulated by their enemies that Choate was to be Mrs.
Eddy's successor. Now, because of their jealousy, these students were
trying to get Mrs. Eddy involved in the fray so that she would punish
Choate for her presumption. To quell this rancor Mrs. Eddy asked
Choate to do her a favor, and she hoped that she would understand her
motive in what she was about to say. Mrs. Eddy asked her to drop the
classes and to devote all of her energy to healing. If she were to continue
teaching, she and Mrs. Eddy would be unable to quiet the ugly rumors
of favoritism.[9]

But the gossip would not abate; it continued to poison the relationship
between Mrs. Eddy and Choate. When Choate had to give up her classes,
the rumor was bruited about that Mrs. Eddy had acted out of jealousy.
As 1883 wound down, Mrs. Eddy decided to send Choate to the Chicago
and Milwaukee area, where the struggling movement needed a firm hand.
Choate, however, suspected that this assignment had nothing to do with
confidence and trust: Mrs. Eddy was trying to undermine her by cutting
into her successful practice in Boston. For Choate, being sent to the
Midwest was like being shuttled off to Siberia; she suspected that her
enemies had gotten Mrs. Eddy's ear and that Mrs. Eddy had sided with
them out of her own jealousy.[10]

In response to one of Choate's letters, Mrs. Eddy declared openly that
she hoped her student did not feel that Mrs. Eddy in any way resented
the fact that she was able to attract fifty pupils in one class. She had
heard thirdhand that Choate claimed that she, Mrs. Eddy, was pre-
venting her from conducting a class. How could that be when she had
done so much to encourage her? The reader senses that Choate's accusation came from a feeling rather than any direct action on Mrs. Eddy's
part. According to her sources, Mrs. Eddy had heard that Choate would
not lecture because she felt too uncomfortable knowing that Mrs. Eddy
was in the room and that somehow she was trying to stop her teaching.[11]

In another letter, Mrs. Eddy tried to assuage Choate's suspicions by
declaring that nobody in her house had taken up Choate mentally, nor
had anyone voiced an opinion one way or the other about Choate's
mission to Chicago and Milwaukee. If there was a problem, it lay within
Choate herself. She was obviously laboring under the beliefs and delusions that had plagued her years earlier. Long before Choate had ever
heard of Christian Science, Mrs. Eddy had received God's commission

to "lead his children out of the darkness of today." Choate would not begin to emulate this until she changed her ways.[12]

Despite Mrs. Eddy's assurances that she was chastising Choate in order to improve her spiritually, Choate continued to harbor the suspicion that Mrs. Eddy had another motive for wanting her to undertake the journey. She intimated as much in a December letter. While Mrs. Eddy was giving short shrift to Choate's thriving practice, to her it was "as great as your Church or college." Mrs. Eddy sent an immediate response, warning her floundering student that the demons were on the verge of conquering her. She urged her to listen to her, the best friend she had, and to go on the assigned mission. If Choate could not hear God's voice speaking through Mrs. Eddy, then those demons would conquer and kill her just as surely as they had killed poor Gilbert Eddy.[13]

This dire prediction came too late. Choate had turned a deaf ear to Mrs. Eddy's spiritual voice; all she heard now was her personal voice. By early January 1884, the die was cast. Mrs. Eddy had been told sometime earlier that Choate had attempted to seduce one of her male patients, a charge substantiated by Mrs. Sarah Crosse, who had treated the same man shortly afterward. On January 5th, Mrs. Eddy wrote a short, direct note to Choate. All things considered, since so many people believed Choate to be the cause of so much dissension and trouble, she should withdraw from the Church and Association. Mrs. Eddy reminded Choate that for the past seven years she had fought for her and defended her from the attacks of others. It saddened her to hear that Choate was publicly attacking her, accusing her of being jealous of Choate's popularity.[14]

On the same day that she received this letter, Choate submitted her resignation, but this hardly severed the emotional tie or ended the correspondence between the two women. Two weeks later in another letter to Choate, Mrs. Eddy showed that they had real trouble disengaging. The long letter rehashed many of the issues that had driven a wedge between the two.

Unwittingly, Mrs. Eddy gave a brief glimpse into the excited byplay within the Christian Science movement. The previous evening Sarah Crosse had read to Mrs. Eddy a recent letter that Choate had addressed to her, Crosse, in confidence. Choate had apparently attacked Mrs. Eddy for her envy and jealousy. Crosse, like Howard earlier, had her own agenda in sharing this letter with Mrs. Eddy. And, like Howard, she would later turn against Mrs. Eddy and defect from the movement. Nevertheless, in this episode she succeeded in further undermining the relationship between Choate and her leader. No wonder, in this climate

of jealousy and anger, that some Christian Scientists felt creeping suspicions that they were the objects of malicious gossip.[15]

But this was not what was on Mrs. Eddy's mind as she accused Choate
of intentionally misrepresenting some of her advice. If only Choate would
take the time to live by the golden rule, she could begin to break the
hold mesmerism had on her. The way things stood now, it had inflamed
"all the evil" in her personality, and she, Mrs. Eddy, had tried, with
patience and love, to extinguish the flames. The rumor that she was
jealous of Choate's popularity was simply unfounded. The truth, wrote
Mrs. Eddy, was that she had initially encouraged Choate to teach, but
when Mrs. Eddy took over Choate's pupils, she discovered that Choate's
mental influence, not her actual words, had caused them severe damage.
Her "sensuality and untruthfulness" had insinuated their way into her
relationships with others, though Choate probably thought she had carefully concealed this part of herself. These were the "two killing errors"
in Choate's character that had impelled Mrs. Eddy to urge her to stop
teaching.

Choate was causing her "*aged Mother*" to age even more rapidly by
trying to hide her sins from her, and then, to make matters worse, Choate
expected her mother to exonerate her for her lapses. Neither Mrs. Eddy
nor her students were trying to injure Choate, and if she tried to "*kill*"
her or her students, then Mrs. Eddy, in the spirit of Christian love, would
not attempt to retaliate, and neither would her students. For years Mrs.
Eddy had not wished to believe that Choate's mental malpractice had
badly divided the movement, but now she had damning evidence that
the accusations were true. Within the past year, she reminded Choate,
she had made many heartfelt promises to reform herself, but each time
she had slid into her old habits. This last time she had actually tried to
stop someone from joining the Church. Mrs. Eddy said that she never
justified or condoned her students' quarrels; moreover, she had supported and defended Choate as long as her conscience would allow, but
now she had to speak out because Choate had been damaging her (Mrs.
Eddy's) reputation and that of her Church. Mrs. Eddy closed her letter
by urging Choate to stop what she was doing and to abide by her
resolutions, for it was Edward Arens and Richard Kennedy who were
prompting Choate to say and do these awful things.[16]

In the late 1880s Mrs. Eddy wrote to Choate with the familiar complaint that there was far too little harmony in her family of believers.
She was plainly weary of the student uprisings that had crippled the
movement every three to seven years. From Mrs. Eddy's perspective, the
trouble began when "malicious minds" sowed the seeds of suspicion
and doubt and then spread harmful lies about people. When jealousy

turned her students against one another, she would try to bring peace by defending both sides. Caught in the middle of their hostilities, Mother Eddy frequently found herself resented by the quarreling children. Because she wished to remain above their disputes, and because her interventions sometimes proved detrimental to her own health, Mrs. Eddy felt that she needed to remain on the sidelines as much as possible. Unfortunately, this hands-off policy did not always produce the intended results. When left to their own devices, she explained to Choate, one student whispered to another what was patently false and "their muddled sense makes them believe it." What was worse, the clever, maligning student was never seen in the open, but quietly worked at building his or her own reputation while pulling hers down.[17]

In his book on the history of Christian Science, William L. Johnson had a shrewd insight into the etiology of the conflicts that beset the movement in 1888. Indeed, Johnson's appraisal clearly underlines one of the real problems facing Mrs. Eddy and the movement, and not just in 1888. The deep emotional attachments between teachers and students—in fact, the psychological dependency fostered in the student-teacher relationship—played havoc with Mrs. Eddy's spiritual intentions. From her perspective, it was as if her children were being lured from the spiritual truths that she had taught them. The all-too-human strivings created the venomous envy that threatened to poison her movement. Johnson, a supporter of Mrs. Eddy, concurred with her view about the origins of the conflicts: her students—her children—were disobedient and thus lost sight of their real mission.[18]

Johnson's insight into the source of the conflicts is a valuable one, but a bit one-sided, neglecting as it does Mrs. Eddy's role. He assumes that her personal side never became engaged in these confrontations, which, of course, was what she always claimed. Naturally, it is hard for anyone to assess his or her role objectively in the subtle dynamics of family relationships, and Mrs. Eddy was no exception. Her involvement in the disputes was complex, just as any mother-and-child relationship is.

The malicious power of Arens and Kennedy carried the day. As Choate made her unscheduled exit from the Christian Science stage, the next star was walking on. In December 1883, Mrs. Eddy had written to Emma Hopkins hoping that she would become a member of her class. She painted a picture of herself as a lone, struggling figure who had only God's love for solace. She seemed to insinuate that if Mrs. Hopkins joined the class, she might make a difference; she might be the one to help spread the word and ease the burdens.[19]

Five days later an eager, enthusiastic Hopkins responded to Mrs.

Eddy's offer, though from the letter it is evident that she came to Christian Science with mixed motives. Though her husband had a job as a high school teacher, for a number of reasons they and their small son were barely scraping by. Money, though, did not seem to be the critical factor. To study with Mrs. Eddy might allow her to fulfill a lifelong dream of establishing a hospital for sick and destitute children. In her fantasy this was not to be the usual barren institution, for the wards would be tended by loving, gentle nurses and caring, competent doctors. The children would play on "sunny playgrounds." Hopkins then asked a question that must have struck a responsive chord in Mrs. Eddy: What if her dream came true and she was able to help the children by "the healing thoughts of your God embued disciples?"[20]

Long after she had become a Christian Scientist and was in hot water with Mrs. Eddy, Hopkins confessed to Julia Bartlett that she had always been an impulsive person. If she made mistakes, it was because she never held her feelings in check. But, she claimed in her own defense, she never had been in a position of responsibility where she was expected to exercise intelligence and restraint. So, added to her other motives, we must include Hopkins's desire to loosen the stays of her Victorian corset, to shuck some of the stereotypes of feminine passivity, and to take an independent step or two.[21]

Despite Hopkins's self-effacing statements, it did not take her long to establish herself as an intelligent woman and an effective healer. Maybe Mrs. Eddy had found the inspired student she desperately needed, and maybe Hopkins could live up to an early promise she had made to Mrs. Eddy: "If the science is really true," and if she accepted it with all of her heart, then she would never do anything to bring discredit or shame to Mrs. Eddy and the movement.[22]

For a while Christian Science was all Hopkins had hoped. She was an apt student, and she said all the right things to Mrs. Eddy. In the spring of 1884, Hopkins was keenly aware of how deeply Mrs. Eddy felt the failures in her movement. She wrote a kind note to say that she wanted to see Mrs. Eddy only when she was in a good mood because in no way did she want to become a burden to her. She understood that Mrs. Eddy had more than a passing acquaintance with the sorrow and grief of the world and that her students must not add to it. And several months later she wrote again, trying to lift Mrs. Eddy's spirits. Mrs. Eddy often seemed like "a tired sobbing body," but simultaneously seemed strong, like Gabriel trumpeting "forth doom to error." If she could, Hopkins would have provided a "sheltering tenderness" for Mrs. Eddy, the woman who had been forced to face so much in life. In

September 1884 Hopkins's dedication and intelligence were rewarded when she was named editor of *The Christian Science Journal*.[23]

As rapid as Emma Hopkins's ascent was, it was more than matched by the swiftness of her descent. Within the year that followed, this admired student disobeyed Mrs. Eddy in publishing a number of ill-conceived articles, and she was relieved of the editorship. Not only that, she aligned herself with Mary Plunkett, a persistent troublemaker in the movement, who wooed her even further from Mrs. Eddy's side. By November 1885, the Christian Scientist Association accepted Hopkins's letter of resignation. The letters between this once-favored student and her teacher bore a familiar refrain: the rumor mill had each woman talking harshly about the other; Hopkins responded that she had been misunderstood, and Mrs. Eddy asserted that she had acted only out of love and concern for her student.[24]

Emma Hopkins was the second strong woman to fall from grace; in subsequent years there would be others, none stranger than Josephine Curtis Woodbury. She was the wife of E. Frank Woodbury, an original trustee of the Massachusetts Metaphysical College. Clara Choate had interested Mrs. Woodbury in Christian Science in 1880, and it did not take long for this new student to establish herself as a healer with special gifts. Surrounded by a group of admiring students at the Massachusetts Academy of Christian Science on Dartmouth Street, Boston, Woodbury had a mercurial rise to the top.

It did not take much time for her to incur the displeasure of Mrs. Eddy. In responding to one of Mrs. Eddy's strong rebukes, Woodbury confessed that it was not unusual for her to fall short of a full understanding of what Mrs. Eddy said and did. Only Mrs. Eddy had reached her high spiritual plane, and if a student entertained any hope of ever attaining this exalted spiritual level, that student had to be around Mrs. Eddy, had to study with her in order to understand the Truth. "No one else can impart that high," Woodbury wrote, and she was sorry to hear that Mrs. Eddy believed that she was criticizing her. Nevertheless, Woodbury would continue to have difficulty abiding by Mrs. Eddy's strict demands. Stories had reached Mrs. Eddy in 1885 that Woodbury was fomenting trouble with other students; she sent a note beseeching her to stop. Mrs. Eddy did not approve of her actions, and she was to halt her disruptive activities; Christian Science could only grow through internal peace and harmony.[25]

By 1886 the gap between Mother Eddy and her student was widening. According to Mrs. Eddy, Woodbury had continued to overstep her bounds, especially in publishing articles in the *Journal* that she had been forbidden to, or about which she should have exercised sounder judgment. In a January letter, Woodbury responded to a rebuke with claims of perplexed innocence. She accepted the truth of Mrs. Eddy's charges not because she understood what she was doing wrong, but because Mrs. Eddy, whom she loved, made the charges. (One can only wonder what Mrs. Eddy made of that line, with its overt compliance and veiled aggression.) Woodbury was positive that she was doing the right thing, that she was reflecting Truth, until the discord among the students indicated just the opposite. The culprit was animal magnetism, but she was ready to do battle with this mental enemy as faithfully as she had fought her fears of sickness in the past. The schemes and plots against her would fail in their attempts to entice her into error, *"for I am not going onto the other side,"* she declared adamantly.[26]

On this side of things, Woodbury continued to bungle. By October 1886 Mrs. Eddy again found reason to scold her, but she expressed her sincere hope that Woodbury would make her Dartmouth Street institute "respectable and Christian" and that it would reflect her leader's confidence in her. That confidence was shown when Mrs. Eddy placed Woodbury on the Committee on Publications of the Christian Scientist Association. In this position, Woodbury continued to be disruptive, making Mrs. Eddy wonder whether her confidence had been well placed. After Woodbury had again disobeyed Mrs. Eddy's explicit directions on publishing certain articles, Mrs. Eddy wrote her in exasperation. Without mincing words, she said that no matter what task Woodbury undertook, misunderstanding and contention soon followed. When things ran smoothly, she invariably disturbed them, and when things ran roughly, she inevitably exacerbated them. Mrs. Eddy had rebuked her on this score many times, and each time Woodbury had confessed to her errors, only to make them again. Her continual backsliding was a result of her lying, or as Mrs. Eddy delicately put it, her tendency of "implying that which is untrue." Unless Woodbury changed her ways, Mrs. Eddy would be forced to bring her "constant quarrels" before the Christian Scientist Association and the Church.[27]

As the 1880s moved on, Mrs. Eddy would need all the earnest prayer she could muster in dealing with Woodbury. By the summer of 1889, if her hands had formerly been clasped in prayer, she now threw them in the air in utter dismay. Woodbury kept falling into the very errors she saw in others. Why could she not see what was happening? She was being used to break up the Church, and Mrs. Eddy vowed that she would not intervene any longer; her most experienced students would have to fend for themselves, "do their own work of salvation."[28]

In the late summer of 1889, Woodbury was frantically trying to work out her salvation. She recognized that her spiritual growth had progressed in fits and starts and that the last year had been an especially trying one. She also voiced a familiar complaint, one that we have seen in the stories of Choate and Hopkins. She was the victim of others' "jealousy and malice"; others were projecting their "evil motives" onto her. The very fact that she had been a staunch defender of Mrs. Eddy and her work made her the object "of hatred and revenge."

Again, this is a familiar story. Woodbury was telling Mrs. Eddy that her spiritual mentor's life had so inspired her that she had tried to imitate it, but her successes had stimulated the envy of others. She was certain that God was using her as a testimony to Mrs. Eddy's Truth. Her successes in healing occurred when she healed in Mrs. Eddy's name, not in her own. Moreover, experience had taught her that if a person believed a lie concerning Mrs. Eddy's motives, it would kill that person, and to believe a lie concerning one of Mrs. Eddy's loyal students would render a person sick. In concluding her long reply to Mrs. Eddy, Woodbury said that through her years of trial and error, God had been testing her and was cleansing her for His greater purposes. If God prompted Mrs. Eddy to withdraw her advice and counsel, then it was His way of making Woodbury turn more fully to His ways. Her withdrawal, moreover, only proved Mrs. Eddy's deep love for her, and it heightened Woodbury's gratitude. It was indeed time that she did her own watching.[29]

In 1889 Woodbury had left Boston for Montreal to undertake missionary work. Throughout her continuing struggles with Mrs. Eddy, Woodbury tried to impress upon her teacher just how much she admired and wished to emulate her. The widening gap between her life and Mrs. Eddy's was almost too much for her to bear. Only because Mrs. Eddy was so kind and gentle did she feel that she had a chance to undo the mistakes of the past, and the only way to perfect herself was to be like Mrs. Eddy. There simply was no other way, she wrote, to demonstrate her love for Mrs. Eddy than by emulating her. If she was able to do that, then one day she might be fortunate enough to hear Mrs. Eddy say that she was her "beloved child" who brought untold pleasure to her heart.[30]

By September and October of 1889, Woodbury's letters to Mrs. Eddy were filled with her wishes for success in her Christian Science work and with her demonstrations that she was Mrs. Eddy's hardest-working, most devoted student. She knew that Mrs. Eddy agonized personally over her students' mistakes, so Mrs. Eddy should know that Woodbury was "constantly being blessed" by her suffering. She discussed the work of malicious animal magnetism that still festered within Christian Science, and she confirmed Mrs. Eddy's long-held belief that Richard Kennedy was behind the current ills. By the beginning of the new year Woodbury was thanking Mrs. Eddy for being a "surgeon as well as mother" to her. Mrs. Eddy had demonstrated her love for her wayward student by doing the most difficult thing any parent had to do with a child: scold and punish her in order to help her grow. In the coming year, Woodbury hoped, she might be a greater comfort to Mrs. Eddy, for she as mother deserved all the help a devoted, "grateful child" could provide.[31]*

At this point, Woodbury might have been having real trouble recognizing the mother-and-child metaphor as an abstraction. By January 1890, she was three months pregnant, and it was an ill-kept secret that she had not had sexual relations with her husband for some time. One may read her letters of love and supplication to Mrs. Eddy as disingenuous and hypocritical, but actually she meant those words of praise and adulation. She idealized Mrs. Eddy and strongly identified with her. Not so ironically, within this glorification of Mrs. Eddy's personality lay the seeds of bitter disillusionment and discontent.

As much as she said she deplored the gap that separated her from Mrs. Eddy, Woodbury widened the breach between them in the fall of 1889 when she closed her Academy of Christian Science, withdrew from the National Christian Scientist Association, and later resigned from the Boston church just before Mrs. Eddy dissolved it. It is not clear why Woodbury initiated these moves; perhaps her private life was inducing too much guilt. Nevertheless, the bombshell hit on June 11, 1890, when she announced that she had given birth to a son. This was not your run-of-the-mill announcement. Woodbury claimed that she had not known she was pregnant. Until her child's birth, she had denied her pregnancy, passing off her "poignant physical discomfort" as some sort of "fungoid formation."[32]

When she held the baby in her arms, Woodbury must have realized that it was a little difficult to talk about fungoid formations, so she shifted her rationalization: her child was a virgin birth. To some Christian Scientists Mrs. Woodbury's pronouncement may not at first have seemed as outlandish as it would have to an outsider. Back when Mrs. Eddy established the Massachusetts Metaphysical College, its prospectus touted her as Professor of Obstetrics, Metaphysics, and Christian Science. In 1887 she conducted two one-week classes on obstetrics. A number of her advanced students took the course and considered it

---

* In an undated letter Woodbury claimed that Richard Kennedy had taken over a meeting being run by Carolyn Roach. Woodbury was becoming increasingly preoccupied by Kennedy, Mrs. Eddy's old nemesis.

among the most stimulating they ever had from her. By "obstetrics" Mrs. Eddy meant the use of Christian Science principles to control, in the words of one historian, "the illusions of childbirth, that is, belief in the reality of anatomy, physiology, physical intercourse, and pain."[33]

The illusion of childbirth simply meant that the true reality was spiritual, not physical. The meaning of this was conveyed by Mrs. Eddy to her students when she said that they reflected the perfection of God in the sense that they were created in His image. They were, moreover, enveloped in His love, protected and sheltered by His strong arms. God was everything to them; His Truth and Love governed their lives so that no evil could touch them. God was the Mother-Father; therefore, they had "no material conception or birth"; they had no parents of the flesh. She underlined this assertion by saying that their birth was something different from the ordinary birth, or the birth of mortal mind. They reflected God, not beliefs. She drove home the point that sensuality had no power over them. They were not fully aware of the temptations of the flesh because they were "the pure conception" of His Truth and His Love. As a result, they reflected the pure qualities of the Father-Mother God.[34]

In a similar vein, in the early 1890s Mrs. Eddy wrote a letter to William G. Nixon, publisher of *The Christian Science Journal*, commenting on the recent birth of his child. She offered congratulations but cautioned him not to be tempted by the belief that he had created a child. God was the creator of all things. In the ordinary way of looking at the birth, Nixon and his wife had created a child, but this was not the Christian Science way of seeing the event. It was true that they had created a baby, "but not in Science have you a mind in matter," any more than they had in sin, sickness, disease, or death. Thus, if he believed that he and his wife had created a mortal child, then that child was subject to those dreaded mortal beliefs; to her, this kind of connection to the material world was impossible.[35]*

Mrs. Eddy also felt strongly that as Christian Science was more fully understood and demonstrated, at some point in the future the pleasures of the body would be destroyed because they detracted from the spiritual and dishonored God. According to Laura Sargent's notes from one of Mrs. Eddy's lessons, she said that when a person was finally able to forsake the material sense, that person would actually love more, not

---

* In the statements compiled by Richard Oakes in his *Mary Baker Eddy's Six Days of Revelation* (Christian Science Research Library, 1981), pp. 301–2, one can read even stronger statements on the issue of childbirth. Some of them indicate Mrs. Eddy's strong desire to overcome limitations of the flesh. The issue is whether or not these statements can be accurately attributed to Mrs. Eddy.

less, because he or she would reflect the spiritual qualities of God, which were total kindness, love, and compassion.

In this same lesson, Mrs. Eddy pointed to a major difference between the material and the spiritual sense of love. The former, she said, degraded the object of one's love through the expression of animal desire or lust. This occurred, for example, in marriage when the husband dishonored his wife "by taking away her virginity," thereby revealing that the so-called love was nothing more than a thinly veiled "lust, i.e., hate." Just the opposite, of course, occurred when the tie between a man and a woman was governed by a spiritual sense of Love.[36]

In statements like these, Mrs. Eddy was arguing within the accepted boundaries of Christian Science regarding the allness of God and the nothingness of matter. At times her language could be dramatic. She was not asking her students to give up marriage; she was not at war against human sexuality. But it is easy to see how some of her students might stretch her words. If the ultimate and desired reality was spiritual, then why not a spiritual birth? Had not Mrs. Eddy, like the Virgin Mary, given spiritual birth to Christian Science?

In the spring of 1894, Mrs. Eddy wrote to one of her students, Julia Field-King, seeking to nip this erroneous thinking in the bud. Rumors had reached Mrs. Eddy's ear regarding Field-King's statements on the virgin birth of Jesus. In a quick reply, Field-King denied that she had said Jesus was the illegitimate child of Mary. Before she had come into the Christian Science fold, she said she had accepted the Congregational Church's teaching regarding the virgin birth, but she had never really understood it. Christian Science made it clear. She vaguely thought, however, as did many other students, that a full spiritual understanding would make such an event possible in today's world. In fact, Mrs. Larminie, a Christian Science teacher in Chicago, told Field-King that she personally knew of "three instances of pure mental conceptions" taking place among her students. While Field-King got off the hook this time, this part of her letter could not have pleased Mrs. Eddy, for it was this kind of apostasy that brought her movement into disrepute. Someone like Field-King could be disabused of her mistaken belief, but someone else, like Woodbury, finding herself consumed in guilt, could take this belief—and others—to another level of meaning.[37]

According to Georgine Milmine, Woodbury and her students had begun to carve their own unique space within the Christian Science sphere; they constructed a reality based upon a primitive, mystical interpretation of Christian Science doctrines and beliefs. They "lived in a kind of miracle play of their own," was the way Milmine described it. They had "inspirations and revelations, and premonitions . . . saw portents and mystic meanings in everything." Woodbury's room was filled with pictures of the Madonna.[38]

Six years after the birth of Woodbury's son, a First Members Meeting was convened to discuss her formal ouster from Christian Science. Many former students testified against her, and they helped to uncover what had transpired in those days before her stunning announcement of a virgin birth. Woodbury told them, according to the testimony of Mary E. Landy, that she was closer to Mrs. Eddy than any of her students. Moreover, Mrs. Eddy was so exalted that she was God. The connection Woodbury was drawing was evident to her followers: Woodbury was as powerful and perfect as Mary Baker Eddy. When she claimed to be in this elevated state, Woodbury could be a compelling, frightening figure. She repeatedly told her most devoted students, Landy testified, that if they did not believe in her, they would die. To underline her prediction, she refreshed her students' memories about a certain Mr. Leighton, a student who had left her and died shortly thereafter. A Mr. Harwood, who had also deserted Mrs. Woodbury, had suffered a similar fate.[39]

Martha Burnes supported Landy's assertions in her testimony and added that Woodbury had decided to leave the Church because she had spiritually outgrown all material organizations. Burnes tried to impress upon the others just how frighteningly seductive Woodbury could be. Burnes had remained loyal to Woodbury because she had threatened death and financial ruin for Burnes's family, and, who knew for certain, she might have been able to do it.[40]

The fullest testimony came from Carolyn Roach, who had been a student of Woodbury's and had known her well for eight years. Around the beginning of June 1890, she was summoned to Woodbury's Dartmouth Street home. This puzzled Roach, for Woodbury had forbidden any of them to see her for several months. When Woodbury entered the room, she was quite obviously pregnant. Roach was shocked, for she had believed that her teacher led a sexually abstemious life. Befuddled, she barely heard Woodbury's oblique reference to her pregnancy and her unusual explanation of it. The struggle had ceased, her teacher said; malicious animal magnetism had been met and conquered, the plot hatched against Woodbury had been exposed and eliminated, and Christian Science had been Woodbury's strength through the whole ordeal. But, while her spiritual sense had remained clear and untroubled, it was evident that Woodbury's body had been put through agony.

One student entered Woodbury's chambers shortly before the birth of the child. She was so shocked that she asked for a room where she could be alone. After several hours, she stepped out of the room and said to Woodbury that the child she had conceived "is of the Holy Ghost. You are Mary!" By the time of the baby's arrival, Woodbury had convinced herself that this identification with the biblical Mary and Mary Baker Eddy was complete. Besides declaring the birth a virgin one, she further claimed to a small group gathered around her that the father and mother of the baby boy was *Science and Health*.

And that was not all: Mrs. Eddy had helped her in the hour of birth, functioning, one supposes, as a spiritual midwife. In fact, Woodbury claimed that just before giving birth, she had a telegram sent to Mrs. Eddy asking for help. While the message was being carried to the telegraph office, Woodbury was convinced that she saw a black cat in the bed. Terrified, she asked a Mrs. Perry to get rid of the frightening animal. One can only guess what Mrs. Perry thought when her cautious steps drew her to the bed and she peered down to see not a black cat, the sign of evil, but a baby boy. Woodbury immediately accepted this as a miraculous transmogrification and told her students to look upon the child as a younger brother, who would one day save the cause of Christian Science and redeem the world. He would be able to talk at the age of three months and thus announce his mission.

While Roach and two other students stayed with Woodbury shortly after the birth, they were genuinely "shocked, puzzled, and skeptical" about the glaring inconsistencies in their teacher's morality. On the one hand, she insisted that his miraculous conception was a sign of her pure spirituality; on the other hand, she led them, out of the blue, into a frank discussion of the meaning of sodomy and buggery. Roach's cheeks reddened when Woodbury said to her one day that if she "let a man roll over" her, she could get anything from him. Woodbury, it seemed, had climbed a few sexual peaks while ascending her spiritual heights.

One evening, while Roach and the other two students were in Woodbury's home, she felt that they were ready to experience "the Vision of the Apocalypse," no doubt with special reference to Revelation 12—the woman clothed with the sun, travailing in birth, and the red dragon standing by to devour her child. Certainly Revelation 12:5 spoke directly to Woodbury: "And she brought forth a man child, who was to rule all nations with a rod of iron: and her child was caught up unto God, and to his throne." That night Woodbury expected her students to retire and to experience the same glorious vision she had. Much to her dismay and anger, they did not. Although they had a vague impression that a robed figure was in the room, this was hardly the confirmatory vision Woodbury had in mind. By the time the three students left her house, they were on the verge of rejecting her, but none of them was strong enough to do so. As a result, the importunings of some of Woodbury's other students led Roach and the other two back into the fold.

One morning in August 1890, at Ocean Point, Maine, where Woodbury and some of her followers had gone shortly after the birth of her baby, she decided to test the limits of *Science and Health*. If it had helped her to give birth to her boy, it could confirm his spiritual purity (and hers) in a baptismal ritual of her choosing. She read to her students an account from the book in which a father taught his son to remain underwater for several minutes without discomfort. What was good enough for this boy was good enough for her two-month-old son. Woodbury took him to the water's edge and submerged him. The onlookers could hear him choking and thrashing about; then it seemed as if he lay perfectly still for a moment. When Mrs. Woodbury lifted his lifeless body out of the water, for a horrifying moment it appeared that he was dead. But then the small gathering heard him gasp for air, and Woodbury immediately blamed her students' mental attitude, their lack of faith, for her son's inability to remain underwater without discomfort.[41]*

In the meantime, she had christened him the "Prince of Peace," and not long after his birth she began to demand that her followers bring him expensive gifts. According to Woodbury, each of her students should feel honored to support the young Prince. Before the child reached the age of one, she announced, he had to have a place large enough for the world to visit him so that he might bestow his blessings. To guarantee the success of this second coming, Woodbury tried to get her students to invest in one of her husband's wild schemes, which quickly went bust.[42]

Instead of immediately severing all ties with this divisive erstwhile student, Mrs. Eddy remained entangled with her for the next six years. Woodbury paid a visit to Mrs. Eddy at Pleasant View on May 2, 1894, and they had an intense tête-à-tête over Woodbury's claims of a virgin birth. At this meeting Woodbury confessed that her child "was incarnated with the devil." Whether it was the black cat or the blackness of sin within her, Woodbury had great difficulty controlling the destructive

* During this period it is evident that Woodbury's identification with Mrs. Eddy was on a primitive level. She had fused with her leader, had grandiose fantasies of absolute perfection (the virgin birth), had moments of destructive anger (holding her infant son under water to the point of threatening his life), and had heightened feelings of persecution (by Richard Kennedy). Even within the framework of the Christian Science movement, Woodbury's thoughts and actions were seen as aberrant. The nature of these issues from a psychoanalytic perspective can be followed in Otto F. Kernberg, *Borderline Conditions and Pathological Narcissism* (New York: Jason Aronson, 1976), especially pp. 175–82.

forces that roiled in her. In 1895 she paid a visit to Julia Bartlett and openly confessed that no one truly knew the egregious sins she had committed. According to Bartlett's memory of the conversation, Woodbury admitted that she had a dark side, that she was filled with evil, that if there were such a thing as a "personal devil," she was that figure. She further acknowledged that she had mentally driven people out of Christian Science, and said that Bartlett simply did not know just how wicked a woman she was. When she took stock of her sinful life, her "agony was almost unbearable." Fortunately, these dark moods did not last long.[43]

In 1895, when Woodbury was seeking admission to the Mother Church, she wrote Mrs. Eddy an interesting letter. Despite her many offenses and despite the fact that she may have been deeply ambivalent about Mrs. Eddy, she needed to be close to her, to feel surrounded by her love so that her considerable anger remained encased in love's arms. What hurt most, Woodbury wrote, was to know that when Mrs. Eddy was "way off in that pure realm," she had somehow disappointed or displeased her. Though Mrs. Eddy promised Woodbury that she would experience a joyous love if she placed her trust in her, Woodbury had her doubts whether even that love would suffice to ameliorate the anguish she now felt. Her end in Christian Science was not far off. Despite Mrs. Eddy's efforts to stall her departure, Woodbury was officially excommunicated in 1896.[44]

Once separated from Mrs. Eddy's love, the devil in Woodbury was given free play. She knew precisely where Mrs. Eddy was vulnerable: the Quimby question. She published an attack on Mrs. Eddy in the journal *The Arena*, in May 1899, openly challenging Mrs. Eddy's assertion that she had originated Christian Science, and she did her best to ridicule Mrs. Eddy's literary output. Woodbury branded her an authoritarian leader and questioned the legitimacy of her healings. Puffing Quimby as the true founder of Mrs. Eddy's healing methods, she mocked Mrs. Eddy's title of Discoverer and Founder and held her up to public humiliation:

> What she had really "discovered" are ways and means of perverting and prostituting the science of healing to her own ecclesiastical aggrandizement, and to the moral and physical depravity of her dupes. As she received this science from Dr. Quimby, it meant simply the healing of bodily ills through a lively reliance on the wholeness and order of the Infinite Mind as clearly perceived and practically demonstrated by a simple and modest love of one's

kind. What she had "founded" is a commercial system monumental in its proportions, but already tottering to its fall.[45]

Woodbury must have had a hard time containing her sadistic glee, knowing what her public attack would do to Mrs. Eddy. In one fell swoop she had succeeded in raising the specters that haunted Mrs. Eddy.

Within a month, Mrs. Eddy went on the offensive. In her annual Communion message to her Church, she depicted the evil symbolized by the "Babylonish woman" of the Apocalypse. Considering that Woodbury's attack had just been published, it seems evident that Mrs. Eddy was launching a counterattack, although she did not mention Woodbury by name. We have already seen that Woodbury identified with the woman in the Book of Revelation, but so did Mrs. Eddy, and this contributed to the blistering attack she levied. Having drunk the blood of saints and Christian martyrs, and having filled her cup with "the wine of her fornication," this woman now had the audacity to enter the Church, the symbolic body of Christ, to corrupt it. If she had her way, this woman would pollute and poison the Church, killing the Truth that could rescue so many lost souls. But she would not have her way, for the vision of the apostle John would hold true. The Babylonish woman would be defeated, and who, Mrs. Eddy asked rhetorically, would mourn the passing of this "widowhood of lust," this representative of everything that was evil and unclean in the world?[46]

This message was blatantly clear to Woodbury. She brought suit for libel. The litigation would drag on for three years. Although Mrs. Eddy eventually triumphed, the heightened public hostility and confusion over the meaning of Christian Science took their toll. During this time Mrs. Eddy suffered physical pains, nightmares, and the belief that Richard Kennedy was again stalking her, and she urged her supporters in Boston to defend mentally against Kennedy and Woodbury. Though Woodbury eventually disappeared from the scene, she left her mark on Mrs. Eddy, who for some time would invoke Woodbury's name in much the same manner that she had warned her students about Richard Kennedy.[47]

Woodbury stood at the far end of the Christian Science spectrum. If, as Frederick Streng observed, religion is a means of ultimate transformation, and if we attribute a psychological dimension to this change, then religion helps people integrate their lives along a wide spectrum of development, from the psychosis of Freud's Schreber, to the adaptation of Erikson's Gandhi, to the call for social justice of Martin Luther King, Jr. Each individual takes his or her chosen religious ideology, with its values, ethics, and beliefs, shapes it, and integrates it according to his or her psychological needs and the level of emotional development he or she has attained.[48]

Beulah Parker has written a poignant story about the deep scars her mother's religion and mental illness left upon each of the children. Parker's description of the role of Christian Science in her mother's life is harrowing:

> Mother really needed her religion. She needed it very badly as a shield against the thoughts and feelings which might have overwhelmed her had she been without such protection. She wore it as an amulet to ward off pain and anxiety and found that the abstract God of Mary Baker Eddy furnished a more effective repellent to evil than the anthropomorphic God of Methodism, who made her feel more helpless and less in command of her own fate. Submission to a totally dominating force in human form already threatened to crush her, and a firm hold on the reality of "divine mind" dispelled the dangerous reality of her very mortal anger, frustration, and despair. By preserving against all attack her "knowledge of the truth," Mother found it possible to maintain her illusions, cope with the emptiness of her daily existence.

As Parker went on to say, her mother's pathology, her excessive need to deny reality, her total plunge into Christian Science ultimately "posed a dire threat to each of us, because it struck at the core of each one's emotional life."[49]

Parker's mother is not being paraded here to illustrate that there is something inherently "sick" about Christian Science, nor am I suggesting that one has to be emotionally ill to believe in it. Rather, I argue that a wide variety of personality types are attracted to religion and that *some* people—not all—bring to it seriously conflicted components of their personalities. Like Parker's mother, Josephine Curtis Woodbury took the doctrines and beliefs of Christian Science and integrated them on a primitive level. There is a big difference between a selective identification with admired traits of Mrs. Eddy and a wish to *become* her.[50]

The most glaring example of the primitive nature of Woodbury's identification with Mrs. Eddy was, of course, Woodbury's belief in the virgin birth of her son. Not only was this a denial of her sexual and aggressive urges, but it emulated Mrs. Eddy, for had she not often talked about giving birth to Christian Science, and was not its father God?

Woodbury's incorporation of Mother Eddy was also a way of protecting herself against her rage toward her. As long as Woodbury could deflect her destructive wishes from Mother Eddy and herself and displace them to another figure, she would be safe. Mrs. Eddy and Christian Science provided Woodbury with a suitable target—the incarnation of evil in Richard Kennedy—and Woodbury became fascinated with him. At times Mrs. Eddy seemed to convey to her students that malicious animal magnetism was a palpable reality. Samuel Bancroft has already spoken about M.A.M.'s being the most vulnerable aspect of her personality, and about the way some of her followers took it to be real. In periods of deep stress, no doubt Mrs. Eddy did see Richard Kennedy and Daniel Spofford as literal evil, but she also had the capacity to pull back from this and discuss evil in more abstract terms as the absence of God. Woodbury lost the capacity to perceive important aspects of her world in these abstract terms; to her, malicious animal magnetism and Kennedy were a terrifying, concrete reality just as the devil in her was.[51]

During the turmoil of the 1880s, Mrs. Eddy seemed to become childish rather than childlike when she was convinced that Kennedy's thoughts from across town could harm her and her students. Evidently Woodbury employed this kind of magical thinking consistently with her followers. They shared the belief that she could mentally cause their financial ruin, illness, and death. It could be argued that this was precisely what Mrs. Eddy told the artist James Gilman about the fate of those who crossed her. There is a difference, however. Mrs. Eddy was showing the failures that befell some of her students when their lives were no longer guided by the principles of Christian Science. Woodbury, on the other hand, was telling her students that her thoughts and wishes could harm them.[52]

To identify with Mrs. Eddy on a childish level meant that Woodbury saw herself and important others in her life through a lens colored by primitive perfectionism. That is, according to the testimony of her followers, she believed Mrs. Eddy was perfect. She was not *like* God; she *was* God, and in her identification with this exalted leader, Woodbury was not *like* Mrs. Eddy, she *was* Mrs. Eddy. As long as this idealization of Mrs. Eddy and her self could be maintained, Woodbury could function in a relatively smooth way and project the image of a powerful, charismatic figure in her own right. But once the idealization began to break down, she found it increasingly difficult to manage her highly conflicted feelings, and she was forced to bring Mrs. Eddy into the fray. Mrs. Eddy and *Science and Health* were there at the birth of Woodbury's son and intimately involved in it. As Woodbury's impulses threatened to break through, her fears of malicious animal magnetism became more intense, and she began to talk about plots and to see the world in a paranoid way. When the idealization finally collapsed, she turned her fury from

Richard Kennedy to Mrs. Eddy. She joined forces with the enemy, Julius Dresser, and remained engaged with Mrs. Eddy in an excited, sadistic way by attacking and humiliating her, first in the *Arena* article and then in the protracted lawsuit.

One must wonder why Mrs. Eddy tolerated her for as long as she did. One might have thought that to protect her movement, she would have cashiered Woodbury long before 1896. We can certainly appreciate Mrs. Eddy's pressing need to find strong people to carry her message to the world, and in these years, when her movement was jolted several times by defecting students, she had to cling to those who showed promise as teachers and healers.

Mrs. Eddy's belief in Christian forgiveness also contributed to her reluctance to take the final step with Woodbury, but one also senses that other factors were involved. In her exaggerated way, Woodbury had the capacity to manipulate people and stir up conflicts within them. It is hard to believe that Mrs. Eddy was not also affected on this level by this gifted but manipulative student. Just what was stirred in Mrs. Eddy, however, must remain in the realm of conjecture, for the evidence simply does not allow anything firmer. Nevertheless, we need to examine more closely why a number of these influential women fell by the wayside.

During the 1880s and 1890s, Mrs. Eddy longed to find students who were able and willing to carry *her* Christian Science message to the world. Through their capacity to heal and to attract other students to the movement, Mother Eddy's child would be properly fed and would grow in strength. Without them, it would starve and die. When we recall the defection of her most trusted students in 1881, we can surely understand Mrs. Eddy's anguish, and we can also understand why she might idealize those special people who showed promise.

Mrs. Eddy once encouraged Clara Choate in a letter to live as closely by the dictates of the golden rule as she could. She should, moreover, never be envious and should extend her goodwill to all except "those whom *God hates*." Honesty was imperative. And there was more. If Choate was able to live by Mrs. Eddy's teachings perfectly—if she was able to live her life according to "the *rules* of science"—then she stood a good chance of becoming one of the world's preeminent healers. At the very moment that Mrs. Eddy confirmed Choate's great potential in the movement, she cautioned her not to let it go to her head; Mrs. Eddy was not elevating her above the other students.[53]

One can well understand why Mrs. Eddy tacked on that caveat, for in the past her movement had experienced dissension over this very issue. One can also understand that Mrs. Eddy was of two minds on this issue; she wished to treat all of her children as spiritual equals, yet she was attracted to some more than others. No doubt part of Choate's reputation as Mrs. Eddy's star pupil came from Choate's own desires and the boasting of her followers. Another part, though, emanated from Mrs. Eddy's own feelings about a promising student. We have earlier heard Mrs. Eddy confess to investing others with her ideal, inflating their potential in her mind (and theirs), and assuming that her students had fully internalized her ideal.[54]

Clara Choate, Emma Hopkins, and Josephine Woodbury: Mother Eddy loved these daughters as her idealized mother had loved her, and she loved them as an idealized aspect of herself. As long as they toed the line of her Christian Science teachings and fulfilled her ideal image of them, then the mutual idealizations could be maintained. In some ways, this method of identification fostered in Choate and Woodbury the kind of idolatry that Mrs. Eddy outwardly eschewed. Moreover, it was this kind of glorification that nudged them across the line; once across, they were unable to live their lives *perfectly* within her doctrines. When this kind of violation occurred, Mrs. Eddy, identifying partly with the punishing mother and partly with the willfully disobedient child, lashed out with her stinging rebukes. This is not to suggest that this process of identification fully colored all of her interactions with Choate. There were times when their relationship was on a more neutral ground, when the reprimands were well deserved, and when they came from Mrs. Eddy's spiritual side. As the relationship grew more strained, however, the personal elements seeped in, from both sides of the relationship.

As was discussed earlier in the incident with the spinning wheel, Mrs. Eddy resolved this overwhelming event by throwing her arms around her mother's neck; the love and the acceptance of guilt would mute the anger provoked by the attack. As an adult, Mrs. Eddy used the same imagery in her conflict with and separation from Choate. In June 1884, she wrote her to say that on that beautiful morning she wished that she could meet with Choate, place her arms around her neck, and tell her how much she loved her. She never felt happier than when thinking of the way their relationship used to be: a loving mother and a loving daughter, with the mother asking God to bless her child over many years. She told Choate that she had forgiven her because she loved her, and she could not hold a grudge against someone who had done as much good work as Choate had. Even if a person had greatly erred, Mrs. Eddy confessed, she still would have nothing but love for that person. That was the way she was; she was incapable of feeling anything else.[55]

But as a result of her overwhelmings earlier in life, Mrs. Eddy, unfortunately, *could* feel otherwise. The repeated plunges from the exalted heights to the despairing depths left an indelible mark on her. Part of her would always seek to master the overwhelmings by repeating variations of them in her current life. For unconscious reasons, then, Mrs. Eddy not only idealized certain promising students and contributed significantly to their spiritual growth and development, but she also contributed unwittingly to the atmosphere of mistrust and to the eventual downfall of some students.

A Big Woman
with a Little Book

*And he had in his hand a little book open: and he set his
right foot upon the sea, and his left foot on the earth.*

Revelation 10:2

AUGUSTA STETSON WOULD PROVE an entirely different problem
for Mrs. Eddy. She grew up in Maine, and after her marriage spent time
in India, Burma, and London. Her husband was an invalid, and to help
make ends meet, Mrs. Stetson began a career as an elocutionist. During
the spring of 1884 she had heard of Christian Science healings and
decided to attend a lecture at a home in Charlestown, Massachusetts.
In the course of the lecture, Stetson felt a lifting of the grief and enervation
that had pressed upon her in the year she had cared for her invalid
husband. While still in this euphoric state, Stetson turned and saw Mrs.
Eddy standing on the stairs. Their eyes met, and unspoken words passed
between the two women. Mrs. Eddy asked Stetson to come to see her
and handed her a card. Stetson hesitated to accept the invitation. According to her account of this first meeting, Mrs. Eddy, sensing her
doubt, urged her again to come, for she was confident that Stetson would
do "a great work in Christian Science."[1]

Whatever the attraction at that first meeting, it deepened when Stetson
overcame her hesitations and joined Mrs. Eddy's class many months
later. She brought her speaking talents into the fold and soon proved a
highly effective healer. By 1886 Mrs. Eddy decided that Stetson's eloquent voice and natural qualities of leadership were exactly what New
York's hustle and bustle needed.

At first the two women seemed to feel mutual respect and admiration.
Through much of the correspondence in the 1880s, Stetson comes across
as an obedient child eager to please her mother. Mrs. Eddy certainly

could have used this support during the late 1880s, when she was again having trouble keeping her students in line and her movement on course. In 1889 Mrs. Eddy wrote Stetson that she greatly appreciated her letters; they were a welcome tonic in her never-ending struggles. She was also thankful that she had as dedicated a student as Stetson. Over the past twenty-five years, she could count on one hand her faithful and devoted students. Pleased that Stetson had followed her directions explicitly, Mrs. Eddy marveled at Stetson's growth in Christian Science. Mother Eddy affirmed lovingly that Stetson was ingesting the truths of Christian Science and "growing like a sweet fat, promising baby."[2]

Stetson in turn reassured Mrs. Eddy that she was her obedient child. In 1900, after a scolding, Stetson apologized and confessed that Mrs. Eddy was a loving mother no matter how naughty her children were. A baby nursing at her mother's breast, feeling discontented or in pain, would "bite the nipple" which was providing the nourishment. The children whom Mrs. Eddy had "fed with the milk of the Mind" had all hurt her when they were babies, but as they grew into spiritual adulthood in Christian Science and experienced the kind of cruelty and sorrow that their mother had, then, in their fight against self and sin, they could eventually make their mother proud of them.[3]

Well before 1900, Augusta Stetson, the spiritual babe, had begun to feel the pangs of pride and ambition and brought more pain than pleasure to Mother Eddy. Writing from New York in the early spring of 1900, Laura Lathrop suggested that Mrs. Eddy summon all her New York students to Pleasant View and give them a good spanking. Truthfully, Lathrop could have written this letter at any time during the preceding fourteen years, probably from the moment Stetson stepped off the train and declared herself the leader of Christian Science in New York.[4]

One can well imagine that Lathrop, who had been laboring long and hard in the New York vineyard, bridled upon hearing Stetson's proclamation that she had been sent by Mrs. Eddy to run things in the city. Actually, tension between the two women had been lying dormant for a number of years, and it did not take much to reawaken it. Lathrop had met Stetson back when Lathrop was taking a course at the Metaphysical College in Boston, and even this early in their careers something told Lathrop to watch out for this woman. She had always felt, Lathrop wrote Mrs. Eddy, that Stetson had the capacity for the greatest good or the greatest evil. Lathrop had to admit, however, that Stetson attracted a large number of wealthy and prominent people to the movement; even so, Lathrop thought she was doing irreparable damage to the Christian Science cause.[5]

According to Lathrop and others, Stetson meddled in the affairs of students and subtly undermined the authority of other teachers, trying to coax students away; in short, she kept the New York movement in turmoil. Throughout all of this, Lathrop carried her grievances to Mrs. Eddy, who was well aware of Stetson's activities. She invariably told Lathrop to be on her guard yet to continue working with Stetson for the greater good of Christian Science. That was easier said than done.

In late January 1888, one of Lathrop's letters to Mrs. Eddy indicates, she was trying her best to accept Stetson and to work with her, but by March things had turned sour. Stetson's machinations only confirmed Lathrop's initial impression: she was exceptionally egotistical, devious in her dealings with others; she could not be trusted. Stetson's avowed purpose in coming to New York was to dominate the Christian Science field in her own name, and she was not above using deceit and outright lies to accomplish this. One incident in particular reveals just how deeply Lathrop and her students feared Stetson's mental powers.[6]

In 1898 Stetson sent a letter to John Lathrop and two other students asking them to meet her. They must have felt that a Siren was luring them to their death, because, after conferring with Laura Lathrop, they decided to delay the meeting for a day. The extra time would be put to good use. Laura Lathrop spent the night in prayer, and when she met with her son and the others, they meditated silently, recited the Lord's Prayer, repeated the Scientific Statement of Being, and said some prayers that Mrs. Eddy had given them. Thus spiritually armed, the students marched off to see Stetson. As Lathrop put it, Love would be their protective shield; their truth and honesty would help open her eyes to the truth, and that was all they really wanted.[7]

"Devil or saint"—those were the words Lathrop used to describe Stetson when they first met at the Metaphysical College. As reluctant as Lathrop might have been to admit it, Stetson had a particular charm that was hard to resist. Lathrop wished that she could fully love and trust Stetson, but she could not. Lathrop came under her spell at times, especially when she heard her preach, but, as Lathrop confided to Mrs. Eddy, she also saw that there was a dark side to Stetson's enchantment.[8]

Stetson had the ability to lure other students into conflicts that aroused envy. Lathrop was not invulnerable. To have any relationship governed by these feelings was to lose sight of the spiritual truth in Christian Science. If this happened, a student might also lose favor with Mrs. Eddy and become separated from her. This was Lathrop's greatest fear: if Stetson succeeded in driving a wedge between her and Mrs. Eddy, Lathrop might lose her mother's love. In an 1894 letter, Lathrop told Mrs. Eddy that she had heard the rumor that Stetson had been called to Pleasant View on a monthly basis. Trying mightily to deny her strong feelings, Lathrop hoped that Mrs. Eddy would not think that just because she was voicing this concern, she was envious of Stetson. If the rumor was true, Lathrop reasoned, Stetson was either in trouble and needed Mrs. Eddy's guidance, or—and she presumably hoped that this was not the case—Mrs. Eddy had grown closer to Stetson spiritually than Lathrop had.[9]

Two days after sending this letter to Mrs. Eddy, Lathrop got a reply. Mrs. Eddy reassured Lathrop that there was no truth to the rumors; in fact she had not seen Stetson for eight months or so. Mrs. Eddy also saw through Lathrop's denials of envy, cautioning her not to let these destructive feelings govern her mind.[10]

Throughout her troubles with Lathrop and other students, Stetson continued to write Mrs. Eddy affectionate, if not ingratiating, letters. In a number she addressed Mrs. Eddy as her "precious Mother," while in others she elevated Mrs. Eddy to a "royal Leader," the "Word made flesh," and the "Mother-in-Israel." Like the three wise men bearing gifts to the baby Jesus, she wished she could bring presents to Mrs. Eddy as expressions of her love and gratitude. In yet another instance, she gushed that she would never be able to show enough gratitude for Mother Eddy's "tender, chiding, and watchful care" of her sometimes disobedient child. In time the veil that hid Mrs. Eddy's true identity from the rest of the world would lift and all would see her "as God manifest."[11]

It would be cynical to dismiss all Stetson's adulation as a self-serving mask for her own ambitions. Part of her genuinely admired Mrs. Eddy and wished to become her favored child. She bestowed lavish gifts upon Mrs. Eddy, and, partly because of her identification with her, she, too, wanted to adopt a student. Just as Mrs. Eddy had adopted Foster Eddy, so Stetson sought Mrs. Eddy's permission in 1890 to adopt Carol Norton, an ardent student. Mrs. Eddy wisely counseled against the adoption. The lavish gifts did not especially please or impress Mrs. Eddy; nevertheless, a strong bond tied these two women together. Just how tight this bond was was revealed indirectly in Stetson's visions or dreams involving Mrs. Eddy.[12]

Stetson's dreams, of course, were her personal creations, and as such they reveal something about her deepest thoughts and feelings. They also reflected something much broader than her personal concerns. Mrs. Eddy and her students saw dreams and visions as valuable forms of communication. In her monumental discovery of Christian Science, Mrs. Eddy had revived and restored the spiritual roots in the healing practices of Jesus. She did not segregate or isolate her discovery from other aspects of primitive Christianity as it was revealed in the Bible. The Old Testament is replete with dreams and visions in which God revealed His will to man. Indeed, as Morton Kelsey points out in abundant detail in his book on dreams, visions, and prophecy, through this form of communication with man, which bypassed the critical, examining ego, God brought to man a special way of knowing the world around him. In so doing, He gave man a more direct understanding of His reality and will. Mrs. Eddy and her students did not, like Freud, look upon the dream as a royal road to the unconscious or a buried past. They focused instead on the dream as a form of spiritual communication pointing through the present to the future.[13]

Martha Harris Bogue came to Christian Science in the late 1880s, attending Mrs. Eddy's Primary Class in 1888 and a year later taking her Normal Class. Bogue was a successful practitioner in Chicago and a charter member of the First Church of Christ, Scientist there. She recalled one class with Mrs. Eddy that revolved around the crucifixion of Jesus. Mrs. Eddy feared that her Christian Science truth was being crucified by Ursula Gestefeld's recent book, which claimed to be Christian Science but grossly distorted her message. When a student asked Mrs. Eddy whether she meant to say that she herself was about to be crucified, she said no, and then clarified her point by recounting three visions she had had.

In the first vision she saw a beautiful maiden, clothed in pure white, who was standing at an altar being married "to a terrible sensuous man." Fearing marriage to this man, Mrs. Eddy fell to her knees in tears, but she was quickly forced back to her feet. About three years later, the man in that vision came to her for treatment; she did not want to accept him because he was a horrible sinner. Despite this, her husband, Dr. Eddy, said that she should see the man. She did and he became her student. Shortly thereafter she had her second vision. This time she saw herself standing with a beautiful child in her arms. This same man approached her, ripped away the bottom part of her garment, dragged it through the dirt, and then placed it around "the neck of a *negro*."

Mrs. Eddy's third vision was on November 11, 1888, the day before Martha Bogue's class with her. Mrs. Eddy saw herself again holding the child in her arms; its once-pure white garments had been stripped away. She was standing on a precipice; a high ledge in front of her made it impossible to climb while holding the baby in her arms. She could not turn back; something was driving her to climb higher. There were no alternative paths; she had to go straight ahead. She placed the child at her feet and held it by a single finger.

With their eyes fixed raptly on Mrs. Eddy, Bogue and the other students heard her interpretation of these visions. She employed them as a way of fortifying herself and the group, as a way of reassuring students that present attacks would not sidetrack her, and as a way of restoring hope about Christian Science's future. At first Mrs. Eddy had read the last vision as a sign that she was about to be crucified again, but now she knew that there would be one more vision which would show her climbing the cliff and rising above all animal magnetism. She and the movement would reach higher spiritual truths, she was convinced, but she needed the unqualified support of her students to reach new heights.[14]

While Mrs. Eddy openly shared her visions and dreams with her students, she was also a willing listener and interpreter. Janet Coleman, who had a distinguished career as a practitioner and, along with her husband, was asked by Mrs. Eddy to help organize the First Church of Christ, Scientist, several times brought her dreams to Mrs. Eddy. In the last, Coleman thought she and some of the other students were at Pleasant View. The older students were slicing a cake, which was very white and filled with fruit. Every time Mrs. Eddy handed out a piece of cake, her hungry students madly scrambled for it, and Coleman was never quick enough to get one. As one student darted for a piece, he left an opening in the crowd; at this moment Mrs. Eddy saw Coleman. She cut a large piece of cake for her, much larger than any of the others had received. Mrs. Eddy then beckoned to Coleman. At this point, Coleman awakened.

Mrs. Eddy interpreted Coleman's dream within a biblical frame of reference, reassuring Coleman that she had not overlooked her. As the dream suggested, Coleman was to receive more than the others; in fact, she was to get the "Benjamin Portion." What Mrs. Eddy was referring to was Genesis 43:34, in which Joseph's youngest brother, Benjamin, received in his sack five times as much as the others.[15]

The dreams that Stetson shared with Mrs. Eddy came in the late 1890s, when the relationship between the two women was becoming increasingly strained. During this time Stetson's success and popularity had, as we have seen, stimulated the jealousy of other Christian Scientists. She was accused—rightly—of tampering with the students of other Christian Science teachers, of telling others that she was Mrs. Eddy's favorite student and heir apparent, of seeking publicity for herself, and of continually fomenting trouble among Christian Scientists in New York.[16]

In the midst of all these charges, Mrs. Eddy was remarkably forbearing; in fact, in her letters to Stetson she seemed genuinely warmer than she was with either Woodbury or Hopkins. Nevertheless, in one ear Mrs. Eddy was hearing increasingly loud whispers of Stetson's machinations, while in the other she was hearing Stetson's equally loud protestations of innocence. The evidence was piling up against Stetson by 1895, and at this time she sent Mrs. Eddy letters describing recent dreams in which she and Mrs. Eddy were the central figures.[17]

The description of one dream is long and highly structured; in fact, it lacks the freshness and spontaneity that one would expect to find in an initial reporting of a dream. Stetson obviously reworked the dream into a coherent narrative that she could share with Mrs. Eddy. Stetson presents herself as a dutiful, loving daughter who is trying her best to close the gap between herself and her spiritually advanced mother. As the dream unfolds, Stetson willingly follows Mrs. Eddy anywhere and suffers any hardship so that she may be like her esteemed leader. Try as she might, however, Stetson can never quite catch up. Mrs. Eddy is clearly the beautiful one, the admired one, the powerful one; she is, in a word, *everything*. Stetson, in marked contrast, is virtually nothing, certainly no match for the idealized figure she so ardently pursues.

According to her letter, when Stetson awoke, she got up and immediately began to read her Bible. Her eyes fastened upon the sixth verse of the sixth chapter of Isaiah. Uplifted by those verses on visions and prophecies, Stetson told Mrs. Eddy that ever since her dream and the reading of these particular verses, she had been seeing "wondrous things out of God's law." What Mrs. Stetson could not admit to herself (and certainly not share with Mrs. Eddy) was that beneath her admiration of Mrs. Eddy lay her competitive wish not merely to catch up with her mother, but to supersede her.

When Stetson showered Mrs. Eddy with expensive gifts in the late 1890s, her gifts had strings attached. In the latter part of 1895, Stetson reported another dream to Mrs. Eddy that shared some of the attributes of the earlier one. The night before she had received Mrs. Eddy's most recent letter, Stetson had dreamed that Mrs. Eddy came to her, took her hand, and placed on her finger a ring with a large, beautifully cut amethyst and a band of gold. Stetson felt both elated and apprehensive. If she wore it, others would try to steal it. Mrs. Eddy allayed her fears by saying that she had given her the ring, and no one would hurt her.[18]

In this second dream, the ring was no ordinary ring; its size and beauty were unmatched. It was indeed the symbol of Mrs. Eddy's power, which she had willingly relinquished to Stetson. Actually, Mrs. Eddy's compliant, loving gesture masked Stetson's envy and jealousy of Mrs. Eddy's position and power. Mrs. Eddy's assurance that she had given the ring to her and that no harm would befall her, assuaged Stetson's guilt for the aggressive wish to possess what belonged to the mother. In a November 1895 letter to Mrs. Eddy that followed one of her rebukes,

Stetson wrote placatingly that she simply could not bear to think that she might be in danger of losing her mother's love. "Do not let go my hand," she pleaded.[19]

In the years that lay ahead, until her dismissal from the Church in 1909, this ambivalence in Stetson continued to disrupt her relationship with Mrs. Eddy. She wanted to cling to Mrs. Eddy's hand; she wanted to feel her arms around her; she wanted to share in her Mother's power and to reflect it. But another part of Stetson wished to throw aside the hand, to unwrap the arms, to usurp the mother's power. Their letters after 1895 follow a familiar pattern: Mrs. Eddy's rebukes elicited Stetson's protestations of innocence; in truth, she loved Mrs. Eddy.

Mrs. Eddy appealed to the loving part of Stetson and tried to enlist it for the greater good of Christian Science. In 1899 she wrote to Laura Lathrop and her son, John, who were busy defending themselves against Stetson, that no matter how disruptive she was, they were to keep cordial ties with her. Such divisiveness among her leading students would result in irreparable damage to the Christian Science cause. If the truth were known, she had suffered more from Stetson's transgressions than they ever had. Moreover, she saw signs of improvement; the rebukes were having their intended effect. Mrs. Eddy recognized Stetson's considerable potential for good, and that was why she kept her in the movement.[20]

As the founder of the First Church of Christ, Scientist in New York City, Stetson had built up a substantial following, and she had raised the money to build her own church in 1903. By this time it was becoming increasingly difficult for Mrs. Eddy to tell for whose greater glory this new church was constructed. Stetson certainly did not cut corners. According to the *Chicago Sunday American*, it was a striking building. Its John LaFarge stained-glass windows were patterned after Michelangelo's designs. The interior was decorated with flowers shaped from ivory and overlaid with gold. Chandeliers of gold graced the hallways; Persian and Turkish rugs covered the floors, while the delicately carved Spanish furniture was made from the finest mahogany. The organ alone cost $25,000. In an interview with the *American*, Stetson emphatically denied that she had any intention of building a bigger church than Mrs. Eddy's or was trying to outshine her. Stetson was so far removed from Mrs. Eddy's spiritual greatness that she counted herself lucky just to "touch the hem of her garment."[21]

No matter how charming and powerful Stetson may have appeared to her New York followers, her relationship to her leader revealed an inner fragility. The dreams and her correspondence with Mrs. Eddy dealt with issues of her self-regard, and exposed her feelings of feminine inadequacy. Stetson admired in order to be admired; she loved in order to be loved; she elevated Mrs. Eddy in order to rise with her. However, as long as Stetson could keep her demands for admiration within the bounds set by Mrs. Eddy's teachings and her goals for Christian Science, as long as there was a close enough fit between Stetson's private dream of glory and Mrs. Eddy's own dreams, then Mrs. Eddy could genuinely admire the speaking and healing gifts that made Stetson a highly attractive figure.

Once Stetson's ambition was placed predominantly in the service of her own needs; that is, once she began to alter Mrs. Eddy's doctrines and tamper with her students in a controlling, seductive manner, she transgressed the spiritual tie, and the ensuing conflict threatened to pull Mrs. Eddy into the whirlpool of personal feelings, an area in which Mrs. Eddy was not invulnerable. However, she had the capacity to step back and disentangle herself. In the end, there could be no room for Stetson in the movement, and, like Woodbury, she was excommunicated from the Church.[22]

Mrs. Stetson's conflicts, along with those of the other women like Woodbury, threw into bold relief an issue that hindered the movement almost from its inception: the overinflation of the spiritual ideal. The tendency of Mrs. Eddy's students to glorify her as the Woman of the Apocalypse, as the second coming of Christ, or even as greater than Jesus, was a central issue in the Woodbury lawsuit. Woodbury charged that Mrs. Eddy considered herself the Woman of the Apocalypse and *Science and Health* divinely inspired. Though Mrs. Eddy won this case, the issues it raised were never fully settled in the movement. Was Mrs. Eddy the prophesied one? If so, then she could be seen as on equal footing with Christ. Or was Mrs. Eddy fulfilling prophecy? If so, then she was a spiritually gifted mortal, who, like other human beings, was still striving to reach the perfection of Christ. Mrs. Eddy's nature, especially how she herself saw it, has been a sensitive issue among Christian Scientists, as the recent uproar over the publication of Bliss Knapp's book indicates. For the outsider, any discussion of this topic is like stepping into a minefield. Perhaps the safest spot is the well-trod area where some of her students unabashedly sang her praises.

All Christian Science students would have agreed that Mrs. Eddy had a greater spiritual sensitivity than any of them. None of them, for instance, could have said what Mrs. Eddy said to Lida Fitzpatrick and some of the other Pleasant View workers in 1903: she knew what the future held, but she could not tell them because they were, spiritually speaking, too young. They had much to learn; it was "the time to experiment." But, she reassured her rapt students, one day they, too, would see what she had seen. Even if she truly believed that all men and women reflected God's idea, to her students Mrs. Eddy mirrored His Truth more flawlessly than they. In 1907, Lida Fitzpatrick recorded Mrs. Eddy saying God spoke to her through the Bible "as a person talks to another," and He had been communicating with her this way for forty years.[23]

Edward Everett Norwood spent most of his Christian Science career in the South. In 1898 he took Mrs. Eddy's last class, where, one day, he had a remarkable experience. Never quite explaining what led up to this supercharged moment, Norwood said that suddenly he felt as if a veil had been lifted and he was able to see the awe-inspiring oneness, vastness, and "eternal silence" of God's realm. As he looked around him and saw the ordinary walls and furnishings of the room, he realized that he had broken through the plane of material reality and everyday perception; he was now seeing reality in all its wonder. For a brief moment Norwood had glimpsed "the Way—the road our great Leader trod," the very same spiritual path that Jesus had earlier walked. Remaining in this blissful state was impossible; the veil lowered, and Norwood returned to the mundane world.[24]

Norwood was not the only student who had this kind of experience in Mrs. Eddy's presence. Joseph Armstrong, a longtime publisher of Mrs. Eddy's journals and writings, told Norwood about the time he was called to Pleasant View to consult with her. In the course of their conversation, Mrs. Eddy told him about a class she would be teaching. The spiritual music accompanying her words uplifted and transformed Armstrong; a marvelous vista opened before him, and for a brief moment he saw the wonderful spiritual reality about which Mrs. Eddy often spoke. Ecstatically, Armstrong said to her that he had never imagined in his wildest dreams that such a marvelous world existed. And to think, Armstrong mused, this was the realm Mrs. Eddy lived in much of the time.[25]

While all Mrs. Eddy's students performed healings, Mrs. Eddy's healings were special in their eyes. We remember that Janet Coleman heard Mrs. Eddy speak at the Chicago Convention in 1888, and that on the second day many people came up to the stage to be healed by her. This sight filled Coleman with an unspeakable joy; that night she had a vision related to this experience, in which she saw Jesus and Mrs. Eddy becoming one.[26]

An even more dramatic healing took place within the walls of Pleasant View. One day Clara Shannon was taking dictation from Mrs. Eddy when she was asked to take a message to Calvin Frye. When Shannon got to his room, she saw him lying face up on the floor; apparently he had fainted. She immediately called Mrs. Eddy, who rushed to the room.

She knelt beside him and healed him with a gentleness, love, and care that Shannon had never before observed. Shortly Frye opened his eyes, whereupon Mrs. Eddy altered her method of treatment; her voice sounded sterner as she strongly reproved him for the error that had led to his collapse.

After Mrs. Eddy helped Frye to his feet, she returned to her room, where she immediately summoned Frye to her side and continued to thunder against his error. She then told him to go to his room, but before he got there, she called him back and spoke against the error. Mrs. Eddy repeated this several times; at one point Shannon interceded, asking her to let Frye rest for a moment or two. Mrs. Eddy replied that if he rested he might die, and they could not permit this to happen. They had to keep him alert and awake. She then told Frye a story that made him laugh. As Mrs. Eddy later explained to Shannon, this was the moment when the error had broken. In healing, as Shannon remembered her leader's words, when you uttered the truth directly to somebody, and if your words evoked an emotional response such as laughter, tears, or anger, then you had succeeded in reaching "the thought that needed correction."[27]

For Bliss Knapp this healing of Frye meant one thing: Mrs. Eddy had emulated the Master when He raised Lazarus from the dead. Indeed, Mrs. Eddy had brought Frye back "from the symptoms of death," which was truly inspiring for any Christian Scientist. Of course, she was not the first to do this kind of healing. The Bible mentions numerous incidents in which Jesus, Daniel, Peter, Paul, and others overcame death through their comprehension of the Fatherhood of God. Now, said Knapp, Mrs. Eddy carried this understanding into the present age as an expression of the Motherhood of God.[28]

If Bliss Knapp connected Mrs. Eddy and her healings to biblical precedents, his father, Ira, was doing the same thing long before his son. Ira scoured the Scriptures, and his active imagination forged indissoluble links between Mrs. Eddy and biblical prophecy: she was God's messenger to this age; she was the Woman of the Apocalypse as foretold in Revelation 12, and Christian Science was nothing less than the second coming of Christ. Some might excuse Ira Knapp's fervor and dismiss him as a wild man, as one of those students better left alone on the radical fringe of the movement. Yet Ira was not alone, for a number of Mrs. Eddy's most experienced and trusted students shared his perceptions, if not the depth of his spiritual enthusiasm.[29]

As rock-solid a student as Caroline Noyes believed in Mrs. Eddy's divine calling. A hallmark of Mrs. Eddy's students and devoted followers was that they recognized and accepted the fact that their leader was the woman prophesied by John in Revelation 12. It was equally clear to them that *Science and Health* was the little book that the angel held in his hand in Revelation 10. The writing of *Science and Health* was inspired; no human hand had created it. This little book was a fulfillment of prophecy; it was indeed a sacred book. In treating woman as the equal of man, Christian Science was the one true religion creating a spiritual wholeness in today's people. Those who followed the tenets of this new religion recognized Mrs. Eddy as its Discoverer and Founder and as the one who linked the modern age directly to the truths of Christ. Her way was the way to the world's salvation.[30]

We have seen how generally competent and efficient Septimus Hanna was in carrying out his responsibilities as editor of *The Christian Science Journal* and as First Reader. His practical, hardheaded business side, however, was fueled by a spiritual intensity not unlike Ira Knapp's and Caroline Noyes's when it came to Mrs. Eddy's place within the movement. In his reminiscences, he told a story about the time when, in 1898, he had felt undue stress related to his work. He asked Mrs. Eddy for permission to resign one of his posts so that he could concentrate his energies and do a good job for her. Mrs. Eddy would not permit this, but she did recommend that he seek solitude for a few hours a day in order to restore his spiritual strength.

Hanna took her advice; he went up to the tower of Mrs. Eddy's Commonwealth Avenue home in Boston, where he lived while he was First Reader. Withdrawing from the hubbub of the world, Hanna concentrated on his Bible reading. One day his eyes became riveted on Chapters 53 and 54 of Isaiah. As he studied the latter, it suddenly came to him as clearly as a voice speaking out loud that this chapter pertained as directly to Mrs. Eddy as it did to Jesus. Chapter 54, too, was literally a prophecy of Mrs. Eddy, just as it was of Jesus. Hanna's new awareness was not, he adamantly declared, the product of emotional excess or momentary ecstasy. It grew out of the roots of a deep spiritual understanding about the meaning of prophecy.[31]

Before Hanna had climbed the stairs to this tower room, he had received a copy of Gardiner Spring's "Fragments from the Study of a Pastor." Spring was a minister at the Brick Presbyterian Church in New York City, and his short book of prophecy dovetailed with Hanna's understanding of Isaiah and added fuel to Hanna's spiritual fire. In the heat of the spiritual moment, Hanna wrote an article for publication in the *Journal* spelling out Mrs. Eddy's direct connection to the biblical prophecies. Although the article got as far as galley proofs, it was never published, though Hanna later included it among his reminiscences.

"The Church of the Wilderness," as the article was called, declared that the age of prophecy and prophets was not confined to biblical times; it was here and now in Mrs. Eddy and Christian Science. Throughout the Bible God manifested Himself to man; His most unique expression of this was as Christ Jesus. Even in biblical times, however, man was reluctant to accept these manifestations of God, and the same was true now, wrote Hanna. Nevertheless, the individual expression of God was with us today in Mary Baker Eddy, and one could prove this by turning to pertinent chapters and verses in Genesis, Isaiah, Jeremiah, and, of course, Revelation.

From the Christian Science point of view, Jesus represented a revelation of God's maleness; His complete revelation would have to include His femaleness. Christian Scientists believed in a whole, integrated God; therefore, they saw in Genesis a prophecy of the second coming in a female form, while Revelation presented the end result of this prophecy. Christian Scientists, claimed Hanna, saw the Woman of the Apocalypse as a type or symbol of the female aspect of God mentioned in Genesis. Moreover, the woman of travail mentioned in Isaiah 54 and again in Jeremiah 4, as well as the woman God spoke of in Isaiah 62 and 66, left no doubt in the mind of anyone familiar with Mrs. Eddy's personal life and career that she was this woman. In light of all this, questioned Hanna rhetorically, would it not be consistent to argue that the second coming was here? And where it was noted in the Bible that a woman was the chosen instrument of this coming, was it not consistent to argue that Mrs. Eddy was "the personal representative" of the second coming? Was there any part of this that might be considered "far-fetched or unreasonable?"[32]

Certainly the Christian Scientists of Kansas City did not think it was either far-fetched or unreasonable. In early July 1897, a small party of Scientists from that city went to Concord to see Mrs. Eddy. When they returned home, they wanted to send her a token of their love and veneration. What seemed appropriate to them was a crown, a symbol which Mrs. Eddy used as an imprint on all her publications. The crown her students sent contained forty-six pearls and twelve diamonds; it recalled the crown worn by the woman described in Revelation 12:1. Moreover, her students believed that Mrs. Eddy's book was the little book referred to in Revelation 10:2–3. *Science and Health* "gives the true idea of God and the spiritual interpretation of the Scriptures, that which heals the sick and reforms the sinner."[33]

As much as Mrs. Eddy appreciated this gift of love from her students, she was also aware that during the late 1880s and 1890s, her students' glorification of her was becoming excessive. She tried to curb it. In 1898 she wrote to Hanna that this "hyperbolic praise" of her in the *Journal* must be stopped. In early September 1895, Mrs. Eddy told Laura Sargent that whenever she taught students, she had to instruct them that she, Mrs. Eddy, was the Wayshower. "I am not the Way," she said with emphasis. God and Christ were the Way; through her writings and teachings of Love, Life, and Truth she could show others the Way. Because excessive flattery erased this distinction between the Wayshower and the Way, Mrs. Eddy tried to divert attention from herself and direct it toward the power that came through her as expressed in her works. She understood that a true Christian Scientist could never build on personality; such a flimsy structure would be pulled down too easily.[34]

A student named William McKenzie remembered Mrs. Eddy's once saying to him that when she heard people mention her in the same breath with Christ, it made her "shiver" because the more she understood "His true character and work," the more clearly she saw how spiritually elevated He was above everyone. In a December 1900 letter, Mrs. Eddy scolded Augusta Stetson for claiming that she, Mrs. Eddy, was the Christ. She tried fruitlessly to set the record straight on this issue, but it was evident that Stetson could not or would not hear her. She was not the Christ, Mrs. Eddy stated unequivocally. If Stetson insisted on making this comparison, she was disobeying her and injuring the cause. Mrs. Eddy urged her to reread some of her writings on this subject. She always explained Christ in spiritual terms, never in corporeal ones. Jesus was a man; Christ was the Holy Ghost, the spiritual idea of God. She, Mrs. Eddy, was corporeal in the same sense that Paul was. Nevertheless, God had chosen her to bring His work and Word to the rest of the world. She was anointed to do the work that nobody, except Jesus, had done before. As both Paul and Christ were misunderstood in their time, she suffered a similar fate in hers. Those who followed them and obeyed Christ and Paul were blessed; the same would hold true for those who followed and obeyed Mrs. Eddy.[35]

Annie Knott recalled a similar incident that occurred in 1903 when she was a guest at Pleasant View. Mrs. Eddy had requested her presence shortly after breakfast. When Knott entered the room, Mrs. Eddy, who had been reading the Bible, said that she had just read John 4:39–42, and she had seen it in a new light. Mrs. Eddy put particular emphasis upon the forty-second verse: "And said unto the woman, Now we believe, not because of thy saying: for we have heard him ourselves, and know that this is indeed the Christ, the Saviour of the world." After reading this, Mrs. Eddy paused thoughtfully and decided to share it with the other members of her household. When they gathered, she reread the passage and reminded them that they believed not because of what she had told them but because they had proved for themselves that Christian Science was indeed the redeemer of the world.[36]

To squelch the enthusiasm of some of her students, Mrs. Eddy declared in a letter to Julia Field-King in 1892 that her official title should be the one God had given her, Discoverer and Founder. While dignified enough, this title was fairly neutral, and Mrs. Eddy hoped that it would go far toward toning down some of the statements of her students. From these and many other examples a strong case could be built that Mrs. Eddy did her best to stifle the excessive idealization of her, because she knew that it did not reflect a true spirituality, that it could lead to dissension within the movement, and that it could incur hostile attacks from outsiders. Yet the picture is not quite this clear-cut; when it comes to Mrs. Eddy, it seems that there is never a simple answer.

One can understand, for instance, why some of her followers reacted so emotionally to the *Christ and Christmas* book and used it for healing purposes. In the picture "Christian Unity," the two figures in the foreground are Jesus and Mary Baker Eddy. Both are clad in white gowns, and both are bathed in haloes of heavenly light. Jesus is seated; Mary is standing to His left, gazing directly into His eyes, her hand in His. Mary's other hand lies diagonally across her body; in it she is holding a scroll with the words "Christian Science" plainly in view. The inscription on the page opposite this picture reads: " 'Tis the same hand unfolds his power, and writes the page."

In another picture, Gilman depicted a scene in a darkened room in which an old man sits in a rocker listening as a girl reads from a book. The Bible rests on a table by the man, while tucked in the background is a grandfather clock showing the little hand on the five and the big hand on the one. It is the little girl, however, who holds our attention. She sits primly in front of a window with a shaft of bright light illuminating her and the book that she holds open. The title, *Science and Health Key to Scriptures*, is easy for all to see. Underneath the picture lies the caption: "I thank Thee, O Father, Lord of heaven and earth, because Thou hast hid these things from the wise and prudent, and hast revealed them unto babes.—*Christ Jesus*. If one of Mrs. Eddy's students were so inspired, he or she might see the hands of the clock as fingers pointing them to Revelation 5:1, where it is revealed: "And I saw in the right hand of him that sat on the throne a book written within and on the backside, sealed with seven seals." The book was obviously *Science and Health*, and just as obviously Mrs. Eddy and biblical prophecy were intimately linked.[37]

These pictures can be read a number of ways, and it is possible to argue that Mrs. Eddy was not portraying herself as the Second Coming. But there were times when she heard students make this direct comparison and did not put a quick end to the talk. During the troubled days in 1907, when Mrs. Eddy's son, George Glover, her adopted son, Ebenezer Foster Eddy, and other relatives initiated a lawsuit to gain control over her finances by having her declared mentally incompetent, Victoria Sargent, Laura's sister, was called to Pleasant View to help combat the mental forces attacking Mrs. Eddy. One day, in an effort to lift her leader's spirits, Victoria told her that her own students believed that God's Word came through Mrs. Eddy. They were convinced that God's hand guided her in her work and felt, moreover, that she fulfilled scriptural prophecies, especially "the God-crowned woman mentioned in the Apocalypse." Mrs. Eddy did not let this statement pass. She might have scolded Victoria, but she did not. Instead, Mrs. Eddy's finger pointed upward, and she said that her power and her special attributes came "from above."[38]

According to Bliss Knapp, much the same thing happened to his father when he was in class with Mrs. Eddy. She had not yet written her chapter on the Apocalypse for *Science and Health*; nevertheless, she took the time to explain Revelation 12 to the class. Though she never made direct reference to herself in the interpretation, Ira Knapp was quick to make the connection, blurting out to Mrs. Eddy and the others that she was the Woman of the Apocalypse. According to Bliss Knapp, Mrs. Eddy turned to his father and smiled sweetly, but she did not reprimand him.[39]

Septimus Hanna had a similar experience. When Mrs. Eddy read his long article about her role in prophecy, she did not rebuke him. In a June 22, 1898, letter to Hanna, Mrs. Eddy mentioned this article. "Your vision article is too grand, *true*" to be altered, said a pleased Mrs. Eddy. In a letter four days earlier, however, it was evident that some tampering was needed. Mrs. Eddy realized that people were not yet ready to accept "the wonderful things" he wrote about her. Instead of being used to elevate Mrs. Eddy to her rightful place, his words could be used by her critics to devalue her. Mrs. Eddy therefore strongly cautioned Hanna not to say that she represented the Second Coming of Christ. That claim would turn others against Christian Science. Though God had inspired Hanna to say it, malicious animal magnetism had evidently been scheming to use it for its own purposes. Mrs. Eddy seemed to be saying that if Hanna wanted to get his point across, he had to use tact, especially when it came to a sensitive issue like this one. So Mrs. Eddy advised Hanna to cast his truths out on the waters of the world not as bold assertions but as hints and suggestions.[40]

When Mrs. Eddy received the crown from her Kansas City students, with its obvious symbolic reference to the Woman in the Apocalypse, she neither returned it nor chided her students for sending it. She sent a letter that the *Kansas City Star* got hold of and published. In it she acknowledged her students for their "regal gift from loyal hearts." She could not thank them enough; her feelings were "too deep for expression." She prayed that she would be able "to reach the crown of divine love, and to be worthy of your crown so emblematical of your love."[41]

There were times when Mrs. Eddy seemed more explicit on this issue, or at least that is how a devoted follower heard and understood her. Edward and Caroline Bates took a number of classes with Mrs. Eddy in the late 1880s. Over the years Edward Bates held a number of prominent positions, such as supervising the construction of the Mother Church in 1894 and serving as a four-term president of the Mother Church. He believed that Mrs. Eddy was as genuinely inspired as any biblical prophet. When she was completely attuned to God, she could hear His voice providing the revelation of Christian Science and how she was to convey it to mankind. His voice had guided her hand in the writing of *Science and Health*; this sacred book was His.[42]

The key issue for Mrs. Eddy and for some of her followers was to what extent they were able to contain the tendency to exaggerate her powers, putting her on a level with Christ. This was not always easy, whether we are talking about the lean years of the 1870s or the fat ones at the turn of the century. Mrs. Eddy's dealings with Julia Field-King in the latter part of the nineteenth century illustrate how muddied these waters could get.

As has been discussed, Field-King was a highly promising student. For a brief time in 1892 she was the editor of *The Christian Science Journal*, and later she was a Christian Science teacher in St. Louis. Her letters to Mrs. Eddy are exhaustively long, filled with apologies, self-abnegation, and lavish praise. In the fall of 1892, Mrs. Eddy tried to curb Field-King's errors and her cloying dependence, but she was never entirely successful in this. Their long correspondence reveals that she fully recognized her student's limitations; nevertheless, she became involved in one of Field-King's pet projects.[43]

Around 1895 Field-King became engrossed with Charles A. L. Totten's *Our Race: Its Origin and Its Destiny*, particularly with its extolment of the Anglo-Saxon race and its treatment of the woman mentioned in Revelation. Fanning the flames of England's imperialistic fervor, Totten traced Britain's genealogical line back to the biblical David. Field-King, unable to control her desire to praise Mrs. Eddy, reasoned that what was good enough for Queen Victoria was good enough for Mrs. Eddy. She took it upon herself to send a researcher to Washington, and presented her project to Mrs. Eddy in such a way as to suggest that it was a virtual certainty that she was a direct descendent of the King of Israel. In February of 1895, she wrote Mrs. Eddy ecstatically that "the glorious proof" of her direct genealogical link to David was close at hand. When this was made known, she would be hailed as the great king's daughter. Beyond any question, Mrs. Eddy's Christian Science had demonstrated and reinvigorated the teachings of Jesus. It was evident that God was behind this effort to establish her "lineal descent" from His royal line.[44]

In early 1896 Field-King was sent to London, where she had great success in attracting new members to the Church. Her pet project did not die, however, and Mrs. Eddy's interest in it was also kept alive. In February Mrs. Eddy wrote enthusiastically about Field-King's assertion that the line of David could be traced to her mother's family. What attracted Mrs. Eddy to this project in the first place, and what maintained her interest in it over the years, emerged from a welter of motives, some spiritual, some personal, and some cultural.[45]

It is not difficult to see why Mrs. Eddy became personally involved in this quest for roots. She was seventy-five years old; how many years did she have left? Foster Eddy would never be her successor; though the movement was growing, would its bright star continue to shine after Mrs. Eddy passed on? It would have comforted Mrs. Eddy to know that she and Christian Science fulfilled the prophecy in Revelation 22:16: "I Jesus have sent mine angel to testify unto you these things in the churches. I am the root and the offspring of David, and the bright and morning star." In the same vein, Gilbert Carpenter once remarked that Mrs. Eddy often yearned for somebody to "bring her the prophetic vision" that she was the one chosen by God, just as Jesus had been earlier, to deliver God's truth to man. And, what is more, she was just as anxious to know that all the evil in the world could not thwart her mission, could not force her off "the predestined path God had prepared for her."[46]

In a letter to Field-King, Mrs. Eddy confirmed Carpenter's observation; she sought a genealogical line of spiritual purity for her cause, not for reasons of personal aggrandizement, she quickly noted, but because if the direct descent could be established, it might convince others of the legitimacy of her mission. In another letter, she expressed a similar sentiment. The historical link to David might be just the thing to cleanse the White House of the "Mind cure pestilence." Mrs. Eddy had heard that President Cleveland's wife accepted Christian Science, but according to the teachings of some of her disloyal students in Washington. Now, she hoped, she could put an end to that malicious error.[47]

As important as it was, the personal was only one dimension of this quest. Mrs. Eddy was hardly alone in this kind of historical search in the latter part of the nineteenth century. Stimulated by the centennial celebration in 1876, Americans became fascinated with the colonial and Revolutionary War periods. The interest reached fever pitch by the 1890s, stimulating research into local histories. A number of genealogical organizations were formed specifically to help Americans trace their heritage to the Revolutionary armies, political groups such as the Society of Cincinnati, and the *Mayflower*. "Americans of Anglo-Saxon descent," notes Harvey Green, "busily plowed through archives in libraries all over the country" hoping to find a family connection linking them to the cherished names, places, and traditions of the past.[48]

Hereditarian doctrines also had an enormous appeal. These doctrines were attractive to many people for a variety of reasons, but according to Charles Rosenberg, they brought emotional and intellectual comfort to a generation of Americans who needed to impose a sense of order and continuity upon a changing, threatening social order. Rosenberg further notes that one can find hints of "a traditional religious commitment in even the most overtly secular visions of eugenicists and social reformers who sought to restore national vitality and racial purity. Social hereditarianism served as one avenue through which pre-bellum activist and reformist, even millennial, trends could find emotional and social policy continuity."[49]

Over the years, Mrs. Eddy went back and forth on this issue of genealogy; one can even find a reference to it in her correspondence with Field-King at the turn of the century. In looking over the evidence on this long-drawn-out episode, as well as a number of the other incidents, we can conclude that Mrs. Eddy closely identified with the Woman of the Apocalypse and that she felt she had fulfilled biblical prophecy. It is also clear that she did not elevate herself to a station equal with Christ. To her this would have been blasphemy. Perhaps the clearest and most systematic expression of her views on this point came more than three decades after her death. In April 1938, the Christian Science Board of Directors commissioned the Church archivists to ascertain what Mrs. Eddy had actually believed regarding her place in scriptural prophecy. After extensive study, the archivists submitted their findings to the Board of Directors, which had them published in 1943 in the *Christian Science Sentinel* and *The Christian Science Journal*.[50]

The findings were formulated as six brief points. Mrs. Eddy, the Discoverer and Founder of Christian Science (the title she preferred), viewed herself as the one chosen by God to bring His word to mankind. Therefore, she was "the revelator of Christ, Truth," for today's world.

She understood parts of Revelation 12 as pointing to her; she was the woman who fulfilled prophecy by revealing God's truth. Her work, then, paralleled Jesus'. Also, since Jesus revealed the "fatherhood of God," Mrs. Eddy revealed "God's motherhood." Mrs. Eddy thus saw herself as the woman God had appointed and anointed to rediscover the true science of Christian healing and to interpret its meaning to the current age. In fact, she was so closely attached to the message of Christian Science that one could not separate the message from the messenger, the revelator from the revelation. Knowing herself to be the chosen instrument of God protected Mrs. Eddy from the attacks of malicious animal magnetism, and she was deeply grateful to all those who saw her prophetic status and supported her in her cause.

After the sixth and final point, the Board of Directors issued a strong warning to Christian Scientists not to distort the meaning of Mrs. Eddy's role. She fulfilled prophecy, but she was not prophesied the way Christ was. The Directors reminded their fellow Scientists of Mrs. Eddy's own words in *Miscellaneous Writings*: "The Scriptures and Christian Science reveal 'the way,' and personal revelators will take their proper place in history, but will not be deified."[51]

This position statement and the Directors' admonition seem about as clear as one can get regarding Mrs. Eddy's beliefs on her role. How, then, are we to explain her apparent acceptance of Ira Knapp's and Septimus Hanna's glorification? They seemed to be telling her directly that she was the one prophesied in the Bible. We can neither dismiss these recollections as sheer fabrications nor slough off her failure to remonstrate with them as a benign toleration for the excessive love her students felt for her. Something was coming from Mrs. Eddy as well. Just what that something was is not easy to tell. We can suggest that when she did seem to elevate herself and seemed to wink at her students' statements exalting her, it was a momentary lapse, occasioned by stress and the need for support.

This explanation, in turn, takes us back to Mrs. Eddy's inability to keep the two halves of her self in harmony. There was the self of flesh and blood, burdened with a personal past and always threatening to pull her back into anguish and despair. Her need for idealization grew out of biographical experiences that could never be fully expunged. The other self, her spiritual side, liberated her; it offered a perfection that was different from human striving. As we have seen, it was essential that she keep her spiritual side in ascendance, for in this realm a genuine humility kept glorification in check. When she felt undermined or threatened, however, the spiritual self was temporarily invaded by the human self. This intrusion affected how Mrs. Eddy momentarily saw herself in relationship to others and to Christ.

To her credit, Mrs. Eddy always remained a reluctant charismatic figure; she was never fully comfortable with the adulation of her followers, and when it was carried to excess, she began to sense that her spiritual self had been overtaken temporarily by her personal needs. She would then regroup and reestablish the spiritual side of things.

BEARING FRUIT IN OLD AGE

They shall still bring forth fruit in old age; they shall be fat and flourishing;

To shew that the Lord is upright: he is my rock, and there is no unrighteousness in him.

Psalms 92:14–15

HENRY DAVID THOREAU frostily noted in *Walden* that "age is no better, hardly so well, qualified for an instructor as youth, for it has not profitted so much as it has lost. One may almost doubt if the wisest man has learned anything of absolute value by living. Practically, the old have no very important advice to give the young. . . . their lives have been such miserable failures."[1]

A number of recent studies have indicated that old age—roughly seventy-five and beyond—embodies much more than decline and depletion. Leon Edel has described the "creative aging" in Tolstoy, Henry James, and William Butler Yeats. Freud's mind remained fertile and creative until virtually the day he died at eighty-three, but it was Longfellow, writing a poem to commemorate the fiftieth anniversary of his Bowdoin College class of 1825, who most succinctly told us that creativity and productivity do not necessarily cease with advancing age:

> *It is too late! Ah, nothing is too late*
> *Till the tired heart shall cease to palpitate.*
> *Cato learned Greek at eighty; Sophocles*
> *Wrote his grand Oedipus, and Simonides*
> *Bore off the price of verse from his compeers,*
> *When each had numbered more than four-score years.*
> *Chaucer, at Woodstock with the nightingales,*
> *At sixty wrote the Canterbury Tales;*

Goethe at Weimar, toiling to the last,
Completed Faust when eighty years were past.[2]

Several lines later Longfellow shared what might have been a nostalgic wish with his classmates as they entered their early seventies, but today a number of geropsychiatrists would agree that:

These are indeed exceptions; but they show
How far the gulf-stream of our youth may flow
Into the arctic regions of our lives . . .
For age is opportunity no less
Than youth itself, though in another dress
And as the evening twilight fades away
The sky is filled with stars, invisible by day.[3]

That Mary Baker Eddy would show signs of old age, from roughly 1896, when she turned seventy-five, to 1910, when she died, was to be expected. At times she seemed to fit the picture of decline and depletion, but at others she was the picture of vitality and creativity. From the appraisals of outsiders, one would never guess that the ravages of time had marred Mrs. Eddy's beauty or her mind. When Michael Meehan, who was not a Christian Scientist, came to Pleasant View, Mrs. Eddy had just passed her eighty-sixth birthday. Meehan came away impressed with how deliberate and forceful she was.[4]

In the 1890s, Arthur Klein, a playwright, noted for the readers of the *Concord World* that Mrs. Eddy had the voice of command, a voice that knew rather than believed. There was no sign of effusive gushing or "over-inflated ecstasy" when she spoke. She was "calm, self-possessed," and exhibited a "well-poised equilibrium." A reporter for another Concord paper, the *People and Patriot*, had pretty much the same impression of Mrs. Eddy's voice: it came across to him as clear, rich, and musical.[5]

Mrs. Eddy's voice also carried darker tones. Advanced age did not reduce the power of her rebukes; this little old lady could still wither the strongest of her students. Cora Reeves Nunn passed on a story that her husband, Henry, told her about the time he visited Mrs. Eddy in 1899. He was sitting by her side on the sofa when she launched into a censure of her older students. Nunn was shocked by "the rugged, vehement manner" in which she scolded them. Nunn barely had time to collect his thoughts when Mrs. Eddy turned to him with a calm, sweet look and said that she was sorry he had heard it; it was "strong meat" for such a young student. It was only later that Nunn came to understand that Mrs. Eddy was so severe in her admonishments because she was trying to lift the mesmerism that infected her students' work.[6]

Her age did not reduce the reams of letters she sent her students in the field. Adelaide Still, her maid, was impressed with the time and energy Mrs. Eddy devoted to her correspondence and articles even when she had reached her upper years. To say that Mrs. Eddy was finicky would be to understate the point. Still recalled that Mrs. Eddy would usually dictate to a helper and then would pore over the paper, correcting it many times until she was satisfied that her meaning was crystal-clear and could not be misinterpreted.[7]

Her words, of course, were misinterpreted. Old conflicts continued to pester her as she and Christian Science moved into the new century. In the summer of 1901, in the midst of the Woodbury trial, she felt as if she had suffered more than even the persecuted Dreyfus in France. At least Dreyfus was never haunted by the ghost of Phineas Quimby. In early 1902, one of Mrs. Eddy's earliest manuscripts—one purportedly showing that she had borrowed heavily from Quimby—fell into the hands of Augusta Stetson. She sent it to Pleasant View, and we can only guess why; she must have known that it would upset Mrs. Eddy. According to Calvin Frye, he showed the manuscript to Mrs. Eddy, and she denied that it was hers. But the mere reading of it upset her so much that "she was under great fear and old beliefs" for most of the evening and early morning. A year later, when the Dresser and Woodbury clique resurrected Quimby's name in the *Boston Manuscript*, it must have seemed to Mrs. Eddy that the charges of borrowing from Quimby would follow her to the grave.[8]

Other issues also refused to fade away. Some rivalries among her students were nipped in the bud, but others bloomed. Though Mrs. Eddy tried to stay disengaged from the angry words and hurt feelings, at times she was pulled into the fray, and it was often difficult to tell who was using whom as a repository for unwanted thoughts and feelings. In one letter to Edward Kimball in late 1903, Mrs. Eddy wearily noted that "another plot is sprung on us" and the students refused to take the responsibility for dealing with it themselves. To her it always seemed as though they would dump the whole mess into her lap, wave goodbye, and "sail on in calm seas."[9]

Mrs. Eddy kept her own course steady. She was an unusual executive in the way she combined the rational and nonrational decision-making processes. She often opened her Bible and read passages at random. This reading, coupled with communication with God through prayer, led to her decision on a particular issue, and it is also evident that she identified with Christ. Just as He took the sufferings of man into his body in order that man might be saved, so she took the growing pains of her Church into her body in order that it might flourish. Calvin Frye told Adam

Dickey, Mrs. Eddy's secretary, that whenever a momentous revelation presented itself to her regarding the course and well-being of Christian Science, "these struggles appeared in her body." Dickey confirmed this by asserting that some of the most important by-laws of the Mother Church—getting rid of the Communion Service and disbanding the executive members, for example—"formulated themselves" in Mrs. Eddy's thought while she was in the throes of suffering. Her anguish continued until the by-law was passed by the Directors; then it ceased.[10]

From the late 1890s to a year or two before her death, Mrs. Eddy instituted and closely supervised a number of significant changes and developments in the movement. In late 1901, she was busy with a major revision of *Science and Health*; she wrote a number of important by-laws that affected Church organization, and in 1908 she requested that the Trustees of the Publishing Society start a daily paper. By November the first issue of *The Christian Science Monitor* was published.[11]

As much as Mrs. Eddy kept an eye on the present and future, she also cast longing glances toward the past. In fact, she used her memories as a way of restoring and maintaining self-continuity in old age. She had always liked singing hymns, and during her later years she particularly enjoyed hearing the hymns she associated with her youth. Camilla Hanna remembered a number of instances when Mrs. Eddy mentioned her first husband and Gilbert Eddy with great affection. During their first years with Mrs. Eddy, the Hannas saw her frequently, and she always chose a spot in their interviews to speak lovingly about her mother. In a 1918 interview, Julia Bartlett remembered that Mrs. Eddy never ceased to enjoy telling stories about her mother and her childhood days in Bow. At one point in the telling of the stories, it sounded as though Mrs. Eddy and her mother were mirror reflections of each other. Mrs. Eddy emphasized the fact that her mother was a deeply spiritual woman. Abigail Baker's theology, recalled Bartlett, in many aspects seemed to have been "as scientific as the concept afterwards revealed to Mrs. Eddy." Moreover, it was clear from Mrs. Eddy's telling that her mother had made a special effort to discuss religious issues with her young daughter.[12]

In August 1910, months away from her death, Mrs. Eddy wistfully recalled an earlier time of separation and sadness in her life. When she was getting ready to move south with her husband George Glover, everyone in the family was against her going, with the exception of her mother. All the arrangements went smoothly until it came time to say goodbye. Because she loved them all so deeply, even the thought of parting was painful. Since then she had tried to love others with the same depth of feeling. Irving Tomlinson remembered that Mrs. Eddy was nostalgic about her childhood home in Bow; she often recalled it

vividly, sometimes with a tear in her eye. Even Mark Baker's gruff image
seemed to be softened by the passing of the years. She now remembered
him as the one who did not want her to marry George Glover and move
away.[13]

Mrs. Eddy vividly recalled the family Bible on its stand and the important role it played in her family's life. She recounted the daily religious
rituals, the long prayers both before and after meals, and Mark Baker's
leading role in this activity. These memories were not clouded by her
struggles with his Calvinism; indeed, she seemed to admire her father.
It did not matter how threatening the weather was or how much hay
had to be cut, Mark never permitted these rituals to be altered in any
way. A stickler for order in her own right, Mary could identify with this
part of her father.[14]

Given Mrs. Eddy's penchant for stability and order, one might think
that she would have spent her final days at Pleasant View. There her
fond reveries could have been reinforced by merely stepping onto the
veranda and gazing over the hills to Bow. But Mrs. Eddy never did things
according to the expectations of others. In 1908 she moved to Chestnut
Hill, Massachusetts, most likely so as to be closer to her Church's
strength in the Boston area. Even so, the move was not a happy one for
her. Adelaide Still said that for the first months at Chestnut Hill, "a
belief of homesickness" had its grip on Mrs. Eddy. She missed Pleasant
View and its magnificent vistas. The new house, though much larger,
did not occupy her attention the way the old house had. We remember
how she used to make her daily pass through the downstairs rooms,
carefully observing each object. She did not do this at Chestnut Hill.
Except when she went on her drive, she rarely spent any time downstairs
and, according to Still, on only one or two occasions did she ever go
through them.[15]

After she arrived at Chestnut Hill, Adam Dickey picked up the story.
When Mrs. Eddy moved in, she paid the same close scrutiny to everyday
details that she had at Pleasant View. Her demands for order did not
lessen with the passing years. One example should suffice. In the winter
of 1908, Martha Wilcox became a member of Mrs. Eddy's Chestnut
Hill household. Like Dickey and the others, she was struck by Mrs.
Eddy's insistence upon orderliness. In her reminiscence she understood
that Mrs. Eddy's demands for order and neatness in the everyday world
reflected her deeper spiritual concerns. Mrs. Eddy knew that if a person's
thought was not "orderly and exact" in every aspect of material life,
then it would not be so in the more important spiritual things. Orderliness and exactness were highly developed in Mrs. Eddy's mind, far
more so than the ordinary mind could comprehend, said an awed Martha

Wilcox. Mrs. Eddy had taught her that her mind reflected God's; thus, she expected Wilcox to reflect "deeper spiritual concerns" and the same kind of discipline, order, and perfection that she did. Mrs. Eddy's pincushion, for example, had pins of different lengths, each firmly stuck in its proper corner. No sensible person would have dared to change the position of a pin, because Mrs. Eddy was so highly sensitive to change and potential disharmony in all earthly things.[16]

Mrs. Eddy's aversion to bad weather followed her to Chestnut Hill. According to Adam Dickey, she considered heavy snowfalls "the damaging results of error," and they were not to be tolerated. While she enjoyed hearing "the patter of a gentle rainfall," she clapped her hands to her ears whenever a noisy electrical storm cut loose. The weather watches were maintained in her new home as they had been in Concord. The regular watches to protect Mrs. Eddy from the mental attacks of her enemies also continued at Chestnut Hill.[17]

The weather was not the only thing she tried to control at Chestnut Hill. Time's inevitable passing became an increasingly important issue to Mrs. Eddy in her advanced years. In her bedroom there were a number of clocks; one was an old-fashioned alarm clock that she had attached to the end of her bed. If she woke up in the dark, she could flick on a light and immediately see what time it was. While this demand to control time clearly had its psychological dimension, Mrs. Eddy and her staff understood it in religious terms. She had spelled this out at some length in *Science and Health*, when she urged her readers not to become preoccupied with birthdates and passing years. "Chronological data," she said, "are not part of the vast forever." Statistical data regarding birth and death rates were "so many conspiracies against manhood and womanhood." When "immortal Mind" governed man, age was not a consideration; he was "always beautiful and grand. Each succeeding year unfolds wisdom, beauty, and holiness."[18]

Despite her precautions, Mrs. Eddy was not freed from the assaults of the outside world. She could not turn to her adopted son, Foster, for consolation because their relationship had deteriorated so badly. To add insult to injury, he joined the "next friends" lawsuit in March 1907, which utterly failed in its attempt to prove that Mrs. Eddy was mentally incompetent to run her affairs.[19]

From the late 1890s on, Mrs. Eddy's emotional and physical health seemed to decline severely at times; indeed, she had a number of harrowing moments. Some of her later episodes at first glance might appear no different from those she had suffered when she was younger, but now she was carrying the added burden of age. Parts of 1898 and 1899 seemed to be particularly difficult for her. Calvin Frye recorded a number of instances in his diary when it seemed that Mrs. Eddy was on the verge of dying, only to be called back by him at the last moment. In February 1898, Mrs. Eddy feared that mental malpractice was so prevalent that her Christian Science movement was on the verge of collapse. Taking these anxieties into her body, she collapsed, and Frye leaped to her side. He shouted for her to awaken, assuring her that she need not fear Theosophy, or a hypnotic influence, or any "hashish dream of death or disease." When she heard these words, Mrs. Eddy responded and quickly regained her health.[20]

The last seven years of Mrs. Eddy's life were punctuated with days, even weeks, of exhausting mental and physical suffering. The ubiquitous Calvin Frye noted in his diary that on May 3 and 4, 1903, Mrs. Eddy had a particularly trying time. She was suddenly struck with a severe pain shortly before midnight, and none of her students seemed able to relieve her suffering. A number of doctors were summoned, but they could not provide any relief. She continued to suffer through the next day "from paroxysms of pain" induced by renal calculi. Finally Dr. E. Morrill was called, and he administered a shot. Again, a brief entry in Frye's diary for August 3, 1909, indicates that Mrs. Eddy was in such intense pain that a doctor was called in to give a painkilling shot. A fuller entry some months earlier revealed that Adam Dickey, acting in the doctor's stead, had informed Mrs. Eddy that she was not to have any more morphine for her pain. For several days she had been "suffering from renal calculi and had voided stones in the urine but yesterday the water seemed normal." Dickey thus determined that she was to have no more shots, particularly since she had had injections of morphine twice within the past few days.[21]

When Mrs. Eddy resorted to morphine, she was open to the charge that she was not living by her own Christian Science teachings. One might think that knowledge of her drug-taking would have been disillusioning for her students. This, however, was not the case, at least not for Gilbert Carpenter, who explained her use of morphine in a way consistent with her Christian Science principles—though his explanation must seem at best problematic to outsiders. When animal magnetism concentrated its full deadly power on Mrs. Eddy, she met it head-on and refused to allow it a victory over her. While she might seem to be taking a regressive step when she chose to use morphine to dull her considerable pain, this was appearance only, according to Carpenter. When she used the drug, she was not succumbing to mortal mind; to the contrary, she was showing her triumph over it. With her spiritual weapons temporarily out of commission, Mrs. Eddy felt momentarily exposed and helpless. To free herself, she took the morphine and "put

God back of it"; she gave no credence to man's mortal mind and the material world's belief in the efficacy of drugs. The meaning of Mrs. Eddy's actions was self-evident to Carpenter. Mrs. Eddy had taken the morphine not for personal reasons but to make a demonstration for her students that when God was behind any act, that person was empowered to fight for His Truth.[22]

Just when it seemed that Mrs. Eddy was about to surrender to the ravages of time, she seemed capable of turning back the hands of the clock. One student with her at Chestnut Hill was William Rathvon. In July 1910, he noted in his diary that late one afternoon the household was called into Mrs. Eddy's room, apparently for a long session. As things turned out, the time raced by. Mrs. Eddy was riveting; her mind was keen, her theological discussions spiritually stimulating. Considering her age and all that she had been through, Rathvon was dumbstruck by her performance.[23]

Despite her moments of rallying, Mrs. Eddy's illnesses seemed to become more severe and debilitating. Shortly before her death, she recounted a dream to Frye wherein she was writing a poem and singing the refrain, "She is not here, she is risen." Frye could not have missed the connection to Christ and the Resurrection. Mrs. Eddy also told Frye that if she appeared to die, he was not to bury her body for three and a half days, nor was he to say a word about her apparent demise during that time. She explained to Frye that while David had died and was buried, and while Jesus had died and His body had risen, her resurrection would be of a different kind. The "demonstration for her would not be in death even, but a body transformed by the renewing of Mind."[24]

For a number of her detractors this was sufficient evidence to confirm their suspicion that Mrs. Eddy harbored grandiose fantasies of being a Christlike figure. No matter how vociferously she disclaimed the connection, she secretly felt herself to be this powerful and this exalted. Perhaps this was why Ernest Bates and John Dittemore chose to include this episode in their highly critical study of Mrs. Eddy. We can, however, view this incident in a different light. Mrs. Eddy was old and sick and momentarily vulnerable. As David Gutmann has shown in his essay on aging, under such pressures older persons may "revive early modes of managing and expressing narcissism. Thus, they may idealize their own wishes, reviving the grandiose self and its . . . demands—to be all-containing, male and female, omnipotential."

In another part of his essay, Gutmann discussed a special capacity that some older people have, which he called the "cathexis of otherness." As some older people lose their investment in the world of things, they are freed to search "for those objects that finally will be sustaining and security giving. . . . Since substance has failed, they seek the sustaining object in the insubstantial abstractions that cannot be lost . . . to search for the trustworthy object in the realm of the impersonal—the realm of otherness." Ever since her fall on the ice, Mrs. Eddy had been deeply invested in this "realm of otherness"—her spiritual realm. Her advancing age and increasing illness led her temporarily to hyperinvest her ideal self and ideal objects in that realm. During the last days of her life, therefore, this process might well have accounted for her temporary identification with Jesus and the Resurrection.[25]

When Mrs. Eddy died on December 3, 1910, one could point to the Mother Church in Boston, with its magnificent domed extension, as a symbol of the success of her religious movement. She, one suspects, would not have been comfortable with this statement, for she was never at ease with the physical grandeur of her Church. From her experiences in the Congregational Church, and from the wider lessons of history, Mrs. Eddy knew that human institutions tended to debase Christ's teachings and God's truth, for at best a church could only point the way. Mrs. Eddy's legacy was in the strict demands she made upon herself and her followers to see the spiritual world as the true reality. She kept the door ajar to Christ's spiritual healings and thus helped to perpetuate spiritual healing in a secular, scientific age.[26]

14

WITH BANNERS STILL FLYING: CHRISTIAN SCIENCE AND AMERICAN CULTURE

We will rejoice in thy salvation, and in the name of our God
we will set up our banners: the Lord fulfill all thy petitions.

Psalms 20:5

MARY BAKER EDDY'S DEATH in 1910 was not the passing of an ordinary woman. Obituaries appeared in big-city tabloids and small-town weeklies across the country. Thumbing through a sample of these editorial comments today, one is struck by their lack of neutrality. Even when progressive America admired her accomplishments, it was uncomfortable with her, not knowing where to fit her into its notions of authority, leadership, and gender.

The *Rochester Times* observed that Mrs. Eddy's death marked the passing of a woman who was "probably the most notable of this generation; certainly none other has had more widespread influence or is regarded with greater reverence by more people." Indulging in hyperbole, the paper noted that "millions of followers" flocked to fill the pews of her worldwide church. The *Chicago Tribune* reflected the same sentiments: with her death, "there passes from this world's activities one of the most remarkable women of her time."[1]

The *Chicago Post* accurately summed up the meaning of Christian Science to Mrs. Eddy's followers. "Without humbug or sentimentalism, any outsider can and must admit that Christian Science people are good people. They not only believe in their church and attend its meetings with a passionate faithfulness that other churches envy, but they also carry their faith with them into their daily lives." Other newspapers were not as perceptive or careful in their assessments of Mrs. Eddy's contributions. A North Carolina paper stated that "her gospel was largely one of sunshine and mental uplift," while a Michigan daily thought that

if Mrs. Eddy was remembered for anything, it would be for the "optimism" that she taught. "Christian Scientists are sunny, hopeful,
cheerful."[2]

Even before Mrs. Eddy died, Georgine Milmine was evaluating Christian Science in terms that made her sound like a precursor of such
positive thinkers as Norman Vincent Peale. "Mrs. Eddy's teachings,"
said Milmine, "brought the promise of material benefits to a practical
people. . . . In the West, especially, where every one was absorbed in a
new and hard-won material prosperity, the healer . . . met with an
immediate response. This religion had a message of cheer for the rugged
materialist as well as for the morbid invalid. It exalted health and self-
satisfaction and material prosperity high among the moral virtues." Mrs.
Eddy would have grumbled at these words, because she saw her ideas
as radical rather than assimilative, and she pushed for religious rigor
rather than comfortable accommodation. Christian Science went against
the grain; it demanded a spiritual inner-directedness that withstood the
whims and fancies of others.[3]

In life, Mrs. Eddy's rigorous spiritual demands and her Christian
Science doctrines had the capacity to disturb the wider culture. The
Springfield Union captured the flavor of Mrs. Eddy's unsettling influence.
"About no personage of her generation has so much and such bitter
controversy raged as around the Founder and Leader of the organization
and doctrines known as Christian Science." The *Concord Monitor*
skated delicately around this issue by noting that whether one was an
admirer of Mrs. Eddy or not, an "impartial pose toward her seems to
have been very difficult to maintain." Both of these papers were ostensibly referring to Mrs. Eddy's radical idealism regarding the meaning of
reality and how man could overcome disease and death. Her theology
sounded strange and threatening to secular ears. Though Mrs. Eddy and
her doctrines repelled some people, the papers indicate that she appealed
to others, and hint that she and her Christian Science touched the core
of American society in diverse, fundamental ways.[4]

One might be hard-pressed to see much of cultural connection in the
early years of the movement. From the time when she lived in her modest,
nondescript home at 8 Broad Street in Lynn, Massachusetts, to her final
days in her tasteful, twenty-five-room gray stone mansion in Chestnut
Hill, Mrs. Eddy—as much as was humanly possible—kept her movement enveloped in the spiritual realm. This was especially true for the
first decades, when she struggled to keep her fledgling movement alive.
Even in its early days, Lynn reflected the disruptive changes of the nineteenth century. As she walked the streets, Mrs. Eddy easily could have
brushed shoulders with Quaker and Methodist dissenters, vocal tem-

perance advocates, and disgruntled shoe workers. Indeed, the Lynn of Mrs. Eddy's day was "notorious as a hotbed of radicalism," according to one historian.[5]

But as Mrs. Eddy took those walks along Lynn's streets, it was as if she and many of her early followers, who came from the city's shoe factories, had spiritual blinders on. They simply did not become involved in the social discontents of the day, and often when they did acknowledge them in *The Christian Science Journal*, they were quickly subsumed under the teachings and meaning of Christian Science. And yet, despite Mrs. Eddy's focus on spiritual matters, the world and its diversity did filter into her movement. A full exploration of this diversity is beyond the scope of this book. The demographic data for any future study of her students would be exceptionally difficult to accumulate; the Mother Church did not keep these kinds of records. Nevertheless, we can make hypotheses based upon some fragmentary, impressionistic evidence about Mrs. Eddy's appeal to the wider culture.[6]*

In the late 1890s, Alfred Farlow was asked where Christian Science students came from, and he replied that there was no single type. They came from all kinds of churches; some did not even have an official church affiliation, and they stood on all rungs of the social ladder. There were hints of this diversity even in the early days of the movement, although most of Mrs. Eddy's students clustered around the lower end of the social scale. Mrs. Eddy attracted a number of men and women in their mid- to late twenties from Lynn's shoe factories. Until he devoted himself to the practice of Christian Science, Samuel Bancroft was a worker in a shoe factory. So were Richard Kennedy and Miss Dorcas Rawson, a member of one of Mrs. Eddy's first classes and one of the eight defectors in 1881. Daniel Spofford worked in a shoe trade in Tennessee, while his wife was a Christian Science practitioner. Others among Mrs. Eddy's early followers came from equally modest beginnings. Delia Manley grew up in Tiverton, Rhode Island; her father was a farmer and made shoes during the winter. Walter Watson came out

---

* The spiritual blinders stem from a number of sources. One was Mrs. Eddy's early tendency to keep disturbing events at arm's length. A second was that this "safe" interaction with reality changed function when she established her Christian Science. The sense of detachment was now being used to keep her students focused on their spiritual tasks, and it was an indication to her that the ultimate reality was spiritual, not material. Finally, this distancing maneuver is an early manifestation of Christian Science's abiding by the dictum in Romans 12:2, "And be not conformed to this world: but be ye transformed by the renewing of your mind, that ye may prove what is that good, and acceptable, and perfect, will of God." On the outsider's position of Christian Science vis-à-vis the wider culture, see R. Laurence Moore, *Religious Outsiders and the Making of Americans* (New York: Oxford University Press, 1986), pp. 105–27.

of the New Hampshire Hills as a house painter, and his wife worked in a glove factory.[7]

Stephen Gottschalk, a close student of Christian Science, noted that until the early 1880s a "significant proportion" of Mrs. Eddy's students came from spiritualism or had some spiritualism in their backgrounds. Indeed, many of Mrs. Eddy's students came from a patchwork quilt of religious backgrounds. Dorcas Rawson, for example, was a "Holiness Methodist," while Laura C. Nourse was raised in a more regular Methodist church. Wallace Wright was a Universalist; so was Mary Godfrey Parker, whose mother was an "ardent Universalist," and her husband was of a similar persuasion. Delia Manley was a churchgoing Baptist; Walter Watson was raised by "good, staunch, New England parents of the Unitarian faith." In looking over her 1880s class, Jennie Sawyer found it remarkable that people representing so many different denominations could find a consensus on such a critical issue as "one's Christian faith."[8]

It is understandable that other Protestants might find Christian Science attractive in the late nineteenth and early twentieth centuries. While Mrs. Eddy's Christian Science may have been cut out of new cloth, in her public writings, and sometimes in her interviews, she wove the threads of the Puritan past into the fabric of her appeal. In *No and Yes*, for example, Mrs. Eddy linked herself and her Christian Science to many of America's cherished values. Her ancestors, she proudly noted, were among the first to settle in New Hampshire, where they raised "the Puritan standard of undefiled religion. As dutiful descendants of Puritans, let us lift their standard higher, rejoicing as Paul did, that we are *free born*."[9]

On many occasions in *Science and Health* Mrs. Eddy spelled out the duty and destiny of her movement. In one instance, her words harked back to John Winthrop's charge to his small band of Puritan followers. In the current age, Christian Scientists occupied the same position that the disciples did when Jesus confirmed the uniqueness of their mission. They were special, and to convey this Mrs. Eddy repeated the biblical phrase that has come to mean so much to America's special mission: "Ye are the light of the world. A city that is set on a hill cannot be hid." Then, much like Winthrop, Mrs. Eddy urged her students to be fully dedicated to their calling so that "this light be not hid, but radiate and glow into noontide glory."[10]

Mrs. Eddy was also forging stronger links between her Christian Science and other Protestant traditions in America. As far back as the Genesis manuscript she hinted at this when she equated the importance of her discovery to Robert Fulton's. In an 1893 article in *The Christian*

Science Journal, her movement was linked to two of America's most resourceful and innovative men, Benjamin Franklin and Thomas Edison. Until Franklin, the article noted, there was no real knowledge of electricity, and until Edison no one realized its potential. The analogy was self-evident: Mrs. Eddy was just as innovative in her spiritual work.[11]

In another article in the *Journal*, not only were Mrs. Eddy's Protestant roots stressed—she was a New England girl raised by "God-fearing parents"—but it was also emphasized that her parents were middle-class. And Mrs. Eddy tried to convince her readers that Christian Science's spiritual rigor was not out of step with the postmillennial secularism in American society after the Civil War. The current age appeared to be moving toward perfectibility on a number of cultural levels, Mrs. Eddy noted in an 1884 article. Why, then, she questioned, should religion not also strive for "a more perfect and practical Christianity?"[12]

By invoking the Puritan past, Mrs. Eddy appealed to those who wished to cling to cherished values and ideals in a rapidly changing America. The intellectual historian Michael Kammen has recently shown that the Puritan past served late-Victorian Americans in a number of ways. At one end of the spectrum, a number of nineteenth-century Americans used it to attack religious bigotry and intolerance, while in the bulging middle were those who saw the Puritan past as "a mixed blessing." "Moving from the center of the spectrum to the end," writes Kammen, "there remained a considerable number of vocal and perfectly sensible individuals who between 1880 and 1910 not only retained an extremely positive view of the Puritans but felt nostalgia for the qualities of intense faith, imagination, and courage that seemed to be in short supply in late Victorian America."[13]

Mrs. Eddy could be counted among those "perfectly sensible individuals" described by Kammen. For her the Puritans came to represent not only a step back into an ideal past, but also a step forward into the future. Evolutionary ideas and a secular optimism helped to reshape the image of the Puritans; increasingly they were seen as having cut the umbilical cord to England. Having thus broken from a confining, immoral past, they were free to invent their own tradition. In the 1884 article, Mrs. Eddy tapped into this radical tradition; thus, her link to the Puritans is much more complicated than it first looks. She was, in effect, allowing people to acknowledge their roots and to break from them, to be conservative and radical simultaneously.[14]

Puritan roots, Benjamin Franklin, science and manufacturing, perfectibility; no wonder Christian Science began to appeal to more and more middle-class people as the nineteenth century gave way to the twentieth.

Businessmen, clergymen, doctors, lawyers, clerks sought out Christian Science. (And it is no wonder that by the turn of the century this connection to basic American values appealed to a number of ethnic minorities such as European Jews who converted to Christian Science as a way of assimilating into American society.) Though Christian Science made headway in small Midwestern towns in this same period, and though Alfred Farlow was probably right in contending that Christian Science drew from all ranks of society, by the late nineteenth century the tone, the attitude, and the language in many of the articles in *The Christian Science Journal* and the *Christian Science Weekly* seemed slanted to a middle-class audience's hopes and fears about life in an urban, increasingly bureaucratized, corporate America.[15]

The historian George Cotkin has characterized the intellectuals of the late nineteenth century as "reluctant modernists." This is an apt phrase, for it could easily apply to a large segment of middle-class men and women. In the case of men, for example, though they made their accommodations to the emerging bureaucratized world of corporate America, and seemed to enjoy the growing leisure time and the cornucopia offered by the emerging consumer culture, this acceptance of the new did not come without serious strain and hesitancy. Christian Science addressed its message to those middle-class men who were highly sensitive to these kinds of tensions.[16]

William Rathvon, a prominent Christian Scientist in Mrs. Eddy's last years, wrote a 1903 article extolling the benefits of the religion, and his language reflected this strong middle-class bent. Nineteenth-century Victorians were obsessed with the meaning of character, as if somehow a person's inner qualities would buttress him or her against the onslaughts of modern life. Christian Science, said Rathvon, stood for a special kind of power and permanence. The mental attitude of every person should be "active, alert, and assiduous." The particular kind of fitness in Christian Science was not limited to any one kind of culture or any one kind of person; it applied to all men in all cultures. Though Christian Science "declares daily dividends, its capital is never impaired." By infusing Christian Science thought into daily business activities, one would begin to guarantee higher returns "than any investment that lies within the scope of our modern man of affairs."[17]

Rathvon was comfortable employing the secular idioms of his day; in this essay he even sounded a bit like William James, who, in his quest for security in a pluralistic world, often combined metaphors from the sacred and the profane. Christian Science, however, was never sanguine about the individual's place in the ever-changing secular world. Psychologically, life was not simple for many well-educated middle-class Americans during the late nineteenth and early twentieth centuries. Many of them were "battling a dread of unreality." These feelings, according to T. J. Jackson Lears, "stemmed from urbanization and technological development; from the rise of an increasingly interdependent market economy; and from the secularization of liberal Protestantism among its educated and affluent devotees."[18]

For many in an emerging consumer culture it felt as if the core meaning of self had been lost. Now the self was nothing more than a mask, a false self a person constructed to "sell" others. As this sense of alienation grew at the end of the nineteenth century and into the next, and as it became increasingly possible to define the self through the desire and enjoyment of things, many middle-class Americans increasingly yearned to rediscover "the real thing" in virtually all aspects of their lives. As Miles Orvell has recently noted:

> Again and again, around the turn of the century, as the saturation of *things* reached the limit of containing space, the social and spiritual grace afforded by material objects was put to the question. And Nietzsche's observation on the European bourgeoisie would apply to America as well: "Men of the seventies and eighties . . . were filled with a devouring hunger for reality, but they had the misfortune to confuse this with matter—which is but the hollow and deceptive wrapping of it. Thus they lived perpetually in a wretched, padded, puffed-out world of cotton-wool, cardboard, and tissue-paper."[19]

Mrs. Eddy never confused matter with reality; in Christian Science, the spiritual core of the self was the "real thing." Some Christian Scientists were lured down the path of material comfort, but Mrs. Eddy always accepted the things of the real world for what they were: illusions, sometimes destructive ones. She held out a warning, for example, that imperialism, monopoly, and a decline in religion posed real threats to the moral fiber of the nation. Yet she also held out a hope for the future if people would only accept "a true Science and Christianity."[20]

A number of Christian Science writers did not sugar-coat their concern that America was deeply divided between the haves and the have-nots. For self-satisfied Americans basking in the sunlight of American prosperity, one writer saw dark clouds gathering, harbingers of a potentially destructive storm that would "threaten our civil institutions, producing universal distrust among all classes." The massive corporations had "grown wealthy and arrogant," and in their rapid growth they had lost sight of the larger community and the meaning of justice. Officeholders were no better. They violated the public trust, lining their own pockets at the public's expense. No matter where one looked, civil and religious institutions had compromised their principles.[21]

What to do about these social ills? By the turn of the century, Americans were offered a variety of social plans that promised a more efficient, equitable world, whether it was from the blueprint of a progressive or a socialist. According to one Christian Scientist writer, socialism, because it aimed at the betterment of all, was an improvement over the "selfish individualism" of capitalism, but like all other "isms" it had a fatal flaw: it mistook institutions and social conditions as "the real and ultimate conditions of earthly existence." From this erroneous assumption emerged a faulty conclusion: if these institutions could be changed and improved, then mankind could attain an earthly paradise. From the Christian Science perspective, this was an illusion.

To achieve true social harmony one had to penetrate beneath the surface of things to get in touch with the spiritual reality. The recognition that what most people took to be real and concrete was actually erroneous belief and illusion is what separated Christian Science reform from "ordinary social reforms." The socialist erred when he or she believed "all discord to be material inequality and individualism." Other reformers were equally mistaken when they considered "competition and private, unchecked capitalism" the major cause of social disharmony.

Christian Science plainly revealed that these causes were not really causes after all; they were effects "of a false sense of Life as material, a false sense of Mind as plural, a false sense of substance as matter, a false sense of existence as temporal." It stood to reason, therefore, that "an entire readjustment of the constituent relations of man to man must be reached and reorganized before we can hope for ultimate harmony." But this could only be accomplished when man understood true spiritual individuality and a true relationship to God. With these understandings, a person could then adjust his or her life to the spiritual reality rather than the material illusion. In *Science and Health*, Mrs. Eddy held out the hope that Christian Science was slowly, inch by inch, leading the way toward a morally reformed society:

> I have never supposed this century would witness the full
> fruitage of Christian Science, or that sin, disease, and
> death would not continue for centuries to come; but this
> I do aver, that, as a result of Christian Science, ethics and
> temperance have received an impulse, health has been
> restored, and longevity increased. If such are the present

fruits, what may not the harvest be, when this Science is more generally understood?[22]

Christian Science's spiritual radicalism was clothed in a gray flannel suit; it promised a transvaluation, but it would not lead an assault on America's corporate walls. Change, when it came, would be evolutionary, not revolutionary. This was a comforting message to an anxious, if not increasingly neurasthenic, middle class that craved order and stability and yearned for verities. While Christian Science produced testimony after testimony confirming its healings of broken bones and major illnesses from tuberculosis to cancer, its healings were also attractive to people suffering from psychosomatic illnesses like neurasthenia. In the late-Victorian era this was a catchall psychological disorder whose long list of symptoms ranged from depression, to male hysteria, to stress, to chronic fatigue. Though neurasthenia crossed class and gender lines, it seemed to find a welcome home among middle- and upper-middle-class men—the very people supposedly adapting the best and making the most out of a rapidly changing social world.

Ironically, as these men exerted themselves to climb economic and social ladders, they suffered a paralysis of will; seemingly the faster they scrambled to get to the top, the further they fell away from old-fashioned values and from a sense of who and what they were. Indeed, it seemed as though they had lost contact with any kind of emotional center, as though they had become detached from "real things." When Christian Science turned its penetrating look into the workplace of middle-class America, it identified the secularization process as a major source of the middle class's ills. Most businessmen kept their Christian ideals separated from their work, content to devote one hour on Sundays to God and to spiritual concerns.[23]

This was an artificial separation that produced a deep alienation. Indeed, Christian Science made it eminently clear that "a business based on Principle" and governed by Christian values was impervious to the wild fluctuations in the marketplace, where today's success was tomorrow's failure. A host of middle-class professionals—"merchants, bankers, traveling salesmen, railroad officials, and busy people in all aspects of industry"—were turning to Christian Science with spectacular results in their businesses and in their private lives, one writer tooted.[24]

Another writer addressed his article to the rising middle-class businessman, encouraging him never to think about "danger, disaster, failure, limitation, discord, confusion," unless he wanted to have these unnerving thoughts "manifested on your body or in your business."

Once a businessman fully accepted the principles of Christian Science; once every act he performed and every relationship he entered into were governed and directed by God, then the vicissitudes of business life could never make him a helpless victim.[25]

Interestingly enough, when Mrs. Eddy died a newspaper in Spokane, Washington, listed Christian Science's spiritual help to the businessman as one of her real contributions. The typical businessman, the paper remarked, was overworked, overanxious, and overwrought. There seemed no place for religion in his practical world, which left him empty and adrift. Above all else the emotionally battered businessman needed a "mental anchorage that . . . maintains and buoys," that allowed him the freedom to move in the world while at the same time he was firmly anchored in "absolute certainty." This is what Christian Science provided.[26]

A number of newspapers turned Mrs. Eddy's life into a reaffirmation of America's most cherished middle-class values and myths. America was the land of unlimited opportunity; like Horatio Alger, Mrs. Eddy had risen from rags to riches; she had moved from a New England saltbox to a Chestnut Hill mansion. A Milwaukee paper pointedly observed that history was full of women who had made their mark in a world dominated by men, but most of those women had to exercise their power indirectly through "their feminine charms." If it was true that behind every great man stood a woman, then it seemed as if Mrs. Eddy had stepped from the shadows and created a niche all her own.[27]

This was quite a niche. By 1906, Mrs. Eddy's *Science and Health* had sold 400,000 copies. In the brief span from 1882 to 1890, Christian Science had grown from a paltry group of fifty to a burgeoning organization of "twenty churches, ninety societies, at least 250 practitioners, and 33 teaching centers scattered across the country." *The Christian Science Monitor* had a healthy daily circulation of 50,000. These accomplishments in corporate America did not escape the eye of the Cleveland *Plain Dealer* and the *Baltimore Sun*. In their evaluations of Mrs. Eddy's achievements they used words and phrases commonly reserved for the careers of powerful men like Andrew Carnegie, John D. Rockefeller, and Teddy Roosevelt. The Ohio paper described her as "virile and vigorous," a "natural commander," a "natural organizer" who possessed "intellectual qualities of the highest order." The *Sun* chipped in by noting that Mrs. Eddy exhibited a "fine business acumen" in managing her church; she had a "tremendous capacity for work" that was coupled to "a great executive ability and penetrating judgment."[28]

Other newspapers, however, had difficulty accepting Mrs. Eddy as a symbol of authority and success in America. They recognized her achievements, but it was as if Mrs. Eddy had crossed gender lines and the newspapers wanted to nudge her back to her proper, feminine side. One newspaper from the West, for instance, lauded her for bringing Christian Science into the crass, materialistic world where success "was the fetish men were worshipping." Even when it praised her, however, the paper did not link her to the great male discoverers and inventors as she and *The Christian Science Journal* had, but to Joan of Arc. A Philadelphia newspaper duly noted that many women had made their marks as humanitarian reformers in a variety of fields where the moral purity of women was permitted active expression. The paper bemoaned the fact that recently Julia Ward Howe and Florence Nightingale had died. Mrs. Eddy, "the leading woman of her time, and among the greatest in history," achieved her status in religion, a field segregated from the economic and political corridors of power, and she chose not to challenge men from her bastion of strength.[29]

As excerpts from these editorial comments reveal, outsiders found much to admire in Mrs. Eddy, but her success and authority made a number of people—especially men—nervous. We earlier saw that James Henry Wiggin gave a flattering assessment of Mrs. Eddy's power and effectiveness as a teacher. Wiggin, we recall, was the ex-Unitarian minister whom Mrs. Eddy hired to help her smooth out the rough edges of her 1886 revision of *Science and Health*. Like any demanding executive, she had high standards, knew what she wanted, and would settle for nothing less. When it came to the publication of her book, Mrs. Eddy would not tolerate shoddiness, and she could be exasperating as she fought over the meaning of a word or phrase. Still, Wiggin had a healthy respect for her—or at least that is the impression he gave in his correspondence with her.[30]

But working with a dynamic religious leader who happened to be a woman pricked the masculine pride of this lapsed Unitarian minister. In 1889 he wrote a college friend, mocking Mrs. Eddy's theology as muddled and as "an ignorant revival of one form of gnosticism." As for Mrs. Eddy herself, well, what he really wanted to say would have to wait until he saw his friend, because it was too hot and damning to put in writing. What he did say was damaging enough. "An awfully (I use the word advisedly) smart woman, acute, shrewd, but not well read, nor in any way learned." Apparently this smart, acute, shrewd woman did not have the ability to create, for as Wiggin saw it, she had borrowed all of her ideas from Quimby. In one fell swoop, Wiggin demeaned Mrs. Eddy, her accomplishments, and her Christian Science.[31]

By the turn of the century, when she was becoming something of a household name, Wiggin was not the only man whose gender anxieties were aroused by Mrs. Eddy, and increasingly these men treated her as an aberration. Sometimes these fears of an assertive woman were masked in wider cultural concerns; for some men Mrs. Eddy became a cultural symbol for all that ailed America. No one manipulated this multilayered symbol better than Mark Twain.

In a provocative analysis of Twain and other male writers in the nineteenth century such as Emerson, Thoreau, Melville, and Cooper, Joyce Warren argues that Twain, like the others, accepted assertive individualism and the American dream of success for men, but when it came to women in his life and fiction, he treated them as "abstract symbols of purity and selflessness." Twain, furthermore, could not conceive of a woman as an independent person. "For Twain, woman existed only as imaged by and in relation to the male self." As Warren notes in a sentence or two, Mrs. Eddy was "the ultimate example of the woman who did not fit the image." In 1899 Twain fired his first salvo at Mrs. Eddy in *Cosmopolitan*, and three years later his sardonic articles on her and Christian Science began to appear in the *North American Review*. In 1907 he wove his articles into an even nastier attack in his book *Christian Science*.[32]

In the early twentieth century, Protestant America was bewildered by the forces that it suspected were invading it. The millions of immigrants from Southern and Eastern Europe not only brought their Catholicism along with their trunks and suitcases, but they also packed their threatening ideologies of anarchism and socialism. Once settled in their urban tenements, these Catholic ethnic groups, it was feared, would breed and overrun the WASPs of America. And for many Americans the threats did not emanate only from without. The changes in urban living and the growth of the large corporations challenged accepted beliefs about the meaning of American individualism and freedom.

Twain adeptly wedded Mrs. Eddy and Christian Science to those forces that were conspiring to undermine traditional American morality. Twain knew precisely what kind of response he would evoke when he asserted that Mrs. Eddy and her Christian Science church were no better than any other monopoly or trust. She was as power-hungry and money-hungry as any grasping business titan, and the authority of her organization constricted liberty and individualism as effectively as any trust did.[33]

To a Protestant nation beset by fears of being smashed in a tidal wave of Catholic immigrants, Twain's symbolic linking of Mrs. Eddy to the Pope and religious authoritarianism was well calculated to stimulate anxieties and inveterate prejudices. The way Twain pictured it, Mrs. Eddy and the Pope, her Christian Science and his Catholicism, were two unnatural peas in a rotten pod. In the preceding ten or fifteen years, as Protestantism had relaxed its guard, Catholicism had slipped in and taken over the public schools, contaminating America's youth and its future. Christian Science was just as invasive a threat as Catholicism. The Scientists, who looked like your everyday Protestants, were already here; they had already invaded the community. "There are families of Christian Scientists in every community in America," Twain warned, "and each family is a factory; each family turns out a Christian Science product at the customary intervals, and contributes to the Cause. . . . Each family is an agency for the Cause, and makes converts among the neighbors, and starts some more factories."[34]*

Guiding this far-flung empire, this monster with its tentacles reaching into every American community, was the authoritarian Mrs. Eddy. Like the Pope, she did not run a democratic organization. To the contrary, she, too, claimed infallibility; she, too, governed with an iron hand. If one looked closely one could see that in her tight-fisted feminine hand she held more power than the Pope. "A marvellous woman; with a hunger for power such as has never been seen in the world before," wrote Twain. He pounded away at Mrs. Eddy's insatiable need for power and dominance:

> No thing, little or big, that contains any seed or suggestion
> of power escapes her avaricious eye; and when once she
> gets that eye on it, her remorseless grip follows. There
> isn't a Christian Scientist who isn't ecclesiastically as much
> her property as if she had bought him and paid for him,
> and copyrighted him and got a charter. She cannot be
> satisfied when she has handcuffed a member, and put a

---

* The irony in Twain's charges was that Christian Science, its roots deeply planted in Protestant soil, was just as wary of Catholicism as he and other Protestants were. Christian Scientists had many of the same prejudices and fears. The Pope was considered autocratic if not dictatorial. This meant that Catholics were under his control, the control of the church hierarchy, and the church's dogma. Thus, Catholics were not free to develop their full spiritual potential. So Christian Scientists were warned to be on their guard against the mental malpractice of Roman Catholics. On expressions of anti-Catholicism among late-nineteenth- and early-twentieth-century Christian Scientists, see Cynthia Grant Tucker, *A Woman's Ministry: Mary Collson's Search for Reform as a Unitarian Minister, a Hull House Social Worker, and a Christian Science Practitioner* (Philadelphia: Temple University Press, 1984), p. 94, where she notes Mrs. Eddy's fear of "the Catholic priests"; where she says that Edward Kimball devoted part of his classroom teaching to the powers of "Romanism"; and where she includes an experience of Mary Collson's with the Scientists' fears of Catholicism. For other warnings about Catholics, see *Course in Divinity and General Collectanea* (privately printed), p. 75; *Mary Baker Eddy's Six Days of Revelation*, compiled by Richard Oakes (Christian Science Research Library, 1981), pp. 450–51.

leg-chain and ball on him and plugged his ears and removed his thinker, she goes on wrapping needless chains
round and round him, just as a spider would. For she
trusts no one, believes in no one's honesty, judges every
one by herself.

She is not merely an autocratic leader; she has become a primitive,
terrifying creature. And when she was not enslaving her followers this
way, her powerful grip was castrating them.[35]

Twain was not the only man to use primitive imagery to convey vividly
her threat to the stability of the social world. As Mrs. Eddy went about
God's business and her movement grew, she began to unnerve men in
the healing professions, particularly the doctors and the clergymen of
the conservative Protestant denominations. In a recent article, Jean A.
McDonald waded through the periodicals and books of the period and
uncovered the primitive fantasies and exaggerated fears that Mrs. Eddy's
success stirred in some doctors and ministers. Feeling threatened by the
appearance of a strong woman on the public stage, they transmogrified
Mrs. Eddy into a witch, a spider, a worm, and an anaconda. As the
giant spider, she lured unsuspecting souls into her web in order to "devour" them, while as the giant snake she "coiled herself around the
Christian system, breaking all the doctrinal bones of Christianity," and
then "slimed it over" so that she could swallow it easily. Like the witch,
Mrs. Eddy could change her form, and in one writer's imagination she
had taken the "slimy, repulsive worm" of her teachings and transformed
them into a beautifully seductive butterfly that would entrap innocent,
simple souls.[36]

To one minister she was "the modern witch of Concord," brewing
God-knew-what in her cauldron. Another distressed minister envisioned
Mrs. Eddy as a seductress enticing young people with "the sweet cup
of her sorcery." Moreover, if Mrs. Eddy denied the literal truth of the
Adam and Eve story, as she wrote in *Science and Health*, then she was
like Satan's serpent in the garden. Her beguiling interpretations could
not hide the fact that in her words there "lurks always the face of that
Evil One who can hiss through a serpent, sin through a woman, shine
in an angel, be a harlequin in logic, and a devil behind it all." For another
anxious clergyman, Mrs. Eddy was Satan disguised as a woman; she
was "the woman who introduced the corrupting leaven into the pure
meal in the Gospel and leavened the whole lump." How could any man
or woman digest what Mrs. Eddy had concocted?

Doctors were not much kinder to Mrs. Eddy. As was to be expected, they used their science to attack hers. Hysteria was one of their old standbys, but sometimes they could be more inventive: "neurotic," "psychotic," "paranoid," and "manic" were some of the terms they used to label and categorize her. No matter which label of pathology one chose to use, Mrs. Eddy clearly had a degenerate mind that employed "morbid symbolism."[37]

These male professionals saw Mrs. Eddy as abnormal. She had surrendered her femininity when she became a strong, competent leader—in short, when she became a man. Mrs. Eddy was not blind to the gender issues her leadership provoked. She knew the risks of being an outspoken woman in late-Victorian America; she knew that for her Christian Science organization to gain a foothold in American culture, she would have to accept some of its expectations regarding gender roles.[38]

An 1895 article in *The Christian Science Journal* again linked Mrs. Eddy to the basic values and ideals of American culture. From her Puritan past she inherited the innate "love of freedom" that was prominent in all she did. The article also praised Mrs. Eddy's work for what it meant for women. Within Christian Science she had opened to women "the two noblest of all avocations, philanthropy and medicine." Her work had "placed women by the side of men in the pulpit." In *No and Yes* Mrs. Eddy championed the role of women as spiritual reformers. Let no one say in Boston, she declared, that a woman had no rights that man had to respect. Natural law and religion both established woman's inalienable right to be educated and to hold important governmental jobs. These rights, moreover, were ably supported by the best people of both genders. As she drew this essay to a close, Mrs. Eddy foresaw a religious change coming to America; she knew that both Christian Science and women would be at the forefront as America began to fulfill its spiritual destiny. America, yearning for health and spiritual rebirth, must accept Christ, whose life and teachings were imparted by Christian Science. In its march toward its destiny, America should not relegate women to the rear. And in a jab at traditional ministers, she said in words that still have a ring of truth today: "Theologians descant pleasantly upon free moral agency; but they should begin by admitting individual rights."[39]

Clearly representative of Mrs. Eddy's thinking about gender roles were her notes "Man and Woman," which she wrote in December 1900 and which Calvin Frye transcribed about five years after her death. She acknowledged that her organization seemed to favor men in positions of influence and power. There was, for example, only one woman compared to three men on the Board of Education. The Board of Trustees, the Board of Directors of the Mother Church, and the Publication Committee were all male. Out of thirteen members on the Board of Lectureship, only two were women.

To some this may have looked hypocritical. After all, this was a church headed by a woman, a church whose healing practitioners were predominantly female. Why did the men in the church—especially this church—control virtually all the positions of influence and power? From Mrs. Eddy's perspective, there was no real inconsistency or hypocrisy. In terms of gender, God was feminine, masculine, even neuter. God was everything; He was the Mother and Father of the entire universe. As such, man, created in His image, reflected both of His qualities, not simply one or the other. It was this unity that Christian Science aspired to recognize in both men and women.

Although the direction that Mrs. Eddy's argument took next has a remarkably modern ring, we must be careful not to read too much of the present into it. She clearly had her own late-Victorian culture in mind when she said that if at any period of history the reflection of God's masculine side seemed ascendant and more dominant than His feminine side, then it was because human perception and understanding had not fully grasped the true meaning of God's dual nature.

One could not deny that men had predominated in positions of power and influence in history, but history was temporal. "The divine data," on the other hand, was spiritual and infinite. It stood to reason, therefore, that men should not complain if in some future period the balance of power shifted to women. Society would then have to recognize that God's feminine nature had come to the forefront. Mrs. Eddy felt that in the eyes of God men and women were equal. In the divine order, man and woman began "in One and as one." There was no artificial sexual division to mar this unity and harmony. Unfortunately, in the world of material beliefs this inherent unity of God was sundered, split into two artificial halves instead of a seamless whole. However, this did not mean that she capitulated to convention regarding gender issues and role relationships. From the day she fell on the ice to the day she died, Mrs. Eddy saw herself and her movement not in terms of gender, but in spiritual terms: they were all reflections of God. From the early days of the Genesis manuscript, through the 1881 revision of *Science and Health*, in which she employed feminine pronouns in referring to God, to her notes on "Man and Woman," Mrs. Eddy wrestled with the issues of gender and the gap between man's personal sense and spiritual reality. It would have taken a Solomon to avoid the psychosocial implications of the Bible's account of Adam and Eve and the secondary status of women. It was also impossible to use gender pronouns and nouns in a spiritual sense without people assuming a social-psychological meaning and thus missing the heart of her message.[40]

Most of the full-time practitioners in Christian Science were women. According to one historian they outnumbered men "five to one by the 1890s and eight to one by the early 1970s." In the late 1880s, a *Chicago Times* reporter was sent to cover a Christian Science meeting. He noted the preponderance of women in the audience and was not too far off the mark when he wrote, "Grammatically viewed, Christian Science is a noun in the feminine gender."[41]*

It is clear that no matter how imperfect Mrs. Eddy might have been in reconciling the gender issue (Mary Collson, for one, found that Christian Science fell short of the feminist expectations she carried into the movement), she provided an arena in which women could demonstrate intellectual, organizational, and publicity skills, a sphere of power in which they could demonstrate moral superiority, a sphere prepared by the culture of domesticity but outside the home on a public scale.[42]

The resistance to Mrs. Eddy's leadership on the grounds of gender was confronted in an article in *The Christian Science Journal* in the spring of 1899. The article hailed Mrs. Eddy as a forceful, active leader whose long years of service had earned her the respect of her followers, much like "a commander whom every private soldier loves and honors." Of course, Mother Eddy was a woman, "and so too is your mother." Was it not obvious that in charitable work and in religion the brunt of the work was borne by women? Was it not also true that "in spiritual perception and intuitive power" women were at least the equal of men?[43]

This was an ingenious argument, for the author placated fears of Mrs. Eddy's strong leadership by claiming that she had not breached the sphere of domesticity; she was merely extending it into the outside world, and, after all, who could deny that a moral woman's place was in religion? But this justification of Mrs. Eddy was also a bit disingenuous, because Mrs. Eddy was being more than a good girl who knew her proper place. She was not merely enlarging a separate sphere for women; other women had been doing this for some time. In terms of gender,

---

* Rennie B. Shoepflin states that "the last two decades of Eddy's life coincided with the rapid growth of Christian Science; membership grew seven-fold, from 8,724 in 1890 to about 55,000 (72 percent of whom were women) by 1906." This preponderant number of women reflects the feminizing process of American Protestantism that had begun long before the advent of Christian Science. The number of women attracted to Christian Science, however, is notable. Shoepflin, "Christian Science Healing in America," in Norman Gevitz, ed., *Other Healers: Unorthodox Medicine in America* (Baltimore: Johns Hopkins University Press, 1988), p. 204. On this point, also see Clifford P. Smith, *Historical Sketches* (Boston: Christian Science Publishing Company, 1941), pp. 139, 140.

she went a long way toward creating interlocking circles rather than separate spheres for the men and women in Christian Science. Women, like men, could exercise a dependent autonomy—as paradoxical as that might sound—within the world shaped by Mrs. Eddy's religious ideology.[44]

It was this kind of feminism and autonomy that Mary Collson measured against the kind she had known at Hull House, and she found it wanting. But it was this kind that allowed Caroline Noyes and Edward Kimball to work side by side despite their disagreements (although Mary Collson and Alfred Farlow could not). As one Christian Science writer put it, "Through the understanding of Christian Science men and women, by one and the same method, can reform the sinner and heal the sick." Throughout the world Mrs. Eddy had "placed woman by the side of man in the pulpit as co-worker and co-equal."[45]

From these pieces of impressionistic evidence, one can also see that Mrs. Eddy provided an arena for men who were looking for nurturing consolation but who for cultural reasons could not find it in Catholicism (here the Mother Mary connection is striking). We recall that Alfred Farlow discovered Christian Science to be a fertile ground for his skills and competence, but he also sought something more than autonomy. As he once put it, "Indeed, we seek [Mrs. Eddy's] advice as a child would seek the advice of its mother, and because of her peculiar relationship to us in this work, we have learned to call her 'Mother.' "

Yet gender stereotypes simply are not adequate to convey the reality of what Mrs. Eddy provided men and women in Christian Science. One crucial aspect of what she did through her connections to a Puritan past and Protestant values was to synthesize Protestant and Catholic images. She legitimated for Protestants the idea of a nurturant-maternal-consoling figure in terms that they could live with and in terms she preferred, as an ideal figure, a vessel for God's intentions, a denial of corporeality, which is consistent with the kind of disciplined rationalization they were learning. As a woman she could not have had such an appeal, especially for men in the nineteenth century, but as an idealized, spiritual figure she could.[46]*

In many respects Mrs. Eddy hit the right note at the right time; she synthesized "science" and nurturance, and she contained the anxiety by taking the process out of the body. She emphasized what many wanted to believe anyway: if they were able to couple the will, belief, and

---

* Though she rejected any comparison to the Virgin Mary, Mrs. Eddy's own thought often invited just such a comparison. On this issue, see Stephen Gottschalk, *The Emergence of Christian Science in American Religious Life* (Berkeley: University of California Press, 1978), p. 167.

discipline to the true spiritual reality, then they could purge from their spirit the kinds of strivings and feelings the capitalist society was imposing. In one of its appeals, at least, Christian Science was a Protestant-capitalist version of nurturance, but precisely for whom will have to await a demographic study, if the data exists. For now, however, we can say that Mrs. Eddy and Christian Science were multivocal symbols. She succeeded in part because of the strength of her religious truth and because she provided an opportunity for different kinds of people. Putting the issue of Christian Science's radical idealism to one side, one can see that her success and the movement's were limited, at the same time, because of their maternal-nurturant-female quality.

Mrs. Eddy's followers, of course, were not swept up in these sociological abstractions; they responded to her in a more immediate, heartfelt way, which was poignantly demonstrated at her funeral. While most of her followers accepted her passing with a sadness moderated by restraint, John Salchow, her "Johnnie," more openly expressed a deep sense of loss. Just as her casket was being placed in the vault at Mount Auburn Cemetery and the door was being closed, Salchow looked at his watch, which read two o'clock. This was the exact time at which Mrs. Eddy used to take her daily drive, and this association had a profound effect upon the grief-stricken Salchow. The emotional pain was too much for him, and he had a brief out-of-body experience. To him it suddenly seemed as if he had become detached from reality. He then felt as if he were "suspended far above the earth," completely unaware of the other mourners. He had a single desire; he wanted to be with his beloved Mother. "I began to separate from myself," he wrote, "rising at an angle of about forty-five degrees and seemed to become two distinct persons, both dressed alike." When he had arisen about a foot or more from what appeared to be his other self, another Christian Science student, sensing his distress, approached him and, gently laying her hand on him, said, "John, she loved you." These comforting words brought Salchow down to earth and slowly he "was again one person." In an exaggerated way, he was expressing what all of the mourners—these children of Christian Science—felt at the loss of their Mother. She had guided them, and especially in "Johnnie's" case, shown them a great deal of love. Now she was gone. Yet as Salchow and the others would rediscover in the days ahead, she still lived through her words: *Science and Health with Key to the Scriptures*, along with her other writings, would continue to guide man into the path of spiritual reality.[47]

NOTES

SHORT FORMS OF CITATION USED IN NOTES

Archives: Archives of The Mother Church
Longyear: Longyear Historical Society

Preface

1. Mark Twain, *Christian Science*, Author's National Edition, The Writings of Mark Twain, vol. XXV (New York: Harper & Bros., 1907), p. 211.
2. William Cole and Louis Phillips, compilers, *Oh, What an Awful Thing to Say!: Needles, Skewers, Pricks, and Outright Nastiness* (New York: St. Martin's Press, 1992), p. 35; Harold Bloom, *The American Religion: The Emergence of the Post-Christian Nation* (New York: Simon & Schuster, 1992), p. 133.
3. Robert Peel, *Mary Baker Eddy: The Years of Discovery*, paperback ed. (New York: Holt, Rinehart & Winston, 1975); *Mary Baker Eddy: The Years of Trial*, paperback ed. (New York: Holt, Rinehart & Winston, 1974); *Mary Baker Eddy: The Years of Authority*, paperback ed. (New York: Holt, Rinehart & Winston, 1980).
4. Twain, *Christian Science*, p. 146.

Chapter 1

1. Archives, James F. Gilman diary; Archives, Frank Phelan reminiscences; Mary Baker Eddy, *Retrospection and Introspection*, in *Prose Works Other Than Science and Health with Key to the Scriptures* (Boston: First Church of Christ, Scientist, 1953), p. 4.
2. Quoted in Clifford P. Smith, *Historical Sketches: From the Life of Mary Baker Eddy and the History of Christian Science* (Boston: Christian Science Publishing Society, 1941), pp. 14–15; Eddy, *Retrospection and Introspection*, p. 5.
3. Of the recent writers, Robert Peel, *Mary Baker Eddy: The Years of Discovery*, paperback ed. (New York: Holt, Rinehart & Winston, 1975), does the best job of revealing the personalities of Mark and Abigail Baker.
4. Eddy, *Retrospection and Introspection*, p. 5; Smith, *Historical Sketches*, p. 11.

5. Longyear, The Covenant of the Congregational Church in Bow (1822); Jewel Spangler Smaus, *Mary Baker Eddy: The Golden Days* (Boston: Christian Science Publishing Society, 1966), p. 17; Irving C. Tomlinson, *Twelve Years with Mary Baker Eddy* (Boston: Christian Science Publishing Society, 1945), p. 17.

6. Smaus, *The Golden Days*, p. 17. On the family prayers, also see Tomlinson, *Twelve Years with Mary Baker Eddy*, pp. 16–17.

7. Peel, *Years of Discovery*, p. 20.

8. Smaus, *The Golden Days*, p. 12.

9. Tomlinson, *Twelve Years with Mary Baker Eddy*, p. 17.

10. Longyear, letter dated Apr. 24, 1836. For the chaise as a status symbol, see Rev. M. T. Runnels, *History of Sanbornton, New Hampshire*, 2 vols. (Boston: Alfred Mudge & Son, 1882), I, p. 57; Smith, *Historical Sketches*, p. 13.

11. Longyear, letter dated Jan. 20, 1836; Longyear, letter dated Aug. 5, 1836; Longyear, letter dated Nov. 20, 1836.

12. William J. Gilmore, *Reading Becomes a Necessity of Life: Material and Cultural Life in Rural New England, 1780–1835* (Knoxville: University of Tennessee Press, 1989), pp. 106, 111.

13. Longyear, letter dated Apr. 24, 1836; Longyear, letter dated Dec. 15, 1835.

14. Longyear, letter dated Sept. 14, 1835.

15. Longyear, letter dated May 1836.

16. Julius Silberger, Jr., *Mary Baker Eddy: An Interpretive Biography of the Founder of Christian Science* (Boston: Little, Brown & Co., 1980), p. 14.

17. Georgine Milmine, "Mary Baker Eddy: The Story of her Life and the History of Christian Science," *McClure's* 28 (Jan. 1907), p. 227; Smith, *Historical Sketches*, pp. 15–16. This idealization of the mother was a wider cultural phenomenon as well. Ann D. Wood, " 'The Scribbling Women' and Fanny Fern: Why Women Wrote," *American Quarterly* 23 (Spring 1971), p. 13; Steven Mintz, *A Prison of Expectations: The Family in Victorian Culture* (New York: New York University Press, 1983), p. 51.

18. Peel, *Years of Discovery*, p. 6.

19. Runnels, *History of Sanbornton*, vol. I, p. 58; Longyear, letter dated May 5, 1844.

20. Longyear, letter dated Aug. 7, 1849; Longyear, letter dated Dec. 26, 1847. For similar expressions regarding separations in the nineteenth century, see Mary P. Ryan, *Womanhood in America: From Colonial Times to the Present*, 2nd ed. (New York: Franklin Watts, 1979), p. 70.

21. Longyear, letter dated May 5, 1844; Archives, no date on letter.

22. Longyear, letter dated Dec. 26, 1847.

23. Archives, Longyear, letter dated Aug. 7, 1849; Archives, no date on letter.

24. Longyear, essay on "Character." Albert's college essays, his quest for status and self-discipline, can be placed in a wide social context. See Burton J. Bledstein, *The Culture of Professionalism: The Middle Class and the Development of Higher Education in America* (New York: W. W. Norton & Co., 1976), pp. 159–78, 248–55; Longyear, essay on "The Mahometan Religion, not the cause of Mahometan degradation."

25. Longyear, letter dated July 6, 1837, addressed to Mrs. McNeil; Albert made these points in a number of essays. See his "Perfectibility of Human Nature," "Temperance," and "Enthusiasm." On the stresses and strains felt by middle-class men as they coped with an expanding democratic society in the nineteenth century, see Robert H. Wiebe, *The Opening of American Society: From the Adoption of the Constitution to the Eve of Disunion* (New York: Alfred A. Knopf, 1984), pp. 265–90; E. Anthony Rotundo, *American Manhood: Transformations in Masculinity from the Revolution to the Modern Era* (New York: Basic Books, 1993), pp. 163–283; Mark Carnes and Clyde Griffen, eds., *Meanings for Manhood: Constructions of Masculinity in Victorian America* (Chicago: University of Chicago Press, 1990); Mary Ann Clawson, *Constructing Brotherhood: Class, Gender, and Fraternalism* (Princeton, N.J.: Princeton University Press, 1989).

26. Longyear, "Essay on Character Delineation"; Longyear, "Perfectibility of Human Nature."

27. Longyear, "Speech Delivered Before the Bay State Association of Democratic Young Men," Feb. 3, 1840.

28. Martha H. Verbrugge, *Able-Bodied Womanhood: Personal Health and Social Change in Nineteenth-Century Boston* (New York: Oxford University Press, 1988), pp. 11–27.

29. Longyear, George S. Baker journal. On the use of oral imagery among Jacksonians, see Michael Paul Rogin, *Fathers and Children: Andrew Jackson and the Subjugation of the American Indian* (New York: Alfred A. Knopf, 1975). Also see George B. Forgie, *Patricide in the House Divided: A Psychological Interpretation of Lincoln and His Age* (New York: W. W. Norton & Co., 1979), pp. 97–110, where the attacks on the past were expressed in bodily metaphors. An article with a broader scope is Martha Banta, "Medical Therapies and the Body Politic," in Jack Salzman, ed., *Prospects* 8 (1983), pp. 59–128.

30. Longyear, letter dated Dec. 15, 1835.

31. Longyear, letter dated Oct. 15, 1837.

32. Longyear, letter dated Nov. 23, 1837.

33. Longyear, George S. Baker journal; Longyear, letter to Mark Baker, dated Jan. 27, 1838; Longyear, George S. Baker journal, Sept. 1836 entry.

34. Longyear, letter dated Nov. 23, 1837. This concern over reading matter, over the need for moral strength, may have reflected gender anxieties in George. If so, he was far from alone in this anxiety. On this issue among nineteenth-century writers, see David Leverenz, *Manhood and the American Renaissance* (Ithaca, N.Y.: Cornell University Press, 1989); Longyear, letter to Jeremiah C. Tilton, dated Mar. 12, 1842.

35. Longyear, George S. Baker journal, entry for 1837.

36. Longyear, Letter dated Aug. 1, 1835.

37. Longyear, letter dated Oct. 13, 1837; Longyear, letter dated Oct. 13, 1837. On her mother's aversion to city life, see Longyear, letter dated Aug. 7, 1849; Longyear, letter dated July 4, 1838.

38. Longyear, letter dated May 1, 1836; Longyear, letter dated Sept. 7, 1835.

39. Longyear, letter dated Jan. 20, 1836; Longyear, letter dated July 18, 1837. On the theme of anxiety, separation, and feelings of loss accompanying marriage, see Ellen K. Rothman, *Hands and Hearts: A History of Courtship in America* (New York: Basic Books, 1984), pp. 60–63; Mary Kelley, *Private Woman, Public State: Literary Domesticity in Nineteenth-Century America* (New York: Oxford University Press, 1984), pp. 217–49.

40. Lewis O. Saum, *The Popular Mood of Pre–Civil War America* (Westport, Conn.: Greenwood Press, 1980), p. xv. The term "gentle melancholy" is his.

41. Longyear, Baker papers.

42. Longyear, letter dated July 6, 1837.

43. Longyear, letter dated June 21, 1836.

44. Marvin Meyers, *The Jacksonian Persuasion* (New York: Vintage Books, 1960), pp. 33–56; John William Ward, in Stanley Coben and Lorman Ratner, eds., *The Development of an American Culture*, 2nd ed. (New York: St. Martin's Press, 1984), pp. 58–79. On the issue of self-control see Anita Clair Fellman and Michael Fellman, *Making Sense of Self: Medical Advice Literature in Late Nineteenth-Century America* (Philadelphia: University of Pennsylvania Press, 1981); John B. Blake, "Health Reform," in Edwin S. Gaustad, ed., *The Rise of Adventism: Religion and Society in Mid-Nineteenth-Century America* (New York: Harper & Row, 1974), pp. 30–49; Robert David Thomas, *The Man Who Would Be Perfect: John Humphrey Noyes and the Utopian Impulse* (Philadelphia: University of Pennsylvania Press, 1977), pp. 56–67; on perfectibility, see James C. Whorton, *Crusaders for Fitness: The History of American Health Reformers* (Prince-

ton, N.J.: Princeton University Press, 1982), p. 7; also see Fellman and Fellman, *Making Sense of Self*, pp. 5–6; Verbrugge, *Able-Bodied Womanhood*, p. 4.

45. Longyear, letter dated Jan. 29, 1840.

46. See Kirk Jeffrey, "The Family as Utopian Retreat from the City: The Nineteenth Century Contribution," in Sallie TeSelle, ed., *The Family, Communes, and Utopian Societies* (New York: Harper & Row, 1972), pp. 21–39; Clifford Edward Clark, Jr., *The American Family Home, 1800–1960* (Chapel Hill: University of North Carolina Press, 1986), pp. 3–71; Edward Halsey Foster, *The Civilized Wilderness: Backgrounds to American Romantic Literature, 1817–1860* (New York: Free Press, 1975), pp. 51–144; Colleen McDannell, *The Christian Home in Victorian America, 1840–1900* (Bloomington: Indiana University Press, 1986), pp. 20–51.

47. Adam H. Dickey, *Memoirs of Mary Baker Eddy* (Boston: Lillian S. Dickey, 1927), p. 132.

Chapter 2

1. Clifford P. Smith, *Historical Sketches: From the Life of Mary Baker Eddy and the History of Christian Science* (Boston: Christian Science Publishing Society, 1941), p. 37; Georgine Milmine, "Mary Baker G. Eddy: The Story of Her Life and the History of Christian Science," *McClure's* 28 (Jan. 1907), p. 235.

2. Archives. See, for example, letter dated May 11, 1836; Archives, letter dated Dec. 20, 1836; Archives, letter dated Sept. 5, 1835, "anticipating receiving George's "*poetical* effusions of love dity. . . .""; Archives, letter dated Apr. 17, 1837; Longyear, letter dated Mar. 27, 1837.

3. Archives, letter dated May 2, 1836.

4. Archives, 11023. On the rise of literacy and its challenge to the order of rural New England communities, see William J. Gilmore, *Reading Becomes a Necessity of Life: Material and Cultural Life in Rural New England, 1780–1835* (Knoxville: University of Tennessee Press, 1989), pp. 131, 134.

5. Longyear, letter dated Dec. 24, 1840; Archives, letter dated May 2, 1836; Archives, letter dated Apr. 17, 1837.

6. Archives, letter dated Apr. 17, 1837.

7. On their relationship, see the following letters: Archives, letter dated Feb. 24, 1843; Archives, letter dated ca. 1841; Archives, letter dated Jan. 28, 1841. A wider context of nineteenth-century female relationships is established by Nancy F. Cott, *The Bonds of Womanhood: "Woman's Sphere" in New England, 1780–1835* (New Haven and London: Yale University Press, 1977), pp. 160–96; Carroll Smith-Rosenberg, *Disorderly Conduct: Visions of Gender in Victorian America* (New York: Alfred A. Knopf, 1985), pp. 53–76.

8. Archives, letter dated Apr. 17, 1837; Longyear, letter dated Jan. 15, 1837.

9. Longyear, George Baker journal, entry for Jan. 1837; Longyear, letter dated Jan. 15, 1837; Longyear, letter dated Oct. 13, 1837; Longyear, letter dated Aug. 5, 1836; Archives, letter dated Apr. 17, 1837.

10. For the literature on this, see Anita Clair Fellman and Michael Fellman, *Making Sense of Self: Medical Advice Literature in Late-Nineteenth-Century America* (Philadelphia: University of Pennsylvania Press, 1981); James C. Whorton, *Crusaders for Fitness: The History of American Health Reformers* (Princeton, N.J.: Princeton University Press, 1982); Longyear, letter dated Oct. 21, 1838; Longyear, letter dated Nov. 19, 1838.

11. Georgine Milmine, *The Life of Mary Baker G. Eddy, and the History of Christian Science* (New York: Doubleday, Page & Co., 1909), p. 57. Milmine turned her *McClure's* articles into a book.

12. See, for example, Ernest Sutherland Bates and John V. Dittemore, *Mary Baker Eddy: The Truth and the Tradition* (New York: Alfred A. Knopf, 1932), p. 8; Edwin Franden Dakin, *Mrs. Eddy: The Biography of a Virginal Mind* (New York: Charles

Scribner's Sons, 1930), pp. 6–10. For a current assessment of the hysterical personality, see Alan Krohn, *Hysteria: The Elusive Neurosis* (New York: International Universities Press, 1978).

13. Milmine, "Mary Baker G. Eddy," p. 235. Robert Peel, *Mary Baker Eddy: The Years of Discovery*, paperback ed. (New York: Holt, Rinehart & Winston, 1975), p. 315, n. 22; p. 318, n. 76; p. 327, n. 74; p. 330, n. 121, succeeds in making any historian wary of accepting Milmine and her informants.

14. Longyear, letter dated Oct. 13, 1837; Longyear, letter dated July 18, 1837.

15. Longyear. Letter dated Feb. 16, 1840; Longyear, letter dated July 18, 1837; Longyear, letter dated Oct. 15, 1837. Ellen White of the Seventh-Day Adventists had similar worries regarding disease and death. See Ronald L. Numbers and Janet S. Numbers, "The Psychological World of Ellen White," *Spectrum* 14 (Aug. 1983), p. 23.

16. On the state of the medical profession, see John Harley Warner, *The Therapeutic Perspective: Medical Practice, Knowledge and Identity in America, 1820–1885* (Cambridge: Harvard University Press, 1986); Richard Harrison Shryock, *Medicine in History: Historical Essays* (Baltimore: Johns Hopkins University Press, 1966), p. 150; William G. Rothstein, *American Physicians in the Nineteenth Century: From Sects to Science* (Baltimore: Johns Hopkins University Press, 1972), pp. 41–121; John S. Haller, Jr., *American Medicine in Transition, 1840–1910* (Urbana: University of Illinois Press, 1981).

17. Peel, *Years of Discovery*, p. 22.

18. There is, of course, a vast literature on this material. See especially Edith Jacobson, *The Self and the Object World* (New York: International Universities Press, 1964); Margaret S. Mahler, Fred Pine, and Annie Bergman, *Psychological Birth of the Human Infant* (New York: Basic Books, 1975); Stanley I. Greenspan and George H. Pollock, eds., *The Course of Life: Psychoanalytic Contributions Toward Understanding Personality Development*, Vol. I: *Infancy and Childhood* (Adelphi, Md.: National Institute of Mental Health, 1980); D. W. Winnicott, *The Maturational Processes and the Facilitating Environment: Studies in the Theory of Emotional Development* (New York: International Universities Press, 1974), p. 58.

19. A superb article here is Erna Furman, "On Fusion, Integration and Feeling Good," *Psychoanalytic Study of the Child* 40 (1985), pp. 81–110.

20. On the meaning of trauma and the attempts at reintegration, see Erna Furman, "On Trauma: When Is the Death of a Parent Traumatic?," *Psychoanalytic Study of the Child* 41 (1986), pp. 191–208. Also see Arnold M. Cooper, "A Limited Definition of Psychic Trauma," in Arnold Rothstein, ed., *The Reconstruction of Trauma*, Workshop Series of the American Psychoanalytic Association, Monograph 2 (Madison, Conn.: International Universities Press, 1986), pp. 41–56.

21. Pinchas Noy, "Originality and Creativity," *The Annual of Psychoanalysis*, vol. XII/XIII (New York: International Universities Press, 1985), pp. 421–46. Also see Gilbert J. Rose, *The Power of Form: A Psychoanalytic Approach to Aesthetic Form*, Psychological Issues, Monograph 49 (New York: International Universities Press, 1980); Rose, "Narcissistic Fusion States and Creativity," in Mark Kanzer, ed., *The Unconscious Today: Essays in Honor of Max Schur* (New York: International Universities Press, 1971), pp. 495–505; Rose, *Trauma and Mastery in Life and Art* (New Haven: Yale University Press, 1987), for his discussion of parallels and differences between pathological and creative responses to traumatic events.

22. On this point, see Leonard Shengold, *Halo in the Sky* (New York: Guilford Press, 1988), pp. 79–91; Mary Baker Eddy, *Science and Health with Key to the Scriptures* (Boston: First Church of Christ, Scientist, 1934), p. 194.

23. Mary Baker Eddy, *Science and Health*, p. 195.

24. See, for example, ibid., pp. 154–55. On p. 237 she states, "The more stubborn beliefs and theories of parents often choke the good seed in the minds of themselves and their offspring"; ibid., p. 352. She uses the same ghost analogy on p. 371.

25. Jewel Spangler Smaus, *Mary Baker Eddy: The Golden Days* (Boston: Christian

Science Publishing Society, 1966), pp. 37–38; Stephen Nissenbaum, *Sex, Diet, and Debility in Jacksonian America: Sylvester Graham and Health Reform* (Westport, Conn.: Greenwood Press, 1980). Also see Shyrock, "Sylvester Graham and the Popular Health Movement, 1830–1870," in *Medicine in History*, pp. 111–25; Whorton, *Crusaders for Fitness*, pp. 38–61, and Whorton's essay "Patient, Heal Thyself: Popular Health Reform Movements as Unorthodox Medicine," in Norman Gevitz, ed., *Other Healers: Unorthodox Medicine in America* (Baltimore: Johns Hopkins University Press, 1988), pp. 52–81.

26. Ronald L. Numbers and Rennie B. Schoepflin, "Ministeries of Healing: Mary Baker Eddy, Ellen G. White, and the Religion of Healing," in Judith Walzer Leavitt, ed., *Women and Health in America: Historical Readings* (Madison: University of Wisconsin Press, 1984), p. 379; Philip Greven, *The Protestant Temperament: Patterns in Child-Rearing, Religious Experience, and the Self in Early America* (New York: Alfred A. Knopf, 1977), p. 43. For the linking of obsessional traits to Calvinism, see David Leverenz, *The Language of Puritan Feeling: An Exploration in Literature, Psychology, and Social History* (New Brunswick, N.J.: Rutgers University Press, 1980), pp. 105–37. For a psychological understanding of obsessive phenomena and ways of relating to the world, see David Shapiro, *Autonomy and Rigid Character* (New York: Basic Books, 1981), pp. 78–100; on Christian physiology, see Catherine L. Albanese's fine chapter, "Physical Religion: Natural Sin and Healing Grace in the Nineteenth Century," *Nature Religion in America: From the Algonkian Indians to the New Age* (Chicago: University of Chicago Press, 1990), pp. 117–52, esp. pp. 117–25.

27. Robert C. Fuller, *Alternative Medicine and American Religious Life* (New York: Oxford University Press, 1989), p. 31; Ronald L. Numbers, *Prophetess of Health: A Study of Ellen G. White* (New York: Harper & Row, 1976), pp. 52–53.

28. Sylvester Graham, *Lectures to Young Men*, 2nd ed. (New York: n.d.), p. 3. On this score, also see Charles E. Rosenberg, "The Therapeutic Revolution: Medicine, Meaning, and Social Change in Nineteenth-Century America," in Morris J. Vogel and Charles E. Rosenberg, eds., *The Therapeutic Revolution: Essays in the Social History of Medicine* (Philadelphia: University of Pennsylvania Press, 1979), pp. 3–22; Fellman and Fellman, *Making Sense of Self*, p. 15; Robert David Thomas, *The Man Who Would Be Perfect: John Humphrey Noyes and the Utopian Impulse* (Philadelphia: University of Pennsylvania Press, 1977), pp. 59–64.

29. Lindley Murray, *The English Reader*, 10th ed. (Keene, N.H.: John Prentiss, 1817), p. 24; Longyear, letter dated Dec. 24, 1840. An excellent article on the body image and body functions in relation to the representation of psychic conflict in adolescence is Samuel Ritvo, "The Image and Uses of the Body in Psychic Conflict," *Psychoanalytic Study of the Child* 39 (1984), pp. 449–69. In addition, see David W. Krueger, "The 'Parent Loss' of Empathic Failures and the Model Symbolic Restitution of Eating Disorders," in David R. Dietrich and Peter C. Shabad, eds., *The Problem of Loss and Mourning: Psychoanalytic Perspectives* (Madison, Conn.: International Universities Press, 1989), p. 224.

30. Archives, notebook. Also see the revised version in her *Poems Including Christ and Christmas* (Boston: n.d.), pp. 32–33.

31. Bruce Haley, *The Healthy Body and Victorian Culture* (Cambridge: Harvard University Press, 1978), p. 19. Also see Martha H. Verbrugge, *Able-bodied Womanhood: Personal Health and Social Change in Nineteenth-Century Boston* (New York: Oxford University Press, 1988), p. 39.

32. Longyear, letter dated Feb. 16, 1840.

33. *Covenant* VI (May 1847), p. 25.

34. Archives, anecdotes, 10134; Julia S. Bartlett reminiscences.

35. Ibid.

36. Sibyl Wilbur, *The Life of Mary Baker Eddy* (New York: Concord Publishing Co., 1908), pp. 28–30.

37. Murray, *English Reader*, p. 24.

38. The episode is mentioned in Peel, *Years of Discovery*, p. 10.

39. Barbara Leslie Epstein, *The Politics of Domesticity: Women, Evangelism, and Temperance in Nineteenth-Century America* (Middletown, Conn.: Wesleyan University Press, 1981), p. 41. While Mary Baker's struggle with her father has oedipal features, I am arguing that the preoedipal factors are just as significant in this crisis. Annie Reich has indicated how one can expect to find a mixture of preoedipal and oedipal factors in narcissistic crises. See her *Annie Reich: Psychoanalytic Contributions* (New York: International Universities Press, 1973), especially the following essays: "Narcissistic Object Choice in Women," pp. 179–208; "Early Identifications as Archaic Elements in the Superego," pp. 209–35; "Pathologic Forms of Self-Esteem Regulation," pp. 288–311.

40. Ann D. Wood, "The Scribbling Women" and Fanny Fern: Why Women Wrote," *American Quarterly* 23 (Spring 1971), p. 13. There is an extensive psychoanalytic literature on the nature of splitting as a function of the ego. The articles that helped in my understanding of Mary Baker Eddy and her kind of splitting are Harold P. Blum, "Splitting of the Ego and its Relation to Parent Loss," in Harold P. Blum, ed., *Defense and Resistance: Historical Perspectives and Current Concepts* (New York: International Universities Press, 1985), pp. 301–22; Joseph D. Lichtenberg and Joseph William Slap, "Notes on the Concept of Splitting and Defense Mechanism of the Splitting of the Ego," *Journal of the American Psychoanalytic Association* 21 (1973), pp. 772–87; Paul W. Pruyser, "What Splits in 'Splitting'? A Scrutiny of the Concept of Splitting in Psychoanalysis and Psychiatry," *Bulletin of the Menninger Clinic* 39 (Jan. 1975), pp. 1–46.

41. Archives, letter dated Apr. 17, 1837.

42. Archives, letter dated Mar. 27, 1837.

43. On Ellen White, see Numbers, *Prophetess of Health*, pp. 1–32; on Lucy Colman, see James Turner, *Without God, Without Creed: The Origins of Unbelief in America* (Baltimore: Johns Hopkins University Press, 1985), p. 143; on Elizabeth Cady Stanton, see Elisabeth Griffith, *In Her Own Right: The Life of Elizabeth Cady Stanton* (New York: Oxford University Press, 1984), pp. 20–21. Also see Nancy Cott, "Young Women in the Second Great Awakening," *Feminist Studies* 3 (Fall 1975), pp. 15–29; Joseph F. Kett, *Rites of Passage: Adolescence in America, 1790 to the Present* (New York: Basic Books, 1977), pp. 62–85.

44. Epstein, *Politics of Domesticity*, pp. 46–58; ibid., p. 58. Also see Virginia Lieson Brereton, *From Sin to Salvation: Stories of Women's Conversions, 1800 to the Present* (Bloomington: University of Indiana Press, 1991), pp. 32–40. For an example of the active-passive dilemma in men and the conversion experience, see Thomas, *The Man Who Would Be Perfect*, pp. 15–18.

45. Archives, I-10032.

46. Nicholson quoted in Martin Price, "The Theatre of Mind: Edward Young and James Thomson," in Harold Bloom, ed., *Poets of Sensibility and the Sublime* (New York: Chelsea House, 1986), p. 74. Young quoted on p. 75.

47. Peel, *Years of Discovery*, p. 46. Peel goes on to recount an incident when Mary had one of her "spells." She regained consciousness to find Albert sitting beside her with Young's "Night Thoughts" in his hand. He read a comforting passage to Mary, which she copied into her notebook.

48. Ibid., p. 48.

49. *An Account of the Seventy-fifth Anniversary of the Congregational Church of Northfield and Tilton* (Concord, 1897), p. 25.

50. Peel, *Years of Discovery*, p. 51.

51. Ibid., p. 64; ibid., p. 62; Isaac Watts, *The Improvement of the Mind*, rev. ed. (Boston: James Loring, 1833), p. 53.

52. Archives, notebook.

53. See, for example, Ann Douglas, *The Feminization of American Culture* (New York: Alfred A. Knopf, 1977), pp. 220–26; Ann Douglas, "Heaven Our Home": Consolation Literature in the Northern United States, 1830–1880," in David E. Stannard,

ed., *Death in America* (Philadelphia: University of Pennsylvania Press, 1975), pp. 49–68; Peel, *Years of Discovery*, p. 63.

54. *New Hampshire Patriot and State Gazette*, Dec. 23, 1840.

55. Longyear, letter dated Aug. 5, 1836.

56. Archives, journal in her notebook; Archives, notebook entry dated Aug. 25, 1843, Barry Cornwall, "Life." From a psychoanalytic perspective, one can observe the dynamics of externalization when Mary invested nature with "symbols of power." Her attempts to provide an inner and outer harmony for herself have wider cultural roots as well. Her externalizing was a variation of what William A. Clebsch has called an "esthetic spirituality." According to Clebsch, this strain of American spirituality "involved not so much the appreciation of beauty attributed to or inhering in objects of artistic creation but rather a consciousness of the beauty of living in harmony with divine things—in a word, being at home in the universe." Clebsch follows this kind of spiritual thinking in Jonathan Edwards, Ralph Waldo Emerson, and William James in his *American Religious Thought: A History*, paperback ed. (Chicago: University of Chicago Press, 1973), p. xvi. In conjunction with this, see Robert C. Fuller, *Americans and the Unconscious* (New York: Oxford University Press, 1986), especially ch. 1, "The Psyche as Symbol: Theological Applications," pp. 11–27.

57. For this kind of thinking in nineteenth-century romanticism, see Robert Langbaum, *The Poetry of Experience: The Dramatic Monologue in Modern Literary Tradition* (London: Chatto & Windus, 1957); David Thoburn and Geoffrey Hartman, eds., *Romanticism: Vistas, Instances, Continuities* (Ithaca, N.Y.: Cornell University Press, 1973); Thomas Weiskel, *The Romantic Sublime: Studies in the Structure and Psychology of Transcendence* (Baltimore: Johns Hopkins University Press, 1976).

58. Archives, notebook.

59. Lyman P. Powell, *Mary Baker Eddy: A Life Size Portrait* (New York: Macmillan Company, 1930), p. 289, fn. 3.

60. Archives, notebook.

61. Ellen K. Rothman, *Hands and Hearts: A History of Courtship in America* (New York: Basic Books, 1984), p. 68; Archives, notebook.

62. Archives, notebook; Child quoted in Carl N. Degler, *At Odds: Women and the Family in America from the Revolution to the Present* (New York: Oxford University Press, 1980), pp. 106–7.

63. Archives, notebook. Entry dated Aug. 19, 1843.

64. Powell, *Mary Baker Eddy*, p. 77. On the popularity of Lydia Sigourney in antebellum America, see Emily Stipes Watts, *The Poetry of American Women from 1632 to 1945* (Austin: University of Texas Press, 1977), pp. 83–97; Douglas, *Feminization of American Culture*, pp. 74–75, 202–6.

65. Rothman, *Hands and Hearts*, p. 68. Also see Judith Walzer Leavitt, *Brought to Bed, Childbearing in America, 1750–1950* (New York: Oxford University Press, 1986).

Chapter 3

1. Longyear, letter dated February 6, 1844.

2. Archives, 1-10001.

3. Longyear. For the deep emotional ties between Mary and her mother, see the letters dated Feb. 6 and May 6, 1844. For these strong mother-daughter ties on a wider social level, see Carl N. Degler, *At Odds: Women in the Family in America from the Revolution to the Present* (New York: Oxford University Press, 1980), p. 109; Mary P. Ryan, *Womanhood in America: From Colonial Times to the Present*, 2nd ed. (New York: Franklin Watts, 1979), p. 104.

4. Archives, notebook. "Written on Leaving N. Carolina July 19th 1844."

5. "Emma Clinton, or a Tale of the Frontiers," *Covenant*, Aug. 1846.

6. Judith Walzer Leavitt, *Brought to Bed, Childbearing in America, 1750–1950* (New York: Oxford University Press, 1986), p. 28. Nelson quoted on p. 32.

7. Sibyl Wilbur, *The Life of Mary Baker Eddy* (Boston: Christian Science Publishing Society, 1933), p. 40. Amos Morrison was a locomotive builder. His wife gave birth to twins a few days before George W. Glover was born.

8. On these issues, see Harold P. Blum, "The Maternal Ego Ideal and the Regulation of Maternal Qualities," in Stanley I. Greenspan and George H. Pollock, eds., *The Course of Life: Psychoanalytic Contributions Toward Understanding Personality Development*, Vol. III: *Adulthood and the Aging Process* (Adelphi, Md.: National Institute of Mental Health, 1981), pp. 91–113; Judith D. Kestenberg, "Regression and Reintegration in Pregnancy," *Journal of the American Psychoanalytic Association*, Supplement, 24 (1976), pp. 213–50; Leo Sadow, "The Psychological Origins of Parenthood," in Rebecca S. Cohen, Bertram J. Cohler, and Sidney H. Weissman, eds., *Parenthood: A Psychodynamic Perspective* (New York: Guilford Press, 1984), pp. 285–96; David M. Terman, "Affect and Parenthood: The Impact of the Past Upon the Present," ibid., pp. 326–36.

9. Degler, *At Odds*, p. 109, notes the difficulty women had breaking from the family of origin even after having a child. For a discussion of these issues from a psychoanalytic perspective, see Therese Benedek, "Motherhood and Nursing," in E. James Anthony and Therese Benedek, eds., *Parenthood: Its Psychology and Psychopathology* (Boston: Little, Brown & Co., 1970), pp. 153–65; Donald Silver and B. Kay Campbell, "Failure of Psychological Gestation," in B. Kay Campbell, ed., *Psychoanalytic Inquiry*, pp. 222–32.

10. Ryan, *Womanhood in America*, p. 100.

11. Archives, Clara Shannon reminiscences; Robert Peel, *Mary Baker Eddy: The Years of Discovery*, paperback ed. (New York: Holt, Rinehart & Winston, 1975), p. 78.

12. Therese Benedek, "The Family as a Psychologic Field," in Anthony and Benedek, eds., *Parenthood*, pp. 112, 117, has good insights on this mother-child interaction.

13. Archives, Mrs. Sarah Clement Kimball reminiscences.

14. Longyear, letter dated Dec. 26, 1847; Longyear, letter dated May 17, 1848.

15. Archives, F00035, letter dated Jan. 22, 1848.

16. Archives, 78-11150, letter dated Mar. 5, 1848.

17. Longyear, letter dated Aug. 7, 1849; Peel, *Years of Discovery*, p. 96. For the role of the father in a child's development and what the absence of the father can mean, see the fine essays in Stanley H. Cath, Alan R. Gurwitt, and John Munder Ross, eds., *Father and Child: Developmental and Clinical Perspectives* (Boston: Little, Brown & Co., 1982). Especially pertinent here is James M. Herzog, "On Father Hunger: The Father's Role in the Modulation of Aggressive Drive and Fantasy," pp. 163–74, and Stanley I. Greenspan, "The 'Second Other': The Role of the Father in Early Personality Formation and the Dyadic-Phallic Phase of Development," pp. 123–38. Also see Melvin R. Lansky, "The Paternal Imago," in Stanley H. Cath, Alan Gurwitt, and Linda Gunsberg, eds., *Fathers and Their Families* (Hillsdale, N.J.: Analytic Press, 1989), pp. 27–45; and Robert M. Friedman and Leila Lerner, eds., *Toward a New Psychology of Men: Psychoanalytic and Social Perspectives*, special issue of *Psychoanalytic Review* 73 (Winter 1986).

18. Archives, F00035, letter dated Jan. 22, 1848; Longyear, letter dated Dec. 26, 1847; Longyear, letter dated Aug. 7, 1849. Also see Longyear, letter dated Sept. 2, 1848.

19. Archives, 78-11150, letter dated Mar. 5, 1848.

20. Susan E. Cayleff, *Wash and Be Healed: The Water-Cure Movement and Women's Health* (Philadelphia: Temple University Press, 1987), p. 14; Robert C. Fuller, *Mesmerism and the American Cure of Souls* (Philadelphia: University of Pennsylvania Press, 1982), p. 50. Also see Arthur Wrobel, "Orthodoxy and Respectability in Nineteenth-Century Phrenology," *Journal of Popular Culture* 9 (Summer 1975), pp. 38–50; from a slightly different perspective, Wrobel, "Phrenology as Political Science," in Wrobel, ed., *Pseudo-Science and Society in Nineteenth-Century America* (Lexington: University Press of Kentucky, 1987), pp. 122–39. Cynthia Eagle Russett, *Sexual Science: The Victorian*

Construction of Womanhood (Cambridge: Harvard University Press, 1989), pp. 20–21, notes that phrenology was cordial to the aspirations of women.

21. John D. Davies, *Phrenology, Fad and Science: A Nineteenth Century American Crusade* (New Haven: Yale University Press, 1955), p. 157.

22. Cayleff, *Wash and Be Healed*, p. 15.

23. Alan Gribben, "Mark Twain, Phrenology and the 'Temperaments': A Study of Pseudoscientific Influence," *American Quarterly* 24 (Mar. 1972), pp. 45–68; Davies, *Phrenology*, p. 163; John S. Haller, Jr., *American Medicine in Transition, 1840–1910* (Urbana: University of Illinois Press, 1981), p. 15.

24. Longyear, letter dated Jan. 22, 1848.

25. For further information on the role of the doctor, see John S. Haller, Jr., and Robin M. Haller, *The Physician and Sexuality in Victorian America* (Urbana: University of Illinois Press, 1981), pp. x–xi; Barbara Sicherman, "The Uses of Diagnosis: Doctors, Patients, and Neurasthenia," *Journal of the History of Medicine and Allied Sciences* 32 (Jan. 1977), pp. 53–54; John Harley Warner points out that being a moral man was critical to the doctor's standing in the community and to his effectiveness as a healer. Anything that undermined the doctor's competence (such as a willful young girl resisting his therapeutic ministrations) threatened his professional identity. Warner also notes that another part of a doctor's duty was "to act as a moral agent in a religious sense." See his *The Therapeutic Perspective: Medical Practice, Knowledge, and Identity in America, 1820–1885* (Cambridge: Harvard University Press, 1986), pp. 15–17.

26. Georgine Milmine, "Mary Baker G. Eddy," *McClure's* 28 (1907), p. 236.

27. On the role of the doctor-patient ritual, see Charles E. Rosenberg, "The Therapeutic Revolution: Medicine, Meaning, and Social Change in Nineteenth-Century America," in Morris J. Vogel and Charles E. Rosenberg, eds., *The Therapeutic Revolution: Essays in the Social History of American Medicine* (Philadelphia: University of Pennsylvania Press, 1979), p. 4. For this struggle on a wider level including gender, see Carroll Smith-Rosenberg, "The Hysterical Woman: Sex Roles and Role Conflict in Nineteenth-Century America," in *Disorderly Conduct: Visions of Gender in Victorian America* (New York: Alfred A. Knopf, 1985), pp. 197–216; Haller and Haller, *The Physician and Sexuality in Victorian America*, p. 274; Barbara Welter, *Dimity Convictions: The American Woman in the Nineteenth Century* (Athens: Ohio University Press, 1976), pp. 57–70.

28. Archives, 78-11150, letter dated Mar. 5, 1848.

29. Peel, *Years of Discovery*, p. 95; Archives, F00035, letter dated Jan. 22, 1848; Longyear, letter dated Sept. 2, 1848.

30. Warner, *The Therapeutic Perspective*, presents an intelligent analysis of the complex relationships among the changing roles and practices of doctors, what caused these changes, and the way doctors were perceived by the public. His book does much to dispel the charge that antebellum therapy was either laughable or tragically inept. Also see Robert C. Fuller, *Alternative Medicine and American Religious Life* (New York: Oxford University Press, 1989), pp. 12–17. For an older view, see Richard Harrison Shryock, *Medicine in History* (Baltimore: Johns Hopkins University Press, 1966), pp. 149–76. R. Laurence Moore, *In Search of White Crows: Spiritualism, Parapsychology, and American Culture* (New York: Oxford University Press, 1977), p. 3, has noted that beginning in 1850 spiritualism became "vastly popular" in America. Lewis O. Saum, *The Popular Mood of Pre–Civil War America* (Westport, Conn.: Greenwood Press, 1980), has found a wide interest in spiritualist mediums and their messages among America's common folk. Ann Braude, *Radical Spirits: Spiritualism and Women's Rights in Nineteenth-Century America* (Boston: Beacon Press, 1989), pp. 28–31, has found an interest in spiritualism among women, Catholics, urban and rural workers, and blacks. Benton Gates Brown, Jr., "Spiritualism in Nineteenth-Century America" (Ph.D. diss., Boston University, 1973), p. 112, argues that only several hundred thousand men and women took an interest—to one degree or another—in spiritualism. This is a far cry from the

enthusiastic claims that there were millions of followers. Over the years Robert W. Delp has written a number of informative articles on Andrew Jackson Davis. See Delp's recent effort, "Andrew Jackson Davis and Spiritualism," in Wrobel, ed., *Pseudo-Science and Society*, pp. 100–18.

31. James Turner, *Without God, Without Creed: The Origins of Unbelief in America* (Baltimore: Johns Hopkins University Press, 1985), p. 81; Braude, *Radical Spirits*, pp. 34–40. Also see Moore, *In Search of White Crows*, pp. 50, 57, 45; Mary Farrell Bednarowski, "Nineteenth-Century American Spiritualism: An Attempt at a Scientific Religion," (Ph.D. diss., University of Minnesota, 1973), pp. 43–46.

32. Werner Sollors, "Dr. Benjamin Franklin's Celestial Telegraph, or Indian Blessings to Gas-Lit American Drawing Rooms," *American Quarterly* 35 (Winter 1983), pp. 470, 474. On the role of the machine and technology, see James W. Carey and John J. Quirk, "The Mythos of the Electronic Revolution," *American Scholar* 39 (Spring 1970), pp. 219–41. The concept of the "technological sublime" is discussed in Leo Marx, *The Machine in the Garden: Technology and the Pastoral Ideal in America*, paperback ed. (New York: Oxford University Press, 1968). Also see Marx's "The Railroad-in-the-Landscape: An Iconological Reading of a Theme in American Art," in Jack Salzman, ed., *Prospects*, Vol. 10 (New York: Cambridge University Press, 1985), pp. 77–115. On the impact of science upon American thought, see Perry Miller, *The Life of the Mind in America, From the Revolution to the Civil War* (New York: Harcourt, Brace & World, 1965), pp. 269–313.

33. Moore, *In Search of White Crows*, p. 62. On this point also see Ernest Isaacs, "The Fox Sisters and American Spiritualism," in Howard Kerr and Charles L. Crow, eds., *The Occult in America: New Historical Perspectives* (Chicago: University of Illinois Press, 1986), p. 80; Bednarowski, "Nineteenth-Century American Spiritualism," pp. 49–56, sees spiritualism as a return to a form of primitive Christianity.

34. Peel, *Years of Discovery*, p. 133; Wilbur, *Life of Mary Baker Eddy*, p. 53. Mrs. Eddy's mature position against spiritualism came well after her fall and discovery. See Mary Baker G. Eddy, "Christian Science and Spiritualism," in *Science and Health with Key to the Scriptures* (Boston: Joseph Armstrong, 1900), pp. 236–65.

35. Braude, *Radical Spirits*, pp. 182–89.

36. Mary Baker G. Eddy, *Science and Health*, (1900), p. 297.

37. *Covenant*, May 1847.

38. Marie Caskey, *Chariot of Fire: Religion and the Beecher Family* (New Haven: Yale University Press, 1978), p. 331. Moore, *In Search of White Crows*, p. 103, talks about the integrative functions of spiritualism.

39. Archives, F00035, letter dated Jan. 22, 1848.

40. "A Strong Reply," *Christian Science Journal* 3 (Apr. 1885), p. 5.

41. Archives, 73-10568, letter dated Nov. 22, 1849.

42. On the sentimentalization of death, see Charles O. Jackson, ed., *Passing: The Vision of Death in America* (Westport, Conn.: Greenwood Press, 1977); James J. Farrell, *Inventing the American Way of Death, 1830–1920* (Philadelphia: Temple University Press, 1980), pp. 30–43; Karen Halttunen, *Confidence Men and Painted Women: A Study of Middle-class Culture in America, 1830–1870* (New Haven: Yale University Press, 1982), pp. 124–53; Ann Douglas, *The Feminization of American Culture* (New York: Alfred A. Knopf, 1977), pp. 200–26; Faye Joanne Baker, "Toward Memory and Mourning," (Ph.D. diss., George Washington University, 1977).

43. Longyear, letter dated Sept. 28, 1849.

44. Archives, copybook, "My Soul Is Dark."

45. Archives, F00036, letter dated Nov. 1850.

46. The poem can be found in Peel, *Years of Discovery*, p. 98.

47. Archives, F00030, letter dated Apr. 22, 1851.

48. Archives, 73-10468, letter dated Jan. 4, 1852.

49. Archives, 62-8901, letter dated Jan. 3, 1853.

50. John L. Thomas, "Romantic Reform in America," in Stanley Katz and Stanley I. Kutler, eds., *New Perspectives on the American Past*, 1 (Boston: Little, Brown & Co., 1969), pp. 466–91; Sarah M. Evans, *Born for Liberty: A History of Women in America* (New York: Free Press, 1989), p. 67. There is a vast literature on the topic of reform organizations. See, for example, Anne Firor Scott, *Natural Allies: Women's Associations in American History* (Urbana: University of Illinois Press, 1991), pp. 11–57; Nancy A. Hewitt, *Women's Activism and Social Change, Rochester, New York, 1822–1872* (Ithaca, N.Y.: Cornell University Press, 1984), pp. 38–68; Nancy F. Cott, *The Bonds of Womanhood: "Woman's Sphere" in New England, 1870–1835* (New Haven: Yale University Press, 1977), pp. 155–59; Catherine Clinton, *The Other Civil War: American Women in the Nineteenth Century* (New York: Hill & Wang, 1984), pp. 166–87; Carl Degler, *At Odds*, pp. 286–306.

51. On Mary Gove Nichols, see Jane B. Donegan, *"Hydropathic Highway to Health: Women and Water-Cure in Antebellum America* (New York: Greenwood Press, 1986), p. 28; John B. Blake, "Mary Gove Nichols, Prophetess of Health," in Judith Walzer Leavitt, ed., *Women and Health in America* (Madison: University of Wisconsin Press, 1984), pp. 359–72. On Catharine Beecher, see Kathryn Kish Sklar, *Catharine Beecher: A Study in American Domesticity* (New York: W. W. Norton & Co., 1976). For a description and analysis of the social disorder and the varied emotional responses to it, see David J. Rothman, *The Discovery of the Asylum: Social Order and Disorder in the New Republic* (Boston: Little, Brown & Co., 1971).

52. Lori D. Ginsberg, *Women and the Work of Benevolence: Morality, Politics, and Class in the Nineteenth-Century United States* (New Haven: Yale University Press, 1990), p. 97.

53. Saum, *Popular Mood of Pre–Civil War America*, p. 131, states that while the writing of poetry in this period involved a wish to order and discipline language, this wish "involved a parallel or yet another extension of the "social" inclination to order and discipline the self." Caskey, *Chariot of Fire*, p. 79, comments on some of the integrative functions of writing for Catharine Beecher. Poets were not the only ones trying to shape and order a reality through words. See Richard M. Rollins, *The Long Journey of Noah Webster* (Philadelphia: University of Pennsylvania Press, 1980); Kenneth Cmiel, *Democratic Eloquence: The Fight over Popular Speech in Nineteenth-Century America* (New York: William Morrow & Co., 1990).

54. On the concept of the mirror, my thinking has been shaped by the following: Anneliese Riess, "The Mother's Eye," *Psychoanalytic Study of the Child* 33 (1978), pp. 381–408; Beatrice Priel, "On Mirror-Image Anxiety," ibid., 40 (1985), pp. 183–92; D. W. Winnicott, *Playing and Reality* (New York: Basic Books, 1971). On the concept of a linking object, see D. W. Winnicott, "Transitional Objects and Transitional Phenomena," in his *Collected Works: Through Pediatrics to Psychoanalysis* (New York: Basic Books, 1958), pp. 229–42. F. A. Moore, *Gems for You: From New Hampshire Authors* (Manchester, N.H.: William H. Fisk, 1850), pp. 35–36, for Hale's "The Light of Home." On Sarah Joseph A. Hale, see William R. Taylor, *Cavalier and Yankee: The Old South and American National Character* (New York: George Braziller, 1961), passim.

55. Informative articles applying Winnicott's theories appear in Simon A. Grolnick and Leonard Barkin, eds., *Between Reality and Fantasy: Transitional Objects and Phenomena* (New York: Jason Aronson, 1978). See especially Ruth Miller, "Poetry as a Transitional Object," pp. 451–68; Susan Deri, "Transitional Phenomena: Vicissitudes of Symbolization and Creativity," pp. 45–60; Gilbert J. Rose, "The Creativity of Everyday Life," pp. 347–62. In addition, see Richard Kuhns, "Loss and Creativity: Notes on Winnicott and Nineteenth-Century American Poets," in Leila Lerner, ed., *Illusion and Culture: A Tribute to Winnicott, Psychoanalytic Review* 79 (Summer 1992), pp. 197–208; Michael Eigen, "The Fire that Never Goes Out," ibid., pp. 271–87; Gilbert J. Rose, *The Power of Form: A Psychoanalytic Approach to Aesthetic Form* (New York: International Universities Press, 1980), pp. 110–29; Paul W. Pruyser, *The Play of the Imag-*

ination: Toward a Psychoanalysis of Culture (New York: International Universities Press, 1983), pp. 56–72; Winnicott quoted in Deri, "Transitional Phenomena," p. 47.

56. "The Moon," *New Hampshire Patriot and State Gazette*, Oct. 1846; "Voices of Spring," ibid., April 27, 1848. Paul H. Tolpin, "The Regulation of Anxiety: Its Relation to the Timelessness of the Unconscious and Its Capacity for Hallucination," in *The Annual of Psychoanalysis*, 2 (New York: International Universities Press, 1975), pp. 150–75; Joseph Barnett, "Dependency Conflicts in the Young Adult," *Psychoanalytic Review* 58 (Spring 1971), pp. 111–24; Irving B. Harrison, "On Merging and the Fantasy of Merging," *Psychoanalytic Study of the Child* 41 (1986), pp. 155–69—all indicate that the wish to merge does not always relate to the original state of the neonate, and the wish does not always have to express pathology. There are ego-enhancing aspects to this wish as well.

57. Archives, F00037, "Wild Rose."

58. For a wider cultural analysis, see Conrad Cherry, *Nature and the Religious Imagination: From Edwards to Bushnell* (Philadelphia: Fortress Press, 1980), p. 22; Murray Roston, *Prophet and Poet: The Bible and the Growth of Romanticism* (Evanston: Northwestern University Press, 1965); Philip E. Gura, *The Wisdom of Words: Language, Theology, and Literature in the New England Renaissance* (Middletown, Conn.: Wesleyan University Press, 1981).

59. Archives, Mrs. Addie Arnold reminiscences. The flavor of Patterson's courting can be savored in a series of letters he wrote to Mary during this period. The letters are in the Patterson file, Archives. Wilbur, *Life of Mary Baker Eddy*, p. 55, describes Patterson as "a big, handsome, healthy man with great animal spirits and excessive confidence in himself." Mrs. Grace Chard, in her reminiscences, recalled Patterson's kindness. Archives.

60. Mary M. Glover, "The Test of Love," *Covenant*, June 1847.

61. Mary Baker Eddy, *Retrospection and Introspection*, in *Prose Works Other than Science and Health with Key to the Scriptures* (Boston: First Church of Christ, Scientist, 1953), p. 20; Julius Silberger, Jr., *Mary Baker Eddy: An Interpretive Biography of the Founder of Christian Science* (Boston: Little, Brown & Co., 1980), p. 53; Archives, 62-8903, letter dated Mar. 29, 1853.

62. Archives, 62-8900, letter dated Apr. 29, 1853; Archives, 62-8899, letter dated May 2, 1853.

63. Archives, Mrs. Addie Arnold reminiscences.

64. Ernest Sutherland Bates and John V. Dittemore, *Mary Baker Eddy: The Truth and the Tradition* (New York: Alfred A. Knopf, 1932), p. 66.

65. Jewel Spangler Smaus, "An Important Historical Discovery," *Christian Science Journal* 101 (May 1983), p. 286; Archives, reminiscences of Elmira Smith Wilson.

66. Archives, Mrs. Sarah C. Turner reminiscences.

67. Eddy, *Retrospection and Introspection*, p. 20.

68. Archives, scrapbook; Longyear, letter dated June 6, 1857. Elizabeth, Mark Baker's second wife, commented on Mary's poor health in a letter dated June 6, 1856 (Longyear). Apparently Mary was very ill, and Patterson was taking care of her. In the letter one senses that the relationship between Mary and her stepmother was still strained.

69. This statement was made by Mrs. M. C. Whittier, a second cousin of Mrs. Eddy. Quoted in Robert Peel, *Mary Baker Eddy: The Years of Authority*, paperback ed. (New York: Holt, Rinehart & Winston, 1980), pp. 327–28, fn. 74. Peel does not give credence to this jaundiced testimony. For the continued belief in witches and magic in the late eighteenth and early nineteenth centuries, see Jon Butler, *Awash in a Sea of Faith: Christianizing the American People* (Cambridge and London: Harvard University Press, 1990), pp. 225–56. Also see Robert H. Abzug, *Passionate Liberator: Theodore Dwight Weld and the Dilemma of Reform* (New York: Oxford University Press, 1980), p. 6.

70. Archives, Mrs. Sarah Clement Kimball reminiscences.

71. Archives, Mrs. Sarah C. Turner reminiscences; Archives, Mrs. Addie Towns Arnold reminiscences; Archives, Elmira Smith Wilson reminiscences.

72. Archives, Elmira Smith Wilson reminiscences. See also Wilbur, *Life of Mary Baker Eddy*, p. 66; Archives, Mrs. Sarah C. Turner reminiscences; Peel, *Years of Discovery*, pp. 121–22.

73. Archives, Elmira Smith Wilson reminiscences; Longyear, letter dated Nov. 1850.

74. Archives, Mrs. Sarah C. Turner reminiscences; Archives, Daniel Kidder reminiscences.

75. Archives, Mrs. Addie Towns Arnold reminiscences.

76. Archives, Elmira Smith Wilson reminiscences; Archives, Elias F. Bailey reminiscences; Archives, Mrs. Sylvester Swett reminiscences.

77. Archives, Mrs. Sarah G. Chard reminiscences.

78. For the threat of the witch to communal harmony and why women were especially singled out as witches, see Carol F. Karlsen, *The Devil in the Shape of a Woman: Witchcraft in Colonial New England* (New York: W. W. Norton & Co., 1987), pp. 117–81. Also see John Putnam Demos, *Entertaining Satan: Witchcraft and the Culture of Early New England* (New York: Oxford University Press, 1982); Paul Boyer and Stephen Nissenbaum, *Salem Possessed: The Social Origins of Witchcraft* (Cambridge: Harvard University Press, 1974).

79. The sense of this humiliating retreat is captured in Wilbur, *Life of Mary Baker Eddy*, p. 63.

80. For the details of this episode, see Peel, *Years of Discovery*, pp. 114–45.

81. Archives, letter dated Dec. 2, 1851.

82. Catherine L. Albanese, *Nature Religion in America: From the Algonkian Indians to the New Age* (Chicago: University of Chicago Press, 1990), p. 133; Ronald L. Numbers, *Prophetess of Health: A Study of Ellen G. White* (New York: Harper & Row, 1977), p. 63. Also see Haller, *American Medicine in Transition*, pp. 104–19; John B. Blake, "Health Reform," in Edwin S. Gaustad, ed., *The Rise of Adventism: Religion and Society in Mid-Nineteenth-Century America* (New York: Harper & Row, 1974), p. 35; William G. Rothstein, *American Physicians in the Nineteenth Century: From Sects to Science* (Baltimore: Johns Hopkins University Press, 1972), pp. 230–46.

83. Eddy, *Retrospection and Introspection*, p. 33.

84. Albanese, *Nature Religion*, p. 133; Fuller, *Alternative Medicine and American Religious Life*, p. 25; Paul Starr, *The Social Transformation of American Medicine* (New York: Basic Books, 1982), p. 96. Peel, *Years of Discovery*, p. 136, indicates another reason for homeopathy's appeal to Mrs. Patterson: she became an effective healer in the community. For additional information on this movement, see Martin Kaufman, "Homeopathy in America: The Rise and Fall and Persistence of a Medical Heresy," in Norman Gevitz, ed., *Other Healers: Unorthodox Medicine in America* (Baltimore: Johns Hopkins University Press, 1988), pp. 100–1, where he discusses its various appeals. Also see his older work, *Homeopathy in America: The Rise and Fall of a Medical Heresy* (Baltimore: Johns Hopkins University Press, 1971); Fuller, *Alternative Medicine and American Religious Life*, pp. 55–56. On p. 56 he notes: "Thus, Transcendentalists such as Theodore Parker, Bronson Alcott, and Elizabeth Palmer Peabody saw homeopathy as a vital aspect of their Swedenborgian-inspired mystical world view. Likewise, prominent homeopaths found in Transcendentalism and Swedenborgianism ready-made systems for articulating their intuitive sense of the physical body as but an outer covering of some inner spiritual energy." Also see Kaufman, "Homeopathy in America," p. 101.

85. Donegan, "*Hydropathic Highway to Health;*" Cayleff, *Wash and Be Healed*; Fuller, *Alternative Medicine and American Religious Life*, pp. 26–30; William Leach, *True Love and Perfect Union: The Feminist Reform of Sex and Society* (New York: Basic Books, 1980), pp. 19–37; quoted in Donegan, "Hydropathic Highway to Health," p. 39; Ronald G. Walters, *American Reformers: 1815–1860* (New York: Hill & Wang, 1978), p. 149.

86. Archives, letter dated May 29, 1862. A number of recent authors have discussed hydropathy's considerable impact on women. While gender issues might have drawn other women to the water-cure sanitariums, feminist considerations were deeply buried

in Mary Patterson, and they did not surface as conscious motives in her decision to go to Vail's. On the gender implications of hydropathy, see Cayleff, *Wash and Be Healed*, pp. 16–18, 145–48; Sklar, *Catharine Beecher*, p. 207. For the expansion of women's roles in the field of health care, see Regina Markell Morantz, "Nineteenth-Century Health Reform and Women: A Program of Self-Help," in Guenter B. Risse, Ronald L. Numbers, and Judith Walzer Leavitt, eds., *Medicine Without Doctors: Home Health Care in American History* (New York: Science History Publications, 1977), pp. 73–93; Morantz, "Making Women Modern: Middle-Class Women and Health Reform in 19th-Century America," in Leavitt, ed., *Women and Health in America*, pp. 346–54.

87. Letter reprinted in Lyman P. Powell, *Mary Baker Eddy: A Life Size Portrait* (New York: Macmillan Company, 1930), p. 100.

Chapter 4

1. On this issue, see Barbara Welter, "The Feminization of American Religion, 1800–1860," in Mary Hartman and Lois W. Banner, eds., *Clio's Consciousness Raised* (New York: Harper & Row, 1974), pp. 137–52; Ann Douglas, *The Feminization of American Culture* (New York: Alfred A. Knopf, 1977); Richard D. Shiels, "The Feminization of American Congregationalism, 1730–1835," *American Quarterly* 33 (Spring 1981), pp. 46–62; Nancy F. Cott, *The Bonds of Womanhood: "Woman's Sphere" in New England, 1780–1835* (New Haven: Yale University Press, 1977), pp. 126–59.

2. On Quimby's background, see Ervin Seale, ed., *Phineas Parkhurst Quimby: The Complete Writings*, vol. 1 (Marina Del Rey, Calif.: Devorss & Company, 1988), pp. 19–20. An older assessment of Quimby worth reading is Charles S. Braden, *Spirits in Rebellion: The Rise and Development of New Thought* (Dallas: Southern Methodist University Press, 1963), pp. 47–88; Emerson quoted in George Perkins et al., eds., *The American Tradition in Literature*, 6th ed. (New York: Random House, 1985), p. 418.

3. Richard Rudisill, *Mirror Image: The Influence of the Daguerreotype on American Society* (Albuquerque: University of New Mexico Press, 1971), p. 233. On the linking of the daguerreotype to nature, also see Barbara Novak, *American Painting of the Nineteenth Century: Realism, Idealism, and the American Experience* (New York: Harper & Row, 1979), p. 197. Miles Orvel, *The Real Thing: Imitation and Authenticity in American Culture, 1880–1940* (Chapel Hill: University of North Carolina Press, 1989), pp. 73–102, has pertinent things to say about the quest for the authentic in photography in the late nineteenth century.

4. On this point, also see Alan Trachtenberg, *Reading American Photographs: Images as History, Mathew Brady to Walker Evans* (New York: Hill & Wang, 1989), pp. 27–29; Louis P. Masur, " 'Age of the First Person Singular': The Vocabulary of the Self in New England, 1780–1850," *Journal of American Studies* 25 (Aug. 1991), pp. 208–9.

5. Robert C. Fuller, *Mesmerism and the American Cure of Souls* (Philadelphia: University of Pennsylvania Press, 1982), pp. 17, 69–104, 43–47; Robert C. Fuller, *Alternative Medicine and American Religious Life* (New York: Oxford University Press, 1989), p. 46; Robert C. Fuller, *Americans and the Unconscious* (New York: Oxford University Press, 1986), pp. 34–45.

6. Seale, ed., *Complete Writings*, vol. 1, journal entry, Friday [January] 17th, 1845, p. 43.

7. Ibid., journal entry, Tuesday [January] 14th, 1845, p. 42.

8. Ibid., journal entry, Sunday [February] 9th, 1845, p. 49.

9. Ibid., journal entry, Thursday [February] 13th, 1845, p. 50; ibid., journal entry, Friday, [February] 14th, 1845, p. 50.

10. Ibid., journal entry, Wednesday [January] 15th, 1845, p. 42; ibid., journal entry, Saturday [February] 15th, 1845, p. 51.

11. Catherine L. Albanese, *Nature Religion in America: From the Algonkian Indians to the New Age* (Chicago: University of Chicago Press, 1990), p. 108.

12. Seale, ed., *Complete Writings*, vol. 3, p. 378; Seale, ed., *Complete Writings*, vol. 2, p. 374.

13. Seale, ed., *Complete Writings*, vol. 3, p. 30.

14. Ibid., vol. 2, p. 183; ibid., p. 96.

15. Ibid., vol. 3, p. 416.

16. Horatio Dresser, ed., *The Quimby Manuscripts* (Secaucus, N.J.: Citadel Press, 1976), p. 78.

17. Ibid., p. 118; Seale, ed., *Complete Writings*, vol. 3, p. 31; ibid., vol. 2, p. 110; ibid., vol. 1, p. 262; ibid., vol. 3, p. 401. For other examples of this kind of absent healing, see ibid., vol. 3, pp. 418–20, 422, 424, 427, 433, 437. A sharp analysis of Quimby's unique linking of spirit and matter (and the contradictions it implied) can be found in Albanese's *Nature Religion in America*, pp. 107–15.

18. Dresser, ed., *Quimby Manuscripts*, p. 144.

19. Seale, ed., *Complete Writings*, vol. 3, p. 342.

20. John Higham, *From Boundlessness to Consolidation: The Transformation of American Culture, 1848–1860* (Ann Arbor, Mich.: William L. Clements Library, 1969); Seale. ed., *Complete Writings*, vol. 3, p. 476.

21. Seale, ed., *Complete Writings*, vol. 3, p. 39; ibid., vol. 2, p. 82; ibid., p. 97.

22. Ibid.; Ibid., p. 374.

23. Ibid., vol. 3, p. 443. A similar view on homeopathy is expressed in vol. 2, p. 86.

24. Ibid. p. 378; ibid. p. 397.

25. Ibid., vol. 1, p. 281.

26. Edward Shorter, *From Paralysis to Fatigue: A History of Psychosomatic Illness in the Modern Era* (New York: Free Press, 1992); Seale, ed., *Complete Writings*, vol. 2, p. 375; ibid., p. 301.

27. On religion as a vast superstition, see Seale, ed., *Complete Writings*, vol. 1, pp. 302–6; on his attacks on the Bible, see ibid., vol. 2, p. 147; ibid., vol. 1, pp. 358–59; on his linking religion and insanity, see ibid., vol. 3, p. 248; ibid., vol. 1, pp. 350–51; ibid., p. 299. An interesting essay on religious insanity is Ronald L. Numbers and Janet S. Numbers, "Millerism and Madness: A Study of 'Religious Insanity' in Nineteenth-Century America," in Ronald L. Numbers and Jonathan M. Butler, eds., *Millerism and Millenarianism in the Nineteenth Century* (Bloomington: Indiana University Press, 1987), pp. 92–117.

28. Seale, ed., *Complete Writings*, vol. 3, p. 434; ibid., p. 300.

29. Ibid., pp. 301–2.

30. On the issue of Christ and institutions, see ibid., vol. 1, p. 373; ibid., vol. 3, p. 142. On the old woman and her Calvinism, see ibid., p. 302.

31. Dresser, ed., *Quimby Manuscripts*, p. 337.

32. Seale, ed., *Complete Writings*, vol. 3, p. 400.

33. Ibid., vol. 1, p. 298; ibid., p. 357.

34. Ibid., p. 231; ibid., vol. 3, p. 142. In his quest for primordial innocence, Quimby was tapping a deep well in American culture. See the essays in Richard T. Hughes and C. Leonard Allen, eds., *Illusions of Innocence: Protestant Primitivism in America, 1630–1875* (Chicago: University of Chicago Press, 1988).

35. Seale, ed., *Complete Writings*, vol. 3, p. 382.

36. Ibid., p. 356.

37. Ibid., vol. 1, p. 380; ibid., vol. 3, p. 374.

38. Ibid., p. 236; ibid., vol. 1, p. 271; ibid., vol. 3, p. 79. Also see ibid., vol. 1, p. 390.

39. Ibid., vol. 3, p. 446; ibid., vol. 2, p. 84; ibid., p. 398.

40. Ibid., p. 450; ibid., p. 462.

41. Dresser, ed., *Quimby Manuscripts*, p. 231.

42. Seale, ed., *Complete Writings*, vol. 3, p. 477; ibid., p. 210.

43. On Quimby's belief that insanity and disease came from the outside world, see

Ibid., vol. 1, p. 243. On the techniques of nineteenth-century psychotherapeutic techniques, see F. G. Gosling, *Before Freud: Neurasthenia and the American Medical Community, 1870–1910* (Urbana: University of Illinois Press, 1987), pp. 69, 72.

44. Seale, ed., *Complete Writings*, vol. 2, pp. 224–25.

45. Ibid., pp. 361–62; ibid., vol. 3, p. 248.

46. Ibid., vol. 3, p. 436. On the mirror and idealizing transferences, see Heinz Kohut, *The Analysis of the Self: A Systematic Approach to the Psychoanalytic Treatment of Narcissistic Personality Disorders* (New York: International Universities Press, 1971).

47. Dresser, ed., *Quimby Manuscripts*, p. 114.

48. Ibid., pp. 341, 118. Also see Seale, ed., *Complete Writings*, vol. 2, p. 311, where Quimby says, "Christ often comes in the form of some good samaritan and saves man from the power of the devil."

49. Ibid., p. 99.

50. Ibid., vol. 1, p. 25. Also see ibid., vol. 3, p. 451.

51. Ibid., vol. 3, p. 455; Dresser, ed., *Quimby Manuscripts*, p. 279.

52. Seale, ed., *Complete Writings*, vol. 3, p. 52.

53. Ibid., p. 413; ibid, p. 406.

54. Catharine E. Beecher, *Letters to the People on Health and Happiness* (New York: Harper & Bros., 1855); Seale, ed., *Complete Writings*, vol. 2, p. 35.

55. Ibid., p. 351. Also, on women's spiritual superiority, see ibid., pp. 366–72; ibid., p. 351.

56. Dresser, ed., *Quimby Manuscripts*, p. 387.

57. Ibid., pp. 393, 387, 394.

58. Robert Peel, *Mary Baker Eddy: The Years of Discovery*, paperback ed. (New York: Holt, Rinehart & Winston, 1975), p. 167.

59. Dresser, ed., *Quimby Manuscripts*, pp. 231, 156. On Quimby's use of water and the laying on of hands, see Peel, *The Years of Discovery*, pp. 164–65. While some of these practices no doubt stemmed from Quimby's mesmeric days, they are also a part of Christian healing. See Morton T. Kelsey, *Healing and Christianity: In Ancient Thought and Modern Times* (New York: Harper & Row, 1976). Quimby was keenly sensitive to the charge that his healing methods bore a striking resemblance to mesmerism and spiritualism, especially in his ability to annihilate conventional time and space and communicate with the "spirit" of his patients. Quimby admitted that he was a medium and could induce trances. Unlike the trances brought on by a spiritualist, however, his did not invest "wisdom" in the dead. His kind of "wisdom" was to be found in the minds of the living. To his critics, Quimby still sounded suspiciously like a spiritualist, and their continued attacks led devoted followers like Mary Patterson to defend him publicly. For Quimby's lengthy statement on his relationship to spiritualism, see Seale, ed., *Complete Writings*, vol. 3, pp. 408–17.

60. This letter is reprinted in Georgine Milmine, *The Life of Mary Baker G. Eddy and the History of Christian Science* (New York: Doubleday, 1909), pp. 58–59.

61. Letter quoted in Julius Silberger, Jr., *Mary Baker Eddy: An Interpretive Biography of the Founder of Christian Science* (Boston: Little, Brown & Co., 1980), p. 67.

Chapter 5

1. Robert Peel, *Mary Baker Eddy: The Years of Discovery*, paperback ed. (New York: Holt, Rinehart & Winston, 1975), p. 173; *Lynn Reporter*, Sept. 12, 1863; ibid., June 11, 1864.

2. Archives, V03344, letter dated Jan. 31, 1863.

3. Archives, F00019, letter dated Nov. 16, 1863.

4. Sarah M. Evans, *Born for Liberty: A History of Women in America* (New York: Free Press, 1989), pp. 113, 118. Also see Lori D. Ginzberg, *Women and the Work of Benevolence: Morality, Politics, and Class in the Nineteenth-Century United States* (New

Haven: Yale University Press, 1990), chap. 5, "A Passion for Efficiency," pp. 133–73; Anne Firor Scott, *Natural Allies: Women's Associations in American History* (Urbana: University of Illinois Press, 1991), pp. 58–77.

5. Philip Shaw Paludan, *"A People's Contest": The Union and Civil War, 1861–1865* (New York: Harper & Row, 1988), p. 365. Other important works exploring the meaning of the Civil War for its surrounding society are Anne C. Rose, *Victorian America and the Civil War* (New York: Cambridge University Press, 1992); James H. Moorhead, *American Apocalypse: Yankee Protestants and the Civil War, 1860–1869* (New Haven: Yale University Press, 1978); Randall Jimerson, *The Private Civil War: Popular Thought During the Sectional Conflict* (Baton Rouge: Louisiana State University Press, 1988). Walt Whitman stands as a good example of the profound effect the war's devastation could have on a person's life and work. See Paul Zweig, *Walt Whitman: The Making of a Poet* (New York: Basic Books, 1984), pp. 18–26. Also worth consulting is Daniel Aaron, *The Unwritten War: American Writers and the Civil War*, paperback ed. (New York: Oxford University Press, 1973).

6. This poem is reprinted in *Mary Baker Eddy's Six Days of Revelation*, compiled by Richard Oakes (Christian Science Research Library, 1981), p. 18.

7. Samplings of these writings can be found in the *Portland Daily Press*, Nov. 21, 1863; ibid., Jan. 7, 1864; ibid., Jan. 29, 1864.

8. Archives, V03345, letter dated Mar. 10, 1863.

9. Peel, *Years of Discovery*, p. 181; Julius Silberger, Jr., *Mary Baker Eddy: An Interpretive Biography of the Founder of Christian Science* (Boston: Little, Brown & Co., 1980), pp. 82–83.

10. Archives, V03347, letter dated Mar. 31, 1864.

11. Peel, *Years of Discovery*, p. 184; Archives, V03348, letter dated Apr. 15, 1864.

12. Archives, V03350, letter dated Apr. 24, 1864.

13. Archives, V03351, letter dated May 1, 1864.

14. Archives, V03352, letter dated May 27, 1864.

15. Archives, V03353, letter dated July 8, 1864; Peel, *Years of Discovery*, p. 185.

16. Peel, *Years of Discovery*, p. 186.

17. Milmine, *Life of Mary Baker G. Eddy*, pp. 66–68.

18. Peel, *Years of Discovery*, pp. 186–87.

19. Archives, 16-2012, letter dated 1864.

20. Peel, *Years of Discovery*, p. 188.

21. Archives, V03356, letter dated July 29, 1865. My emphasis.

22. Archives, 78-11151, letter dated Sept. 7, 1865.

23. "Interview with Mary Baker Eddy at Pleasant View, August 31, 1890," [Fannie L. Pierce], in *Miscellaneous Documents relating to Christian Science* (privately printed), p. 101; Archives, *Lynn Reporter*, Feb. 3, 1866.

24. Fuller, *Alternative Medicine and American Religious Life*, p. 36.

25. Archives, George Newhall statement. In a statement he made in 1920 regarding his knowledge of Mrs. Eddy's state of health after her fall, Newhall (a milkman who had delivered her milk) said that she had attended "a Temperance Society," where she was active in the meetings. My thoughts on the role of fantasy and its relationship to reality have been influenced by Fred Weinstein, *History and Theory After the Fall: An Essay on Interpretation* (Chicago: University of Chicago Press, 1990).

26. My thinking on Mary Baker Eddy's gradual detachment from traditional institutions has been shaped by Peter Homans's discussion of deidealization in his *The Ability to Mourn: Disillusionment and the Social Origins of Psychoanalysis* (Chicago: University of Chicago Press, 1989).

27. Archives, Rev. Frank L. Phalen reminiscences.

28. In early editions of *Science and Health*, Mrs. Eddy cited Mark 3. Later she said she had read Matthew 9:2. Peel, *Years of Discovery*, p. 346, fn. 17.

29. An interesting discussion of the religious conversion experience in terms of the

cognitive, affective, and moral levels is found in Walter Conn, *Christian Conversion: A Developmental Interpretation of Autonomy and Surrender* (New York: Paulist Press, 1986). Archives, Rev. Frank L. Phalen reminiscences.

30. Peel, *Years of Discovery*, p. 197.

31. "Interview with Mary Baker Eddy at Pleasant View," p. 102. Creativity in religious experience has close connections to that in artistic endeavors, especially since creative people have kept a close tie to transitional phenomena. On this point, see Jerome D. Oremland, *Michelangelo's Sistine Ceiling: A Psychoanalytic Study of Creativity* (Madison, Conn.: International Universities Press, 1989), pp. 27–29; Oremland, "Michelangelo's *Pietàs*," *Psychoanalytic Study of the Child* 33 (1978), p. 566. A psychoanalytic perspective on the sudden emotional breakthrough experience in religious conversion can be found in John Frosch, "The Morning Ruminative State—The Flash Phenomenon," *International Journal of Psychoanalysis* 58 (1977), pp. 301–9; Nathaniel Ross, "Affect as Cognition: With Observations on the Meanings of Mystical States," *International Review of Psychoanalysis* 2 (1975), pp. 79–92; Sheldon Bach, "On the Narcissistic State of Consciousness," *International Journal of Psychoanalysis* 58 (1977), pp. 209–32; W. W. Meissner, *Ignatius of Loyola: The Psychology of a Saint* (New Haven: Yale University Press, 1992), pp. 48–54. I am aware of the danger of reducing religious experience to psychoanalytic categories. One of the best warnings on this comes from Stanley A. Leavy, *In the Image of God* (New Haven: Yale University Press, 1988), p. 74, where he argues that the domains of psychology (all psychologies including psychoanalysis) and religion should be kept separate; "the two orders of existence—earthly and divine—are equally real and interactive; but we must be content in this life to keep them intellectually apart."

32. From a psychoanalytic perspective, my thinking about Mrs. Eddy's experience has been influenced by W. W. Meissner, *Psychoanalysis and Religious Experience* (New Haven: Yale University Press, 1984); W. W. Meissner, "Religious Thinking as Transitional Conceptualization," in Leila Lerner, ed., *Illusion and Culture: A Tribute to Winnicott, Psychoanalytic Review* 79 (Summer 1992), pp. 175–96; and Ana-Maria Rizzuto, *The Birth of the Living God: A Psychoanalytic Study* (Chicago: University of Chicago Press, 1979), especially by their uses of the concepts of developmental phases and Winnicott's theories of transitional objects, transitional space, and phenomena. Also worth reading in this context is James W. Jones, *Contemporary Psychoanalysis and Religion: Transference and Transcendence* (New Haven: Yale University Press, 1991); Paul W. Pruyser, *The Play of the Imagination: Toward a Psychoanalysis of Culture* (New York: International Universities Press, 1983), p. 67. The emphasis on "transcendent" is Pruyser's.

33. Peel, *Years of Discovery*, p. 238; Adam H. Dickey, *Memoirs of Mary Baker Eddy* (Brookline, Mass.: Lillian S. Dickey, 1927), p. 33.

34. Archives, 38-4945, letter dated Feb. 24, 1893; Archives, Julia Bartlett reminiscences.

35. Mary Baker G. Eddy, *Historical Sketch of Metaphysical Healing* (Boston: published by author, 1885), p. 7; "Mrs. Eddy—the Woman," *Christian Science Journal* 27 (Mar. 1910), p. 705.

36. Henri F. Ellenberger, *The Discovery of the Unconscious: The History and Evolution of Dynamic Psychiatry* (New York: Basic Books, 1970), pp. 447–48. On Pollock's concept of mourning-liberation, see his collection of essays in George H. Pollock, *The Mourning-Liberation Process*, 2 vols. (Madison, Conn.: International Universities Press, 1989).

Chapter 6

1. Cynthia Grant Tucker, *Prophetic Sisterhood: Liberal Women Ministers of the Frontier, 1880–1930* (Boston: Beacon Press, 1990), p. 1. Also see Barbara Welter, "She Hath Done What She Could, Protestant Women's Missionary Careers in Nineteenth-

Century America," in Janet Wilson James, ed., *Women in American Religion* (Philadelphia: University of Pennsylvania Press, 1980), pp. 111–25; Virginia Lieson Brereton and Christa Ressmeyer Klein, "American Women in Ministry, A History of Protestant Beginning Points," ibid., pp. 171–80; Leonard I. Sweet, "The Female Seminary Movement and Woman's Mission in Antebellum America," *Church History*, 54 (March, 1985), pp. 41–55. On the cultural stereotypes and hostility that greeted women who stepped out of their traditional roles, see Mary P. Ryan, *Women in Public: Between Banners and Ballots, 1825–1880* (Baltimore: Johns Hopkins University Press, 1990), p. 86; Cynthia Eagle Russett, *Sexual Science: The Victorian Construction of Womanhood* (Cambridge: Harvard University Press, 1989); Joy S. Kasson, *Marble Queens and Captives: Women in Nineteenth-Century American Sculpture* (New Haven: Yale University Press, 1990), pp. 203–40.

2. Archives, letter dated Feb. 15, 1866.

3. Archives, letter dated Mar. 2, 1866.

4. *Lynn Reporter*, Sept. 12, 1866. Also see her mournful poem, "To Ellen—Sing Me that Song," ibid., Aug. 25, 1866.

5. Ibid., Aug. 4, 1866.

6. Ernest Sutherland Bates and John V. Dittemore, *Mary Baker Eddy: The Truth and the Tradition* (New York: Alfred A. Knopf, 1932), pp. 118–24.

7. Archives, Testimonies of Cure. Ingham said that he was suffering from pulmonary difficulties, fever, and a wracking cough. He was so weak that he could not walk, and under her care his health was restored.

8. Longyear, letter dated Aug. 4, 1867. On the healing of Ellen Pilsbury, see Archives, Testimonies of Cure.

9. Although "Alone" was written in 1867, it was not published until June 1911, in the *Ladies' Home Journal*. See Bates and Dittemore, *Mary Baker Eddy*, p. 122.

10. Robert Peel, *Mary Baker Eddy: The Years of Discovery*, paperback ed. (New York: Holt, Rinehart & Winston, 1972), p. 220.

11. Mary Baker Eddy, *Science and Health with Key to the Scriptures* (Boston: First Church of Christ, Scientist, 1934), p. ix. Also see Mary Baker G. Eddy, *Mind-Healing: Historical Sketch* (Boston: published by the author, 1886), pp. 17–18. On the conflict between religion and science, see David C. Lindberg and Ronald L. Numbers, eds., *God and Nature: Historical Essays on the Encounter between Christianity and Science* (Berkeley: University of California Press, 1984), especially the pertinent essays by James R. Moore, A. Hunter Dupree, and Frederick Gregory; for the particulars of this argument, see the fine introductory essay in Lindberg and Numbers, eds., *God and Nature*, pp. 1–14. On the wider aspects of Victorian culture, see Daniel Walker Howe, "American Victorianism as a Culture," in Daniel Walker Howe, ed., *Victorian America* (Philadelphia: University of Pennsylvania Press, 1976), pp. 3–28; Frederick Gregory, "The Impact of Darwinian Evolution on Protestant Theology in the Nineteenth Century," in Lindberg and Numbers, ed., *God and Nature*, p. 388. Also see Jon H. Roberts, *Darwinism and the Divine in America: Protestant Intellectuals and Organic Evolution, 1859–1900* (Madison: University of Wisconsin Press, 1988); Paul A. Carter, *The Spiritual Crisis of the Gilded Age* (DeKalb: Northern Illinois University Press, 1972); for Moore's statement, see James R. Moore, "Geologists and Interpreters of Genesis in the Nineteenth Century," in Lindberg and Numbers, eds., *God and Nature*, pp. 326, 344.

12. See D. W. Winnicott, *Playing and Reality* (New York: Basic Books, 1971), p. 99, for his statement on the paradoxical need for roots and the wish to move ahead.

13. Mrs. Eddy's creative synthesis indirectly shares some qualities with the creative painters and writers of the period. See, for example, Bryan Jay Wolf, *Romantic Revision: Culture and Consciousness in Nineteenth-Century American Painting and Literature* (Chicago: University of Chicago Press, 1982), p. 245.

14. Archives, Genesis manuscript. No other footnote citations will be used when it is evident that the quotation comes from this manuscript. Mrs. Eddy often jotted down

her thoughts without paying attention to proper spelling and punctuation. For the sake of clarity I have tried to clean this up.

15. Thomas C. Johnsen, "Christian Science and the Puritan Tradition" (Ph.D. diss., Johns Hopkins University, 1983). Also important in this context of the Puritans is Sacvan Bercovitch, *The Puritan Origins of the American Self* (New Haven: Yale University Press, 1976); on Baconianism, see Richard T. Hughes and C. Leonard Allen, *Illusions of Innocence: Protestant Primitivism in America, 1630–1875* (Chicago and London: University of Chicago Press, 1988), pp. 154–55. Also see George M. Marsden, "Everyone One's Own Interpreter? The Bible, Science, and Authority in Mid-Nineteenth Century America," in Nathan O. Hatch and Mark A. Knoll, *The Bible in America: Essays in Cultural History* (New York: Oxford University Press, 1982), pp. 79–95; Theodore Dwight Bozeman, *Protestants in an Age of Science: The Baconian Ideal and Antebellum Religious Thought* (Chapel Hill: University of North Carolina Press, 1977); Herbert Hovencamp, *Science and Religion in America, 1800–1860* (Philadelphia: University of Pennsylvania Press, 1978); Roberts, *Darwinism and the Divine in America*, p. 22; Mahan quoted in Marsden, "Everyone One's Own Interpreter?," p. 85; Hodge quoted in Roberts, *Darwinism and the Divine in America*, p. 22.

16. Stephen Gottschalk, *The Emergence of Christian Science in American Religious Life* (Berkeley: University of California Press, 1978), p. 26; Catherine L. Albanese, *America: Religions and Religion*, 2nd ed. (Belmont, Calif.: Wadsworth, 1992), p. 238. Also see James Turner, *Without God, Without Creed: The Origins of Unbelief in America* (Baltimore: Johns Hopkins University Press, 1985), pp. 171–202, for his discussion of the intellectual's crisis of belief and the period's desire for a scientific way of knowing God.

17. Mrs. Glover's ideas reflect the Swedenborgian idea of correspondence. On the role of Swedenborg's influence in the nineteenth century and upon the ideas of Quimby, see Robert C. Fuller, *Mesmerism and the American Cure of Souls* (Philadelphia: University of Pennsylvania Press, 1982), pp. 90–104, 118–39. On p. 91, he writes: "Communitarians, Transcendentalists, faith healers, spiritualists . . . were alike encouraged by his expansive doctrines." Also see Jon Butler, "The Dark Ages of American Occultism, 1760–1848," in Howard Kerr and Charles L. Crow, eds., *The Occult in America: New Historical Perspectives* (Urbana: University of Illinois Press, 1986), pp. 7–72. Also in this collection of essays, see R. Laurence Moore, "The Occult Connection? Mormonism, Christian Science, and Spiritualism," p. 145, where he states that Mrs. Eddy owed her most important intellectual debt to Quimby. Quimby in turn was influenced by Andrew Jackson Davis and his version of Harmonial Philosophy. Robert S. Ellwood, Jr., *Alternative Altars: Unconventional and Eastern Spirituality in America* (Chicago: University of Chicago Press, 1979), pp. 86–96; Catherine L. Albanese, *Corresponding Motion: Transcendental Religion and the New America* (Philadelphia: Temple University Press, 1977), passim.

18. For a strong argument against linking Christian Science to harmonialism, see Stephen Gottschalk, "Christian Science and Harmonialism," in Charles H. Lippy and Peter W. Williams, eds., *Encyclopedia of the American Religious Experience: Studies of Traditions and Movements*, 3 vols. (New York: Charles Scribner's Sons, 1988), vol. 2, pp. 901–16.

19. Archives, Charles Allen Taber, affidavit given Jan. 1913.

20. Peel, *Years of Discovery*, pp. 221–22.

21. Archives. See the letters, 59-8306; 55-7798, letter dated June 10, 1869; Archives, 59-8306, letter dated Oct. 20; Archives, 55-7800, letter dated Sept. 14, 1869.

22. Archives, Lucy Wentworth Holmes, letter to Mrs. Longyear, dated Feb. 10, 1922.

23. Quoted in Peel, *Years of Discovery*, p. 230.

24. Archives, Charles Wentworth, dated Mar. 27, 1909.

25. Mary Baker Eddy, *Miscellaneous Writings, 1883–1896*, in *Prose Works, Other than Science and Health with Key to the Scriptures* (Boston: First Church of Christ, Scientist, 1953), p. 105.

Chapter 7

1. Reminiscences of Mary Baker Eddy, by Mrs. Camilla Hanna and Septimus J. Hanna (privately printed), p. 5; Gilbert C. Carpenter and Gilbert C. Carpenter, Jr., *Mary Baker Eddy: Her Spiritual Footsteps* (privately printed), p. 181. For similar recollections see *We Knew Mary Baker Eddy* (Boston: Christian Science Publishing Society, 1979), p. 56; Sibyl Wilbur, "Cradled Obscurity" (privately printed), pp. 7–8.

2. *We Knew Mary Baker Eddy*, p. 140.

3. Samuel Putnam Bancroft, *Mrs. Eddy as I Knew Her in 1870* (Boston: Geo. H. Ellis Co., 1923), p. 52; *We Knew Mary Baker Eddy*, p. 114.

4. Clara Shannon, *Golden Memories* (privately printed), pp. 2–3. This letter also appears in Bliss Knapp, *The Destiny of the Mother Church* (Boston: Christian Science Publishing Society, 1991), pp. 42–43; ibid., pp. 9–10.

5. Quoted in Robert Peel, *Mary Baker Eddy: The Years of Trial*, paperback ed. (New York: Holt, Rinehart & Winston, 1974), p. 191.

6. Archives, Jennie Sawyer reminiscences; *We Knew Mary Baker Eddy*, p. 65. For an understanding of this kind of idealization from a different cultural perspective, see Sudhir Kakar, *Shamans, Mystics and Doctors: A Psychological Inquiry into India and Its Healing Traditions* (New York: Alfred A. Knopf, 1982).

7. Georgine Milmine, *The Life of Mary Baker G. Eddy and the History of Christian Science* (New York: Doubleday, Page & Co., 1909), p. 156.

8. Archives, Mrs. Grace Choate Huse reminiscences; Archives, Clara Choate reminiscences. For other statements regarding Mrs. Eddy's strong demands for neatness and order, see Archives, J. Henry Jones reminiscences, and Emma Shipman reminiscences. Obsessive traits were not peculiar to Mrs. Eddy. On the role of obsessive-compulsive traits in Puritanism, see David Leverenz, *The Language of Puritan Feeling: An Exploration in Literature, Psychology, and Social History* (New Brunswick, N.J.: Rutgers University Press, 1980), pp. 105–37; Philip Greven, *Spare the Child: The Religious Roots of Punishment and the Psychological Impact of Physical Abuse* (New York: Alfred A. Knopf, 1991), pp. 135–41; John Owen King III, *The Iron of Melancholy: Structures of Spiritual Conversion in America from the Puritan Conscience to Victorian Neurosis* (Middletown, Conn.: Wesleyan University Press, 1983).

9. Archives, Emma Shipman reminiscences; Archives, J. Henry Jones reminiscences; Mary Baker Eddy, *Retrospection and Introspection*, in *Prose Works, Other than Science and Health with Key to the Scriptures* (Boston: First Church of Christ, Scientist, 1953), p. 28.

10. "The Science of Man," in Bancroft, *Mrs. Eddy as I Knew Her*, pp. 69, 74.

11. "Introduction," ibid., p. ix.

12. Mary Baker Eddy, *Miscellaneous Writings, 1883–1896*, in *Prose Works*, p. 102; Irving C. Tomlinson, *Twelve Years with Mary Baker Eddy* (Boston: Christian Science Publishing Society, 1973), pp. 74–75.

13. Stanley A. Leavy, *In the Image of God: A Psychoanalyst's View* (New Haven: Yale University Press, 1988), p. 38.

14. Ernest Kafka, "The Uses of Moral Ideas in the Mastery of Trauma and in Adaptation, and the Concept of Superego Severity," *Psychoanalytic Quarterly* LIX (1990), pp. 255–56, 268.

15. Bancroft, *Mrs. Eddy as I Knew Her*, p. 8; Robert Peel, *The Years of Discovery*, paperback ed. (New York: Holt, Rinehart & Winston, p. 278.

16. Quoted in Peel, *Years of Trial*, p. 79.

17. Archives, 59-8304; letter dated Sept. 16.

18. Bancroft, *Mrs. Eddy as I Knew Her*, pp. 2–3.

19. Ibid., p. 75. On pp. 59–60, Bancroft said that this rubbing would eventually cause Mrs. Eddy a great deal of grief. On the methods Jesus used to heal and cure, see

Morton T. Kelsey, *Healing and Christianity* (New York: Harper & Row, 1976), pp. 69–103.

20. Archives, 31-3921, letter dated Apr. 10, 1871/1872.
21. "Moral Science alias Mesmerism, No. 2," *Lynn Transcript*, Jan. 27, 1872.
22. "Moral Science alias Mesmerism, No. 3," *Lynn Transcript*, Feb. 3, 1872.
23. Archives, 31-3923; *Lynn Transcript*, Feb. 17, 1872.
24. Archives, 20-2464, letter dated Jan. 25, 1879; Bancroft, *Mrs. Eddy as I Knew Her*, p. 11. On the need of some religious "outsiders" to keep their distance from the mainstream, and how they turned persecution to their own advantage, see R. Laurence Moore, *Religious Outsiders and the Making of Americans* (New York: Oxford University Press, 1986), especially chap. 4, "Christian Science and American Popular Religion," pp. 105–27.

Chapter 8

1. Samuel Putnam Bancroft, *Mrs. Eddy as I Knew Her in 1870* (Boston: Geo. H. Ellis Co., 1923), p. 52.
2. Ibid., p. 10; Archives, Jennie Sawyer reminiscences. Sawyer made a similar observation.
3. Mary Baker Eddy, *Science and Health with Key to the Scriptures* (Boston: First Church of Christ, Scientist, 1934), pp. 368–69, 375–76.
4. Archives, 17-2044, letter dated Nov. 27, 1876.
5. Bancroft, *Mrs. Eddy as I Knew Her*, p. 16; ibid., p. 29.
6. Heinz Kohut, "Creativeness, Charisma, Group Psychology," in John E. Gedo and George H. Pollock, eds., *Freud: The Fusion of Science and Humanism*, Psychological Issues, IX, monograph 34/35 (New York: International Universities Press, 1976), p. 403.
7. Quoted in Robert Peel, *Mary Baker Eddy: The Years of Discovery*, paperback ed. (New York: Holt, Rinehart & Winston, 1975), pp. 220–30. Stephen Gottschalk, *The Emergence of Christian Science in American Religious Life* (Berkeley: University of California Press, 1978), pp. 164–65, briefly comments on this loneliness.
8. Archives, letter dated Apr. 26, 1875.
9. Archives, *Boston Investigator* and a long review of the book in an unidentified paper.
10. Archives, 55-7809, letter dated Oct. 1, 1876.
11. Archives, 55-7810, letter dated Oct. 22, 1876.
12. Archives, 59-9897, letter dated July 14, no year given.
13. Mary Beecher Longyear, *The Genealogy and Life of Asa Gilbert Eddy* (Boston: Geo. H. Ellis, Co., 1922), pp. ix, 13.
14. Archives, Mary Godfrey Parker reminiscences.
15. Archives, 55-7811.
16. Archives, Emma Shipman reminiscences.
17. Clara Shannon, *Golden Memories* (privately printed), p. 10.
18. Archives, 17-2048, letter to Eldridge J. Smith, dated Oct. 19, 1877; Archives, Clara Choate reminiscences.
19. Poem quoted in Georgine Milmine, *The Life of Mary Baker G. Eddy and the History of Christian Science* (New York: Doubleday, 1909), p. 161.
20. Archives, 86-12621, letter dated Jan. 13, 1879 (or maybe 1880); *Newburyport Herald*, May 16, 1878. On the second court case involving Arens, see Peel, *Mary Baker Eddy: The Years of Trial*, paperback ed. (New York: Holt, Rinehart & Winston, 1974), pp. 50–57.
21. Archives, Clara Choate reminiscences; Mary Baker Eddy, *Science and Health*, pp. 233, 254.
22. Quoted in Robert Peel, *The Years of Trial*, pp. 95–96.

23. Archives, Julia S. Bartlett reminiscences; prophecies quoted in Bates and Dittemore, *Mary Baker Eddy*, p. 214.

24. Archives, Julia S. Bartlett reminiscences; 75-10643, letter dated July 28, 1883.

25. Archives, 91-13476, letter dated June 3, 1882.

26. Boston *Post*, June 5, 1882.

27. Archives, 32-4089, letter dated July 16, 1883.

28. Archives, 75-10643, letter dated July 28, 1883; 63-8956, letter dated Oct. 9, 1882.

29. Bancroft, *Mrs. Eddy as I Knew Her*, pp. 38–39.

30. Mary Baker Glover Eddy, *Science and Health*, Vol. II (Lynn, No. 8 Broad Street: published by Dr. Asa G. Eddy, 1878), pp. 136–37. This volume was reproduced by the Rare Book Company, New York.

31. Archives, 90-13376, letter dated Oct. 8, 1878.

32. Bancroft, *Mrs. Eddy as I Knew Her*, pp. 42–43.

33. Mary B. Glover Eddy, *Science and Health* (1881), pp. 1–46.

34. *Visions of Mary Baker Eddy* (Rumford, R.I.: Gilbert C. Carpenter, 1935), p. 33.

35. Ibid., pp. 43, 46, 54; Bates and Dittemore, *Mary Baker Eddy*, p. 230, discuss this in terms of her "intense hysterical beliefs" which spread like "a miasma"; Frye quoted in Edwin Franden Dakin, *Mrs. Eddy: The Biography of a Virginal Mind* (New York: Charles Scribner's Sons, 1930), p. 527.

36. Bates and Dittemore, *Mary Baker Eddy*, p. 228; Milmine, *Life of Mary Baker G. Eddy*, p. 266.

37. Mary Baker Eddy, *Unity of Good*, in *Prose Works, Other than Science and Health with Key to the Scriptures* (Boston, First Church of Christ, Scientist, 1953), pp. 55–57; Mary Baker G. Eddy, *Science and Health with Key to the Scriptures* (Boston: Joseph Armstrong, 1900), p. 253.

38. Robert Peel, *Health and Medicine in the Christian Science Tradition* (New York: Crossroad, 1988), pp. 66–67.

39. Ralph Waldo Emerson, "Nature," in Cleanth Brooks, R. W. B. Lewis and Robert Penn Warren, eds., *American Literature: The Makers and the Making*, I (New York: St. Martin's Press, 1973), p. 691.

40. Mary Baker Eddy, "Ways That Are Vain," *Christian Science Journal* 5 (May 1883), p. 92. My thinking about the dynamics of mesmerism, animal magnetism, and malicious animal magnetism has been influenced by my reading on the concept of projective identification. See Thomas H. Ogden, *Projective Identification and Psychotherapeutic Technique* (New York: Jason Aronson, 1982); Thomas H. Ogden, *The Matrix of the Mind: Object Relations and the Psychoanalytic Dialogue* (Northvale, N.J.: Jason Aronson, 1986), pp. 150–65, 227–31; Joseph Sandler, ed., *Projection, Identification, Projective Identification* (Madison, Conn.: International Universities Press, Inc., 1987); Robert A. Furman, "A Pathological Form of Projective Identification" (unpublished paper); Michael S. Poder, "Projective Identification," *Psychoanalytic Quarterly* 56 (1987), pp. 431–51.

41. My thinking about the paranoid qualities embedded in the fears of malicious animal magnetism has been shaped by a number of psychoanalytic writers. Arnold M. Cooper, "Paranoia: A Part of Most Analyses," *Journal of the American Psychoanalytic Association* 41 (1993), pp. 423–42, discusses paranoid defenses. On p. 438 he notes that in his patients paranoia "represents an available defensive mode that can appear in varying degrees of intensity, whenever there is a threat to higher-level narcissistic defenses." Elizabeth L. Auchincloss and Richard Weiss, "Paranoid Character and the Intolerance of Indifference," ibid., 40 (1992), pp. 1021–23, 1035–36, discuss paranoia and the need for "magical connectedness." Also, Harold P. Blum, "Object Inconstancy and Paranoid Conspiracy," ibid., 29 (1981), pp. 788–813, especially p. 790, analyzes "transitional paranoid states" and their varying degrees of reversibility. The best discussion of the dynamics of paranoia in the leader and the group process is Fred Weinstein, *The Dynamics*

of Nazism: Leadership, Ideology, and the Holocaust (New York: Academic Press, 1980), pp. 110–12, fn. 22. On the linking of obsessive behavior and paranoid dynamics, see David Shapiro, *Neurotic Styles* (New York: Basic Books, 1965), pp. 54–107. On the connections between narcissism and paranoia, see Annie Reich, "Pathologic Forms of Self-Esteem Regulation," in her *Psychoanalytic Contributions* (New York: International Universities Press, 1973), pp. 288–311; W. W. Meissner, *The Paranoid Process* (New York: Jason Aronson, 1978), pp. 615–42; W. W. Meissner, *Psychotherapy and the Paranoid Process* (Northvale, N.J.: Jason Aronson, 1986), pp. 95–98, 163–210. Thomas Simmons, *The Unseen Shore: Memories of a Christian Science Childhood* (Boston: Beacon Press, 1991), p. 74, sensed these qualities in the Christian Science religion as it was practiced in the world he was familiar with. "*Mental malpractice*—the phrase haunted me for years, nurturing my unstated awareness of the dark, paranoic side of my religion."

42. Martha H. Bogue, "Notes from Mrs. Eddy's Primary and Normal Classes of 1888 and 1889, in *Miscellaneous Documents Relating to Christian Science* (privately printed), p. 73. I have omitted most of the underlining which appears in the document.

43. Ibid., pp. 76–77.

44. On the issue of good and evil presences in the Bible, see Morton T. Kelsey, *God, Dreams, and Revelation: A Christian Interpretation of Dreams* (Minneapolis, Minn.: Augsburg Publishing House, 1974), p. 98. The problems in trying to label any religious belief system as pathological or delusional are superbly discussed by W. W. Meissner, "The Pathology of Belief Systems," in Leo Goldberger, ed., *Psychoanalysis and Contemporary Thought: A Quarterly of Integrative and Interdisciplinary Studies* 15 (1992), pp. 99–126. Also see W. W. Meissner, "The Phenomenology of Religious Psychopathology," *Bulletin of the Menninger Clinic* 55 (1991), pp. 281–98.

45. Cynthia Grant Tucker, *A Woman's Ministry: Mary Collson's Search for Reform as a Unitarian Minister, a Hull House Social Worker, and a Christian Science Practitioner* (Philadelphia: Temple University Press, 1984), p. 96.

46. Ibid., p. 97. For Collson's experiences in Evansville, Boston, and London, see pp. 100–23.

47. Ibid., pp. 126–27.

48. Ibid., p. 127.

49. Peel, *The Years of Trial*, pp. 284–85, also notes that in the fiftieth edition of *Science and Health* Mrs. Eddy cut by almost half the already shortened chapter "Animal Magnetism." Also on this point, see Gottschalk, *Emergence of Christian Science in American Religious Life*, pp. 147–49.

50. On the role of the Puritans and the jeremiad, see Sacvan Bercovitch, *The American Jeremiad* (Madison: University of Wisconsin Press, 1978), pp. 6–8.

Chapter 9

1. Rennie B. Schoepflin, "Christian Science Healing in America," in Norman Gevitz, ed., *Unorthodox Medicine in America* (Baltimore: Johns Hopkins University Press, 1988), p. 199.

2. Robert Peel, *Mary Baker Eddy: The Years of Trial*, paperback ed. (New York: Holt, Rinehart & Winston, 1974), pp. 237–44.

3. For background information on Foster Eddy, see ibid., pp. 221–22. My thoughts on Mrs. Eddy's health and the reasons for her adopting Foster have been influenced by an informal discussion with Tom Johnsen, Lee Johnson, and Stephen Gottschalk.

4. Peel, *Years of Trial*, pp. 247–48.

5. On the role of time in the organization of experience, see Irvine Schiffer, *The Trauma of Time* (New York: International Universities Press, 1978); Peter Hartocollis, *Time and Timelessness: The Varieties of Temporal Experience* (New York: International Universities Press, 1983); Thomas J. Cottle and Stephen L. Klineberg, *The Present of Things Future* (New York: Free Press, 1974).

6. *The Autobiography of Ben Franklin and Selections from His Writings*, introduction by Henry Steele Commager, Illustrated Modern Library (n.p.: Random House, 1944), pp. 98–99.

7. Archives, M. Adelaide Still reminiscences. Gilbert Carpenter has different times for the meals during the year he was at Pleasant View. Nevertheless, Mrs. Eddy's demands for promptness and order were the same. Gilbert C. Carpenter, Sr., and Gilbert C. Carpenter, Jr., *Mary Baker Eddy: Her Spiritual Footsteps* (privately printed), p. 55.

8. Archives, M. Adelaide Still reminiscences.

9. Carpenter and Carpenter, *Spiritual Footsteps*, p. 6. Victorians furnished their parlors with high moral seriousness. Louise L. Stevenson, *The Victorian Homefront: American Thought and Culture, 1860–1880* (New York: Twayne, 1991), p. 5, notes, "Victorians associated parlor decor from the natural world with a larger world of meaning and believed that all elements of the temporal world suggested or stood before a larger moral and divine world of meaning." As the nineteenth century drew to a close, the Victorians' association of the parlor's objects and furnishings with spiritual values declined. For Mrs. Eddy, however, this association was always a close one. For an account of the Victorians becoming less religious and more secular, see pp. 27–29. Also see Clifford Edward Clark, Jr., *The American Family Home, 1800–1960* (Chapel Hill: University of North Carolina Press, 1986), pp. 3–102.

10. Carpenter and Carpenter, *Spiritual Footsteps*, p. 138; ibid., pp. 5–6.

11. Ibid., pp. 222–23.

12. Ibid., p. 245.

13. Ibid., p. 56.

14. Ibid., p. 169.

15. Ibid., p. 52; ibid., p. 235.

16. Archives, M. Adelaide Still reminiscences; Carpenter and Carpenter, *Spiritual Footsteps*, p. 194; ibid., p. 46.

17. Carpenter and Carpenter, *Spiritual Footsteps*, p. 53.

18. Ibid., p. 193; ibid., p. 132.

19. Ibid., p. 52; Mary B. G. Eddy, "Mistaken Views," *Christian Science Journal* 8 (Sept. 1889), p. 277. From a psychoanalytic viewpoint, it is hard to miss the masochistic elements in Mrs. Eddy's suffering. There is a vast literature on masochism; a good starting point is the strong selection of essays in Robert A. Glick and Donald I. Meyers, eds., *Masochism: Current Psychoanalytic Perspectives* (Hillsdale, N.J.: Analytic Press, 1988). See especially Arnold M. Cooper, "The Narcissistic-Masochistic Character," pp. 117–38; Stuart S. Asch, "The Analytic Concepts of Masochism: A Reevaluation," pp. 93–115. Mrs. Eddy and her followers, of course, did not see her suffering in psychoanalytic terms. For the meaning of suffering in religious terms, see Robert Schreiter, ed., *The Schillebeeckx Reader* (New York: Crossroad, 1984), pp. 51–59, 186–87, 265; Jan Lambrecht, "Paul and Suffering," in Jan Lambrecht and Raymond F. Collin, eds., *God and Human Suffering* (Louvain: Peeters Press, 1990), pp. 47–67; John Bowker, *Problems of Suffering in Religions of the World* (Cambridge, England: Cambridge University Press, 1970), pp. 42–98.

20. Archives, John G. Salchow reminiscences.

21. Carpenter and Carpenter, *Spiritual Steps*, p. 217; ibid., p. 276.

22. Ibid., p. 170; ibid., p. 185. Also see ibid., p. 210.

23. *Course in Divinity and General Collectanea* (Freehold, N.J.: Rare Book Company, n.d.), p. x.

24. Carpenter and Carpenter, *Spiritual Footsteps*, p. 48.

25. *Course in Divinity and General Collectanea*, pp. xi–xii.

26. Clara Shannon, *Golden Memories* (privately printed), p. 5.

27. Carpenter and Carpenter, *Spiritual Footsteps*, pp. 134–36.

28. These watches and others are in *Course in Divinity and General Collectanea*, pp. 36, 38, 41–42, 44, 46.

29. A good example of this is the letter she sent to the Board of Directors, Aug. 1900. See ibid., p. xii.

30. Carpenter and Carpenter, *Spiritual Footsteps*, p. 144.

31. Adele Godchaux Dawson, *James Franklin Gilman: Nineteenth-Century Painter* (Canaan, N.H.: Phoenix Publishing, 1975), pp. 24–37, 45. For a wider perspective on romantic artists of the nineteenth century, see Barbara Novak, *American Painting of the Nineteenth Century: Realism, Idealism, and the American Experience*, 2nd ed. (New York: Harper & Row, 1979), pp. 44–164; Joshua C. Taylor, *America as Art* (New York: Harper & Row, 1976), pp. 96–131.

32. Dawson, *James F. Gilman*, p. 13.

33. Archives, James F. Gilman diary. All further citations are from this diary.

34. On the role of the diary for Gilman, see Robert Peel, *Mary Baker Eddy: The Years of Authority*, paperback ed. (New York: Holt, Rinehart & Winston, 1980), p. 384, fn. 44.

35. Archives, James F. Gilman diary. The first entry is Nov. 28, 1892. Gilman first saw Mrs. Eddy on Dec. 17 and recorded it on Dec. 18th; Peel, *Years of Authority*, pp. 30–34.

36. The italics are my own.

37. Carpenter and Carpenter, *Spiritual Footsteps*, p. 36; ibid., p. 262.

38. *Mary Baker Eddy's Six Days of Revelation*, compiled by Richard Oakes (n.p.: Christian Science Research Library, 1981), p. 469.

39. Ibid., p. 470.

40. Jewel Spangler Smaus, *Mary Baker Eddy: The Golden Days* (Boston: Christian Science Publishing Society, 1966), pp. 17–18, contains further examples of Abigail's warmth and Mary's closeness to her.

41. On the role of memory, see Hans W. Loewald, "Perspectives of Memory," in Merton M. Gill and Philip S. Holzman, eds., *Psychology versus Metapsychology: Psychoanalytic Essays in Memory of George S. Klein*, Psychological Issues, Monograph 36 (New York: International Universities Press, 1976), pp. 298–324. More specifically, Mrs. Eddy's memory here seems to reflect the qualities of a screen memory. See, for example, Eric LaGuardia, "The Return of Childhood in Autobiography: Freud's 'Screen Memories,' " in Leo Goldberger, ed., *Psychoanalysis and Contemporary Thought* 5 (1982), pp. 293–305; Phyllis Greenacre, "On Reconstruction," *Journal of the American Psychoanalytic Association* 23 (1975), pp. 706–10, for pertinent information on memory and screen memories. This memory can also be treated as a variation of a beating fantasy. There is a vast literature on this topic, but one is especially noteworthy because it stresses the role of the mother-child relationship in the fantasy instead of the father-child role. See Ruth F. Lax, "A Variation on Freud's Theme in 'A Child Is Being Beaten'—Mother's Role: Some Implications for Superego Development in Women," *Journal of the American Psychoanalytic Association* 40 (1992), pp. 455–73.

42. Greven's examples are drawn from modern fundamentalists, but this was also a pattern in evangelical families in the nineteenth century and earlier in Puritan homes. Philip Greven, *Spare the Child: The Religious Roots of Punishment and the Psychological Impact of Physical Abuse* (New York: Alfred A. Knopf, 1991) pp. 46–54, especially pp. 46–47. Also see Greven, *The Protestant Temperament: Patterns of Child-Rearing, Religious Experience, and the Self in Early America* (New York: Alfred A. Knopf, 1977).

43. Greven, *Spare the Child*, pp. 29–30.

44. Shannon, *Golden Memories*, p. 2; Adam H. Dickey, *Memoirs of Mary Baker Eddy* (Brookline, Mass.: Lillian S. Dickey, 1927), pp. 133–34.

45. Mary Baker Eddy, *Retrospection and Introspection*, in *Prose Works Other than Science and Health with Key to the Scriptures* (Boston: First Church of Christ, Scientist, 1953), pp. 3–9. Also see Archives, Julia S. Bartlett reminiscences.

46. Julius Silberger, Jr., *Mary Baker Eddy: An Interpretative Biography of the Foun-*

der of Christian Science (Boston: Little, Brown & Co., 1980), p. 21, states that she was "the youngest of the family, spoiled, petted, and much valued."

47. For Clara Shannon's statement, see her *Golden Memories*, p. 2. For an understanding of the role and function of personal myths, see André Green, "On the Constituents of the Personal Myth," in Peter Hartocollis and Ian Davidson Graham, eds., *The Personal Myth in Psychoanalytic Theory* (Madison, Conn.: International Universities Press, 1991), pp. 63–86; Otto F. Kernberg, " 'Mythological Encounters' in the Psychoanalytic Situation," ibid., pp. 37–48; Ernest S. Wolf, "The Personal Myth and the History of the Self," ibid., pp. 89–107; Jacob A. Arlow, "Ego Psychology and the Study of Mythology," *Journal of the American Psychoanalytic Association* 9 (1961), pp. 371–93.

48. Mary Baker G. Eddy, *Science and Health with Key to the Scriptures*, 46th ed. (Boston: Author, 1890), pp. 205, 206.

49. Ibid., pp. 442–43. Also see Annie M. Knott, "Reminiscences of Mary Baker Eddy," in *We Knew Mary Baker Eddy* (Boston: Christian Science Publishing Co., 1979), pp. 76–77. While the mirror had become secularized by the eighteenth century, and while Mrs. Eddy could use it in conventional secular ways, there was a part of her that used the mirror in an older religious sense. On this point, see Benjamin Goldberg, *The Mirror and Man* (Charlottesville: University of Virginia Press, 1985), pp. 112–75.

50. Highly suggestive here is what D. W. Winnicott has written about the mirror role of the mother's face. See his "Mirror-role of Mother and Family in Child Development," in *Playing and Reality* (New York: Basic Books, 1971), pp. 111–18. A number of important articles in *Psychoanalytic Inquiry* 5 (1985) explore the relationship of looking into a mirror and the developmental mirroring experiences that give emotional sustenance throughout life. See, for example, Joseph D. Lichtenberg, "Mirrors and Mirroring: Developmental Experiences," pp. 199–210; Malcolm Pines, "Mirroring and Child Development," pp. 211–31; Ernest Wolf, "The Search for Confirmation: Technical Aspects of Mirroring," pp. 271–82. Also pertinent is Leonard Shengold, Ch. 6, "The Metaphor of the Mirror," in *"Father Don't You See I'm Burning?," Reflections on Sex, Narcissism, Symbolism, and Murder: From Everything to Nothing* (New Haven: Yale University Press, 1991), pp. 61–82.

51. Archives, H133, letter dated Jan. 22, 1894, to Augusta Stetson. Mrs. Eddy's disenchantment with *Christ and Christmas* can be followed in "Christ and Christmas," *Christian Science Journal* XI (Jan. 1894), pp. 427–29. On p. 429, she said that pictures reflected part "of one's ideal," but this ideal did not represent "one's personality." Also see "Hear, O Israel," *Christian Science Journal* XI (Feb. 1894), pp. 471–73, where she canceled the book, and "Queries," on p. 474, where she said that the clergy of other denominations probably would not understand the illustrations. They did not reflect her human personality; they presaged "the typical appearing of the womanhood . . . [and] the manhood of God." And in a letter to Foster Eddy (Archives, 15-1883, dated Jan. 10, 1894), she told him that she had stopped publication of the book because her students were making "a golden calf of it." She never intended the book to heal; those students who healed with it were misusing it.

Chapter 10

1. Mary B. G. Eddy, "Fallibility of Human Concepts," *Christian Science Journal* VII (July 1889), p. 160.

2. Archives, letter dated June 19, 1889; Archives, letter dated Dec. 18, 1891.

3. Archives, 19-2345, letter dated Oct. 11, 1891.

4. My thinking on the leader as a transitional object has been influenced by the brilliant discussion in Fred Weinstein, *History and Theory After the Fall: An Essay on Interpretation* (Chicago: University of Chicago Press, 1990), pp. 128–32.

5. Cynthia Grant Tucker, *A Woman's Ministry: Mary Collson's Search for Reform*

as a Unitarian Minister, a Hull House Social Worker, and a Christian Science Practitioner
(Philadelphia: Temple University Press, 1984). The Archives of the Mother Church have
no letters or other data regarding Collson's career in Christian Science.

6. *Miscellaneous Documents relating to Christian Science* (privately printed), p. 53.

7. Septimus J. Hanna reminiscences (privately printed), p. 11.

8. Archives, John G. Salchow reminiscences.

9. Georgine Milmine, *The Life of Mary Baker G. Eddy, and the History of Christian
Science* (New York: Doubleday, Page & Co., 1909), p. 306.

10. Archives. For her matter-of-fact tone, see the letters dated Oct. 23 and 28, 1884;
on the attacks of the press and ministry, see the letter dated Mar. 30, 1885.

11. Archives, letter dated June 18, 1885; Archives, Lo5972, letter dated July 15,
1892.

12. Archives, letter dated May 31, 1886.

13. Archives, Lo5950, letter dated July 3, 1888; Archives, Lo5951, letter dated July
30, 1888.

14. Chester C. Muth, *Victoria H. Sargent and Laura E. Sargent: A Biographical
Sketch* (privately printed), p. 29; ibid., p. 32.

15. Archives. For samples of the rebukes, see Laura Sargent diary, entry dated Friday,
Apr. 12, 1907; Archives, Vo1654, letter dated June 11, 1899; on being driven to tears,
see John G. Salchow reminiscences; Archives, Vo0433, letter dated July 26, 1903.

16. Archives, letter dated Oct. 30, 1884.

17. Archives, letter dated Sept. 10, 1888.

18. Archives, letter dated May 28, 1886.

19. Archives, letter dated May 8, 1887.

20. Archives, letter dated July 3, 1901.

21. Archives, letter dated June 17, 1898; Archives, letter dated Oct. 22, 1910.

22. Archives, letter dated Sept. 13, 1897; Archives, Lo4376. Letter dated Sept. 15,
1897.

23. Archives, Tuesday, 1899, no other date on letter; Archives, Lo4383, letter dated
Sept. 9, 1899.

24. Archives, Lo2443, letter dated Dec. 18, 1898.

25. Archives, letter dated Dec. 20, 1898.

26. Archives, letter dated June 2, 1903. Also see Archives, Lo4391, letter dated May
14, 1903, where Mrs. Eddy asks for John for a year. And see Archives, letter dated Nov.
20, 1903, for Laura's acceptance of John's working for Mrs. Eddy.

27. Septimus J. Hanna reminiscences, p. 13.

28. Archives, letter dated Feb. 23, 1895; Septimus J. Hanna reminiscences, p. 14.

29. Archives, Camilla Hanna reminiscences.

30. Archives, 14478, letter dated Aug. 5, 1897.

31. Archives, see the letter dated Dec. 15, 1885, where Noyes confesses that
at one point she did not clearly see the difference between mind cure and Christian
Science.

32. Archives, letter dated July 25, 1887.

33. Archives, letter dated Jan. 9, 1891; Archives, letter dated Feb. 10, 1891.

34. Archives, letter dated Sept. 7, 1893; Archives, letter dated Jan. 9, 1894. On these
same topics, see the letters dated Sept. 9, 1890, and Nov. 24, 1891.

35. Archives, letter dated Jan. 15, 1892; Archives, letter dated Sept. 18, 1898.

36. *Miscellaneous Documents relating to Mary Baker Eddy* (privately printed), p.
226.

37. Archives, letter dated Nov. 24, 1891.

38. Archives, letter dated Oct. 9, 1891.

39. Archives, 41-5429, letter dated Mar. 14, 1887; Archives, 41-5417, letter dated
Aug. 2, 1885. Also see Archives, 41-5441, letter dated Jan. 26, 1889.

40. Tucker, *A Woman's Ministry*, p. 86.

41. Archives, 13-1576, letter dated Dec. 5, 1887; Robert Peel, *Mary Baker Eddy: The Years of Authority*, paperback ed. (New York: Holt, Rinehart & Winston, 1980), p. 157. For an example of Farlow's ability to straddle the sacred and the secular, see "A Critic Answered," *Christian Science Journal* XXII (June 4, 1904), pp. 130–52.

42. Alfred Farlow, "Christianity Made More Practical Through Christian Science," *Christian Science Journal* XVII (July 1899), pp. 253, 255, 257, 263, 266.

43. Archives, 13-1595, letter dated Jan. 11, 1899; Archives, 13-1596, letter dated Jan. 21, 1899.

44. Archives, 13-1617, letter dated "————— 21, 1901."

45. Bliss Knapp, *The Destiny of the Mother Church* (Boston: Christian Science Publishing Society, 1991) p. 117. Also see Peel, *Years of Authority*, p. 221.

46. Archives, letter dated Jan. 20, 1888; Peel, *Years of Authority*, pp. 168–70, 190–94, 248–51.

47. Archives, letter dated Feb. 21, 1893.

48. Archives, diary of Laura Sargent, Sept. 19, 1893, entry. On the World's Parliament of Religions, see Martin E. Marty, *Modern American Religion*, vol. 1, *The Irony of It All, 1893–1919* (Chicago: University of Chicago Press, 1986), pp. 17–24; Robert T. Handy, *Undermined Establishment: Church-State Relations in America, 1880–1920* (Princeton, N.J.: Princeton University Press, 1991), pp. 74–76; Eric J. Ziolkowski, "Heavenly Visions and Worldly Intentions: Chicago's Columbian Exposition and World's Parliament of Religions," *Journal of American Culture* 13 (Winter, 1990), pp. 9–15; Grant Wacker, "A Plural World: The Protestant Awakening to World Religions," in William R. Hutchinson, ed., *Between the Times: The Travail of the Protestant Establishment in America, 1900–1960* (New York: Cambridge University Press, 1989), pp. 253–57. On Kimball's evaluation of Hanna's speech, see Peel, *Years of Authority*, pp. 53–54.

49. Archives, letter dated Sept. 24, 1893. Also see the letter dated Sept. 30, 1893.

50. Archives, 53-7430, letter dated Oct. 5, 1893.

51. Archives, letter dated Sept. 29, 1893.

52. Archives, 53-7430, letter dated Oct. 5, 1893.

53. Archives, letter dated Oct. 5, 1893.

54. Archives, letter dated Oct. 6, 1893.

55. Archives, 41-5453, letter dated Oct. 5, 1893.

56. Archives, 41-5454, letter dated Oct. 8, 1893.

57. Archives, H27. The letter was to Augusta Stetson. Earlier, in September 1893, Mrs. Eddy had written to Stetson, voicing her displeasure that the *Chicago Inter-Ocean* had published the address and listed Hanna as the author. H23, letter dated Sept. 26, 1893.

58. Archives, 53-7434, letter dated Oct. 1893. Also in this correspondence between Mrs. Eddy and Kimball, see the letters in the Archives dated Oct. 8, 1893, and 53-7433, dated Oct. 15, 1893. Some of Mrs. Eddy's hesitations stemmed from her fears that the press might not only distort her message but group Christian Science with the rising tide of religious mysticism and interest in Oriental religions. See T. J. Jackson Lears, *No Place of Grace: Antimodernism and the Transformation of American Culture, 1880–1920* (New York: Pantheon, 1981), p. 175. Also see Steven F. Walker, "Vivekananda and American Occultism," in Howard Kerr and Charles L. Crow, eds., *The Occult in America: New Historical Perspectives* (Urbana: University of Illinois Press, 1986), pp. 162–73, and the essays in that book by Robert S. Ellwood, Jr., "The American Theosophical Synthesis," pp. 111–31, and Mary Farrell Bednarowski, "Women in Occult America," pp. 177–92.

59. Archives, letter dated Oct. 29, 1893.

60. Archives, letter dated Oct. 31, 1893.

61. Archives, letter dated Dec. 8, 1893.

62. Archives, 41-5456, letter dated Dec. 9, 1893. For letters that indicate the tensions were decreasing, see Archives, letters dated Oct. 13, and Dec. 8, 1893.

63. Archives, letter dated Dec. 15, 1893. Some of the low moments occurred in late 1897 and early 1898. During this time Kimball was besieged with psychosomatic symptoms. See the letters in the Archives dated Nov. 29, 1897, and Mar. 11, 1898. In an Apr. 27, 1898, letter, Kimball seemed depressed. For the loss of some of his power, see 21-2613, letter dated Apr. 27, 1904.

64. "New Commandment," *Christian Science Journal* VII (Oct. 1889), p. 340.

65. Archives, 20-2533, letter dated May 23, 1888. For another example, see Archives, 32-4097, letter dated July 17, 1886.

66. Mary B. G. Eddy, "Parting Makes Tender," *Christian Science Journal* VII (Jan. 1890), p. 477.

67. Archives, 20-2536, letter dated Feb. 22, 1895; Archives, F00133, letter dated Nov. 11, 1896.

68. Archives, Grace Choate Huse reminiscences.

69. Archives, 21-2642, letter dated July 6, 1894.

70. On turning passivity into activity as a defense, see Anna Freud, *The Ego and the Mechanisms of Defense, The Writings of Anna Freud*, Vol. II, rev. ed. (New York: International Universities Press, 1973), pp. 113, 134. Also note this defense's close connection to identification with the aggressor.

Chapter 11

1. Georgine Milmine, *The Life of Mary Baker G. Eddy, and the History of Christian Science* (New York: Doubleday, Page & Co., 1909), p. 364.

2. Archives, 20-2498, letter dated Feb. 6, 1882.

3. Archives, Clara Choate reminiscences.

4. Archives, letter dated Dec. 9, 1879.

5. Robert Peel, *Mary Baker Eddy: The Years of Trial*, paperback ed. (New York: Holt, Rinehart & Winston, 1974), p. 74.

6. Ibid., p. 72. Peel emphasizes Choate's jealousy and claims that there was "little love lost between the two." It stands to reason that this jealousy was not solely lodged in Choate; she probably inflamed it in Howard as well as some of Mrs. Eddy's other students.

7. Archives, 20-2492, letter dated Nov. 8, probably 1881.

8. Archives, 20-2494, letter, approximately 1881–82; Archives, 20-2498, letter dated Feb. 6, 1882; Archives, 32-4088, letter dated Mar. 15, probably 1882.

9. Archives, 20-2506, letter dated Dec. 22, no year given.

10. Archives, 20-2520, letter dated Dec. 12, doubtless 1883.

11. Archives, 20-2524, no date, probably 1883–84.

12. Archives, 20-2519, letter dated Dec. 11, 1883.

13. Archives, 32-4093, letter before 1884; Archives, letter dated Dec. 12, 1883; Archives, 20-2520, letter dated Dec. 12, doubtless 1883.

14. Peel, *Years of Trial*, pp. 143–44; Archives, 20-2527, letter dated Dec. 12, doubtless 1883.

15. On Crosse's character, see Peel, *Years of Trial*, pp. 239–41, 263.

16. Archives, 20-2529, letter dated Jan. 19, 1886.

17. Archives, 32-4099, letter dated June 20, 1888.

18. William Lyman Johnson, *The History of the Christian Science Movement* (Brookline, Mass.: Zion Research Foundation, 1926), pp. 51–52. Also see "Modus Operandi of Demonology," *Christian Science Journal* VI (Sept. 1888), p. 303.

19. Archives, letter dated Dec. 13, 1883.

20. Archives, letter dated Dec. 18, 1883, from Manchester, N.H.

21. Archives, Statement of Emma Hopkins in Julia S. Bartlett reminiscences.

22. Archives, letter dated Dec. 17, 1883.

23. Archives, letter dated Apr. 18, 1884; Archives, letter dated July 19, 1884.

24. Archives, Mrs. Eddy's letters: V00904, Oct. 16, 1885; V00984, Dec. 20, 1886; V01015, Aug. 22, 1887.

25. Archives, no date on letter, probably late 1884; Archives, 21-2633, no date on letter.

26. Archives, letter dated Jan. 19, 1886.

27. Archives, 21-2635, letter dated Oct. 15, 1886; Archives, 21-2636, letter dated Oct. 17, 1886.

28. Archives, 21-2639, letter dated July 21, 1889.

29. Archives, letter dated Aug. 4, 1889.

30. Archives, undated letter.

31. Archives, letter dated Sept. 8, 1889; Archives, letter dated Sept. 18, 1889; Archives, letter dated Jan. 3, 1890.

32. Quoted in Peel, *Years of Trial*, p. 269.

33. Ibid., p. 237; Rennie B. Schoepflin, "The Christian Science Tradition," in Ronald L. Numbers and Darrel W. Amundsen, eds., *Caring and Curing: Health and Medicine in the Western Religious Traditions* (New York: MacMillan, 1986), p. 432.

34. *Course in Divinity and General Collectanea* (privately printed), p. 80.

35. *Mary Baker Eddy's Six Days of Revelation*, compiled by Richard Oakes (n.p.: Christian Science Research Library, 1981), pp. 386–87.

36. Ibid., p. 493.

37. Archives, Mrs. Eddy's letter is dated Apr. 9, 1894. Mrs. Field-King's reply is dated Apr. 12, 1894.

38. Milmine, *Life of Mary Baker G. Eddy*, p. 425. For an inkling of Woodbury's machinations and her ability to instill fear in her students, see the reminiscences of Helen Andrews Nixon (privately printed).

39. Archives, testimony of Mary E. Landy.

40. Archives, testimony of Martha E. Burnes.

41. Archives. This material has been drawn from the Carrie Roach testimony and the Carolyn Roach statement.

42. Archives. According to the statement of Charles Nash, Mrs. Woodbury tried to talk his daughter into investing $200 in her husband's air engine stock.

43. Archives, 21-2652, letter dated Mar. 24, 1896. In the letter she refers to the May 2, 1894, meeting; Archives, Julia S. Bartlett testimony.

44. Archives, letter dated Mar. 11, 1895.

45. The article on Mary Baker Eddy in the May issue of *The Arena* was in two parts; the first part was written by Horatio W. Dresser, the second by Woodbury. "Christian Science and Its Prophetess," *Arena* 5 (May 1899), "Part II, The Book and the Woman," p. 570.

46. Robert Peel, *Mary Baker Eddy: The Years of Authority*, paperback ed. (New York: Holt, Rinehart & Winston, 1980), p. 164; ibid., pp. 153–54.

47. Julius Silberger, Jr., *Mary Baker Eddy: An Interpretive Biography of the Founder of Christian Science* (Boston: Little, Brown & Co., 1980), p. 213.

48. Frederick J. Streng, *Understanding Religious Life*, 2nd ed. (Encino, Calif.: Dickenson, 1976), p. 7. On the connections among paranoia, psychosis, and religion, see Freud's analysis of Schreber's *Memoirs* in "Psycho-Analytic Notes on an Autobiographical Account of a Case of Paranoia (Dementia Paranoides)," in *The Standard Edition of the Complete Psychological Works of Sigmund Freud*, trans. by James Strachey, XII (London: Hogarth Press, 1975), pp. 9–108. One may consult Erik H. Erikson's well-known *Gandhi's Truth*, but also see his companion pieces "On the Nature of Psycho-Historical Evidence" and "Freedom and Nonviolence," in his *Life History and the Historical Moment* (New York: W. W. Norton & Co., 1975), pp. 113–89. On Martin Luther King, Jr., see David J. Garrow, *Bearing the Cross: Martin Luther King, Jr., and the Southern Christian Leadership Conference* (New York: William Morrow & Co., 1986). On the link between religious beliefs and psychological levels of development, see W. W. Meiss-

ner, *Psychoanalysis and Religious Experience* (New Haven: Yale University Press, 1984), pp. 137–59. Also see Ana-Marie Rizzuto, *The Birth of the Living God: A Psychoanalytic Study* (Chicago: University of Chicago Press, 1979), pp. 206–7. Less helpful here, but worth consulting, is Philip M. Helfaer, *The Psychology of Religious Doubt* (Boston: Beacon Press, 1972), pp. 36–59, and his case studies on pp. 63–223.

49. Beulah Parker, *A Mingled Yarn: Chronicle of a Troubled Family* (New Haven: Yale University Press, 1978), pp. 87–88; Ibid., p. 88.

50. On this issue, see Roy Schafer, *Aspects of Internalization* (New York: International Universities Press, 1968), p. 31; Samuel Putnam Bancroft, *Mrs. Eddy as I Knew Her in 1870* (Boston: Geo. H. Ellis Co., 1923), p. 38.

51. On the internal sources of aggression, see Louis Berkowitz, "The Devil Within," *Psychoanalytic Review* 55 (1968), pp. 28–36. The best discussion of the role of language, its flexibility, and the metaphoric and concrete levels of thought is Fred Weinstein, *The Dynamics of Nazism: Leadership, Ideology, and the Holocaust* (New York: Academic Press, 1980), pp. 17–19, 87–90. Also see Anneliese Riess, "The Mother's Eye," *Psychoanalytic Study of the Child* 33 (1978), p. 387, for the preverbal forms of communication, and her "The Power of the Eye in Nature, Nurture, and Culture: A Developmental View of the Mutual Gaze," Ibid. 43 (1988), pp. 399–421. Hans W. Loewald, *Psychoanalysis and the History of the Individual* (New Haven: Yale University Press, 1978), pp. 55–77, draws connections among language, the primary process, and the religious experience.

52. On the connections between the ego ideal and a heightened sense of paranoia, see Janine Chasseguet-Smirgel, *The Ego Ideal: A Psychoanalytic Essay on the Malady of the Ideal*, trans. by Paul Barrows (New York: W. W. Norton & Co., 1985), pp. 121, 122, 127. Also Eli Marcovitz, "Some Aspects of Aggression in the Concept of Narcissism," *Bulletin of the Philadelphia Psychoanalytic Association* 22 (1972), pp. 276–83, especially p. 282, where he discusses narcissistic injury and the attempt to regain esteem by annihilating the one who has caused the injury.

53. Archives, 20-2471.

54. "Mind-Healing History," *Christian Science Journal* V (June 1887), p. 115.

55. Archives, 32-4095, letter dated Jan. 17, 1884.

Chapter 12

1. Augusta E. Stetson, *Reminiscences, Sermons and Correspondence: Proving Adherence to the Principle of Christian Science as Taught by Mary Baker Eddy* (New York: G. P. Putnam's Sons, 1913), p. 1.

2. William Lyman Johnson, *The History of the Christian Science Movement* (Brookline, Mass.: Zion Research Foundation, 1926), pp. 51–52, 59–72, on the defection of students in 1888; Archives, H001, letter dated Mar. 21, 1889.

3. Archives, letter dated June 1900.

4. Archives, letter dated May 11, 1900.

5. Archives, letter dated July 9, 1897.

6. Archives, letter dated Oct. 26, 1892; Archives, letter dated Jan. 31, 1888; Archives, letter dated Mar. 1, 1888.

7. Archives, undated letter, 1898?

8. Archives, letter dated July 9, 1897; Archives, letter dated Jan. 31 (no year).

9. Archives, letter dated Feb. 10, 1894.

10. Archives, letter dated Mar. 8, 1894.

11. Archives, letter dated May 15, 1893 (also see the letters dated July 19, 1890; Nov. 7, 1892; Feb. 8, 1893; Mar. 14, 1893); Archives, letter dated June 15, 1893.

12. Archives, letter dated June 11, 1896. In this letter Stetson said that six years before, she had gone to Mrs. Eddy seeking her advice on adopting Carol Norton. Mrs. Eddy advised her not to. Mrs. Eddy's advice was probably appropriate, for Stetson's interest

in Norton may have been something more than altruism. Norton apparently attracted a number of women, and Stetson had to shoo them away.

13. Morton T. Kelsey, *God, Dreams, and Revelation: A Christian Interpretation of Dreams* (Minneapolis, Minn.: Augsburg Publishing House, 1974), p. 18. On biblical dreams, also see Martin Grotjahn, *The Voice of the Symbol* (Los Angeles: Mara Books, 1971), p. 65. Prophetic dreams and visions and other occult phenomena were a part of religion in seventeenth-century New England, and they continued to be practiced by some members of nineteenth-century religious groups. On visions, dreams, and voices in the seventeenth century, see David D. Hall, *Worlds of Wonder, Days of Judgment; Popular Religious Belief in Early New England* (New York: Alfred A. Knopf, 1989), pp. 74, 86–91, 93–97, 106–7. For the eighteenth and nineteenth centuries, see Jon Butler, *Awash in a Sea of Faith: Christianizing the American People* (Cambridge: Harvard University Press, 1990), pp. 225–47, on the persistence of occult beliefs among Methodists and Mormons. Ellen G. White made extensive use of her trancelike visions in her leadership of the Seventh-Day Adventists. See Ronald L. Numbers, *Prophetess of Health: A Study of Ellen G. White* (New York: Harper & Row, 1976); Jonathan M. Butler, "Prophecy, Gender, and Culture: Ellen Gould Harmon [White] and the Roots of Seventh-Day Adventism," *Religion and American Culture: A Journal of Interpretation* 1 (1991), pp. 3–29.

14. Martha H. Bogue, "Notes from Mrs. Eddy's Primary and Normal Classes of 1888 and 1889," in *Miscellaneous Documents Relating to Christian Science* (privately printed), pp. 63–64.

15. Janet T. Coleman reminiscences, ibid., p. 59. For another example of visions and dreams see Bliss Knapp, *The Destiny of the Mother Church* (Boston: Christian Science Publishing Company, 1991), p. 21.

16. Archives, V00985, letter dated Dec. 27, 1886. Mrs. Eddy accuses Stetson of telling students in New York that she had been sent there under Mrs. Eddy's direct orders. In H8, letter dated Feb. 10, 1890, Mrs. Eddy tells her to come to terms with her anger and grievances. In Stetson's Feb. 27, 1893, letter to Mrs. Eddy, she talks about the jealousies and gossip that were undermining her work. Also see 33-4235, letter dated Sept. 5, 1891, in which Mrs. Eddy warns Stetson about tampering with the minds of her (Mrs. Eddy's) students; Archives, LXXVIII–11229, letter dated Sept. 10, 1895, in which she again accuses Stetson of meddling with her students; Archives, LXXVIII–11228, letter dated Nov. 22, 1895, in which she points out Stetson's weak point: her narcissism and inability to accept criticism.

17. Archives, letter dated Oct. 28, 1889, or 1890; Archives, H003, letter dated Nov. 12, 1888.

18. Stetson, *Reminiscences*, pp. 163–64; Archives, letter dated Dec. 11, 1895.

19. Archives, letter dated Nov. 25, 1895.

20. Archives, 19-2446, letter dated Apr. 8, 1899.

21. Archives, letter dated Nov. 29, 1903.

22. For a full treatment of Stetson's overthrow, see Ernest Sutherland Bates and John V. Dittemore, *Mary Baker Eddy: The Truth and the Tradition* (New York: Alfred A. Knopf, 1932), pp. 426–42. From her correspondence with Mrs. Eddy over the years, it is evident that Stetson's relationship with Mrs. Eddy was pitched on a higher developmental level than, say, Woodbury's. For a fuller understanding of the narcissistic features involved in the Stetson-Eddy relationship, see Rose Edgcumbe and Marion Burgner, "The Phallic-Narcissistic Phase: A Differentiation between Preoedipal and Oedipal Aspects of Phallic Development," *Psychoanalytic Study of the Child* 30 (1975), pp. 161–79, and in this context, especially pp. 177–78. On the conflicts within Christian Science in terms of organizational structure and personality, see the suggestive material in Part 3, Chapters 11, 12, and 13, of Otto Kernberg, *Internal World and External Reality: Object Relations Theory Applied* (New York: Jason Aronson, 1980), pp. 211–73.

23. Lida Fitzpatrick, "Notes on the Course in Divinity," in *Divinity Course and*

General Collectanea (Freehold, N.J.: Rare Book Company, n.d.), p. 2, entry dated May 18, 1903.

24. Edward Everett Norwood, "Reminiscences of Mary Baker Eddy," in *Miscellaneous Documents*, pp. 112–13.

25. Ibid., p. 113.

26. Janet T. Coleman reminiscences, in Ibid., p. 53.

27. Clara Shannon, *Golden Memories* (privately printed), pp. 34–35.

28. Knapp, *Destiny of the Mother Church*, pp. 118–20.

29. Ibid., p. 214.

30. Caroline D. Noyes, "Christian Science Notes," in *Miscellaneous Documents*, p. 227.

31. Septimus J. Hanna reminiscences (privately printed), p. 72.

32. Ibid., pp. 78–83.

33. *Kansas City Star*, Tuesday, Oct. 12, 1897.

34. Archives, 39-5213, letter dated Feb. 25, 1898; Archives, 19-2342, letter dated July 10, 1891.

35. Quoted in Peel, *Years of Authority*, p. 169; Archives, H69, letter dated Dec. 17, 1900; Archives, ibid.

36. Archives, Annie M. Knott reminiscences.

37. Mary Baker Eddy, "Christ and Christmas: A Poem" (Boston: First Church of Christ, Scientist, 1925), n.p.

38. Chester C. Muth, *Victoria H. Sargent and Laura E. Sargent: A Biographical Sketch* (privately printed), pp. 46–47.

39. Knapp, *Destiny of the Mother Church*, p. 58.

40. Septimus J. Hanna reminiscences, p. 74.

41. *Kansas City Star*, Oct. 12, 1897.

42. Edward P. Bates reminiscences (privately printed), pp. 38–39.

43. For examples of the correspondence, see the following in the Archives: F00091, letter dated Sept. 23, 1892; F00092, letter dated Jan. 29, 1893; F00095, letter dated Sept. 5, 1893; letter dated October 21, 1893; letter dated Oct. 23, 1893; letter dated June 9, 1892.

44. Archives, F00115, letter dated Feb. 15, 1895.

45. Archives, F00116, letter dated Feb. 8, 1896.

46. Gilbert C. Carpenter and Gilbert C. Carpenter, Jr., *Mary Baker Eddy: Her Spiritual Footsteps* (privately printed), p. 185.

47. Archives, 21-2592, letter dated Mar. 13, 1895; Archives, F00116, letter dated Feb. 8, 1896.

48. Harvey Green, *Fit for America: Health, Fitness, Sport, and American Society* (New York: Pantheon, 1986), p. 223. Also see Michael Kammen, *Mystic Chords of Memory: The Transformation of Tradition in American Culture* (New York: Alfred A. Knopf, 1991), pp. 206, 217, for examples of this idealization of the past and one's ancestors.

49. Charles E. Rosenberg, *No Other Gods: On Science and American Social Thought* (Baltimore: Johns Hopkins University Press, 1978), p. 52. Also see T. J. Jackson Lears, *No Place of Grace: Antimodernism and the Transformation of American Culture, 1880–1920* (New York: Pantheon, 1981), pp. 107–17.

50. "Mrs. Eddy's Place," *Christian Science Sentinel* XLV (June 5, 1943), pp. 985–86; "Mrs. Eddy's Place," *Christian Science Journal* LXI (July 1943), pp. 412–13. This is also reprinted in Knapp, *Destiny of the Mother Church*, pp. 253–55.

51. Archives, letter dated Mar. 3, 1902. But also see the following letters on this issue of the genealogy: Archives, 21-2592, letter dated Mar. 13, 1895; Archives, F00105, letter dated Mar. 24, 1895; Archives, letter dated July 23, 1895; Archives, F00127, letter dated Sept. 2, 1896; Archives, F00128, letter dated Sept. 3, 1896; Archives, letter dated Mar. 3, 1901; Field-King was still broaching the subject to Mrs. Eddy.

Chapter 13

1. Thoreau quoted in David Hackett Fischer, *Growing Old in America* (New York: Oxford University Press, 1977), p. 115. On the changing attitudes toward aging and death in the nineteenth century, see Thomas R. Cole, *The Journey of Life: A Cultural History of Aging in America* (New York: Cambridge University Press, 1992).

2. The definition of old age is a troubling one. Does one determine it chronologically, mentally, physiologically, or culturally? In this instance I am following the age patterns discussed by George H. Pollock, "Aging or Aged: Development or Pathology," in George H. Pollock, *The Mourning-Liberation Process*, 2 vols. (Madison, Conn.: International Universities Press, 1989), vol. 1, p. 351; Leon Edel, "Portrait of the Artist as an Old Man," in David D. Van Tassel, ed., *Aging, Death, and the Completion of Being* (Philadelphia: University of Pennsylvania Press, 1979), p. 212. Actually, the concept of creative aging applied to James and Yeats. Tolstoy never managed to reach this level, as Edel points out.

3. Quoted in Pollock, "Aging or Aged," pp. 363–64. Also see the interesting article by Francis V. O'Connor, "Albert Berne and the Completion of Being: Images of Vitality and Extinction in the Last Paintings of a Ninety-six-year-old Man," in Van Tassel, ed., *Aging, Death, and the Completion of Being*, pp. 255–289.

4. Archives, Michael Meehan reminiscences.

5. Quoted in Jean Angela McDonald, "Mary Baker Eddy at the Podium: The Rhetoric of the Founder of the Christian Science Church," (M.A. thesis, University of Minnesota, 1969), pp. 158–60. Also see Adam H. Dickey, *Memoirs of Mary Baker Eddy* (Brookline, Mass., Lillian S. Dickey, 1927), p. 30.

6. Archives, Mrs. Cora Nunn Reeves reminiscences.

7. Archives, Adelaide M. Still reminiscences.

8. Appendix A: The Frye Diaries, in Edwin Franden Dakin, *Mrs. Eddy: The Biography of a Virginal Mind* (New York: Charles Scribner's Sons, 1930), p. 528; Archives, 11-5299, letter dated Sept. 17, 1903.

9. Archives, LIV-7603, letter dated Dec. 26, 1903. Archives, 13-1604, letter to Alfred Farlow, dated Apr. 26, 1900, mentions the discord in the New York churches. Archives, H123, letter dated Apr. 15, 1903, Mrs. Eddy refuses to get embroiled in Augusta Stetson's conflict with Anne Dodge.

10. Dickey, *Memoirs of Mary Baker Eddy*, pp. 45, 47.

11. For the history of these developments, see Robert Peel, *Mary Baker Eddy: The Years of Authority*, paperback ed. (New York: Holt, Rinehart & Winston, 1980), passim.

12. Ibid., p. 512, fn. 90; Archives, Camilla Hanna reminiscences. The importance of reminiscences for the mental health of the elderly is discussed by George H. Pollock, "Reminiscences and Insight," in his *The Mourning-Liberation Process*, vol. 1, pp. 369–76. Also see Bertram J. Cohler and Robert M. Galatzer-Levy, "Self, Meaning, and Morale Across the Second Half of Life," in Robert A. Nemiroff and Calvin A. Colarusso, eds., *New Dimensions in Adult Development* (New York: Basic Books, 1990), pp. 227–28, 237; Bernard Chodorkoff, "The Catastrophic Reaction: Developmental Aspects of a Severe Reaction to Loss in Later Life," ibid., pp. 380–81.

13. Archives, William R. Rathvon diary, entry dated Aug. 5, 1910; Irving C. Tomlinson, *Twelve Years with Mary Baker Eddy* (Boston: Christian Science Publishing Society, 1925), pp. 12, 22.

14. Tomlinson, *Twelve Years with Mary Baker Eddy*, p. 17. For some of her other memories of Mark Baker, see "Statement by Helen W. Bingham," in *Miscellaneous Documents relating to Christian Science* (privately printed), pp. 147–48; Lida Fitzpatrick, "Notes on the Course in Divinity," in *Divinity Course and General Collectanea* (Freehold, N.J.: Rare Book Company, n.d.), entry dated Dec. 27, 1903, p. 17. Jerome M. Grunes, "Reminiscences, Regression, and Empathy—A Psychotherapeutic Approach to the Impaired Elderly," in Stanley I. Greenspan and George H. Pollock, eds., *The Course of*

Life: Psychoanalytic Contributions Toward Understanding Personality Development, vol. III: *Adulthood and the Aging Process* (Adelphi, Md.: National Institute of Mental Health, 1981), pp. 545–548, especially p. 546, where he discusses memory in the elderly as a source of mastery and gratification.

15. Archives, M. Adelaide Still reminiscences.

16. Martha W. Wilcox, "A Worker in Mrs. Eddy's Chestnut Hill Home," in *We Knew Mary Baker Eddy* (Boston: Christian Science Publishing Society, 1979), p. 201. On Mrs. Eddy's demands for order at Chestnut Hill, also see, Dickey, *Memoirs of Mary Baker Eddy*, pp. 61–66, and Archives, Cora Reeves Nunn reminiscences.

17. Dickey, *Memoirs of Mary Baker Eddy*, pp. 5, 20, 45, 47–50, 54–55. On these points, also see Dakin, *Mrs. Eddy: The Biography of a Virginal Mind*, Appendix A: The Frye Diaries, p. 528; Archives, John G. Salchow reminiscences.

18. Dickey, *Memoirs of Mary Baker Eddy*, p. 66; Mary Baker Eddy, *Science and Health with Key to the Scriptures* (Boston: First Church of Christ, Scientist, 1934), p. 246.

19. Through her lengthy correspondence with Foster Eddy, Mrs. Eddy tried repeatedly to get him to toe the line, but Foster managed to go his self-seeking way. For a sample of this long correspondence, see the following letters in the Archives: 16-1941, Mar. 17, probably 1895; 16-2003, Feb. 7, 1897, and the long letter, 16-1962, July 12, 1895. On the details of the next friends suit, see Peel, *Years of Authority*, pp. 280–91.

20. Ernest Sutherland Bates and John V. Dittemore, *Mary Baker Eddy: The Truth and the Tradition* (New York: Alfred A. Knopf, 1932), p. 359.

21. Ibid., pp. 338–39, 445.

22. Gilbert C. Carpenter and Gilbert C. Carpenter, Jr., *Mary Baker Eddy: Her Spiritual Footsteps* (privately printed), p. 271.

23. Archives, William R. Rathvon diary, entry dated July 18, 1910.

24. Bates and Dittemore, *Mary Baker Eddy*, pp. 357–58.

25. David L. Gutmann, "Psychoanalysis and Aging: A Developmental View," in Greenspan and Pollock, eds., *The Course of Life*, pp. 509, 492.

26. See the statements and testimony in Robert Peel, *Spiritual Healing in a Scientific Age* (San Francisco: Harper & Row, 1987).

Chapter 14

1. *Editorial Comments on the Life and Work of Mary Baker Eddy* (Boston: Christian Science Publishing Company, 1911), pp. 9–10, 64.

2. "Excerpts from Editorial Comments," *Christian Science Sentinel* XIII (Dec. 17, 1910), pp. 306, 308; ibid., pp. 309, 305. On the association of Christian Science to mind cure, see Gail Thain Parker, *Mind Cure in New England: From the Civil War to World War I* (Hanover, N.H.: University Press of New England, 1973). For Christian Science's relationship to American churches in the late nineteenth century, see Raymond J. Cunningham, "The Impact of Christian Science on the American Churches, 1880–1910," *American Historical Review* 72 (Apr. 1967), pp. 885–905; Stephen Gottschalk, *The Emergence of Christian Science in American Religious Life* (Berkeley: University of California Press, 1978); and, more briefly, Martin E. Marty, *Modern American Religion: The Irony of It All, 1893–1919*, vol. I (Chicago: University of Chicago Press, 1986), pp. 251–68.

3. Georgine Milmine, *The Life of Mary Baker G. Eddy and the History of Christian Science* (New York: Doubleday, Page & Co., 1909), p. 375. On the link to positive thinking, see Donald Meyer, *The Positive Thinkers: Religion as Pop Psychology from Mary Baker Eddy to Oral Roberts*, reissue paperback (New York: Pantheon, 1980). On the issue of social change and the transformation of the American character from inner- to other-directed, see T. J. Jackson Lears, "From Salvation to Self-Realization, Advertising and the Therapeutic Roots of the Consumer Culture, 1880–1920," in Richard Wightman

Fox and T. J. Jackson Lears, eds., *The Culture of Consumption: Critical Essays in American History, 1880–1980* (New York: Pantheon, 1983), pp. 3–17; Susan Curtis, "The Son of Man and God the Father: The Social Gospel and Victorian Masculinity," in Mark C. Carnes and Clyde Griffen, eds., *Meanings for Manhood: Constructions of Masculinity in Victorian America* (Chicago: University of Chicago Press, 1990), p. 67.

4. "Excerpts from Editorial Comments," p. 307.

5. Alan Dawley, *Class and Community: The Industrial Revolution in Lynn* (Cambridge: Harvard University Press, 1976), p. 8. Also see Paul G. Faler, *Mechanics and Manufacturers in the Early Industrial Revolution: Lynn, Massachusetts, 1780–1860* (Albany: State University of New York Press, 1981), pp. 222–33, for the growth of class and class-consciousness in Lynn; Mary H. Blewett, *Men, Women, and Work: Class, Gender, and Protest in the New England Shoe Industry, 1780–1910* (Urbana: University of Illinois Press, 1988).

6. This quality of being in the world but not of it contributed to what historian Sydney Ahlstrom has called Christian Science's "this-worldly otherworldliness." Sydney E. Ahlstrom, "Mary Baker Eddy," in Edward T. James, Janet Wilson James, Paul S. Boyer, eds., *Notable American Women, 1607–1950, A Biographical Dictionary*, 3 vols. (Cambridge: Belknap Press, 1971), vol. 1, p. 559. Also see Catherine L. Albanese, *America: Religions and Religion*, 2nd ed. (Belmont, Calif.: Wadsworth, 1992), p. 238.

7. Alfred Farlow, "Christianity Made More Practical Through Christian Science," *Christian Science Journal* XVII (July 1899), p. 253; Robert Peel, *Mary Baker Eddy: The Years of Discovery*, paperback ed. (New York: Holt, Rinehart & Winston, 1975), p. 252; Archives, Delia S. Manley reminiscences.

8. Gottschalk, *Emergence of Christian Science in American Religious Life*, p. 142; Peel, *Years of Discovery*, p. 252; *Christian Science Journal* 9 (Jan. 1892), p. 413, on Nourse; Archives, Mary Godfrey Parker reminiscences; Archives, Delia S. Manley reminiscences; Archives, Jennie Sawyer reminiscences. Also see Robert Peel, *Mary Baker Eddy: The Years of Trial*, paperback ed. (New York: Holt, Rinehart & Winston, 1974), p. 165.

9. Mary Baker Eddy, *No and Yes*, in *Prose Works other than Science and Health with Key to the Scriptures* (Boston: First Church of Christ, Scientist, 1953), p. 46.

10. Mary Baker Eddy, *Science and Health with Key to the Scriptures* (Boston: First Church of Christ, Scientist, 1934), p. 367. Also see the statements she made to the Reverend R. S. Rust. Archives, letter from Rachel F. Marshall, dated Oct. 11, 1902.

11. "The Resurrection and the Life," *Christian Science Journal* 11 (Apr. 1893), p. 5. On the wider implications of technological inventions in the late nineteenth century and the anxieties they created (and implicitly how Christian Science may have helped some people adapt to these changes), see Carolyn Marvin, *When Old Technologies Were New: Thinking About Electric Communications in the Late Nineteenth Century* (New York: Oxford University Press, 1988); Stephen Kern, *The Culture of Time and Space: 1880–1918* (Cambridge: Harvard University Press, 1983).

12. "Christian Science and Its Revelator," *Christian Science Journal* 1 (Apr. 1889), p. 4; *Christian Science Journal* 1 (Feb. 2, 1884), p. 2. On the theme of postmillennialism, see Jean B. Quandt, "Religion and Social Thought: The Secularization of Postmillennialism," *American Quarterly* 25 (Oct. 1973), pp. 390–409.

13. Michael Kammen, *Mystic Chords of Memory, The Transformation of Tradition in American Culture* (New York: Alfred A. Knopf, 1991), pp. 206–12.

14. On the concept of inventing traditions, see Eric Hobsbawm's "Introduction: Inventing Traditions," pp. 1–14, and his chapter, "Mass Producing Traditions: Europe, 1870–1914," pp. 263–307, in Eric Hobsbawm and Terence Ranger, eds., *The Invention of Tradition* (New York: Cambridge University Press, 1983). It is also evident that Mrs. Eddy and Christian Science share some of those qualities of "innovative nostalgia" that Robert M. Crunden has discussed in his *Ministers of Reform: The Progressives' Achievement in American Civilization, 1889–1920* (New York: Basic Books, 1982), pp. 116–

62; and the tension between innovation and tradition as discussed in Peter Conn, *The Divided Mind: Ideology and Imagination in America, 1898–1917,* paperback ed. (New York: Cambridge University Press, 1988).

15. According to Sue Harper Mims, "An Intimate Picture of Our Leader's Final Class," *We Knew Mary Baker Eddy* (Boston: Christian Science Publishing Society, 1979), p. 129. A solid book on the middle class's rise is Stuart M. Blumin, *The Emergence of the Middle Class: Social Experience in the American City, 1760–1900* (New York: Cambridge University Press, 1989), especially pp. 192–229, 258–97. On the rural Midwestern experience, see Archives, Miss Marion McDonald reminiscences, for her work in the backwoods of Wisconsin. Also see Ary Johannes Lamme III, "The Spatial and Ecological Characteristics of the Diffusion of Christian Science in the United States: 1876–1910," (Ph.D. diss., Syracuse University, 1968). I am not arguing that ethnic minorities first and foremost sought Christian Science as a means of assimilation. In their testimonies these people stressed the healing aspects of Christian Science as the primary appeal. See, for example, "Letters to Mrs. Eddy," *Christian Science Journal* XV (Apr. 1897), p. 36, where Carol Norton tells her that he has "two former Hebrews" in one of his classes; "From Judaism to Christian Science," *Christian Science Weekly* 1 (Sept. 15, 1898), p. 3; "Testimonies," ibid., (Nov. 17, 1898), p. 6.

16. George Cotkin, *Reluctant Modernism: American Thought and Culture, 1880–1900* (New York: Twayne Publishers, 1992), p. xi. On the rise of corporate America, see Alan Trachtenberg, *The Incorporation of America: Culture and Society in the Gilded Age* (New York: Hill & Wang, 1982); Alfred D. Chandler, Jr., *The Visible Hand: The Managerial Revolution in American Business* (Cambridge: Belknap Press of Harvard University Press, 1977); David F. Noble, *America by Design: Science, Technology, and the Rise of Corporate Capitalism,* paperback ed. (New York: Oxford University Press, 1979). On the consumer culture, see Cotkin, *Reluctant Modernism,* pp. 101–29; William R. Leach, "Transformations in a Culture of Consumption: Women and Department Stores, 1890–1925," *Journal of American History* 71 (Sept. 1984), pp. 319–42; T. J. Jackson Lears, *No Place of Grace: Antimodernism and the Transformation of American Culture, 1880–1920* (New York: Pantheon, 1981). For the anxiety and hopes engendered by the incorporation process, see Lears, "From Salvation to Self-Realization," pp. 3–38; Clyde Griffen, "Reconstructing Masculinity from the Evangelical Revival to the Waning of Progressivism: A Speculative Hypothesis," in Mark C. Carnes and Clyde Griffen, eds., *Meanings for Manhood,* p. 8; Susan Curtis, *A Consuming Faith: The Social Gospel and Modern American Culture* (Baltimore: Johns Hopkins University Press, 1991).

17. On the meaning of character, see Burton J. Bledstein, Chapter 4, "Character," in his *The Culture of Professionalism: The Middle Class and the Development of Higher Education in America* (New York: W. W. Norton, 1976), pp. 129–78; Karen Halttunen, *Confidence Men and Painted Women: A Study of Middle-Class Culture in America, 1830–1870* (New Haven: Yale University Press, 1982), pp. 25–29, 47–50, 201–7. For Rathvon's article, see William R. Rathvon, "A Protecting Religion," *Christian Science Journal* XXI (Sept., 1903), p. 339.

18. On James, see George Cotkin, *William James, Public Philosopher* (Baltimore: Johns Hopkins University Press, 1990). On the feelings of unreality, see Lears, "From Salvation to Self-Realization," p. 6; Cotkin, *William James,* pp. 73–94. On the "real thing," see Miles Orvell, *The Real Thing: Imitation and Authenticity in American Culture, 1880–1940* (Chapel Hill: University of North Carolina Press, 1989).

19. Orvell, *The Real Thing,* p. 69.

20. *Christian Science Weekly* 1 (June 8, 1899), p. 2.

21. O. Henry Clark, "Christian Science and its Relation to the Present Crisis," *Christian Science Journal* XI (Oct., 1893), p. 308.

22. Reuben Pogson, "Christian Science and Economic Reform," ibid., pp. 288–89; Mary Baker G. Eddy, *Science and Health with Key to the Scriptures* (Boston: Joseph Armstrong, 1894), p. 294.

23. "What There Is in Christian Science for Business Men," *Christian Science Weekly* I (Jan. 12, 1899), p. 14. On neurasthenia in this time, see Tom Lutz, *American Nervousness, 1903: An Anecdotal History* (Ithaca, N.Y.: Cornell University Press, 1991), for his interesting discussion of neurasthenia as a transitional object (not in Winnicott's terms) that allowed Americans to negotiate the vast social changes between the Civil War and World War I. Also see F. G. Gosling, *Before Freud: Neurasthenia and the American Medical Community, 1870–1910* (Urbana: University of Illinois Press, 1988); Edward Shorter, *From Paralysis to Fatigue: A History of Psychosomatic Illness in the Modern Era* (New York: Free Press, 1992), pp. 220–32; James Gilbert, *Work Without Salvation: America's Intellectuals and Industrial Alienation, 1880–1910* (Baltimore: Johns Hopkins University Press, 1977), pp. 31–43; Lears, "From Salvation to Self-Realization," p. 7.

24. "What There Is in Christian Science for Business Men," p. 14.

25. "Christian Science and the Business Life," *Christian Science Journal* XXII (Sept. 1904), p. 347. Also see John Carroll Lathrop, "Business Men," ibid. XV (July 1897), p. 205; J. U. Higinbotham, "In the Business World," Ibid. XX (Nov., 1902), p. 471.

26. "Excerpts from Editorial Comments," p. 307.

27. Ibid., p. 309.

28. Ahlstrom, "Mary Baker Eddy," pp. 556–57; "Excerpts from Editorial Comments," p. 305.

29. Ibid., p. 308. Virginia Lieson Brereton, "United and Slighted: Women as Subordinated Insiders," in William R. Hutchinson, ed., *Between the Times: The Travail of the Protestant Establishment in America, 1900–1960* (New York: Cambridge University Press, 1989), p. 145, points out that by 1900 most people agreed that women should have a voice in the church but "that voice was still to be ladylike and severely circumscribed." Needless to say, Mrs. Eddy was not demure; her voice disturbed others.

30. See the Archives for the Wiggin correspondence.

31. Milmine, *Life of Mary Baker G. Eddy*, p. 337.

32. Joyce Warren, *The American Narcissus: Individualism and Women in Nineteenth-Century American Fiction* (New Brunswick, N.J.: Rutgers University Press, 1984), pp. 184–85. Warren's feminist perspective captures one aspect of Twain's reasons for attacking Mrs. Eddy. For a fuller treatment of Twain's personal reasons for vilifying her and Christian Science, see Thomas Johnsen, "Christian Science and the Puritan Tradition" (Ph.D. diss., Johns Hopkins University, 1983), pp. 289–356. Hamlin Hill, *Mark Twain: God's Fool* (New York: Harper & Row, 1973), p. 52, notes that Twain had begun to write about Mrs. Eddy in Vienna in 1898.

33. Mark Twain, *Christian Science*, Author's National Edition, The Writings of Mark Twain, vol. XXV (New York: Harper & Row, 1907), pp. 82–83, 86.

34. Ibid., p. 95.

35. Ibid., pp. 185, 190, 197, 209; ibid., p. 210; ibid., p. 230. On p. 208, Twain says: "I have been misled all this time by that word Member, because there was no one to tell me that its spiritual meaning was Slave."

36. Mrs. Eddy did not fit the nineteenth century's conventional stereotype of an older woman: the smiling grandmother, plump, married, and the very image of domesticity. Mrs. Eddy was thin, unmarried (in a sense, also childless because of her strained relationship with her son, George, and her adopted son, Ebenezer), and autonomous. In fact, nothing was conventional about Mrs. Eddy; she was "unnatural." On the images of the older woman in the nineteenth century, see Lois W. Banner, *In Full Flower: Aging Women, Power, and Sexuality*, Vintage Books (New York: Random House, 1993), pp. 237–72, especially pp. 250–53. On the woman as a demonic force, see Joy S. Kasson, *Marble Queens and Captives: Women in Nineteenth-Century American Sculpture* (New Haven: Yale University Press, 1990), Chapter 8, "Domesticating the Demonic," pp. 203–240. It is hard to miss the underlying sexual implications in these fantasies about Mrs. Eddy's control and power. Elaine Tyler May, *Homeward Bound: American Families in the Cold*

War Era (New York: Basic Books, 1988), p. 93, notes that "fears of sexual chaos tend to surface during times of crisis and rapid social change."

37. All quotations from Jean A. McDonald's article, "Mary Baker Eddy and the Nineteenth Century "Public" Woman: A Feminist Reappraisal," *Journal of Feminist Studies in Religion* 2 (Spring 1986), pp. 96–97, 99.

38. For the way a strong woman like Mrs. Eddy disrupted the conventional expectations of how women were to conduct themselves in public, see John F. Kasson, *Rudeness and Civility: Manners in Nineteenth-Century Urban America* (New York: Hill & Wang, 1990), pp. 112–46; Mary P. Ryan, *Women in Public: Between Banners and Ballots, 1825–1880* (Baltimore: Johns Hopkins University Press, 1990).

39. "Woman Cause," *Christian Science Journal* 13 (July 1895), pp. 149, 151; *No and Yes*, in *Prose Works*, pp. 45, 46.

40. Archives, A10142B, "Man and Woman" (in Calvin Frye's handwriting); Mrs. Eddy dated this Dec. 8, 1900. Frye transcribed it on Aug. 26, 1915.

41. Rennie B. Shoepflin, "The Christian Science Tradition," in Ronald L. Numbers and Darrel W. Amundsen, eds., *Caring and Curing: Health and Medicine in the Western Religious Tradition* (New York: MacMillan, 1986), p. 431.

42. On Mary Collson's feminism, how it contributed to her gender conflicts with Alfred Farlow and to her disenchantment with the kind of feminism within Christian Science, see Cynthia Grant Tucker, *A Woman's Ministry: Mary Collson's Search for Reform as a Unitarian Minister, a Hull House Social Worker, and a Christian Science Practitioner* (Philadelphia: Temple University Press, 1984), pp. 80–85. For the kind of feminism encouraged at Hull House (and how, by inference, it differed from the feminism in Christian Science), see Robyn Muncy, *Creating a Female Dominion in American Reform, 1890–1935* (New York: Oxford University Press, 1991), chap. 1, "Origins of the Dominion: Hull House, 1890–1910," pp. 1–37.

43. "Christian Science, What It Is and What It Is Not," *Christian Science Journal* XVI (Mar. 1899), p. 316.

44. On the enlarging of the woman's sphere, see Mary Ryan, *Cradle of the Middle Class: The Family in Oneida County, New York, 1790–1865* (New York: Cambridge University Press, 1981); Sarah M. Evans, *Born for Liberty: A History of Women in America* (New York: Free Press, 1989), p. 125; and, from a working-class perspective, Joanne J. Meyerowitz, *Women Adrift: Independent Wage Earners in Chicago, 1880–1930* (Chicago: University of Chicago Press, 1988). A thoughtful article that examines the viability of the metaphor "woman's sphere" is Linda K. Kerber, "Separate Spheres, Female Worlds, Woman's Place: The Rhetoric of Woman's History," *Journal of American History* 75 (June 1988), pp. 9–39. Also see Margaret Marsh, "From Separation to Togetherness: The Social Construction of Domestic Space in American Suburbs, 1840–1915," *Journal of American History* 76 (Sept. 1989), pp. 512–515; Marsh, "Suburban Men and Masculine Domesticity, 1870–1915," in Carnes and Griffen, eds., *Meanings for Manhood*, pp. 111–27; Marsh, *Suburban Lives* (New Brunswick, N.J.: Rutgers University Press, 1990); Paula Baker, "Domestication of Politics: Women and American Political Society," *American Historical Review* 89 (June 1984), pp. 620–47; Rosalind Rosenberg, *Beyond Separate Spheres: Intellectual Roots of Modern Feminism* (New Haven: Yale University Press, 1982). Others have addressed the issue of Mrs. Eddy and feminism, with varying degrees of success. See, for example, Penny Hansen, "Woman's Hour: Feminist Implications of Mary Baker Eddy's Christian Science Movement, 1885–1910," (Ph.D. diss., University of California, Irvine, 1981); Margery O. Fox, "Power and Piety: Women in Christian Science," (Ph.D. diss., New York University, 1973); Susan M. Setta, "Denial of the Female-Affirmation of the Feminine, The Father-Mother God of Mary Baker Eddy," in Rita M. Gross, ed., *Beyond Androcentrism: New Essays on Women and Religion* (Missoula, Mont.: Scholars Press, 1977), pp. 289–301; John K. Maniha and Barbara B. Maniha, "A Comparison of Psychohistorical Differences Among

Some Female Religious and Secular Leaders," *Journal of Psychohistory* 5 (Spring 1978), pp. 523–49.

45. Carol Norton, "Woman's Cause," *Christian Science Journal* XIII (July 1895), pp. 151–52.

46. Farlow, "Christianity Made More Practical," p. 266. Also see W. P. McKenzie, "Childlike," *Christian Science Journal* XV (Oct. 1897), p. 389.

47. Archives, John G. Salchow reminiscences.

INDEX

A Note About the Author

Robert David Thomas was born in 1939 in Akron, Ohio. He received his M.A. from Case Western Reserve University and his Ph.D. from the State University of New York, Stony Brook, and was trained at the Cleveland Psychoanalytic Institute. From 1966 to 1972 he taught at Friends Academy in Locust Valley, New York, and since 1974 has taught at University School in Hunting Valley, Ohio. Thomas is the author of *The Man Who Would Be Perfect: John Humphrey Noyes and the Utopian Impulse* (1977). He and his family live in Chagrin Falls, Ohio.

A Note on the Type

The text of this book was set in Sabon, a type face designed by Jan Tschichold (1902–1974), the well-known German typographer. Based loosely on the original designs of Claude Garamond (c. 1480–1561), Sabon is unique in that it was explicitly designed for hot-metal composition on both the Monotype and Linotype machines as well as for film setting. Designed in Frankfurt, Sabon was named for the famous Lyon punchcutter Jaques Sabon, who is thought to have brought some of Garamond's matrices to Frankfurt.

Composed by PennSet, Inc.,
Bloomsburg, Pennsylvania

Printed and bound by R. R. Donnelley & Sons,
Harrisonburg, Virginia

Designed by Robert C. Olsson